SOUTHEY'S
LIFE OF NELSON

AMS PRESS
NEW YORK

SOUTHEY'S
LIFE OF NELSON

EDITED WITH INTRODUCTION AND CRITICAL NOTES

BY

GEOFFREY CALLENDER

M.A., F.R.Hist.S.

*Professor of History and English, Royal Naval College,
Greenwich ; Vice-President of the Navy Records
Society ; Hon. Secretary of the Society
for Nautical Research*

WITH TWELVE MAPS
AND PLANS

By

Robert Southey

1922
LONDON: PUBLISHED BY J. M. DENT
AND SONS LTD., AND IN NEW YORK
BY E. P. DUTTON AND COMPANY

Library of Congress Cataloging in Publication Data

Southey, Robert, 1774-1843.
    Southey's Life of Nelson.

    Bibliography: p.
    1. Nelson, Horatio Nelson, Viscount, 1758-1805.
I. Callender, Sir Geoffrey Arthur Romaine, 1875-1946,
ed. II. Title. III. Title: Life of Nelson.
DA87.1.N4S7 1973   359.3'31'0924 [B]   71-153357
ISBN 0-404-07828-1

Reprinted with permission of J. M. Dent & Sons, Ltd.,
London, England

From the edition of 1922, London and New York
First AMS edition published in 1973
Manufactured in the United States of America

AMS PRESS INC.
NEW YORK, N. Y.   10003

CONTENTS

INTRODUCTION

PAGE

SOUTHEY vii

SOUTHEY'S " NELSON " xxi

BIBLIOGRAPHY xxxv

PART   I.—BOYHOOD AND YOUTH I

PART   II.—EARLY SERVICES 15
   Chap.   I. During the War of American Independence . . 16
   Chap. II. Cruise of the *Boreas* 31

PART III.—CRUISE OF THE " AGAMEMNON " 49
   Chap.   I. Lord Hood being Commander-in-Chief . . . 49
   Chap. II. Admiral Hotham being Commander-in-Chief . . 69
   Chap. III. A Digression 78
   Chap. IV. Sir John Jervis being Commander-in-Chief . . 88

PART   IV.—ST. VINCENT AND TENERIFFE 96

PART   V.—THE BATTLE OF THE NILE 117

PART   VI.—NAPLES 149

PART VII.—THE BALTIC CAMPAIGN OF 1801 206
   Chap.   I. The Battle of Copenhagen 206
   Chap. II. After the Battle 237

PART VIII.—AT HOME 251

PART   IX.—THE CAMPAIGN OF TRAFALGAR 264
   Chap.   I. The Blockade of Toulon 264
   Chap. II. The Pursuit of Villeneuve 280
   Chap. III. Dramatic Pause before the Catastrophe . . 293
   Chap. IV. The Battle 301
   Chap.   V. The Death of Nelson 313

APPENDIX—QUESTIONS 323

INDEX 333

LIST OF MAPS AND PLANS

PAGE

THE SIEGE OF THE NORTH POLE, 1616–1909 7

THEATRE OF WAR IN THE WEST INDIES, 1778–83 . . . 19

WESTERN MEDITERRANEAN, 1793–96 52

THE ITALIAN CAMPAIGN OF 1795 78

JERVIS'S TACTICS AT THE BATTLE OF ST. VINCENT . . . 99

" NELSON'S PATENT BRIDGE FOR BOARDING FIRST-RATES ". . 102

THE FRENCH POSITION IN ABOUKIR BAY 128

THE TACTICS OF THE NILE 131

THE FIGHTING AT THE NILE 134

THE APPROACHES TO COPENHAGEN 211

THE FIGHTING AT COPENHAGEN 221

THE " VICTORY'S " PART AT TRAFALGAR 310

INTRODUCTION

SOUTHEY

No more striking contrast could be devised by the ingenious than that which is afforded by the life of England's Admiral and the life of his most famous biographer. Nelson's career was varied, adventurous, exciting; Southey's monotonous, sequestered, and serene. For the poet there were no single-handed conflicts with boat-loads of assassins; no hair-breadth escapes from fire and wounds and shipwreck; no rescuing of royal families and re-establishment of dynasties; no destruction of fleets or overthrow of Emperors. The greatest days in Southey's life were days when he first made the acquaintance of one of the world's classics; received the proofs of a *magnum opus* which was to rank him with the Immortals; or met in the flesh some literary giant whose work he had read and admired.

The main facts of his life can therefore be sketched in rapid outline.

Born on 12th August, 1774, he was the son of a Bristol linendraper who came of good yeoman stock in the Quantocks, and who married Margaret Hill, an accomplished lady of gentle parentage. The drapery business unhappily did not flourish; and Robert in infancy was transferred from his parents' care to the household of Miss Elizabeth Tyler, his mother's half-sister. This lady, who in many essentials resembled David Copperfield's aunt, Miss Betsy Trotwood, was prepared to play the part of fairy godmother so long as her nephew allowed his career to be moulded by her imperious hands. Robert's education from the first was carefully conducted; and, after the rudiments of knowledge had been acquired in Bristol and the neighbourhood, the future Poet Laureate, aged fourteen and a half, went up to Westminster.

This ancient foundation still prided itself upon main-

taining in pristine vigour the flogging principles of the
famous Doctor Busby; and against these principles Robert
Southey, in the fourth year of his school-time, matched
himself in unequal strife. An article from his pen condemning
heartily the use of the rod as an inducement to study appeared in a magazine run by the boys; and its author, with
every accompaniment of ignominy, was as a consequence
expelled. Southey's motives were honourable, even if his
defiance of authority was injudicious; and his aunt, who
could not pronounce the word "expulsion" without
shuddering, satisfied herself that her nephew's martyrdom
had been suffered for principles of which she might justly
be proud. The boy's uncle, the Rev. Herbert Hill, Chaplain
to the English factory at Lisbon, reached a similar conclusion, and very generously provided funds so that the
youthful anti-flagellant could continue his studies at Oxford.
    Christ Church College, outraged in its tenderest feelings
by the news from Westminster, hurriedly closed its doors
with what to-day will be thought a ludicrous lack of dignity,
and Southey in the eighteenth year of his age matriculated
at Balliol.
    It is unnecessary to take too seriously his own statement
that, of all the attractions that Oxford offered, he availed
himself only of swimming and boating, paying as little
regard to serious study as he had done at Westminster.
To such an omnivorous reader as Southey, the cut-and-
dried curricula of school and college must have seemed too
narrow and restricted; and one who had revelled in Beau-
mont and Fletcher before the age of eight could be trusted
ten years later to feed his mind on strong meats, though
they may not have been such as the dons recommended.
    Michaelmas term, 1792, brought him into residence;
and in the summer term of 1794 there occurred a casual
interview which profoundly affected his outlook on life,
and to some extent shaped his whole career. A close friend
of his, Allen of University, brought round to his rooms at
Balliol a visitor from the Cam, a young man called Samuel
Taylor Coleridge. Southey himself was ripe for the meeting.
Deeply versed in all kinds of learning, widely read in many
subjects and many tongues, he was like a torch ready
primed to give light, and Coleridge with his faculty for

inspiring others was the spark that set him aflame. The two men talked the sun down and the night away, while the deepest veins of philosophy were mined to furnish them with material for fresh discourse. Southey's proposal to complete the unfinished works of Ovid and Spenser now seemed lacking in ambition. What was needed was to refashion the world and restore the Golden Age.

In the long vacation the two dreamers met again near Bristol and defined their plans, which included a model republic based very largely on the teaching of Jean Jacques Rousseau. Having furnished themselves with comely wives, the founders were to shake the dust of England off their feet, and in the beautiful valley of the Susquehanna build up their commonwealth, where no right to private property would be admitted, where all mundane things would be shared in common, where the fields would make merry with music and song, and where the barren hillsides would blossom as the rose. Southey's friend, Lovell, cheerfully agreed to emigrate to the valley beautiful; and the three liberators of a world enchained offered marriage to three fair ladies, Mary, Sarah, and Edith, daughters of one Fricker, a merchant.

The great scheme budded, but never bloomed. Money was required, and none was forthcoming. Nor was this the worst of the matter. Southey's aunt lost patience with what she not unnaturally considered the fanaticism of her nephew, and turned him remorselessly out of doors. The whole affair formed a very painful episode; and the permanent estrangement from his benevolent godmother made a greater chasm in the road which Southey travelled than his expulsion from Westminster. Once more, however, his uncle the Chaplain came to his assistance, and carried him off for a trip to Portugal in order that the breath of a new world might bring his spirit peace. On the eve of his departure Southey was secretly married to Edith Fricker, who bade him good-bye at the door of the church and under her maiden name went back to live with her sisters.

The trip to Lisbon was of incalculable benefit to the young poet, and he returned to England, aged twenty-three, with a fervent resolve to settle down and earn an income suitable for the maintenance of his wife. The next few years were years of anxiety and disquiet. Southey wanted to adopt the advice of the uncle whose kindness had twice been his salvation; but a freedom of thought, which Coleridge had encouraged, quite unfitted him for Holy Orders. He turned from the Church to Medicine; but the anatomy classes and the dissecting-room nauseated him, and with an earnest desire to persevere he turned his back on them. He went up to London, took rooms in Gray's Inn, and with a wet towel round his head endeavoured pluckily to qualify for a legal career. But though libraries of all kinds had ever held him captive, the books of the law enfranchised him. He hated their style and he hated their contents, and could not keep his eyes on the page. Very quickly the Inns of Court closed their gates behind him, and his living was still to seek. He accepted gratefully a private secretaryship to no less a person than the Chancellor of the Exchequer for Ireland. But Dublin Castle proved even less congenial than deeds and indentures, and the boat that carried Southey to Ireland very quickly brought him home again. It would be a mistake to suppose that, like his father, he was un-methodical. It would be a mistake to suppose that by temperament he was unable to settle down to a profession. He was careful, punctilious, and painstaking: he never spared himself in the matter of toil. He worked so hard, achieved so little, and worried his nerves so much, that before long another visit to Portugal was necessary to restore him to health. The truth is that no one who ever lived was more completely the man of letters than Robert Southey. Literature demanded not merely his leisure, but his whole life and soul and strength.

This was definitely recognised at the time of his second return from Lisbon; and henceforth he resolved to dedicate himself wholly to the work of authorship. There was not more wealth to be derived from poetry in those days than in these; but the admiration of an old Oxford friend brought him an annuity of £160, and Southey hoped to augment this by literary hackwork, which would yet leave him time for epics comparable with those of Dante, Tasso and Milton. About this time too—the hour in which Nelson, with his flag in the *Victory*, set sail for the blockade of Toulon—Southey after hesitating between this berth and that came

to an anchor in the Lake District. He was invited there by
Coleridge, who wrote from Greta Hall, Keswick; and Greta
Hall, Keswick, was found on inspection to comprise two
houses under one roof. Charmed by the scenery, and
gladdened by the joy of his wife's reunion with her sister,
Southey decided to take the spare half of the residence
and make it his permanent home. By the time that he
settled down Coleridge had departed to act as secretary
to Nelson's friend, Sir Alexander Ball, the Governor of
Malta; and Keswick knew this wayward genius no more.
In time Southey became the sole owner of the double mansion, making himself responsible for the care of Coleridge's
family in addition to his own.

At Greta Hall, Keswick, Southey resided for the remainder
of his life. An occasional visit to London or the Continent
only served to enhance the affection he felt for the lake
below him and the hills above. His children, whom he
idolised, filled his heart alternately with hopes and fears.
Their love for him gave new zest to his life; and when three
of them, including his first-born son, died in infancy or
early youth, the cup of his sorrow overflowed. Such a
succession of tragedies bereft the poor mother first of her
reason and then of her life; and Southey himself, brave
as he was, was never the same man again. In his later years
he ceased to write books, and at length found himself without
the heart, or even the mind, to read them. He fingered
their backs in a listless way, or rearranged them on the
shelves. Life had become a weariness to him; and in March
1843, taking a last look at the country he loved, he closed
his eyes and fell asleep. On a dark and stormy day his body
was laid to rest in the beautiful churchyard of Crosthwaite
under the shadow of Skiddaw.

Before taking stock of Southey's work, the reader will do
well to remember the influences that determined its character.

His aunt, with whom he spent some of his most impres-
sionable years, was devoted to the theatre; and Robert
was taken to see Sheridan played at an age when other boys
fed their imagination on fights with pirates, or scalp-hunting
Indians, or packs of pursuing wolves. The pageantry of
the stage filled all his life with colour; and his efforts to
recall favourite snatches of dialogue sent him to the volumes

of plays that stacked his aunt's bookshelves. By eight he had sampled all the Elizabethan dramatists and his passion for Shakespeare and the "Mermaid Tavern" group led him by a natural transition to Spenser. Then was his spirit uplifted indeed. When he opened the *Faërie Queene*, his feelings were those of a navigator entering undreamed-of seas where all is new. Worshipping the "Poet's Poet" with knightly adoration, he read the book and read it again, and wept because there was no more. A stage had been reached in this precocious youth's career. He was not yet in his teens, but had already resolved to enrich the world with an epic.

More authors than one, with an epic in view, have found their chief difficulty in the choice of a fitting subject. But while Southey was at Westminster his ideas began to take shape. A copy of Picart's *Religious Ceremonies* was read by stealth, and strongly impressed his imagination. At length he determined to exhibit in a great heroic poem all the more prominent forms of mythology which have swayed the heart of mankind. The greatness of the theme required years of contemplation; and in the meantime his intellectual development was given a new turn by Gibbon's *Decline and Fall*. This book influenced his mind profoundly. It uprooted some of his beliefs; cast others into the crucible of doubt; and convinced him that his proper mission in life was to write History on the imperial scale. For this a new subject was needed.

Southey reached Westminster in 1788, and in the following year the States-General assembled at Versailles. The great upheaval that followed caused a very sharp division of English thought. But when the would-be author of epics and monumental chronicles reached Oxford, it seemed to him that, by all sane men, there was only one tenable view of things. Rousseau was the heaven-sent Prophet whose teaching must liberate the world. All men had been born free, and despotism had shackled them with chains. Tyrants must be punished according to their deserts, and the peoples labouring in bondage set free. The same generous impulse that set the poet in sympathy with Coleridge's Susquehanna project fired his bosom with a sense of indignant outrage at what the Third Estate suffered from Monarchy.

In after years detractors attempted to prove that Southey of Balliol had been a *sans-culotte*, and had renounced his allegiance to God as well as to Cæsar. But there was not a vestige of ground for such a reproach. Southey may have been by conversion a Republican, but he was never an atheist. Gibbon may have shaken his faith in revelation, but he remained throughout his life an intensely religious man; and of all the books that he read at Oxford, none held him so much in thrall as Epictetus. " Look up to God," said the Stoic philosopher, " and say to Him, ' Henceforth use me as Thou wilt. I am of one mind with Thee. I am Thine. I deprecate nothing that seems right to Thee. Where Thou wishest, lead me; and choose for me even the garments that I shall wear.' " Such precepts struck an echoing chord in Southey's heart, and helped to make him what he was. But there was nothing in Epictetus to save him from Pharisaical complacency; and he grew to be an austere moralist, hating unrighteousness, but condemning all those who failed to lift their spiritual being to the ethical standards he had chosen for himself.

When the Susquehanna settlement failed, and Southey accepted his uncle's offer to travel abroad, he found in Portugal the subject he wanted for the historical work that was to rival Gibbon's. From this time onwards to the end of his life he collected with unflagging energy books and documents and manuscripts on which his work was to be based. In these he delved with patient scholarship, garnering annually an amazing harvest of illustrative facts and cited passages.

Nothing less like a " Lake Poet " can well be imagined than Southey at work transcribing from his vellum-covered quartos. But to say the truth, Southey's connection with Cumberland was accidental rather than real. His relationship with Coleridge brought him to Keswick at a time when he was looking for a home and could find rest nowhere else. He loved the seclusion that the place afforded him, but he was no self-proclaimed apostle of nature and naturalism. He knew Wordsworth, and the two occasionally exchanged visits; but there does not appear to have been much cordiality in the acquaintance, or any tendency to ripen. De Quincey, while testifying to the prodigious scholarship of his neighbour, describes Southey as reserved and academic. But there is no dishonour in this. It was Southey's misfortune rather than his fault that Wordsworth eventually made the Lake District sacred for poesy of a kind that the historian of Portugal did not write. The proximity of such a giant as Wordsworth might have converted Southey into a mere imitator. Originality of thought and art are masculine virtues, and Southey deserves credit for his independence. However often he may be labelled a " Lake " poet and then be dismissed as insignificant, the fact remains that his mind had received its determining bent before he visited Cumberland, and that his new environment was powerless to change his predilections.

Among these a foremost place must be assigned to his books, which he loved above all earthly possessions. Though he never knew what it was to be rich, he always had more books than he could easily accommodate. Like Erasmus, he put the need of new volumes above necessity of food and clothing. Friends knew his weakness, and welcomed a way of showing their affection; booksellers sent him notice of bargains, and enabled him to acquire Colgar's *Irish Saints*, Ariosto's works, and Casaubon's *Epistles* without incurring financial ruin. In Greta Hall the books overflowed from room to room, stretched up to the ceiling, and lined the passages. The Spanish and Portuguese collection was probably the most remarkable ever assembled in England; but Southey was catholic in his tastes and, like a true bibliophile, lavished affection on handsome tomes in gilded parchment which he took from the shelves to fondle awhile, or open only to shut. At its greatest extent his library included some fourteen thousand volumes; and yet all had a place in his memory, and fresh acquisitions were never allowed to dethrone old friends. Wordsworth did not more surely draw his inspiration from wayside flowers, nor Coleridge from opium, than Southey from his books.

> With them I take delight in weal,
>   And seek relief in woe;
> And while I understand and feel
>   How much to them I owe,
> My cheeks have often been bedewed
> With tears of thoughtful gratitude.

Southey owed more, then, to what he called the " mighty minds of old " than to the society or the friendship of contemporary men of letters. He incurred Shelley's anger by uninvited admonition; he trespassed on the patience of sweet-natured Elia; he invoked the passionate invective of Byron. But on the other side of the account must be set the names of Savage Landor and Sir Walter Scott. With both of them Southey maintained a sweet and unbroken communion. Landor gallantly offered to bear the cost of publishing all the epics that his fellow-bard found time to write; and it was on the urgent recommendation of the author of *Waverley* that the Government appointed Southey Poet Laureate.

But the sweetest influence in Southey's life was his own family circle. His loving wife and adoring children made known to him sources of happiness unrevealed by Epictetus. The stoicism which had done duty in Oxford days melted in the warmth of that divine faith first taught on the slopes of Olivet and the coasts of Galilee. His austere regulations for the proper conduct of life were forgotten when sickness invaded the nursery; and the sententious pomposity which alienated brother-scribes fell off him like a cloak when he romped with the kiddies, or brought them home toys from his travels:

> The Ark well-filled with all its numerous hives:
> Noah and Shem and Ham and Japhet and their wives.

In the sunny Eden of Greta Hall his opinions, both political and religious, underwent a complete change. Freedom of thought gave way to something like veneration for the Fathers of the Church; and enthusiastic rapture for the Tree of Liberty was replaced by a heartfelt loathing for Napoleon Bonaparte.

> Woe, woe to England! woe and endless shame,
> 　If this heroic land
> False to her feelings and unspotted fame
> Hold out the olive to the Tyrant's hand!
> 　Woe to the world if Bonaparte's throne
> 　　Be suffered still to stand!
> 　For by what names shall Right and Wrong be known,
> What new and courtly phrases must we feign
> For Falsehood, Murder, and all monstrous crimes,
> If that perfidious Corsican maintain
> 　　Still his detested reign;
> And France, who yearns even now to break her chain,
> 　Beneath his iron rule be left to groan?
> No! by the innumerable dead
> Whose blood has for his lust of power been shed
> 　Death only can for his foul deeds atone!
> That peace which Death and Judgment can bestow,
> 　That peace be Bonaparte's . . . that alone!

It was this reversal of attitude that was hailed in many quarters as apostasy, and invited the mocking raillery and scathing satire of Byron. Southey, it must be admitted, brought his fate on his own head. Intolerant in youth to every opinion which he did not hold himself, he could hardly in his grey hairs expect to recant without enduring persecution. Yet he had the grace to perceive his own shortcomings and the wit to plead for their forgiveness. Look at the Holly Tree, he writes. Near the ground its keen and wrinkled leaves oppose a circling fence to repel and wound all that approach unwarily; but nearer to Heaven the prickles disappear and the leaves grow unarmed and barbless:

> Thus, though abroad perchance I might appear
> Harsh and austere,
> To those who on my leisure would intrude
> Reserved and rude;
> Gentle at home amid my friends I'd be
> Like the high leaves upon the Holly Tree.

If Southey had been blessed with a profusion of this world's goods, he would still have been dragged in opposite directions by his desire to write History and his desire to write Epics. But the state of his exchequer left him little freedom of choice; and the task of providing for Coleridge's family in addition to his own forced him in his own despite to use his pen for such things as would sell. In his young days there was quite a brisk market for occasional verse; and he turned out ballads at a guinea apiece with no more scruple for the worth of his wares than a jingling troubadour. Years afterwards, when the *Quarterly* was inaugurated as a rival to the *Edinburgh Review*, he gladly accepted an invitation to make regular contributions, and wrote ninety-five articles at £100 apiece, suffering in silence when his copious sentences were trimmed by the editorial shears. He would gladly have shaken from his sleeve the badge of servitude; but there was hardly a year which brought with it any promise but of penury and want. Southey worked with his pen as manfully as any son of the soil with pick and spade. "How many mouths," he once exclaimed pathetically, "have I to feed from a single inkstand!"

But in all his years of underpaid and unremunerative labour he never lost sight of his life's ambitions. He read extensively, and made voluminous notes for histories of

" English Literature," of the " Monastic Orders," and of
" Portugal "; and he consecrated dearly-purchased hours
of leisure to the epic poems on which he confidently hoped
that his fame would rest secure. While still an Oxford
undergraduate he wrote his *Joan of Arc*, and this to his
joy was published by a Bristol bookseller within a year or
two of its composition. The poem, which was less a tribute
to the sainted maid of Domremy than to the spirit of freedom and fraternity that had reawakened in France, brought
him fifty pounds in solid cash, and sufficient encouragement
to persevere. *Thalaba the Destroyer*, which appeared in 1801,
and the *Curse of Kehama*, which appeared in 1810, fulfilled
in part the cycle of poetic mythologies which he had planned
in boyhood; the former dealing with a Mohammedan theme,
the latter with an Hindu. To these were added *Madoc*, on
which great hopes were based, *Roderick the Last of the Goths*,
suggested by his love of Spanish lore, and the *Vision of
Judgment*, which appeared as a laureate's set task on the
death of George III.

Macaulay's verdict on Southey's epics has been often
quoted, but quoted wrongly. Macaulay did not say that in
half a century the whole series would be dead. He said,
" We doubt greatly whether they will be read fifty years
hence. But that, if they are read, they will be admired, we
have no doubt whatever." Such words rather suggest that
Southey's longer poems reached a wide circle in their own
day. But this was not the case. The great reading public
required no assistance from the *Edinburgh Review* in deciding
to avoid them. And one or two reasons for this callous treatment are not hard to discover. The world's greatest epics deal
with simple stories, already widely known; they are instinct
with passions and emotions common to the whole human
race. But Southey's epics are steeped in learning of an
exotic and unusual kind. They make no appeal to human
hearts, but soar out of range to lofty themes alien to this
world's sympathies. Nor is there any attempt to catch the
atmosphere of the Arabian desert, or paint the gardens and
bazaars of the Orient with realistic colour. The princes of
Ormuz and the rajahs of Hindustan are actuated by
impulses similar to those of English middle-class society.
Moreover, the reader who is not prepared to study English

B

literature for its own sake is hardly likely to be set on fire by Southey's intellectual eminence and moral ardour.

But if the poems were above the heads of the crowd, they evoked genuine praise from the best-qualified judges. Coleridge admired the " pastoral charm and wild streaming lights of the *Thalaba.*" Landor's generous tribute made amends to Southey for years of disappointment. Sir Walter Scott, by his own admission, read *Madoc* four times, liking it better at each perusal; and Charles James Fox stayed up until midnight, unable to put the book down. Modern critics confirm these judgments, tracing the influence of Southey's style on the nineteenth-century poets who followed him, and regretting that the notable splendour of his muse should lie buried beneath a century of neglect. Even for the *Vision of Judgment* Professor Saintsbury finds excuse. It failed, he maintains, not on any of the scores for which Byron overwhelmed it with his irony. It failed partly on account of its subject, and partly on account of its form. It is difficult to write a good official panegyric in English; it is practically impossible to write good English hexameters. Southey, unconscious of his own limitations, attempted to do both things at once.

With the best will in the world the author of *Madoc* was never able to execute his other resolve, and enrich the world with a noble monument of historical research. He did complete his chronicles of the *Peninsular War*; but his volumes in the hour of their publication were eclipsed by those of Napier. His annals of " English Literature " and of the " Monastic Orders " were delayed so long that they never even took shape; and his mighty scheme for the history of Portugal, which no one so well as himself was qualified to write, is known to-day only by the tremendous fragment that deals with the story of Brazil.

But though the achievement of Gibbon remained without a peer, in actual bulk its voluminousness was surpassed. A complete bibliography of Southey's prose works would fill a moderate-sized pamphlet. In 1803 he translated *Amadis de Gaul*, in 1807 *Palmerin of England*, and in 1808 the *Cid*. In the *Book of the Church* he described striking episodes in ecclesiastical annals; and in the *Colloquies* (which roused Macaulay's wrath) he reviewed the progress, the problems, and the prospects of society. He edited *Specimens of Later English Poets*, and reprinted Malory's *Morte D'Arthur.* He issued the collected works of Chatterton and Kirke White with memoirs; he composed *Letters from England* supposedly written by Don Manuel Espriella; and he contributed to Lardner's Encyclopædia *Lives of the British Admirals.* Translations, inscriptions, introductions, reminiscences, newspaper articles, and commonplace books came splashing from his inkpot with a velocity unequalled even by the Cataract of Lodore. And among these there flashed out three sparkling gems of biography, the lives of a poet, a prophet, and a paladin—Cowper, Wesley, and Nelson.

  Like Anthony Trollope, Southey wrote so much, and wrote in such a business-like, methodical fashion, that it was impossible for him to devote much time to the work of recasting and polishing. There was always at least one wolf at the door; and when payment was made at so much a sheet there was little temptation to excise. But Southey, if prolific, was never careless. He was an artist first, and a breadwinner afterwards; and he never allowed himself to pass a single clause that wore the look of slovenliness. He wrote so much, so often and so long, that he evolved a style, at once limpid and perspicuous, which fitted his own requirements to a nicety. Some critics have gone so far as to describe his prose as faultless; but it would be truer perhaps to call it inimitable. There are no tricks of expression, no foibles, no mannerisms; just a pleasant flow of cultured phrasing, which no parodist could caricature, no Byron burlesque. It would be a mistake to press the resemblance between the author of *Kehama* and the author of *Cato*, though both wrote poetry which is left unread. But what Dr. Johnson said of Addison may surely be repeated for the guidance of latter-day authors, with the change of the final name: " Whoever wishes to attain an English style, familiar but not coarse, and elegant but not ostentatious, must give his days and nights to the volumes of Robert Southey."

  The list of these volumes may not at first commend itself to those whose fancy dwells on trifles. Yet Southey, like Lewis Carroll and Sir James Matthew Barrie, out of

the mouths of babes perfected praise. Not Hans Andersen
or the Brothers Grimm knew better how to take a gossamer
thread and turn it into a solid staircase down which the
Fairies might glide; and neither Alice in Wonderland nor
Peter Pan can spoil our relish for *The Three Bears*.

It has been said by one of his kindest and most sym-
pathetic critics that "there is not perhaps any single work
of Southey's the loss of which would be felt by us as a
capital misfortune. . . . We could lose the *History of
Brazil*, or the *Peninsular War*, or the *Life of Wesley*, and
feel that if our possessions were diminished, we ourselves
in our inmost being had undergone no loss which might
not easily be endured. But he who has once come to know
Southey's voice as the voice of a friend, so dear, so brave,
so honest, so full of boyish glee, so full of manly tenderness,
feels that if he heard that voice no more a portion of his
life were gone. To make acquaintance with the man is better
than to study the subjects of his books." And the best
way to make the acquaintance of Southey is to seek him,
not in any of his formal compositions, but in the copious
harvest of his correspondence. His letters deserve to rank
beside Cowper's, and to be cherished with the same affection.
They show us one who was uncharitable only to strange
opinions; one who distributed his bounties with un-
grudging hand, and found that kindnesses, like perennial
flowers, multiply a hundredfold from the roots of those
already planted; one who accepted a life of drudgery with
a genial cheerfulness that made the drudgery itself as
bright as a window filled with varicoloured glass; one who
could not refuse the flattery of kindred hearts, but who had
strength to decline a baronetcy, a seat in the House of
Commons, and two thousand pounds a year for uncon-
genial work. Byron scoffingly professed himself ready to
acknowledge Sapphics as bad as the Laureate's if Nature
would only have endowed him with a tithe of the Laureate's
good looks. The gibe, though effective, was cheap, and went
astray; for Southey's handsome face reflected a beauty
of soul more precious than metrical perfection.

"No, thank God," exclaims Thackeray (concluding his
Four Georges with an estimate of that last whom contem-
poraries flattered as the "First Gentleman in Europe"),

"'we can tell of . . . some who merit indeed the title of
gentlemen, some who make our hearts beat when we hear
their names and whose memory we fondly salute when that
of yonder imperial manikin is tumbled into oblivion. I
will take men of my own profession of letters. I will take
Walter Scott, who loved the King, and who was his sword
and buckler, and championed him like the brave Highlander
in his own story, who fights round his craven chief. What a
good gentleman! What a friendly soul, what a generous
hand, what an amiable life was that of the noble Sir Walter!
I will take another man of letters, whose life I admire even
more—an English worthy, doing his duty for fifty noble
years of labour, day by day storing up learning, day by day
working for scant wages, most charitable out of his small
means, bravely faithful to the calling which he had chosen,
refusing to turn from his path for popular praise or prince's
favour—I mean *Robert Southey.* We have left his old
political landmarks miles and miles behind; we protest
against his dogmatism; nay, we begin to forget it and his
politics. But I hope his life will not be forgotten, for it is
sublime in its simplicity, its energy, its honour, its affection.
In the combat between Time and Thalaba, I suspect the
former destroyer has conquered. Kehama's curse frightens
very few readers now. But Southey's private letters are
worth piles of epics and are sure to last among us as long
as kind hearts like to sympathise with goodness, and purity,
and upright life.''

SOUTHEY'S " NELSON "

THE first biography of Nelson appeared within a few months
of his death. It was compiled by an obscure person called
Harrison, of whom nothing is known beyond the fact that
he wrote at Lady Hamilton's dictation. The book, which
appeared in two octavo volumes, contained stories such
as that quoted on page 295 of this edition: " He looked at
her with tears in his eyes. ' Brave Emma! Good Emma!
If there were more Emmas, there would be more Nelsons.' "[1]

[1] *Cp.* also pp. 252-3.

The work was altogether unworthy of its theme, and merely
served to emphasise the need for a comprehensive and
authoritative memorial.   .
Happily, suitable editors were available in the persons of
Messrs. Clarke and McArthur. The first named was Rector
of a Sussex parish and, on the outbreak of war with the
French Revolution, went to sea as a Naval Chaplain. He
served in the Channel fleet for a number of years, and made
quite a name for himself by his sermons, some of which
were afterwards printed. It is clear that he had distinct
literary gifts; and earning the good opinion of his Captain,
whose word carried weight in royal circles, he was appointed
in 1799 Domestic Chaplain and Librarian to the Prince
Regent. He thereupon gave himself wholly to authorship,
his experience at sea suggesting subjects for his pen. In
1803 he published the *Progress of Maritime Discovery*, and
in 1805 *Naufragia*, a collection of notable shipwrecks. He
subsequently attempted a life of the sailor-king James II.,
making use of papers in the royal possession. But long
before this he had made the acquaintance of John McArthur,
who gave a new turn to his literary activities.

McArthur entered the Navy as a Clerk, and early distinguished himself by his plucky conduct in the capture
of a prize. For this he was promoted at the early age of
twenty-four to be Purser, or (as we should say to-day)
Paymaster-Captain. He rose steadily in the estimation
of all under whom he served, putting the utmost keenness
into every kind of work he undertook. He was one of the
pioneers in the reformation of the signalling system; and
codified the procedure of naval courts martial in a " Manual "
which at once became a classic. When Lord Hood hoisted
his flag in the *Victory* and proceeded to the Mediterranean,[1]
McArthur was specially selected to act as his secretary,
and his organising genius and knowledge of three languages
served the Admiral in good stead. He probably received
direct from Admiral Hood his first knowledge of the Captain
of the *Agamemnon*; and in the Corsican campaign [2] met
Nelson in the flesh and learned to know him well. Ten
years later he received the offer of his old privileged position
when the *Victory* carried Nelson's own flag; but by then

---

[1] See below, p. 50.   [2] See below, pp. 53-68.

he was immersed in literary pursuits, and had joined forces with Clarke.

The work on which they were employed was a nautical monthly called *The Naval Chronicle*. It was inaugurated in 1799, and for nearly twenty years enjoyed a well-deserved popularity. Both editors received doctoral degrees from admiring universities; and Clarke, whose elegance of diction proved an unfailing delight to his colleague, became in due course a Canon of Windsor and a Fellow of the Royal Society. *The Naval Chronicle* sustains to this day a unique authority for all subjects dealt with in its pages; and is eagerly hunted and highly prized. In 1806 it pointed, as clearly as a signpost, to the authors best qualified to undertake an adequate Life of Nelson.

No pains were spared in the preparation for this tremendous work. McArthur with his customary zeal collected the material, and Clarke invested the compilation with literary grace. The work was completed in 1809; and the seven hundred and seventy-five subscribers who had ordered copies beforehand were satisfied that their money had been well spent. The two handsome volumes in royal quarto were embellished by a splendid series of engravings from pictures specially painted at McArthur's command. Those by Richard Westall, R.A., showed Nelson boarding a prize in a gale, Nelson fighting the Spanish launch, and Nelson wounded at Teneriffe. They were much admired at the time, and have been frequently reproduced. To-day they seem wildly theatrical and out of place in their surroundings. The ship-pictures of Nicholas Pocock are infinitely better; indeed, that of Copenhagen will give those unacquainted with maritime warfare a better impression of what the battle looked like than a library full of books.

The letterpress had even greater claims to distinction. McArthur brought under contribution all the family papers then available, and obtained access to the correspondence which had passed between Nelson and his life-long friend the Duke of Clarence, afterwards William IV. So many letters were gathered together that it seemed to the editors the wisest plan to give their narrative an epistolary basis. But other invaluable documents were procured. With commendable foresight McArthur had persuaded Nelson (when the two had worked together in Corsica) to supply an autobiographical sketch of his earlier career; and Doctor Beatty, the surgeon of the *Victory*, was prevailed upon to write all that he could remember of the Admiral's last moments in the cockpit.

The book was great alike in conception and achievement, and was not an unworthy memorial of the nation's hero. And yet, in addition to the price (which was excessive), the work suffered from other serious blemishes. It was unscholarly, in the sense that doubtful and questionable matter was accepted in an uncritical spirit and was interspersed among documents of unchallenged authenticity. Moreover, Dr. Clarke failed in his ambitious scheme of telling Nelson's story in Nelson's own words. Novelists like Smollett and Richardson, it is true, had utilised a series of letters in which to unfold a romance; but then the letters were all of them make-believe. Nelson's letters were genuine, and bore no relation to an argument or plot. Dr. Clarke might have discarded the letters altogether and told the story in his own words; or he might have retained the letters and made them intelligible by notes and exposition. But he did neither one thing nor the other. He left the letters to convey what they would; and he mended what he considered Nelson's faulty syntax, converting the Admiral's whimsical turns of speech into a dignified and ornate diction of a piece with his own. Finally, the volumes were like elephants in bulk and unwieldiness. They measured fourteen inches by eleven, and weighed very nearly twenty-three pounds. They looked well enough on a library table, but the keenest reader could not nurse them for long.[1]

In 1810 Southey received these ponderous tomes, together with Harrison's book, Dr. Beatty's *Authentic Narrative* (now published separately), and one or two other kindred works that need not be specified. He unpacked the bundle, mastered its contents, and proceeded to write one more essay for the *Quarterly*,[2] after the fashion familiar to all who have read Macaulay's contributions to the *Edinburgh*. First came

---

[1] An abridgment of the work, in a single octavo volume without the illustrations, was published in 1810.
[2] Vol. III., pp. 218-62.

destructive criticism of the books under review, and then a carefully constructed account of Nelson, himself. The essay closely resembled his other articles in the same magazine. But to John Murray, the publisher of the *Quarterly*, it afforded unusual satisfaction, and he suggested to the Laureate that he should take this little vignette of Nelson, and expand it into a book. The idea was agreeable to Southey, and he set to work with a will. Always conscientious, he tossed his earlier effort aside and turned again to a fresh perusal of the books which he had hastily reviewed. To these he may have added one or two more which an interest in the subject had made him curious to see; but he made no elaborate preparations as for the *History of Portugal*, because Murray insisted that the book must be short. The result may be best described as an attractive and palatable digest of Clarke and McArthur. Southey began his labours in 1812, and completed them in the following year. John Murray probably expected that sales would be brisk, but he can hardly have anticipated that his casual suggestion was to endow the world with a classic.

Macaulay has asserted in his emphatic way that no writer ever lived better qualified than Southey to write the life of Nelson. The assertion is rather a sweeping one, and the grounds on which Macaulay bases it can hardly be said to lend it weight. Southey had but a meagre equipment for a naval historian. In early boyhood he had seen Rodney fêted in the streets of Bristol on his return from the Battle of the Saints; his younger brother Thomas was a naval officer and fought at Copenhagen; and he himself had traversed the Bay of Biscay on his journeys to Lisbon and back. But his knowledge of the navy and naval ways was almost as meagre as Wordsworth's; and there was little reason why he should have acceded to Murray's request, apart from his keenness to earn one hundred pounds. What made for success in his undertaking was the wide range of subjects which had employed his pen, and the diversity of elements which he had transmuted into prose.

Of the success of the venture there can be no doubt. The book was greeted with a sustained pæan of praise. Sir Humphry Davy, who was a personal friend and admirer both of Southey and of Nelson, declared that the work was an "immortal monument raised by genius to valour." Macaulay in a very dashing style turned out a phrase that smacked of the sea: " It would not be easy to find," he said, " an instance of a more exact *hit between wind and water.*" Even the merciless Byron exclaimed meekly enough that the *Life of Nelson* was beautiful. The American Government printed an edition on fine paper for every officer, and on coarse paper for every rating in the navy of the United States. The book, it was generally agreed, must have been written out of the fulness of knowledge by one whom destiny had shaped for this special end. These highly favourable opinions have long gone unchallenged and may be thought to have stood the test of time. Yet in Nelson's interest, after the lapse of a century, they demand some scrutiny and revision.

Southey's work, as already suggested, sprang like a rich orchid from the rugous flank of dry-as-dust Clarke and McArthur. So closely did the Laureate cling to these prime authorities, that many a passage of his book is not now intelligible without reference to the parent stock. McArthur was an authority on naval lore, and his partner was no mean exponent. Their narrative, though very often as unintelligible as Sanskrit to the multitude, is, nautically speaking, unexceptionable. Southey, as a rule, attempts an easy paraphrase. But sometimes he misses the point of an anecdote; sometimes he finds the jargon too much for him. In the former case he blunders unwittingly; in the latter he simply transcribes verbatim and leaves his reader to look after himself. In short, where Clarke and McArthur are at their best, Southey flies ahead with a fair wind abaft; but where Clarke and McArthur are ineffective or incomprehensible, Southey makes heavy weather.

For such a period as the blockade of Toulon (1803–5), we rely to-day on the memoirs of Nelson's chaplain, Rev. A. J. Scott, and the physician, Dr. Leonard Gillespie. These, however, were not available for Clarke and McArthur, who could devise no better way of filling the void than with a number of letters more or less relevant. A glance at Chapter I. of Part IX. below will show how slavishly Southey followed them. This is the more to be regretted because the most readable parts of his book are those in which he breaks away from their leading-strings. Particularly memorable is the touching passage in which he describes Nelson's wound and death. Dr. Beatty's account had proved longer than McArthur had bargained for, and its pathos and intimacy had not commended themselves to the statuesque dignity of Dr. Clarke. The blue pencil had been freely used, and the twin editors had retained a mere fragment of the original. But Southey recognised at once the truth and beauty which his guides had rejected; and taking the gracious little pamphlet bodily into his pages, gave it a distinction which it might otherwise have missed. Incidentally he conferred a benefit on himself; for few are the readers who disdain to inspect the end of a book before the beginning; and those who submit Southey's *Nelson* to such a test turn back to the title-page and devour the whole.

It was no part of the Laureate's desire to rest satisfied with a brief abstract of Clarke and McArthur. If he had been given a free hand, he would have poured into the composition illustrative material of every description from his commonplace books and encyclopædic researches: for it was always a delight to him, when journeying along the highroad of a literary theme, to dash, with the insatiable curiosity of a dog, up every lane and byway. Had he pursued his bent in the present case, the compilation might well have run into eight or ten volumes; and such a *Life of Nelson*, it is safe to affirm, would be less read to-day than Clarke and McArthur's. But from such a fate the work was saved by John Murray's stringent injunction that the size of the book must be small. Southey in self-despite was compelled to conform, and after a little practice he grew tractable and docile. But in the earlier pages he kicked violently against the pricks of Murray's goad. In Part I. he only just managed to rein his muse as she dashed off tangentially to write up Polar Exploration: and in Part III. he inserts without a shadow of excuse an entirely superfluous history of Corsica.[1]

The bigoted intolerance of his judgment, especially in regard to personalities, constitutes a more serious defect.

[1] See below, pp. 54-60.

His hatred and loathing for Napoleon burn him up like a fire; if only the monster had been killed on his way to Egypt, he says, " he would have escaped the perpetration of those crimes which have incarnadined his soul with a deeper dye than that of the purple for which he committed them—those acts of perfidy, midnight murder, usurpation, and remorseless tyranny which have consigned his name to universal execration, now and for ever."[1] There is something almost unmanly in such vapourings; something in marked contrast to Nelson's boyish eagerness " to try Boney on a wind."[2] Yet Southey's denunciation of public misdemeanours seem charitable when compared with his domestic invectives. His wife's sister was the unhappy woman whom Coleridge married and forsook. And by the stern censor of Greta Hall Coleridge was never forgiven. Wife-desertion seemed to Southey the blackest of atrocities; and as such he labelled it, wherever found. He did not choose or care to consider the sad causes that separated Lord and Lady Nelson. From Coleridge's behaviour he formed his own conclusions; and leaning scornfully against the pedestal of stoic self-control, he drew around him the moral garments of propriety. Against Lady Hamilton no words were too bad, no insinuations too vile. Without waiting for an invitation, he cast the first stone; and many others, knowing him upright and believing him just, have followed his unchristian example.

Southey's hatred of Napoleon (and all that Napoleon stood for) exposed him to the ridicule of those who knew how hotly he had in Balliol days supported the French Revolution. But the Laureate's change of opinion was more apparent than real. He welcomed the Girondins and espoused their cause, because he believed that it would enfranchise the masses and break the rod of their oppressor. But when he saw how hideous was the tree that sprang from the acorn of Liberty, and when he recognised in the Corsican an hypertrophied growth of the despotism he hated, he shifted his standpoint rather than his convictions. In the *Life of Nelson* will be found, side by side with anti-Jacobin outbursts, expressions of sympathy with those who groaned under the heel of continental kingship.[3]

---

[1] See below, p. 124.   [2] See below, p. 123.   [3] See below, pp. 165-6, 192.

Southey was not such a fool in politics as Macaulay would have us believe. He confidently prophesied that interference in Spain would cause Napoleon's overthrow; and he looked forward to the eventual spread of the democratic ideal. It was this liberalism, so antagonistic to the beliefs of the British Navy, which commended his *Nelson* to the nineteenth-century reformers; and the nineteenth-century reformers, applauding the justice of his views concerning the Neapolitan monarchy, applauded also the injustice of his views concerning the admiral whom he condemned.

The truth is that Southey lived too near to the Napoleonic period to write a true or reliable history of it. Time and again he assumes in his readers a fairly intimate acquaintance with minor events on which the larger text-books of to-day throw no light whatever; [1] and on problems of the most debatable and puzzling kind, he lays down the law without waiting for the necessary evidence or even reconciling the scraps already collected. [2] His comments are too often those of a carping critic at a first performance, who niggles at this and misunderstands that, and leaves the theatre without for a moment suspecting that he has misconstrued what posterity will salute as a masterpiece.

It was unfortunate for him that he should have been so ill-instructed in all that appertained to his hero's profession. Maritime strategy is an elusive subject on which few specialists to-day will commit themselves; and those, like Admiral Mahan, who have dared to do so have had their theories torn to shreds. But Southey with his amazing complacency found no necessary limitations to his powers, and sat in judgment on the disposition and movements of fleets as if they were as comprehensible to a well-read man as the ethics of Aristotle or the prosody of Milton. Thousands of those who have read his book have closed it with the conviction that in 1805 Nelson was hoodwinked by Napoleon and betrayed himself by pursuing Villeneuve across the Atlantic to the Indies. In reality Southey was the strategist misled; and those only have suffered betrayal who have blindly followed him.

It is fortunately not on every page that strategic questions arise. But Southey is quite as much out of his depth in the

[1] See below, pp. 80-7.   [2] See below, pp. 132-3, 291-2.

matter of naval tactics. In his account of the Battle of St. Vincent he creates more dire confusion than Jervis effected in the ranks of the Spaniards. At the Nile he attributes the winning gambit not to Nelson at all, but to Captain Foley. And at Trafalgar, the tactical masterpiece in all the annals of maritime warfare, he leaves the English plans severely alone, apparently by an oversight. Nelson, by the confession of all who are competent to judge, was the greatest genius that ever marshalled fleets or ever won battles at sea. As a youth of twenty-five he was commended to the Duke of Clarence by the exacting Lord Hood as the most knowledgeable tactician in the fleet; and this reputation he continued to enjoy until Southey shattered it. Nelson pored over such treatises as Clerk of Eldin and *The Manœuverer* with unflagging and assiduous toil; and, half a century before Moltke, he evolved a marine *Kriegspiel* by means of which he taught his " band of brothers " how to fight. But of this infinite capacity for taking pains there is not so much as a hint in Southey's book. Instead, there has grown from its pages a mischievous heresy that England's greatest admiral owed his amazing success to a rather brainless habit of rushing at his foe head down like a maddened bull. This mischievous impression, so derogatory to Nelson's intellect, found favour with the masses who knew less of sea-warfare even than Southey; and to it may be traced much misdirected aim alike in action and thought ever since.

But though a land-lubber in his ignorance of battles at sea, Southey has been very generally congratulated for his skill in avoiding any glaring mistakes in his terminology. Even naval officers, it has often been said, can find no fault in his use of nautical phrases; and some have thought that he must surely have coaxed his brother Thomas, if not actually to collaborate, at least to teach him the ropes.

Southey was not one who suffered from undue humility; but he certainly cherished no illusions in regard to his seamanship. He trod as delicately among sea-terms (on his own confession) " as a cat among crockery." And this is evident in every part of his work. Either he tells the story in his own words, and avoids the smallest mention of technicalities, or he props in front of him the ponderous tomes of Clarke and McArthur and borrows their narrative without altering a word; brailing up and shivering the driver and after sails, shooting away a cro'jeck yard, or, with the enemy under his lee bow, signalling the van ships to wear, and standing away to windward. There was little enough reason why naval officers should complain; they understood the language. The long-suffering ones were the uninitiated; and they, never having read Messrs. Clarke and McArthur, gave Southey credit for a practical knowledge which he certainly never possessed.

Burdened, then, with so many drawbacks, wherein resides the supreme merit of this acknowledged masterpiece? Not surely in its superiority in point of style over its author's other prose works. Southey told Sir Walter Scott that his *Nelson* could not fail of being a good book; but he never regarded it as surpassing his *Wesley* or his *Cowper*, and would assuredly be disappointed to hear it rated above his *History of Brazil*. At the same time he intuitively gauged what it was that would make his book " sublime." It was Nelson himself; Nelson who had caused everything to succeed with which he was ever connected—Nelson, not only the greatest conqueror of modern times, not only a lover beside whom even Abelard, Paris, and Paolo wax pale, but Nelson the human creature whom all his fellow-countrymen place first among those who have won their affection.

And what is it that has made Nelson, and will continue to make him, the idol of successive generations? Not his strategy, not his tactics, not even his love-romance: for if it had been, Southey's volume, which mutilates them all, would have failed, and the failure would have been great. No: like Dr. Samuel Johnson, Nelson grips all hearts by the beauty and force of his character.

England has produced many world-famous admirals; patriots like Howard of Effingham, disciplinarians like Jervis, tacticians like Monk and Rodney, administrators like Anson, reformers like Howe, conquerors like Blake, knights-errant like Grenville, scientists like Davis, world-circlers like Drake. But there is only one Nelson; only one who combined the virtues of all the rest and added thereto that intangible something which we vaguely label charm. No other admiral in his teens fought a polar-bear single-handed, or as a post-captain raced his middies to the main-top. No other, like the majority of those for whom he fought, was seasick whenever the wind grew wild. No other, after boarding a ship through its windows, utilised its deck as a bridge to capture the biggest craft afloat. No other lost an eye and made less of his loss, or turned it to gain with a telescope. No other lost his right arm and, in the hour of its shattering, used his left to rescue drowning men. No other, after months of neglect and affronts, pleaded so pathetically for command of a cockle-boat. No other caused the surging holiday crowds to kneel and kiss his shadow as it passed.

" Determination," writes one of our greatest living poets, " will always command respect, and genius reverence, and kindness love. All these were in Nelson, together with much passion, much wisdom, a great deal of nervous sensibility and some vanity. There was also something wistful, magnetic and compelling which cannot be explained or ignored. It does not get into books, it cannot be put into words, it is simply mysterious, and very beautiful. It was this quality in him which made his rough sea-captains shed tears when he explained his plans to them. It was by this quality that he bound men's hearts together, and gave to their virtue purpose, and to their strength an aim." [1]

When he crowned a life of patient service and sacrifice by a death whose sweetness the narrow cockpit could not mar, all true men and women desired in the stillness of their homes to study the true lineaments of his character. It was this that Southey's book enabled them to do; and that is the reason why its pages are as fresh to-day as in the hour when they were written.

Between the character of Nelson and the character of Southey there was an attraction which may be styled magnetic. But the two had something else in common: for Nelson, more than any British admiral since Raleigh, had the gift of self-expression in prose. He inherited the precious talent from his father, the Vicar of Burnham Thorpe, whose whimsical muse finds fresh expression in the outpourings of his favourite son. Not that Nelson ever found time to write a book, or even compose a pamphlet.

[1] John Masefield.

But his was the pen of a ready writer; and of the number-less letters which he sent to his friends hundreds happily survive. In fact (if the tactics of Trafalgar be excluded), it may truthfully be said that since Southey's day the study of Nelson has centred round the documents traceable to his own hand. Between 1844 and 1846 a great scholar, Sir Harris Nicolas, published three thousand five hundred which he had patiently collected. They fill seven thick volumes of small print, and constitute the noblest memorial to the admiral's personality. No such assemblage of self-revealing papers is available for the study of any other English seaman; and those who have read Nicolas's volumes all through know Nelson better than they know their best friends. Other letters have been discovered since the *Dis-patches and Letters* were published; and a very important collection, known till recently as the "Morrison Manu-scripts," formed the backbone of Pettigrew's *Memoirs of Lord Nelson* which appeared in 1849.

With such masses of new information it was inevitable that sooner or later an attempt would be made to dethrone Southey and provide the great reading public with a new and up-to-date biography. The task was at length under-taken by the great apostle and exponent of sea-power, Admiral Mahan, of the United States Navy; and his *Nelson : the Embodiment of the Sea Power of Great Britain* appeared in 1897. Mahan enjoyed all the qualifications which were denied to Southey. He was a distinguished naval officer; he had handled battleships under sail; he had applied himself exclusively to the science and art of maritime warfare; and he had a scholar's knowledge of the Napoleonic epoch. Moreover, he left no document of Nicolas unanalysed, no transcript of Pettigrew unread. As a result, his book is one which the student of Nelson cannot afford to ignore; but as a rival to Southey it is simply not to be named. With prolixity of iteration and verbose redund-ancy, with philosophical reflections and repeated use of the same illustrative material, the long phrases and clauses and unpruned paragraphs lift the great little sailor so high above us that he stands, like the figure in Trafalgar Square, so far removed that the man in the street can hardly discern his features.

c

" A peculiar austerity," wrote Macaulay, " marks almost all Mr. Southey's judgments of men and actions. We are far from blaming him for fixing on a high standard of morals and for applying that standard to every case. But rigour ought to be accompanied by discernment; and of discernment Mr. Southey seems to be utterly destitute. His mode of judging is monkish. It is exactly what we should expect from a stern old Benedictine who had been preserved from many ordinary frailties by the restraints of his situation." When we remember how Southey was misled about Nelson's conduct at Naples by such worthless witnesses as Captain Foote and Miss Williams, we can only nod our agreement as we read Macaulay's words. But after all, Southey only went wrong in one chapter; whereas Mahan's whole book is warped by the point of view. Lady Hamilton makes her appearance, like the bad fairy with her curse, quite early in the story, and flutters in and out from page to page until the reader begins to feel that Nelson was born into the world simply to be dogged by an evil ogress to whose wiles he eventually succumbed. This false interpretation spoils a marvellous array of facts, and leaves the Poet Laureate of 1805 in possession of the field.

To Southey, then, we owe an unfading portrait of the greatest English seaman. But we owe him also another debt which is insufficiently recognised. Before Waterloo brought the war of that day to an end, he had created a literary masterpiece with the Navy for its theme. Our ancestors, in consequence, when they welcomed the peace, knew what was due to the silent sailors who had cleared the seas and returned to their homes without expecting praise.

Only once during the Great War of our own time did the main forces that covered the vitals of Germany turn their backs in flight without hope or thought of entering the arena again. And that was at Jutland. Yet the seamen, who inherited Nelson's spirit and fought there as Nelson would have had them fight, were greeted home-returning like Hawke and Howe, with hisses and ironical cheers.

Let it be remembered, then, that on 21st October, 1805, the opposing ships were constructed entirely of wood and continued to float even when riddled with shot-holes. Being wind-propelled, they could not upon the day of battle move at more than one or two knots. In plain English, when vanquished they could neither hope to run away, nor yet by sinking to bury their shame. Out of thirty-three ships opposed to him Nelson captured twenty. At Jutland a single salvo was sufficient to destroy the mightiest vessel afloat, and internal mechanism gave to the slowest ship power to run in any direction. Nothing resembling Nelson's victory was therefore possible. But once more the destinies of nations were at stake; once more the ocean lists were set; and once more the sons of Nelson at the battle's end found themselves alone upon the tumbling waves. Englishmen, however, have been slow with their huzzas. They wait a Southey to lead the applause.

BIBLIOGRAPHY

IN our day it is by no means an unheard-of thing for a popular book to run through twelve impressions in as many years, or attract in its author's lifetime as many as seventy thousand purchasers. But in Southey's day the book-buying public was more select. There were no cheap illuminants to read by after the day's work was done; and no Education Acts had, by their passage through Parliament, made reading a national accomplishment. Southey's *Nelson* certainly conquered the world, but cannot be said to have taken it by storm. First appearing in 1813, it was reprinted in the following year; but the second impression,[1] it is instructive to note, satisfied all immediate requirements.

---

[1] I use the word " impression " advisedly in order to emphasise the resemblance between this issue of the book and the earlier one; but there are, for all that, in the second version some differences worth noting; in particular, the withdrawal of the prophecy at the beginning of Part III. (below, p. 50); and the apology for Hyde Parker's signal of recall at the Battle of Copenhagen (below, pp. 225–6). Moreover, by way of appendix to the second volume the verses entitled *Ulm and Trafalgar* were printed in full. Southey had already quoted eight lines from the poem on the title-page of the original edition—without, apparently, knowing for certain that Canning was the author. In printing the entire " Monody " in his second edition, he reminded his readers that the lines were " written while the event was yet recent and commonly attributed to a gentleman high in office and distinguished no less by his public services than his transcendent abilities." This second edition seems to be the rarest and hardest to come by nowadays; there is no copy either at the British Museum, the Bodleian, the Royal United Service Institution or the Admiralty Library.

The dress in which the work first made its bow will to modern taste appear a little peculiar. The contents of the book, though eminently modest in quantity, were submitted to the public in a two-volume edition, the volumes being slim little tomes measuring four inches by six and a half, and turning the scale at a figure markedly in contrast with the ponderous quartos of Clarke and McArthur.

It has been suggested that this format, which was repeated in the 1814 issue, may be accepted as a satisfactory explanation why nearly twelve years were to elapse before there was any further call for the book.[1] But there is nothing at all to support this reasoning; the work, as Southey suggested in his preface,[2] was of a convenient size to carry in the pocket, and the duodecimo was quite a fashionable vogue for the bookworms of that day.[3]

As the Pre-Raphaelites had to wait for recognition until Ruskin came forth as their champion and their trumpeter, so the great little life of the great little Admiral had to wait its real triumph until Macaulay proclaimed it an essential factor in every self-respecting Englishman's education. It was in January 1830 that *The Edinburgh Review* printed the well-known essay, now referred to as *Southey*. It had as its immediate subject the Poet Laureate's *Colloquies on Society*; but Macaulay laid under review all that Southey had written, and with oracular impressiveness pronounced *The Life of Nelson* "the most perfect and the most delightful of his works." This verdict from their arbiter of excellence filled the men of 1830 with penitence and amazement when they found that the book was out of print. A promising market was thus opened; and, treading on the heels of Macaulay's essay, came a "Revised" or "Fourth" edition of the book.

This important re-issue was christened "Number Twelve" in Murray's "Family Library," a home-educating venture (like the Encyclopædias of our own day) which set forth all that was known of Alexander and Napoleon, the British Artists and the British Physicians, Cervantes and Cicero, Mutinies and State Trials, Demonology, Witchcraft, Isaac Newton, Africa, Fairy Tales, Natural Philosophy, and Ali Pasha. The whole in eighty duodecimo volumes with bijou little woodcuts,[4] at five shillings apiece, "to be sold separately." The size of the fourth edition of Southey's *Nelson* was thus the same as the first three, but instead of two volumes of 250 pages each, there was now only a single volume of 350. The book forthwith penetrated into every English home, and became a standard work of which fresh impressions followed each other at

[1] The "Third" edition of the work appeared in 1825; but although on its title-page it proclaims itself "new," it is in reality no more than a word-for-word reprint of the second edition of 1814. The only copy of this book that I have seen is in the Royal United Service Institution, to which it was "presented by John Murray." My attention was called to it by Mr. W. G. Perrin, the Admiralty Librarian.

[2] Below, p. xliii.

[3] To the first volume alike of the 1813, 1814 and 1825 editions was prefixed a little steel engraving after the pencil portrait of the Admiral done in 1800 by S. de Koster, and to the second volume some facsimiles of Nelson's handwriting.

[4] The "Nelson" illustrations, including a portrait (after de Koster), were drawn by George Cruikshank.

regular intervals. In 1844 the seventh appeared,[1] and in 1857 the fourteenth.[2] And from 1857 to our own day the book has been re-issued in a long array of shapes and sizes; their style proportional to every length of purse, and their number past finding out. Between the first issue of the book and the fourth or "new" edition of 1830 several important works on naval history and the Nelson epoch made their appearance: James's *Naval History* (five volumes), a painstaking chronicle completed in 1824; Brenton's *Naval History*, by a well-known naval officer; Marshall's *Royal Naval Biography*, a clumsy and inartistic production, but with memoirs supplied by the subjects thereof;[3] best of all, perhaps, Ralfe's *Naval Biography of Great Britain*, issued (four volumes) in 1828 and recognised to-day as no mean authority. Here were books which Southey doubtless bought and studied and packed away upon his shelves. And then there were others, which clearly made a deeper impression upon his mind because they concerned his own masterpiece more nearly: a sensational work, veiled in anonymity, styled *Letters of Lord Nelson to Lady Hamilton*,[4] possibly genuine, and by some critics attributed to the author of Harrison's *Life*; and the invaluable *Selection from the Public and Private Correspondence of Vice-Admiral Collingwood*, collected and edited by that admiral's son-in-law.[5]

Armed with fresh information from these and other sources, Southey set himself to revise the book which he had not touched since 1814. He did not, of course, re-write the entire work. Far from it. Indeed, he left severely alone many passages that called loudly for correction. But, where the new material seemed to him important, he busied himself with scissors and paste-pot, recasting one chapter, amending another, and appending subsidiary illustrative matter in expanded paragraphs and footnotes. Some hasty judgments, formed by him when first he wrote, seemed to him to derive confirmation from the Nelson-Hamilton letters, and these he quoted, perhaps rather too copiously, seeing that the authenticity of the collection was not established. But on the other hand, he detected and set right some false conclusions and blunders, notably his unwarranted strictures on Collingwood in connection with Nelson's dying injunction, "Anchor, Hardy, anchor!"

[1] I mention the 1844 issue because, being labelled "seventh," it enabled me to discover what I had long sought in vain, viz., the exact number of editions of the book published during Southey's life. I have examined all of these, and append a tabular view of them.

FIRST	.	.	. 1813, original edition.
SECOND	.	.	. 1814, much the same as 1813, but with some important changes.
THIRD	.	.	. 1825, same as 1814.
FOURTH	.	.	. 1830, new and heavily revised edition.
FIFTH	.	.	. 1831, same as 1830.
SIXTH	.	.	. 1840, same as 1830.

[2] As far as I have been able to discover, the fourteenth edition of 1857 was the earliest to adopt the octavo size. The first edition, however, was obtainable in a large-paper issue, which resembled an octavo in outward appearance. The Admiralty Library has a copy in this style.

[3] See below, Note 1, p. 133.

[4] Two vols., octavo, 1814.

[5] 1828.

From a copy of the thirteenth edition [1] in the British Museum, it appears that Murray incorporated the very latest emendations from Southey's hand some ten years after the author's death. But these last alterations were quite ordinary *corrigenda*, and do not call for special notice. The 1830 edition constitutes Southey's final verdict on Nelson's life and character.

Recent editors of the biography, with commendable zeal and a scholarly desire to reach the fountain-head, have almost without exception made their transcripts from the first edition of 1813. Enough, however, has been said to show that present study, if it is to be profitable, must centre round the particular issue which incorporates Southey's second thoughts. On the 1830 version, therefore, is based the present edition, which a few words will suffice to characterise.

When we consider the absolute dependence of Britain on sea-supremacy and maritime power, when we remember how this country's rise to pre-eminence has been secured by sea-victories and naval commanders, there is good reason to feel surprise at the meagre harvest of first-class books having the Navy for their theme. In 1805 the scarcity was still more pronounced; and, if we except Campbell's *Lives of the Admirals* (1742–5) as lacking almost all the essentials of greatness, it would be hard to name any book except *Robinson Crusoe* which would in that day have appealed with equal force both to the literary critic and to the officers of the Navy and Mercantile Marine.

Southey's *Life of Nelson* was the first work on naval history since the *Traffics and Discoveries* of Richard Hakluyt to be absorbed without question, comment, or challenge, into the elect body of universal literature.

This fact is of all facts the most significant in connection with this remarkable work. And yet in a twofold sense it is apt to be overlooked. Students of history, noting Southey's false perspective, his biased judgments, and misinterpretation of motives, are inclined to turn impatiently to the pages of Mahan, forgetting entirely that the " Nelson " whom we know to-day is almost as truly Southey's creation as " Henry the Fifth " and " Richard the Third " are Shakespeare's. On the other hand, students of English literature, magnetically drawn to an acknowledged masterpiece on a subject so much out of the regular beat as " naval history," are somewhat prone to appraise the merits of the work without sufficiently often reminding themselves that the book is not biography at all in the twentieth-century use of the word, but an impressionistic sketch by a prejudiced contemporary who completed his task before it was possible to collect the material out of which a real biography could be evolved.

The present edition, it is hoped, will assist both classes of readers to approach the work with more profit than they could obtain from any version that was not annotated. No attempt has been made to supplement Southey's very inadequate material by an abstract of what has been discovered since Southey himself died. No attempt has been made to complete even the unfinished fragments on St. Vincent or Trafalgar. Nothing has been added for

[1] 1853.

the sake of making additions. The aim has been so to edit the book
that the author's judgments, when based on untrustworthy evidence,
may be impartially reconsidered, and some effort made to sift the
author's meaning from the clogging encumbrances of an obsolete
nautical jargon: in a word, to clear a highway for truth, and make
the rough passages plain.

The " New " or revised edition of 1830 has been followed verbatim.
But the text has been carefully collated with the editions of 1813,
1814 and 1825, and all the discrepancies made apparent in footnotes.
All four editions, when originally issued, divided their contents
with mechanical precision into nine portions, or " chapters," which
bore little, if any, relation to the course of Nelson's life. This
arrangement imposes a real obstacle to any earnest person desiring
to do his author justice. It has in consequence been dispensed with,
and in its place a scheme of subdivision adopted that attunes itself
more nearly to the natural breaks in the story; the needful references,
however, are given to show where Southey's chapters begin and
end. No other liberties have been taken beyond the modernising of
punctuation and paragraphs and the spelling of proper names.

Undoubtedly the best and most interesting way to read *The Life
of Nelson* would be to approach it after a fairly close perusal of a
modern work on the same subject. Southey has much to give, but
he yields it most readily to those who already have some store of
knowledge to exchange. In particular this edition is recommended
to those who are sufficiently versed in Nelsonian studies to advance
from secondary authorities to an original source, and sufficiently
interested in that source to enquire how far its verdicts stand unchallenged before the findings of modern criticism. For those who
like to read slowly and meditate on what they read, and for those
also who are working together in groups, a number of questions
have been added at the end. They concern themselves, of course,
with only a tithe of the topics that might profitably be discussed;
but they may be of assistance in paving the way to others more
valuable, and may even perhaps lead insensibly to a juster and
keener appreciation of the masterpiece on which they are based.

For the kind help which they have given me in my search after
the rather obscure details concerning the early history of Southey's
book, I desire to thank Mr. W. G. Perrin, the Admiralty Librarian,
Mr. Francis Edwards, Mr. Gibson of the Bodleian, Mr. Sladen
of the British Museum, and in particular Dr. Richard Wilson of
Aldine House.

SOUTHEY'S DEDICATION

JOHN WILSON CROKER, ESQ.

LL.D., F.R.S.

SECRETARY TO THE ADMIRALTY

WHO

BY THE OFFICIAL SITUATION WHICH HE SO ABLY
FILLS IS QUALIFIED TO APPRECIATE
THEIR HISTORICAL ACCURACY

AND WHO

AS A MEMBER OF THE REPUBLIC OF LETTERS IS
EQUALLY QUALIFIED TO DECIDE UPON
THEIR LITERARY MERIT

THESE VOLUMES

ARE RESPECTFULLY DEDICATED
BY HIS FRIEND

THE AUTHOR

Bursting through the gloom
With radiant glory from thy trophied tomb,
The sacred splendour of thy deathless name
Shall grace and guard thy Country's martial fame.
Far-seen shall blaze the unextinguished ray,
A mighty beacon lighting Glory's way;
With living lustre this proud land adorn
And shine and save through ages yet unborn.

GEORGE CANNING.

Quoted by Southey (without attribution) on the title-page of the First Edition ; cp. note on page xxxv, above.

SOUTHEY'S PREFACE

MANY lives of Nelson have been written. One is yet wanting, clear and concise enough to become a manual for the young sailor, which he may carry about with him, till he has treasured up the example in his memory and his heart. In attempting such a work, I shall write the eulogy of our great naval hero; for the best eulogy of Nelson is the faithful history of his actions; the best history, that which shall relate them most perspicuously.

THE LIFE OF NELSON

PART I—BOYHOOD AND YOUTH

[*SOUTHEY. CHAPTER I*]

HORATIO, son of Edmund and Catherine Nelson, was born 29th September, 1758, in the parsonage house of Burnham Thorpe, a village in the county of Norfolk, of which his father was Rector. The maiden name of his mother was Suckling. Her grandmother was an elder sister of Sir Robert Walpole, and this child was named after his godfather, the first Lord Walpole.[1] Mrs. Nelson died in 1767, leaving eight out of eleven children. Her brother, Captain Maurice Suckling of the navy, visited the widower upon this event and promised to take care of one of the boys. Three years afterwards, when Horatio was only twelve years of age, being at home during the Christmas holidays, he read in the county newspaper that his uncle was appointed to the *Raisonnable*,[2] of sixty-four guns.[3] " Do, William," said

[1] Southey is in error here. Nelson's godfather was the *second* Lord Walpole.

[2] Captured ships taken into the English service usually retained their original names. Compare *Temeraire*.

[3] It is not perhaps untrue to say of all His Majesty's ships now, as in the past, that they belong to two main classes:

I. Those that are built to take their place in the line of battle, *i.e.* BATTLESHIPS.
II. Those that, whatever fighting they may see, are in their functions subsidiary to the battleships.

Battleships again may be subdivided into four categories:
(*a*) The dominant type of the moment.
(*b*) Ships still serviceable, but inferior to the dominant type.
(*c*) Improvements on the dominant type.
(*d*) The very latest thing.

According to this classification we can tabulate side by side the ships of Nelson's day and the ships of the Great War of 1914.

	1914	Nelson's Day
(*b*)	Pre-Dreadnought	Sixty-four
(*a*)	Dreadnought	Seventy-four
(*c*)	Super-Dreadnought	Eighty or Ninety
(*d*)	Hyper-super-Dreadnought	Hundred

The names of big ships in Nelson's day were derived from their armament. To all big battleships of 1914 the epoch-making *Dreadnought* stood godmother.

he to a brother who was a year and a half older than himself,
" write to my father and tell him that I should like to go
to sea with Uncle Maurice." Mr. Nelson was then at Bath,
whither he had gone for the recovery of his health. His
circumstances were straitened, and he had no prospect of
ever seeing them bettered. He knew that it was the wish
of providing for himself by which Horatio was chiefly
actuated, and did not oppose his resolution. He understood
also the boy's character, and had always said that, in
whatever station he might be placed, he would climb if
possible to the very top of the tree. Accordingly Captain
Suckling was written to. " What," said he in his answer,
" has poor Horatio done, who is so weak, that he, above all
the rest, should be sent to rough it out at sea? But let
him come; and the first time we go into action, a cannon-
ball may knock off his head, and provide for him at once."

It is manifest from these words that Horatio was not
the boy whom his uncle would have chosen to bring up in
his own profession. He was never of a strong body; and the
ague, which at that time was one of the most common
diseases in England, had greatly reduced his strength.
Yet he had already given proofs of that resolute heart and
nobleness of mind which during his whole career of labour
and of glory so eminently distinguished him. When a mere
child, he strayed a-birds'-nesting from his grandmother's
house in company with a cow-boy. The dinner-hour elapsed;
he was absent, and could not be found; and the alarm of
the family became very great, for they apprehended that
he might have been carried off by gipsies. At length, after
search had been made for him in various directions, he was
discovered alone, sitting composedly by the side of a brook
which he could not get over. " I wonder, child," said the
old lady when she saw him, " that hunger and fear did
not drive you home." " Fear! grandmama," replied the
future hero, " I never saw fear. What is it? " Once, after
the winter holidays, when he and his brother William had
set off on horseback to return to school, they came back
because there had been a fall of snow; and William, who
did not much like the journey, said it was too deep for them
to venture on. " If that be the case," said the father, " you
certainly shall not go; but make another attempt, and I

will leave it to your honour. If the road is dangerous, you may return: but remember, boys, I leave it to your honour!" The snow was deep enough to have afforded them a reasonable excuse; but Horatio was not to be prevailed upon to turn back. "We must go on," said he. "Remember, brother, it was left to our honour!" There were some fine pears growing in the schoolmaster's garden, which the boys regarded as lawful booty, and in the highest degree tempting; but the boldest among them were afraid to venture for the prize. Horatio volunteered upon this service. He was lowered down at night from the bedroom window by some sheets, plundered the tree, was drawn up with the pears, and then distributed them among his schoolfellows without reserving any for himself. "He only took them," he said, "because every other boy was afraid."

Early on a cold and dark spring morning Mr. Nelson's servant arrived at this school (at North Walsham) with the expected summons for Horatio to join his ship. The parting from his brother William, who had been for so many years his playmate and bedfellow, was a painful effort, and was the beginning of those privations which are the sailor's lot through life. He accompanied his father to London. The *Raisonnable* was lying in the Medway. He was put into the Chatham stage,[1] and on its arrival was set down with the rest of the passengers, and left to find his way on board as he could. After wandering about in the cold without being able to reach the ship, an officer observed the forlorn appearance of the boy, questioned him; and, happening to be acquainted with his uncle, took him home and gave him some refreshments. When he got on board, Captain Suckling was not in the ship, nor had any person been apprised of the boy's coming. He paced the deck the whole remainder of the day, without being noticed by any one; and it was not till the second day that somebody, as he expressed it, "took compassion on him." The pain which is felt when we are first transplanted from our native soil, when the living branch is cut from the parent tree, is one of the most poignant which we have to endure through life. There are aftergriefs which wound more deeply, which leave behind them scars never to be effaced, which bruise the spirit, and some-

[1] The stage coach that ran regularly from London to Chatham.

times break the heart: but never do we feel so keenly the want of love, the necessity of being loved, and the sense of utter desertion, as when we first leave the haven of home, and are, as it were, pushed off upon the stream of life. Added to these feelings, the sea-boy has to endure physical hardships, and the privation of every comfort, even of sleep. Nelson had a feeble body and an affectionate heart, and he remembered through life his first days of wretchedness in the service.

The *Raisonnable*, having been commissioned on account of the dispute respecting the Falkland Islands,[1] was paid off[2] as soon as the difference with the court of Spain was accommodated, and Captain Suckling was removed to the *Triumph*, seventy-four,[3] then stationed as a guardship[4] in the Thames. This was considered as too inactive a life for a boy, and Nelson was therefore sent a voyage[5] to the West Indies in a merchant-ship, commanded by Mr. John Rathbone, an excellent seaman, who had served as master's mate[6] under Captain Suckling, in the *Dreadnought*.[7] He

[1] In 1770 the Spaniards made an unprovoked attack upon an English settlement in the Falkland Isles. Public indignation in this country rose to fever heat and a naval force was at once mobilised. The quarrel, however, was adjusted without resorting to armed force.

[2] When a man-of-war was not on active service she was *laid up* in one of the harbours adjacent to a royal dockyard. When her services were required, she was taken into commission and fitted out for a cruise. When the cruise was complete she returned to the port where she was commissioned; and her company, receiving their wages, dispersed. Thus a ship, when " paid off," closed a chapter in her life, and rested awhile from her labours.

[3] See Note 3, p. 1.

[4] A vessel of war appointed in general to superintend the maritime affairs in a harbour, and in particular, by sending out her guard-boats every night, to see that the ships which are not in commission have their proper watch kept.

[5] About June, 1771.

[6] The work on board a man-of-war in Nelson's time was distributed by the captain among a certain number of heads of departments, known as warrant officers. Of these the " Master " was the most important. He was responsible for the navigation of the ship; that is, he took her wherever she wanted to go, like the pilot of a modern aeroplane. He was a mathematician of sound capacity, and could construct hydrographical charts, and guide his vessel through storms and sandbanks with unerring skill and resource. He was assisted by a certain number of petty officers called quartermasters; but these men were able seamen, they were promoted for merit, and seldom rose any higher. The officer qualifying for a Master's warrant was known as " Master's Mate."

[7] This was the fifth vessel of her name. She has gone the way of nearly all wooden ships; but five of her guns may still be seen at the edge of the pavement in St. James's Square. They were brought home by Boscawen (called by the adoring tars " Old Dreadnought "), whose brother, Lord Falmouth, lived at No. 2. Nelson's uncle, Captain Suckling, on 21st October, 1757 (note the date), also fought a very gallant action in this *Dreadnought* No. 5. *Dreadnought* No. 1 was so christened by good Queen Bess just after the massacre of St. Bartholomew's Eve. In her plucky way Elizabeth chose the name to signify the defiance which her trust in the navy emboldened her to fling at her foes.

returned a practical seaman, but with a hatred of the king's service and a saying then common among the sailors: "Aft the most honour; forward the better man." [1] Rathbone had probably been disappointed and disgusted in the navy; and, with no unfriendly intentions, warned Nelson against a profession which he himself had found hopeless. His uncle received him on board the *Triumph* on his return,[2] and discovering his dislike to the navy, took the best means of reconciling him to it. He held it out as a reward that, if he attended well to his navigation, he should go in the cutter and decked long-boat, which was attached to the commanding-officer's ship at Chatham.[3] Thus he became a good pilot, for vessels of that description, from Chatham to the Tower and down the Swin Channel [4] to the North Foreland, and acquired a confidence among rocks and sands of which he often felt the value.[5]

Nelson had not been many months on board the *Triumph* when his love of enterprise was excited by hearing that two ships were fitting out for a voyage of discovery toward the North Pole.[6] In consequence of the difficulties which were

[1] Many of our nautical expressions date back to a time when the largest sailing vessel afloat had only a single mast. This served, in addition to other duties, as a convenient boundary-post between the sphere of those who held command and the sphere of those who did not; even to this day the expression " before the mast " survives as a description of those whose whole duty is obedience. In the phrase here quoted " aft " and " forward " may be translated " commissioned officers " and " subordinates." " Captains and lieutenants may get the decorations, but where would the service be without the petty officers? " There is little doubt that, by adopting such a sentiment thus early, Nelson learnt to treat the foremast hand with a consideration which throughout his career was repaid by something like idolatry.

[2] In July 1772 Nelson was rated midshipman of the *Triumph*; see Note 10, p. 12.

[3] Every man-of-war had her retinue of ministering craft. Her smallest servitor was the jolly-boat, and her biggest the long-boat or launch. The jolly-boat was pulled by four-oars; the long-boat was a ship in miniature. The cutter was something between the two, and was used for the conveyance of stores to the ship and liberty men to the land.

[4] The mouth of the Thames has a submerged delta, whose depths are very difficult to negotiate. The " Swin " is one of the chief avenues of traffic and leads from the mouth of the Medway to the open sea.

[5] For example, at the battles of the Nile and Copenhagen.

[6] The first epoch of English Arctic exploration opened in the reign of Elizabeth, when men still thought it feasible to find a route to India by a circumnavigation of North America. This epoch ended in 1616 when Baffin pronounced the " North-West " project impracticable. The second epoch did not open until the battle of Waterloo had given the world the promise of a century of peace. Between the two epochs there were so few voyages to the frozen North that the expedition in which Nelson took so romantic a part figured more largely than we can nowadays clearly understand. It was in every sense of the word a pioneer venture; for, instead of reviving the search for the " North-West Passage," it had as its object the investigation of the earth's frozen cap in the interests of science and truth. To those who judge by results it may not seem to have been very successful, but

D

expected on such a service, these vessels were to take out
effective men instead of the usual number of boys. This,
however, did not deter him from soliciting to be received,
and, by his uncle's interest, he was admitted as coxswain [1]
under Captain Lutwidge, second in command. The voyage
was undertaken in compliance with an application from
the Royal Society. The Hon. Captain Constantine John
Phipps, eldest son of Lord Mulgrave, volunteered his services.
The *Racehorse* and *Carcass* bombs [2] were selected, as the
strongest ships, and therefore best adapted for such a
voyage; and they were taken into dock and strengthened,
to render them as secure as possible against the ice. Two
masters of Greenlandmen were employed as pilots for each
ship. No expedition was ever more carefully fitted out;
and the First Lord of the Admiralty, Lord Sandwich, with
a laudable solicitude, went on board himself, before their
departure, to see that everything had been completed to
the wish of the officers. The ships were provided with a
simple and excellent apparatus for distilling fresh from
salt water, the invention of Dr. Irving, who accompanied
the expedition. It consisted merely in fitting a tube to the
ship's kettle and applying a wet mop to the surface as the
vapour was passing.[3] By these means from thirty-four
to forty gallons were produced every day.

They sailed from the Nore on the 4th of June.[4] On the
6th of the following month they were in lat. 79° 56′ 39″;
long. 9° 43′ 30″ E. The next day, about the place where
most of the old discoverers had been stopped, the *Racehorse*
was beset with ice; but they hove her through with ice-

it undoubtedly increased men's knowledge of the path to the Pole and so helped
modestly to pave the way for Peary's triumph in 1909. Its real author was
Daines Barrington, brother of the famous admiral, though the Royal Society lent
his scheme its patronage.

[1] The captain of a man-of-war had the right to choose certain personal attendants without consulting the Navy Board. One of these attendants was nominally
selected to act as helmsman of his pinnace or gig.

[2] The bomb-vessel was a ship mounting bombardment guns, mortars and
weapons of the howitzer type. As her armament tended to make her self-
destructive, her designers rejected every element that did not make for tough-
ness and durability. She was ketch-rigged, mainmast and mizzen, so as to allow
plenty of room for the guns in her bows.

[3] Raleigh invented a similar apparatus and used it with effect in the Islands
voyage of 1597. His cleverness, however, was regarded in those days as savouring
too much of witchcraft; and Doctor Irving's device for procuring water by the
condensation of steam was welcomed by Lord Sandwich's administration as a
brilliant novelty.

[4] 1773.

anchors.[1] Captain Phipps continued ranging along the ice, northward and westward, till the 24th; he then tried to the eastward. On the 30th he was in lat. 80° 13'; long. 18° 48' E. among the islands and in the ice, with no appearance of an opening for the ships. The weather was exceedingly fine, mild, and unusually clear. Here they were becalmed in a large bay, with three apparent openings between the islands which formed it; but everywhere, as far as they could see, surrounded with ice. There was not a breath of air, the water was perfectly smooth, the ice covered with snow, low and even, except a few broken pieces, near the edge; and the pools of water in the middle of the ice-fields just crusted over with young ice. On the next day the ice closed upon them, and no opening was to be seen anywhere, except a hole or lake, as it might be called, of about a mile and a half in circumference, where the ships lay fast to the ice with their ice-anchors.

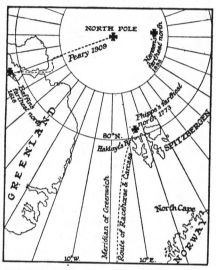

THE SIEGE OF THE NORTH POLE, 1616–1909

From these ice-fields they filled their casks with water, which was very pure and soft. The men were playing on the ice all day; but the Greenland pilots, who were farther than they had ever been before, and considered that the season was far advancing, were alarmed at being thus beset.

The next day there was not the smallest opening. The ships were within less than two lengths of each other, separated by ice, and neither having room to turn. The ice, which the day before had been flat and almost level with the water's edge, was now in many places forced higher

[1] A bar of round iron tapered to a point and bent into the shape of a pot-hook. The point is inserted in a hole in the ice, and the mooring hawser is attached to the shorter arm of the hook.

than the mainyard by the pieces squeezing together. A day of thick fog followed. It was succeeded by clear weather; but the passage by which the ships had entered from the westward was closed, and no open water was in sight either in that or any other quarter. By the pilots' advice the men were set to cut a passage and warp [1] through the small openings to the westward. They sawed through pieces of ice twelve feet thick; and this labour continued the whole day, during which their utmost efforts did not move the ships above three hundred yards; while they were driven, together with the ice, far to the N.E. and E. by the current. Sometimes a field of several acres square would be lifted up between two larger islands, and incorporated with them; and thus these larger pieces continued to grow by aggregation. Another day passed, and there seemed no probability of getting the ships out, without a strong E. or N.E. wind. The season was far advanced, and every hour lessened the chance of extricating themselves.

Young as he was, Nelson was appointed to command one of the boats which were sent out to explore a passage into the open water. It was the means of saving a boat belonging to the *Racehorse* from a singular but imminent danger. Some of the officers had fired at and wounded a walrus. As no other animal has so human-like an expression in its countenance, so also is there none that seems to possess more of the passions of humanity. The wounded animal dived immediately, and brought up a number of its companions; and they all joined in an attack upon the boat. They wrested an oar from one of the men; and it was with the utmost difficulty that the crew could prevent them from staving or upsetting her, till the *Carcass's* boat came up, and the walruses, finding their enemies thus reinforced, dispersed. Young Nelson exposed himself in a more daring manner. One night, during the mid-watch,[2] he stole from

---

[1] To change the position of a ship by pulling with a hawser attached to a ring-bolt, a tree, a post, another ship, or, most commonly, an anchor.
[2] A ship, unlike a land institution, does not rest from her labours at night. There is always work to be done. To make the incidence of service the same for all, the twenty-four hours are divided into seven periods: five of four hours each from 8 p.m. to 4 p.m., and two of two hours each (the " Dog Watches ") from 4 p.m. to 8 p.m. The ship's company is divided into two working parties (the Port Watch and the Starboard), who relieve each other alternately. The Middle Watch or Midwatch (12 midnight to 4 a.m.) is the least-loved period of duty, but the Dog Watches prevent two such penalties in succession.

the ship with one of his comrades, taking advantage of a
rising fog, and set off over the ice in pursuit of a bear. It
was not long before they were missed. The fog thickened,
and Captain Lutwidge and his officers became exceedingly
alarmed for their safety. Between three and four in the
morning the weather cleared, and the two adventurers
were seen, at a considerable distance from the ship, attacking
a huge bear. The signal for them to return was immediately
made. Nelson's comrade called upon him to obey it, but
in vain. His musket had flashed in the pan; [1] their ammunition was expended; and a chasm in the ice, which divided
him from the bear, probably preserved his life. " Never
mind," he cried; " do but let me get a blow at this devil
with the butt-end of my musket, and we shall have him."
Captain Lutwidge, however, seeing his danger, fired a gun,
which had the desired effect of frightening the beast; and
the boy then returned, somewhat afraid of the consequences
of his trespass. The captain reprimanded him sternly for
conduct so unworthy of the office which he filled, and
desired to know what motive he could have for hunting a
bear. " Sir," said he, pouting his lip, as he was wont to do
when agitated, " I wished to kill the bear, that I might
carry the skin to my father." [2]

A party were now sent to an island, about twelve miles
off (named Walden's Island in the charts from the midshipman who was entrusted with this service), to see where the
open water lay. They came back on the 6th [3] with information that the ice, though close all about them, was open
to the westward round the point by which they came in.
They said also that upon the island they had had a fresh
east wind. This intelligence considerably abated the hopes
of the crew; for where they lay it had been almost calm,
and their main dependence had been upon the effect of an
easterly wind in clearing the bay. There was but one alternative; either to wait the event of the weather upon the

[1] The pan contained the priming-powder, and this, when ignited, was expected
to transmit a spark to the charge in the barrel. If it failed in what was expected
of it, there was nothing more than a " flash in the pan " and the piece did not go off.
[2] " I chose Nelson in preference to the others because near bed-time in the
evening my father told me stories of our hero of the day, and neither Pitt nor
Shakespeare lost an eye, or an arm, or fought with a huge white bear on the ice
to make himself interesting."—GEORGE MEREDITH, *The Adventures of Harry
Richmond.*
[3] Of August.

ships, or to betake themselves to the boats. The likelihood
that it might be necessary to sacrifice the ships had been
foreseen. The boats accordingly were adapted (both in
number and size) to transport in case of emergency the
whole crew, and there were Dutch whalers upon the coast
in which they could all be conveyed to Europe. As for
wintering where they were, that dreadful experiment had
been already tried too often. No time was to be lost. The
ships had driven into shoal water, having but fourteen
fathoms. Should they, or the ice to which they were fast,
take the ground, they must inevitably be lost: and at this
time they were driving fast toward some rocks on the N.E.
Captain Phipps sent for the officers of both ships, and told
them his intention of preparing the boats for going away.
They were immediately hoisted out, and the fitting begun.
Canvas bread-bags were made, in case it should be necessary
suddenly to desert the vessels; and men were sent with the
lead and line [1] to the northward and eastward to sound
wherever they found cracks in the ice, that they might have
notice before the ice took the ground; for, in that case, the
ships must instantly have been crushed or overset.

On the 7th of August they began to haul the boats over
the ice, Nelson having command of a four-oared cutter.
The men behaved excellently well, like true British seamen.
They seemed reconciled to the thought of leaving the ships,
and had full confidence in their officers. About noon the
ice appeared rather more open near the vessels; and as the
wind was easterly, though there was but little of it, the sails
were set, and they got about a mile to the westward. They
moved very slowly, and were not now nearly so far to the
westward as when they were first beset. However, all sail
was kept upon them, to force them through whenever the
ice slacked the least. Whatever exertions were made, it
could not be possible to get the boats to the water's edge
before the 14th; and if the situation of the ships should not
alter by that time, it would not be justifiable to stay longer
by them. The commander therefore resolved to carry on
both attempts together, moving the boats constantly, and
taking every opportunity of getting the ships through. A

[1] The sounding apparatus; at this time consisting of a tapered cylinder of
lead, weighing 7, 14 or 28 pounds, attached to a line marked at regular intervals
to indicate in fathoms the depth of water.

party was sent out next day to the westward to examine
the state of the ice. They returned with tidings that it was
very heavy and close, consisting chiefly of large fields. The
ships, however, moved something, and the ice itself was
drifting westward. There was a thick fog, so that it was
impossible to ascertain what advantage had been gained.
It continued on the 9th; but the ships were moved a little
through some very small openings. The mist cleared off in
the afternoon; and it was then perceived that they had
driven much more than could have been expected to the
westward, and that the ice itself had driven still farther.
In the course of the day they got past the boats, and took
them on board again. On the morrow the wind sprang up
to the N.N.E. All sail was set, and the ships forced their
way through a great deal of very heavy ice. They frequently
struck, and with such force that one stroke broke the
shank [1] of the *Racehorse's* best bower-anchor.[2] But the
vessels made way; and by noon they had cleared the ice,
and were out at sea. The next day they anchored in Smeerenberg Harbour, close to that island of which the western-
most point is called Hakluyt's Headland, in honour of
the great promoter and compiler of our English voyages
of discovery.

Here they remained a few days, that the men might rest
after their fatigue. No insect was to be seen in this dreary
country, nor any species of reptile; not even the common
earth-worm. Large bodies of ice called icebergs filled up
the valleys between high mountains, so dark as, when
contrasted with the snow, to appear black. The colour of
the ice was a lively light green. Opposite to the place where
they fixed their observatory was one of these icebergs,
above three hundred feet high. Its side towards the sea
was nearly perpendicular, and a stream of water issued from
it. Large pieces frequently broke off, and rolled down into
the sea. There was no thunder nor lightning during the
whole time they were in these latitudes. The sky was
generally loaded with hard white clouds, from which it was

[1] The bar or shaft of an anchor, at one end of which the stock is fixed and at
the other end the arms.
[2] The two chief anchors of a ship were put to bed right forward of a ship, and
on this account they were described as " bow "-ers. That on the starboard side
was the " best," that on the port the " small." They were both, however,
exactly the same size.

never entirely free even in the clearest weather. They always knew when they were approaching the ice, long before they saw it, by a bright appearance near the horizon, which the Greenlandmen called the blink of the ice. The season was now so far advanced that nothing more could have been attempted, if indeed anything had been left untried: but the summer had been unusually favourable,[1] and they had carefully surveyed the wall of ice extending for more than twenty degrees between the latitudes of 80° and 81°, without the smallest appearance of any opening. The ships were paid off shortly after their return to England; and Nelson was then placed [2] by his uncle with Captain Farmer,[3] in the *Seahorse*, of twenty guns,[4] then going out to the East Indies in the squadron under Sir Edward Hughes.[5] He was stationed in the foretop [6] at watch and watch.[7] His good conduct attracted the attention of the master [8] (afterwards Captain Surridge), in whose watch [9] he was ; and, upon his recommendation, the captain rated him as midshipman.[10] At this time his

[1] Modern historians of this Arctic voyage agree in thinking that climatic conditions could not possibly have been worse.

[2] About March 1774.

[3] Chiefly remembered now for his heroic fight, when captain of the *Quebec*, against the French frigate *Surveillante*, 6th October, 1779. See Cory's " A Ballad for a Boy," in *Ionica*.

[4] According to the classification given in Note 3, p. 1, His Majesty's ships were divided in Nelson's day into vessels intended for the line of battle and vessels intended for other purposes. Of the latter the most important were the frigates, or " eyes of the fleet "; ships that subordinated strength to speed like the light cruisers of 1914. The largest frigate mounted fifty guns and the smallest only twenty.

[5] Admiral Mahan, the famous naval historian, considers that France produced in the Bailli de Suffren an admiral of unmatched resource and superlative skill. Sir Edward Hughes (1720–94) enjoys the reputation of having stood up to De Suffren in five pitched battles off the coast of India (1782–3), and of having supported the English flag throughout the series, not only against the scheming of genius, but against the dead weight of superior forces.

[6] A mast could be elongated telescope-wise according to the strength of the wind. The summit, whatever its height, was known as the " masthead." The " top " was a platform, for fighters with small arms, surrounding the head of that part of the mast which was built into the fabric of the hull.

[7] Alternate watches; see above, Note 2, p. 8.

[8] See above, Note 6, p. 4.

[9] See above, Note 2, p. 8.

[10] In Nelson's day the rule was that a youngster, unless the son of a naval officer, could not go to sea until he was thirteen. After serving as " volunteer " or " cadet " for two years he was then rated midshipman; that is, by interpretation, a *seaman* serving *amidships*. He continued in this status until six years' service afloat entitled him to sit for his lieutenant's examination. In theory no midshipman was more than nineteen years of age. In practice only too many failed to pass for a commission, and the habitué of the midshipmen's berth was in consequence not always quite so juvenile as he is painted.

Southey, however, goes wrong over this matter. Nelson was by this time over

countenance was florid, and his appearance rather stout and athletic; but when he had been about eighteen months in India he felt the effects of that climate, so perilous to European constitutions. The disease baffled all power of medicine. He was reduced almost to a skeleton; the use of his limbs was for some time entirely lost; and the only hope that remained was from a voyage home. Accordingly he was brought home by Captain Pigot, in the *Dolphin*:[1] and had it not been for the attentive and careful kindness of that officer on the way, Nelson would never have lived to reach his native shores. He had formed an acquaintance with Sir Charles Pole, Sir Thomas Troubridge, and other distinguished officers, then, like himself, beginning their career: he had left them pursuing that career in full enjoyment of health and hope, and was returning from a country in which all things were to him new and interesting, with a body broken down by sickness, and spirits which had sunk with his strength. Long afterwards, when the name of Nelson was known as widely as that of England itself, he spoke of the feelings which he at this time endured. " I felt impressed," said he, " with a feeling that I should never rise in my profession. My mind was staggered with a view of the difficulties I had to surmount, and the little interest I possessed. I could discover no means of reaching the object of my ambition. After a long and gloomy reverie, in which I almost wished myself overboard, a sudden glow of patriotism was kindled within me, and presented my king and country as my patron. ' Well, then,' I exclaimed, ' I will be a hero! and, confiding in Providence, I will brave every danger! ' "

Long afterwards Nelson loved to speak of the feelings of that moment: and from that time, he often said, a radiant orb was suspended in his mind's eye which urged

---

seventeen; and was not now rated midshipman for the first time. He had served as midshipman of the *Triumph* and of the *Carcass*, and had been rated midshipman on first joining the *Dolphin* in March 1774. On 5th April Farmer took the rating from him and bestowed it on his own son, Nelson figuring as A.B. (able seaman). There was no degradation in this; and as soon as there was a vacancy (31st October, 1775) Farmer restored his rating as midshipman. The midshipman was in practice a private qualifying for a naval commission by learning the seaman's art. He was theoretically only higher than an A.B., because the term " midshipman " before it was applied to " young gentlemen " had been the designation of a petty officer.

[1] 14th March, 1776; the *Dolphin* paid off on 24th September in the same year.

him onward to renown. The state of mind in which these
feelings began is what the mystics mean by their season
of darkness and desertion. If the animal spirits fail, they
represent it as an actual temptation. The enthusiasm of
Nelson's nature had taken a different direction, but its
essence was the same. He knew to what the previous state
of dejection was to be attributed; that an enfeebled body
and a mind depressed had cast this shade over his soul:
but he always seemed willing to believe that the sunshine
which succeeded bore with it a prophetic glory, and that the
light which led him on was " light from heaven."

His interest, however, was far better than he imagined.
During his absence Captain Suckling had been made Comptroller of the Navy;[1] his health had materially improved
upon the voyage; and as soon as the *Dolphin* was paid
off he was appointed acting lieutenant in the *Worcester*,
sixty-four, Captain Mark Robinson, then going out with
convoy to Gibraltar. Soon after his return, on the 8th of
April, 1777,[2] he passed his examination for a lieutenancy.
Captain Suckling sat at the head of the board; and, when
the examination had ended in a manner highly honourable
to Nelson, rose from his seat, and introduced him to the
examining captains as his nephew. They expressed their
wonder that he had not informed them of this relationship
before. He replied that he did not wish the younker to be
favoured; he knew his nephew would pass a good examination,[3] and he had not been deceived. The next day
Nelson received his commission as second lieutenant of the
Lowestoft frigate,[4] Captain William Locker, then fitting
out for Jamaica.

[1] To-day the whole of the sea-service is administered by the Board of Admiralty.
In Nelson's day the Admiralty confined its attention to the most important duties
only, and left the building and repair of ships and the mustering of men to the
" Navy Board," of which the " Comptroller" was chief. Captain Suckling, as
head of the Navy Office, exercised an influence at least as great as the First Lord
of the Admiralty.
[2] Nelson confirms this date in one of his letters. He was not often at fault,
but the date of the examination was the 9th inst.
[3] For a graphic description of a lieutenant's examination similar to that which
Nelson underwent, see Captain Marryat, *Peter Simple*, Chapter xxxix.
[4] See above, Note 4, p. 12.

PART II.—EARLY SERVICES

1777–93

CHAPTER I

DURING THE WAR OF AMERICAN INDEPENDENCE
(APRIL 1777–JULY 1783)

THIS section requires a few words of introduction because Southey's narrative presumes a knowledge of the history of the period which the modern reader may not possess. Part I. ended with Nelson's appointment to the *Lowestoft* frigate then fitting out for Jamaica. There were at that time three naval stations on the other side of the Atlantic, which we may describe in terms of modern geography as (1) the Greater Antilles station; (2) the Lesser Antilles station; and (3) the New York station. "The War of American Independence" had already been in progress for two years when Nelson received his commission; but up to this point the quarrel had been confined to England and her colonies. The year of Nelson's appointment to the *Lowestoft* was the year of Saratoga, the disaster to British arms which persuaded the European Powers to intervene in the struggle. In 1778 France entered the war on the side of the Americans; in 1779 she was joined by Spain; and in the following year by Holland. In 1780 also arose the "Armed Neutrality of the North," a league of nations (Russia, Prussia, the "Empire," Denmark and Sweden) jointly organised to resist Britain's "Right of Search."

Happily, so vast a coalition against this country could only be made effective by the employment of naval force, and in home waters England could still hold her own against the world. The interest of the maritime war, therefore, centred round the three transatlantic stations in which her foes did their utmost to work her ruin, with the knowledge that the bulk of the Royal Navy would be kept at home to guard an anxious people from the threat of invading armies.

The English admirals on the other side of the ocean did marvels with the meagre forces at their disposal. In 1778 Barrington conducted to admiration the St. Lucia campaign; in 1779 Byron, though worsted by D'Estaing, fought with dashing gallantry at Grenada; in 1780 Rodney redressed the balance by his superlative skill off Martinique; in 1781, though failing to relieve Cornwallis at Yorktown, Graves had much the best of the battle of the Chesapeake; and in 1782 Rodney and Hood won the greatest victory of the war, when on 12th April off a group of islands called "The Saints" they defeated and scattered the vainglorious fleet that was sailing to occupy Jamaica.

15

Now Nelson appeared in West Indian waters before the French came into the war; and yet in every successive year, with a lack of fortune that looked persistent, he missed every battle of importance and was debarred from participation in every notable campaign. The *Lowestoft*, the *Badger*, the *Hinchinbrook*, the *Janus*, and the *Albemarle* were all vessels of the frigate type; and Nelson, whose steadfast ambition it was to command a ship of the battle line, was perforce employed upon the minor duties which Southey in this part describes.

To assist the reader through this bustling but confused period, a chronological table is appended.

1777. April.   Nelson appointed to the *Lowestoft*.
1778. July–Dec.   In the flagship *Bristol*.
      December.   BARRINGTON'S ST. LUCIA CAMPAIGN.
      December.   Nelson in command of the *Badger*.
1779. June.   Nelson captain of *Hinchinbrook*.
      July.   BYRON'S BATTLE OFF GRENADA.
1780. January.   Nelson employed in the San Juan expedition.
      April.   Appointed to the *Janus*.
      April.   RODNEY'S MARTINIQUE CAMPAIGN.
      August.   Nelson invalided home in the *Lion*.
(Then for nearly a year on half-pay, chiefly at Bath.)
1781. August.   Appointed to the *Albemarle*.
      September. BATTLE OF THE CHESAPEAKE.
      October.   CORNWALLIS'S SURRENDER AT YORKTOWN.
      (date?)   Nelson visits Elsinore.
1782. 12th April. BATTLE OF THE SAINTS.
      17th April. Nelson sails with a convoy to Canada.
      July–Sept. Cruising. Falls in with French squadron which he outwits.
      October.   Sails with a convoy to New York.
      December.   Sails with Lord Hood to the West Indies.
1783. Jan.–Sept. Congress of Versailles. End of War.
      July.   Nelson pays off the *Albemarle*.

[*SOUTHEY. CHAPTER I.—continued*]

American, and French privateers [1] under American colours, were at that time harassing our trade in the West Indies. Even a frigate was not sufficiently active for Nelson, and he repeatedly got appointed to the command of one of the *Lowestoft's* tenders. During one of their cruises the *Lowestoft* captured an American letter-of-marque.[2] It was blowing a gale, and a heavy sea running. The first lieutenant being ordered to board the prize, went below to put on his hanger.[3] It happened to be mislaid; and, while he

[1] Men-of-war equipped by individuals to operate against the enemy's shipping.
[2] Properly the licence issued to a privateer; here used of the privateer herself.
[3] Short curved sword.

EARLY SERVICES

was seeking it, Captain Locker came on deck. Perceiving the boat still alongside, and in danger every moment of being swamped, and being extremely anxious that the privateer should be instantly taken in charge, because he feared that it would otherwise founder,[1] he exclaimed, " Have I no officer in the ship who can board the prize? " Nelson did not offer himself immediately, waiting, with his usual sense of propriety, for the first lieutenant's return; but, hearing the Master volunteer, he jumped into the boat, saying, " It is my turn now; and if I come back, it is yours." The American, who had carried a heavy press of sail [2] in hope of escaping, was so completely water-logged [3] that the *Lowestoft's* boat went in on deck, and out again with the sea.[4]

About this time he lost his uncle. Captain Locker,[5] how-ever, who had perceived the excellent qualities of Nelson, and formed a friendship for him which continued during his life, recommended him warmly to Sir Peter Parker,[6] then commander-in-chief upon that station.[7] In conse-quence of this recommendation he was removed into the *Bristol* flagship,[8] and Lieutenant Cuthbert Collingwood, who had long been in habits of great friendship with him, succeeded him in the *Lowestoft*. Sir Peter Parker was the

[1] Fill with water and go to the bottom.
[2] As much sail as the state of the wind will allow a ship to carry.
[3] Full of water, and yet, from the buoyancy of her cargo, continuing to float.
[4] The information contained in this paragraph was supplied in 1799 by Nelson himself to McArthur, who invited him to contribute a memoir of his early services for publication in the *Naval Chronicle*. The facts, as stated by Nelson, are clear enough: (1) The first lieutenant attempted to board the prize and failed; (2) the second lieutenant (Nelson) then made trial and succeeded; (3) even such incidents were not exciting enough, and he got transferred to a schooner, which cruised with the *Lowestoft* and served her as a retriever serves a sportsman. Southey not only implies that Nelson left the *Lowestoft* before the capture of the American privateer, but he seems to suggest that the first lieutenant's failure to capture the prize was due to a rather superfluous sword-hunt. If this had been the case, Nelson would merely have been guilty of theatrical bombast; whereas he earned Captain Locker's undying regard by succeeding where a more experienced officer had failed. (For Nelson's original statement, see Clarke and McArthur, Vol. I. p. 5, and for McArthur's comments, *ibid*, p. 16.)
[5] Nelson's connection with Locker is the more interesting because the captain of the *Lowestoft* was a favourite disciple of Lord Hawke. One may be forgiven for supposing that he would be certain to convey something of the spirit of his own great admiral to the greater admiral who was at this time only his disciple.
[6] The value of this recommendation lay in the fact that the Jamaica station in those days was too far away to communicate easily with England, and the Com-mander-in-Chief had therefore the power to make appointments without reference to the Admiralty. Compare Nelson's selection for the *Badger* and *Hinchinbrook*.
[7] There were *two* naval stations in the West Indies; see Introductory Note to this chapter. Here the Jamaica station is meant.
[8] The vessel that carries the admiral commanding the fleet.

friend of both, and thus it happened that whenever Nelson
got a step in rank, Collingwood succeeded him. The former
soon became first lieutenant; [1] and on the 8th of December,
1778, was appointed commander of the *Badger* brig, [2]
Collingwood taking his place in the *Bristol*.

While the *Badger* was lying in Montego Bay, Jamaica,
the *Glasgow* of twenty guns came in and anchored there,
and in two hours was in flames, the steward having set fire
to her while stealing rum out of the after-hold. Her crew
were leaping into the water, when Nelson came up in his
boats, made them throw their powder overboard, and
point their guns upward; and, by his presence of mind and
personal exertions, prevented the loss of life which would
otherwise have ensued. On the 11th of June, 1779, he was
made post [3] into the *Hinchinbrook*, of twenty-eight guns,
an enemy's merchantman sheathed with wood which had
been taken into the service. Collingwood was then made
commander into the *Badger*. A short time after he left
the *Lowestoft*, that ship, with a small squadron, stormed the
fort of San Fernando de Omoa, on the south side of the
Bay of Honduras, and captured some register [4] ships which
were lying under its guns. Two hundred and fifty quintals
of quicksilver and three millions of piastres were the reward
of this enterprise: and it is characteristic of Nelson that
the chance by which he missed a share in such a prize is
never mentioned in any of his letters; nor is it likely that
it ever excited even a momentary feeling of vexation.

Nelson was fortunate in possessing good interest at the
time when it could be most serviceable to him. His promotion had been almost as rapid as it could be; and, before
he had attained the age of twenty-one, he had gained that
rank which brought all the honours of the service within
his reach. No opportunity, indeed, had yet been given him
of distinguishing himself; but he was thoroughly master

[1] At this time the officer next in rank to the captain, the term " commander "
being applied only to those who held independent control of a very small ship.

[2] A two-masted square-rigged vessel; properly a merchantman, but often
mounting guns and employed by the navy for duties analogous to those of a
T.B.D. to-day.

[3] Became a captain. A *post*-captain was so called (between 1713-1824) to
distinguish him from a *flag*-captain; that is, an admiral's understudy.

[4] Every ship trading from Spain to America had to be " registered " on a list
kept by the Council of the Indies. " Treasure-ships " would have here been more
expressive.

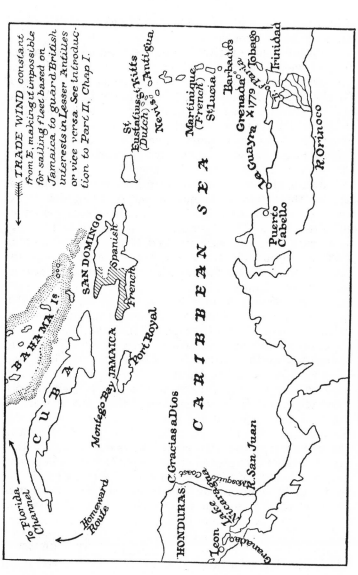

THEATRE OF WAR IN THE WEST INDIES, 1778–83

of his profession, and his zeal and ability were acknowledged wherever he was known.

Count d'Estaing,[1] with a fleet of one hundred and twenty-five sail, men-of-war and transports, and a reputed force of five-and-twenty thousand men, threatened Jamaica from St. Domingo.[2] Nelson offered his services to the Admiral and to Governor General Dalling, and was appointed to command the batteries of Fort Charles at Port Royal. Not more than seven thousand men could be mustered for the defence of the island, a number wholly inadequate to resist the force which threatened them. Of this Nelson was so well aware, that when he wrote to his friends in England, he told them they must not be surprised to hear of his learning to speak French. D'Estaing, however, was either not aware of his own superiority, or not equal to the command with which he was entrusted. He attempted nothing with his formidable armament, and General Dalling was thus left to execute a project which he had formed against the Spanish colonies.

This project was to take Fort San Juan on the river of that name, which flows from Lake Nicaragua into the Atlantic; make himself master of the lake itself, and of the cities of Granada and Leon; and thus cut off the communication of the Spaniards between their northern and southern possessions in America. Here it is that a canal between the two seas may most easily be formed, a work more important in its consequences than any which has ever yet been effected by human power. Lord George Germaine, at that time secretary of state for the American Department, approved the plan: and as discontents at that time were known to prevail in the Nuevo Reyno, in Popayan, and in Peru, the more sanguine part of the English began to dream of acquiring an empire in one part of America more extensive than that which they were on the point of losing in another. General Dalling's plans were well formed; but the history and the nature of the country had not been studied as accurately as its geography. The difficulties which occurred in fitting out the expedition delayed it till

---

[1] Fresh from his victory over Byron at Grenada; see Introductory Note.
[2] The island known indifferently as Hayti, Hispaniola, or San Domingo; at this time shared by Spaniards and French. See map.

the season was too far advanced; and the men were thus
sent to adventure themselves, not so much against an enemy
whom they would have beaten, as against a climate which
would do the enemy's work.

Early in the year 1780, five hundred men destined for
this service were convoyed by Nelson from Port Royal to
Cape Gracias a Dios, in Honduras. Not a native was to be
seen when they landed. They had been taught that the
English came with no other intent than that of enslaving
them and sending them to Jamaica. After a while, however,
one of them ventured down, confiding in his knowledge of
one of the party; and by his means the neighbouring tribes
were conciliated with presents, and brought in. The troops
were encamped on a swampy and unwholesome plain,
where they were joined by a party of the Seventy-ninth
Regiment, from Black River, who were already in a deplorable state of sickness. Having remained here a month they
proceeded, anchoring frequently, along the Mosquito shore,
to collect their Indian allies, who were to furnish proper
boats for the river, and to accompany them. They reached
the river San Juan, March 24th; and here, according to his
orders, Nelson's services were to terminate. But not a man
in the expedition had ever been up the river, or knew the
distance of any fortification from its mouth; and he, not
being one who would turn back when so much was to be
done, resolved to carry the soldiers up. About two hundred, therefore, were embarked in the Mosquito shore craft
and in two of the *Hinchinbrook's* boats, and they began
their voyage.

It was the latter end of the dry season, the worst time
for such an expedition. The river was consequently low.
Indians were sent forward through narrow channels between
shoals and sand-banks, and the men were frequently obliged
to quit the boats and exert their utmost strength to drag
or thrust them along. This labour continued for several
days, when they came into deeper water. They had then
currents and rapids to contend with, which would have
been insurmountable but for the skill of the Indians in such
difficulties. The brunt of the labour was borne by them
and by the sailors, men never accustomed to stand aloof
when any exertion of strength or hardihood is required.

E

The soldiers, less accustomed to rely upon themselves, were of little use. But all equally endured the violent heat of the sun, rendered more intense by being reflected from the white shoals, while the high woods on both sides of the river were frequently so close as to prevent any refreshing circulation of air; and during the night all were equally exposed to the heavy and unwholesome dews.

On the 9th of April they reached an island in the river, called San Bartolomeo, which the Spaniards had fortified, as an outpost, with a small semicircular battery, mounting nine or ten swivels,[1] and manned with sixteen or eighteen men. It commanded the river in a rapid and difficult part of the navigation. Nelson, at the head of a few of his seamen, leaped upon the beach. The ground upon which he sprang was so muddy that he had some difficulty in extricating himself, and lost his shoes. Bare-footed, however, he advanced, and, in his own phrase, " *boarded the battery.*" In this resolute attempt he was bravely supported by Despard, at that time a captain in the army, afterward unhappily known for his schemes of revolutionary treason.[2]

The castle of San Juan is situated about sixteen miles higher up. The stores and ammunition, however, were landed a few miles below the castle, and the men had to march through woods almost impassable. One of the men was bitten under the eye by a snake, which darted upon him from the bough of a tree. He was unable to proceed from the violence of the pain: and when, after a short while, some of his comrades were sent back to assist him, he was dead, and the body already putrid. Nelson himself narrowly escaped a similar fate. He had ordered his hammock to be slung under some trees, being excessively fatigued, and was sleeping, when a monitory lizard passed across his face. The Indians happily observed the reptile, and knowing what it indicated, awoke him. He started up, and found one of the deadliest serpents of the country coiled up at his feet. He suffered from poison of another kind; for, drinking at a spring in which some boughs of the manchineel had been thrown, the effects were so severe, as, in

---

[1] Guns turning on pivots.
[2] After reaching the rank of colonel, he was in 1802 executed on a charge of conspiring to kill the king and set up a republic.

the opinion of some of his friends, to inflict a lasting injury upon his constitution.

The castle of San Juan is thirty-two miles below the point where the river issues from the Lake of Nicaragua, and sixty-nine from its mouth. Boats reach the sea from thence in a day and a half; but their navigation back, even when unladen, is the labour of nine days. The English appeared before it on the 11th, two days after they had taken San Bartolomeo. Nelson's advice was that it should instantly be carried by assault: but Nelson was not the commander; and it was thought proper to observe all the formalities of a siege. Ten days were wasted before this could be commenced. It was a work more of fatigue than of danger; but fatigue was more to be dreaded than the enemy. The rains set in: and, could the garrison have held out a little longer, disease would have rid them of their invaders. Even the Indians sank under it, the victims of unusual exertion and of their own excesses. The place surrendered on the 24th. But victory procured to the conquerors none of that relief which had been expected. The castle was worse than a prison; and it contained nothing which could contribute to the recovery of the sick or the preservation of those who were yet unaffected. The huts which served for hospitals were surrounded with filth and with the putrefying hides of slaughtered cattle— almost sufficient of themselves to have engendered pestilence: and when at last orders were given to erect a convenient hospital, the contagion had become so general, that there were none who could work at it; for, besides the few who were able to perform garrison duty, there were not orderly men enough to assist the sick. Added to these evils there was the want of all needful remedies; for, though the expedition had been amply provided with hospital stores, river-craft enough had not been procured for transporting the requisite baggage; and when much was to be left behind, provision for sickness was that which of all things men in health would be most ready to leave. Now, when these medicines were required, the river was swollen, and so turbulent that its upward navigation was almost impracticable. At length even the task of burying the dead was more than the living could perform, and the bodies were tossed into the stream, or left for beasts of prey, and for the gallinazos, those dreadful carrion birds, which do not always wait for death before they begin their work. Five months the English persisted in what may be called this war against Nature. They then left a few men, who seemed proof against the climate, to retain the castle till the Spaniards should choose to retake it, and make them prisoners. The rest abandoned their baleful conquest. Eighteen hundred men were sent to different posts upon this wretched expedition: not more than three hundred and eighty ever returned. The *Hinchinbrook's* complement consisted of two hundred men; eighty-seven took to their beds in one night; and of the whole crew not more than ten survived.

[The transports' men all died, and some of the ships, having none left to take care of them, sunk in the harbour: but transport ships were not wanted, for the troops which they had brought were no more. They had fallen, not by the hand of an enemy, but by the deadly influence of the climate.] [1]

Nelson himself was saved by a timely removal. In a few days after the commencement of the siege he was seized with the prevailing dysentery. Meantime Captain Glover (son of the author of *Leonidas*) died and Nelson was appointed to succeed him in the *Janus*, of forty-four guns; Collingwood being then made post into the *Hinchinbrook*. He returned to the harbour the day before San Juan surrendered, and immediately sailed for Jamaica in the sloop [2] which brought the news of his appointment. He was, however, so greatly reduced by the disorder, that when they reached Port Royal he was carried ashore in his cot; and finding himself, after a partial amendment, unable to retain the command of his new ship, he was compelled to ask leave to return to England, as the only means of recovery. Captain (afterwards Admiral) Cornwallis took him home in the *Lion*; and to his care and kindness Nelson believed himself indebted for his life. He went immediately to Bath, in a miserable state; so helpless, that he was carried to and

---

[1] This paragraph does not occur in the first edition.
[2] Sloop-of-war, or corvette, a small vessel armed with ten or twelve guns; speedy, but inferior in strength to a frigate, who stood to her as a light cruiser to-day stands to a T.B.D.

from his bed; and the act of moving him produced the most violent pain. In three months [1] he was recovered, and immediately hastened to London, and applied for employment. After an interval of about four months he was appointed to the *Albemarle* of twenty-eight guns, a French merchantman which had been purchased from the captors for the king's service.

His health was not yet thoroughly re-established; and while he was employed in getting his ship ready, he again became so ill as hardly to be able to keep out of bed. Yet in this state, still suffering from the fatal effect of a West Indian climate, as if, it might almost be supposed, he said, to try his constitution, he was sent to the North Seas, and kept there the whole winter.[2] The asperity with which he mentioned this so many years afterwards evinces how deeply he resented a mode of conduct equally cruel to the individual and detrimental to the service. It was during the Armed Neutrality; and when they anchored off Elsinore, the Danish Admiral sent on board, desiring to be informed what ships had arrived, and to have their force written down. " The *Albemarle*," said Nelson to the messenger, " is one of his Britannic Majesty's ships: you are at liberty, sir, to count the guns as you go down the side: and you may assure the Danish Admiral that, if necessary, they shall all be well served."

During this voyage he gained a considerable knowledge of the Danish coast, and its soundings; greatly to the advantage of his country in after times. The *Albemarle* was not a good ship, and was several times nearly overset, in consequence of the masts having been made much too long for her. On her return to England they were shortened, and some other improvements made at Nelson's suggestion. Still he always insisted that her first owners, the French, had taught her to run away, as she was never a good sailer except when going directly before the wind.

On their return to the Downs, while he was ashore visiting the senior officer, there came on so heavy a gale, that almost all the vessels drove, and a store-ship came athwarthawse

---

[1] Nelson's illness lasted from August 1780 to August 1781. During most of this period he resided at Bath. See Introductory Note.

[2] Of 1781, some fifteen months after his return from Jamaica.

of the *Albemarle*.[1] Nelson feared she would drive on the Goodwin Sands. He ran to the beach; but even the Deal boatmen thought it impossible to get on board, such was the violence of the storm. At length some of the most intrepid offered to make the attempt for fifteen guineas; and to the astonishment and fear of all the beholders, he embarked during the height of the tempest. With great difficulty and imminent danger he succeeded in reaching her. She lost her bowsprit and foremast, but escaped further injury. He was now ordered to Quebec: where, his surgeon told him, he would certainly be laid up by the climate. Many of his friends urged him to represent this to Admiral Keppel: [2] but having received his orders from Lord Sandwich, there appeared to him an indelicacy in applying to his successor to have them altered.

Accordingly he sailed for Canada.[3] During her first cruise on that station, the *Albemarle* captured a fishing schooner,[4] which contained, in her cargo, nearly all the property that her master possessed, and the poor fellow had a large family at home, anxiously expecting him. Nelson employed him as a pilot in Boston Bay, then restored him the schooner and cargo, and gave him a certificate to secure him against being captured by any other vessel. The man came off afterwards to the *Albemarle*, at the hazard of his life, with a present of sheep, poultry, and fresh provisions. A most valuable supply it proved; for the scurvy [5] was raging on board. This was in the middle of August, and the ship's company had not had a fresh meal since the beginning of April. The certificate was preserved at Boston in memory of an act of unusual generosity; and now that the fame of Nelson has given interest to everything connected with his name, it is regarded as a relic.

[1] Across the bows of the *Albemarle*.

[2] In March 1782 Minorca was captured, and Lord North, who had held office since the beginning of the war, immediately resigned. Lord Sandwich, the " First Lord," retired with his leader, and was replaced by Admiral Keppel, who earlier in the war had commanded the main fleet and, after engaging the enemy, had been tried by court-martial in order to distract attention from the glaring faults of Lord Sandwich's administration.

[3] 17th April, 1782; five days after the battle of the Saints.

[4] A two-masted vessel, rigged fore and aft ; a two-masted vessel with square sails is known as a brig. See above, Note 2, p. 18.

[5] A prostrating sickness that afflicts those who are deprived of wholesome food. The disease played havoc in the squadron which accompanied Anson on his voyage of circumnavigation. See " Everyman's Library," Vol. 510.

The *Albemarle* had a narrow escape upon this cruise. Four French sail of the line [1] and a frigate, which had come out of Boston harbour, gave chase to her; and Nelson, perceiving that they beat him in sailing, boldly ran among the numerous shoals of St. George's Bank, confiding in his own skill in pilotage. Captain Salter, in the *St. Margaretta*, had escaped the French fleet, by a similar manœuvre, not long before. The frigate alone continued warily to pursue him; but, as soon as he perceived that this enemy was unsupported, he shortened sail and hove to; [2] upon which the Frenchman thought it advisable to give over the pursuit, and sail in quest of his consorts.

At Quebec Nelson became acquainted with Alexander Davison; [3] by whose interference he was prevented from making what would have been called an imprudent marriage. The *Albemarle* was about to leave the station. Her captain had taken leave of his friends and was gone down the river to the place of anchorage; when the next morning, as Davison was walking on the beach, to his surprise he saw Nelson coming back in his boat. Upon enquiring the cause of this reappearance, Nelson took his arm to walk towards the town, and told him he found it utterly impossible to leave Quebec without again seeing the woman whose society had contributed so much to his happiness there, and offering her his hand. " If you do," said his friend, " your utter ruin must inevitably follow." " Then let it follow," cried Nelson, " for I am resolved to do it." "And I," replied Davison, " am resolved you shall not." Nelson, however, upon this occasion, was less resolute than his friend, and suffered himself to be led back to the boat.

The *Albemarle* was under orders to convoy [4] a fleet of transports [5] to New York. " A very pretty job," said her captain, " at this late season of the year " (October was far advanced), " for our sails are at this moment frozen to

---

[1] Ships strong enough to take their place in the fighting line—*i.e.*, what we call " battleships."
[2] Brought his ship to a standstill by making one set of sails pull against another.
[3] Afterwards his prize-agent and business adviser.
[4] To conduct unarmed vessels through a danger zone and defend them in case of attack.
[5] Vessels carrying troops.

the yards." On his arrival at Sandy Hook,[1] he waited on the commander-in-chief, Admiral Digby, who told him he was come on a fine station for making prize-money. " Yes, sir," Nelson made answer; " but the West Indies is the station for honour."

Lord Hood, with a detachment of Rodney's victorious fleet, was at that time at Sandy Hook. He had been intimate with Captain Suckling; and Nelson, who was desirous of nothing but honour, requested him to ask for the *Albemarle*, that he might go to that station where it was most likely to be obtained. Admiral Digby reluctantly parted with him. His professional merit was already well known: and Lord Hood, on introducing him to Prince William Henry, as the Duke of Clarence[2] was then called, told the prince if he wished to ask any questions respecting naval tactics, Captain Nelson could give him as much information as any officer in the fleet. The Duke, who, to his own honour, became from that time the firm friend of Nelson, describes him as appearing the merest boy of a captain he had ever seen, dressed in a full laced uniform, an old-fashioned waistcoat with long flaps, and his lank unpowdered hair tied in a stiff Hessian tail of extraordinary length; making, altogether, so remarkable a figure, that, says the Duke, " I had never seen anything like it before, nor could I imagine who he was, nor what he came about. But his address and conversation were irresistibly pleasing; and when he spoke on professional subjects, it was with an enthusiasm that showed he was no common being."

It was expected that the French would attempt some of the passages between the Bahamas.[3] And Lord Hood, thinking of this, said to Nelson, " I suppose, sir, from the length of time you were cruising among the Bahama Keys, you must be a good pilot there." He replied, with that constant readiness to render justice to every man, which

---

[1] New York harbour.

[2] Afterwards King William IV.

[3] After their defeat by Rodney at the battle of the Saints the French ships fled westwards in confusion. Those that assembled at San Domingo were anxious to get home to France. The sailing route led round the western end of Cuba and so through the Florida Channel, *i.e.*, the narrow passage between the coast of North America and the extensive zone of Bahama coral keys (dotted on the map). As it would take weeks to beat back against the Trades in the Caribbean, and as it was easy to block the Florida Channel, the French were expected to grope their way through the labyrinth of the Bahama shoals.

was so conspicuous in all his conduct through life, that he was well acquainted with them himself, but that in that respect his second lieutenant was far his superior.

The French got into Puerto Cabello on the coast of Venezuela.[1] Nelson was cruising between that port and La Guayra, under French colours, for the purpose of obtaining information; when a king's launch, belonging to the Spaniards, passed near, and being hailed in French, came alongside without suspicion, and answered all questions that were asked concerning the number and force of the enemy's ships. The crew, however, were not a little surprised when they were taken on board, and found themselves prisoners. One of the party went by the name of the Count de Deux-Ponts. He was, however, a prince of the German Empire, and brother to the heir of the Electorate of Bavaria. His companions were French officers of distinction, and men of science, who had been collecting specimens in the various branches of natural history. Nelson having entertained them with the best his table could afford, told them they were at liberty to depart with their boat and all that it contained: he only required them to promise that they would consider themselves as prisoners, if the commander-in-chief should refuse to acquiesce in their being thus liberated—a circumstance which was not by any means likely to happen.

Tidings soon arrived that the preliminaries of peace had been signed; and the *Albemarle* returned to England, and was paid off.[2] Nelson's first business, after he got to London, even before he went to see his relations, was to attempt to get the wages due to his men for the various ships in which they had served during the war. " The disgust of seamen to the navy," he said, " was all owing to the infernal plan of turning them over from ship to ship; so that men could not be attached to the officers, nor the officers care the least about the men." Yet he himself was so beloved by his men, that his whole ship's company offered, if he could get a ship, to enter for her immediately. He was now, for the first time, presented at

---

[1] After the rout at the Saints, Bougainville, who led the van of the French fleet, carried his fugitives to the coast of Venezuela.
[2] 3rd July, 1783.

court. After going through this ceremony, he dined with his friend Davison at Lincoln's Inn. As soon as he entered the chambers, he threw off what he called his iron-bound coat; and putting himself at ease in a dressing-gown, passed the remainder of the day in talking over all that had befallen them since they parted on the shore of the River St. Lawrence.

CHAPTER II

WHEN the *Albemarle* brought her commission to a close Nelson was put for a while on half pay, and took the opportunity of visiting France. But in the spring of 1784 he received sailing orders to return to West Indian seas. Peace duties there did not hold out the expectation of much excitement; and yet the cruise served to bring the captain of the *Boreas* very much before the public eye.

[*SOUTHEY. CHAPTER II*]

" I HAVE closed the war," said Nelson, in one of his letters, " without a fortune; but there is not a speck in my character. True honour, I hope, predominates in my mind far above riches." He did not apply for a ship, because he was not wealthy enough to live on board in the manner which was then become customary. Finding it, therefore, prudent to economise on his half-pay during the peace, he went to France, in company with Captain Macnamara, of the navy, and took lodgings at St. Omer. The death of his favourite sister, Anne, who died in consequence of going out of the ball-room at Bath when heated with dancing, affected his father so much, that it had nearly occasioned him to return in a few weeks. Time, however, and reason, and religion, overcame this grief in the old man; and Nelson continued at St. Omer long enough to fall in love with the daughter of an English clergyman. This second attachment appears to have been less ardent than the first; for, upon weighing the evils of a straitened income to a married man, he thought it better to leave France, assigning to his friends something in his accounts as the cause. This prevented him from accepting an invitation from the Count of Deux-Ponts to visit him at Paris, couched in the handsomest terms of acknowledgment for the treatment which he had received on board the *Albemarle*.

The self-constraint which Nelson exerted in subduing this attachment made him naturally desire to be at sea; and when, upon visiting Lord Howe at the Admiralty, he was asked if he wished to be employed, he made answer that he did. Accordingly, in March, he was appointed to the *Boreas*, twenty-eight guns, going to the Leeward Islands,[1] as a cruiser,[2] on the peace establishment. Lady Hughes and her family went out with him to Admiral Sir Richard Hughes, who commanded on that station. His ship was full of young midshipmen, of whom there were not less than thirty on board; and happy were they whose lot it was to be placed with such a captain. If he perceived that a boy was afraid at first going aloft, he would say to him, in a friendly manner, " Well, sir, I am going a race to the mast-head, and beg that I may meet you there." The poor little fellow instantly began to climb, and got up how he could,—Nelson never noticed in what manner; but, when they met in the top, spoke cheerfully to him, and would say how much any person was to be pitied who fancied that getting up was either dangerous or difficult. Every day he went into the schoolroom, to see that they were pursuing their nautical studies; and at noon he was always the first on deck with his quadrant.[3] Whenever he paid a visit of ceremony, some of these youths accompanied him; and when he went to dine with the governor at Barbados, he took one of them in his hand, and presented him, saying, " Your Excellency must excuse me for bringing one of my midshipmen. I make it a rule to introduce them to all the good company I can, as they have few to look up to, besides myself, during the time they are at sea."

When Nelson arrived in the West Indies, he found himself senior captain, and consequently second in command on that station. Satisfactory as this was, it soon involved

---

[1] The technical way of describing in 1784 the " Lesser Antilles " station.

[2] A vessel commissioned to beat backwards and forwards over the same stretch of sea, almost invariably for the protection of trade. In 1784 the word was used to define a particular frigate's occasional duty. To-day " cruiser " has rendered the name " frigate " obsolete and betokens a certain class of ship.

[3] The quadrant, devised by John Davis in 1594, superseded all other nautical devices for taking the height of the sun until 1757, when the Royal Navy substituted an instrument having its arc, not the fourth part, but the sixth part of a circle. It was long, however, as this sentence shows, before the exacter term " sextant " displaced the older word.

him in a dispute with the Admiral, which a man less zealous for the service might have avoided. He found the *Latona* in English Harbour, Antigua,[1] with a broad pendant hoisted; and, upon enquiring the reason, was presented with a written order from Sir R. Hughes, requiring and directing him to obey the orders of Resident Commissioner [1] Moutray during the time he might have occasion to remain there; the said Resident Commissioner being, in consequence, authorised to hoist a broad pendant on board any of his Majesty's ships in that port that he might think proper. Nelson was never at a loss how to act in any emergency. " I know of no superior officers," said he, " besides the lords commissioners of the Admiralty, and my seniors on the post-list." [2] Concluding, therefore, that it was not consistent with the service for a Resident Commissioner, who held only a civil situation, to hoist a broad pendant, the moment that he had anchored he sent an order to the captain of the *Latona* to strike it, and return it to the dockyard. He went on shore the same day, dined with the Commissioner, to show him that he was actuated by no other motive than a sense of duty, and gave him the first intelligence that his pendant had been struck. Sir Richard sent an account of this to the Admiralty; but the case could admit of no doubt, and Captain Nelson's conduct was approved.

He displayed the same promptitude on another occasion. While the *Boreas*, after the hurricane months [3] were over, was riding at anchor in Nevis Roads, a French frigate passed to leeward,[4] close along shore. Nelson had obtained information that this ship was sent from Martinique, with two general officers and some engineers on board, to make a survey of our sugar-islands. This purpose he was deter-

[1] The chief base of the Leeward Islands, or Lesser Antilles, station was English Harbour on the south coast of the island of Antigua. At English Harbour was the dockyard of the station, and the dockyard was at this time, like all other dockyards at home and abroad, controlled by a naval captain on half-pay, called the Commissioner, or Resident Commissioner. No officer on half-pay could properly wield any executive authority; but Sir Richard Hughes, an easy-tempered, amiable man who preferred to live ashore at Barbados and practise his violin, gave the dockyard Commissioner acting rank, second only to his own. Any captain less spirited than Nelson would certainly have saluted the *Latona's* broad pendant, for it symbolised the presence of a commodore.

[2] On active service: see above, Note 3, p. 18.

[3] June to October.

[4] Nelson was nearer the wind than the intruders. He therefore had the legs of them and could overtake them if he desired.

mined to prevent them from executing, and therefore he gave orders to follow them. The next day he came up with them at anchor in the roads of St. Eustatius, and anchored at about two cables'[1] length on the frigate's quarter.[2] Being afterwards invited by the Dutch governor to meet the French officers at dinner, he seized that occasion of assuring the French captain that, understanding it was his intention to honour the British possessions with a visit, he had taken the earliest opportunity in his power to accompany him, in his Majesty's ship the *Boreas*, in order that such attention might be paid to the officers of his Most Christian Majesty as every Englishman in the islands would be proud to show. The French, with equal courtesy, protested against giving him this trouble; especially, they said, as they intended merely to cruise round the islands, without landing on any. But Nelson, with the utmost politeness, insisted upon paying them this compliment, followed them close in spite of all their attempts to elude his vigilance, and never lost sight of them; till, finding it impossible either to deceive or escape him, they gave up their treacherous purpose in despair, and beat up for Martinique.

A business of more serious import soon engaged his attention. The Americans were at this time trading with our islands, taking advantage of the register[3] of their ships, which had been issued while they were British subjects. Nelson knew that, by the Navigation Act, no foreigners, directly or indirectly, are permitted to carry on any trade with these possessions. He knew, also, that the Americans had made themselves foreigners with regard to England; they had disregarded the ties of blood and language, when they acquired the independence which they had been led on to claim, unhappily for themselves, before they were fit for it; and he was resolved that they should derive no profit from those ties now. Foreigners

---

[1] Six feet make one fathom; one hundred fathoms make one cable. Two cables, therefore, meant four hundred yards, or about a quarter of a mile.

[2] That part of a vessel's side from abaft the mainmast to the stern.

[3] The Americans had so recently been British citizens that their ships were still registered as British ships, and therefore by the Navigation Act were permitted to trade with British possessions. The question for England's representatives in the West Indies to decide was this: Shall we observe the letter of the Navigation Act and allow the Americans to do as they like; or shall we have regard to the spirit of the Act and exclude them as foreigners?

they had made themselves, and as foreigners they were to
be treated. " If once," said he, " they are admitted to any
kind of intercourse with our islands, the views of the
loyalists, in settling at Nova Scotia, are entirely done away;
and when we are again embroiled in a French war, the
Americans will first become the carriers of these colonies,
and then have possession of them. Here they come, sell
their cargoes for ready money, go to Martinique, buy
molasses, and so round and round. The loyalist cannot do
this, and consequently must sell a little dearer. The re-
sidents here are Americans by connection and by interest,
and are inimical to Great Britain. They are as great rebels
as ever were in America, had they the power to show it."

In November, when the squadron, having arrived at
Barbados, was to separate, with no other orders than
those for examining anchorages, and the usual enquiries
concerning wood and water, Nelson asked his friend Collingwood, then captain of the *Mediator*, whose opinions he knew
upon the subject, to accompany him to the commander-
in-chief, whom he then respectfully asked whether they
were not to attend to the commerce of the country, and
see that the Navigation Act was respected—that appearing
to him to be the intent of keeping men-of-war upon this
station in time of peace? Sir Richard Hughes replied he
had no particular orders, neither had the Admiralty sent
him any acts of parliament. But Nelson made answer,
that the Navigation Act was included in the statutes of
the Admiralty, with which every captain was furnished,
and that act was directed to admirals, captains, etc., to
see it carried into execution. Sir Richard said he had never
seen the book. Upon this Nelson produced the statutes,
read the words of the act, and apparently convinced the
commander-in-chief that men-of-war, as he said, " were
sent abroad for some other purpose than to be made a
show of." Accordingly orders were given to enforce the
Navigation Act.

Major-General Sir Thomas Shirley was at this time
governor of the Leeward Islands; and when Nelson waited
on him, to inform him how he intended to act, and upon
what grounds, he replied that " old generals were not in
the habit of taking advice from young gentlemen." " Sir,"

said the young officer, with that confidence in himself which never carried him too far and always was equal to the occasion, " I am as old as the prime minister of England, and think myself as capable of commanding one of his Majesty's ships as that minister is of governing the state."

He was resolved to do his duty, whatever might be the opinion or conduct of others: and when he arrived upon his station at St. Kitts, he sent away all the Americans, not choosing to seize them before they had been well apprised that the act would be carried into effect, lest it might seem as if a trap had been laid for them. The Americans, though they prudently decamped from St. Kitts, were emboldened by the support they met with and resolved to resist his orders, alleging that king's ships had no legal power to seize them without having deputations from the customs. The planters were to a man against him; the governors and the presidents of the different islands, with only a single exception, gave him no support: and the Admiral, afraid to act on either side, yet wishing to oblige the planters, sent him a note, advising him to be guided by the wishes of the President of the Council.[1]

There was no danger in disregarding this, as it came unofficially, and in the form of advice. But scarcely a month after he had shown Sir Richard Hughes the law, and, as he supposed, satisfied him concerning it, he received an order from him, stating that he had now obtained good advice upon the point, and the Americans were not to be hindered from coming, and having free egress and regress, if the governor chose to permit them. An order to the same purport had been sent round to the different governors and presidents; and General Shirley and others informed him, in an authoritative manner, that they chose to admit American ships, as the commander-in-chief had left the decision to them. These persons, in his own words, he soon " trimmed up, and silenced "; but it was a more delicate business to deal with the Admiral. " I must either," said he, " disobey my orders or disobey acts of parliament. I determined upon the former, trusting to the uprightness of my intentions, and believing that my country would not let me be ruined for protecting her commerce." With

---

[1] *I.e.* the governor of St. Kitts.

this determination he wrote to Sir Richard; appealed again
to the plain, literal, unequivocal sense of the Navigation
Act; and in respectful language told him he felt it his duty
to decline obeying these orders till he had an opportunity
of seeing and conversing with him.

Sir Richard's first feeling was that of anger, and he
was about to supersede Nelson; but having mentioned the
affair to his captain, that officer told him he believed all
the squadron thought the orders illegal, and therefore did
not know how far they were bound to obey them. It was
impossible, therefore, to bring Nelson to a court-martial,
composed of men who agreed with him in opinion upon
the point in dispute; and luckily, though the Admiral
wanted vigour of mind to decide upon what was right, he
was not obstinate in wrong, and had even generosity enough
in his nature to thank Nelson afterwards for having shown
him his error.

Collingwood, in the *Mediator*, and his brother, Wilfred
Collingwood, in the *Rattler*, actively co-operated with
Nelson. The custom-houses were informed that after a
certain day all foreign vessels found in the ports would be
seized; and many were, in consequence, seized, and condemned in the Admiralty court. When the *Boreas* arrived
at Nevis, she found four American vessels deeply laden,
and what are called the Island colours flying—white, with
a red cross. They were ordered to hoist their proper flag,
and depart within eight-and-forty hours; but they refused
to obey, denying that they were Americans. Some of their
crews were then examined in Nelson's cabin, where the
judge of admiralty happened to be present. The case was
plain; they confessed that they were Americans, and
that the ships, hull and cargo, were wholly American property; upon which he seized them. This raised a storm.
The planters, the custom-house, and the governor were
all against him. Subscriptions were opened, and presently
filled, for the purpose of carrying on the cause in behalf
of the American captains: and the Admiral, whose flag
was at that time in the roads, stood neutral. But the
Americans and their abettors were not content with defensive
law. The marines, whom he had sent to secure the ships,
had prevented some of the masters from going ashore;

F

and those persons, by whose depositions it appeared that
the vessels and cargoes were American property, declared
that they had given their testimony under bodily fear, for
that a man with a drawn sword in his hand had stood over
them the whole time. A rascally lawyer, whom the party
employed, suggested this story; and as the sentry at the
cabin-door was a man with a drawn sword, the Americans
made no scruple of swearing to this ridiculous falsehood,
and commencing prosecutions against him accordingly.
They laid their damages at the enormous amount of £40,000;
and Nelson was obliged to keep close on board his own ship,
lest he should be arrested for a sum for which it would have
been impossible to find bail. The marshal frequently came
on board to arrest him, but was always prevented by the
address of the first lieutenant, Mr. Wallis. Had he been
taken, such was the temper of the people, that it was certain
he would have been cast for the whole sum. One of his
officers, one day, in speaking of the restraint which he was
thus compelled to suffer, happened to use the word *pity!*
" Pity! " exclaimed Nelson. " Pity! did you say? I shall
live, sir, to be envied! And to that point I shall always
direct my course."

Eight weeks he remained in this state of duresse. During
that time the trial respecting the detained ships came on
in the court of admiralty. He went on shore under a protection for the day from the judge: but, notwithstanding
this, the marshal was called upon to take that opportunity
of arresting him, and the merchants promised to indemnify
him for so doing. The judge, however, did his duty, and
threatened to send the marshal to prison if he attempted
to violate the protection of the court. Mr. Herbert, the
president of Nevis, behaved with singular generosity upon
this occasion. Though no man was a greater sufferer by the
measures which Nelson had pursued, he offered in court
to become his bail for £10,000, if he chose to suffer the
arrest. The lawyer whom he had chosen proved to be an
able as well as an honest man; and, notwithstanding the
opinions and pleadings of most of the counsel of the different
islands, who maintained that ships of war were not justified
in seizing American vessels without a deputation from the
customs, the law was so explicit, the case so clear, and

Nelson pleaded his own cause so well, that the four ships were condemned.

During the progress of this business he sent a memorial home to the King: in consequence of which, orders were issued that he should be defended at the expense of the crown. And upon the representations which he made at the same time to the secretary of state, and the suggestions with which he accompanied it, the Register Act [1] was framed. The sanction of government, and the approbation of his conduct which it implied, were highly gratifying to him. But he was offended, and not without just cause, that the treasury should have transmitted thanks to the commander-in-chief, for his activity and zeal in protecting the commerce of Great Britain. " Had they known all," said he, " I do not think they would have bestowed thanks in that quarter, and neglected me. I feel much hurt, that, after the loss of health and risk of fortune, another should be thanked for what I did against his orders. I either deserved to be sent out of the service, or at least to have had some little notice taken of what I had done. They have thought it worthy of notice, and yet have neglected me. If this is the reward for a faithful discharge of my duty, I shall be careful, and never stand forward again. But I have done my duty, and have nothing to accuse myself of."

The anxiety which he had suffered from the harassing uncertainties of law is apparent from these expressions. He had, however, something to console him, for he was at this time wooing the niece of his friend the president, then in her eighteenth year, the widow of Dr. Nisbet a physician. She had one child, a son, by name Josiah, who was three years old. One day Mr. Herbert, who had hastened, half-dressed, to receive Nelson, exclaimed, on returning to his dressing-room, " Good God! if I did not find that great little man, of whom everybody is so afraid, playing in the next room, under the dining-table, with Mrs. Nisbet's child! " A few days afterwards Mrs. Nisbet herself was first introduced to him, and thanked him for the partiality which he had shown to her little boy. Her

[1] Passed in 1786, this law confined the privilege of trading under the Navigation Act to vessels registered as British ships in British possessions.

manners were mild and winning: and the captain, whose heart was easily susceptible of attachment, found no such imperious necessity for subduing his inclinations as had twice before withheld him from marrying. They were married on March 11, 1787; Prince William Henry, who had come out to the West Indies the preceding winter, being present, by his own desire, to give away the bride. Mr. Herbert, her uncle, was at this time so much displeased with his only daughter, that he had resolved to disinherit her, and leave his whole fortune, which was very great, to his niece. But Nelson, whose nature was too noble to let him profit by an act of injustice, interfered, and succeeded in reconciling the president to his child.

" Yesterday," said one of his naval friends, the day after the wedding, " the navy lost one of its greatest ornaments, by Nelson's marriage. It is a national loss that such an officer should marry. Had it not been for this, Nelson would have become the greatest man in the service." The man was rightly estimated. But he who delivered this opinion did not understand the effect of domestic love and duty upon a mind of the true heroic stamp.

" We are often separate," said Nelson, in a letter to Mrs. Nisbet, a few months before their marriage; " but our affections are not by any means on that account diminished. Our country has the first demand for our services; and private convenience or happiness must ever give way to the public good. Duty is the great business of a sea-officer: all private considerations must give way to it, however painful." " Have you not often heard," says he, in another letter, " that salt water and absence always wash away love? Now I am such a heretic as not to believe that article. For, behold, every morning I have had six pails of salt water poured upon my head, and instead of finding what seamen say to be true, it goes on so contrary to the prescription, that you must, perhaps, see me before the fixed time." More frequently his correspondence breathed a deeper strain. " To write letters to you," says he, " is the next greatest pleasure I feel to receiving them from you. What I experience when I read such as I am sure are the pure sentiments of your heart, my poor pen cannot express; nor, indeed, would I give much for any pen or head which could express feelings of that kind. Absent from you, I feel no pleasure. It is you who are everything to me. Without you, I care not for this world; for I have found, lately, nothing in it but vexation and trouble. These are my present sentiments. God Almighty grant they may never change! Nor do I think they will. Indeed there is, as far as human knowledge can judge, a moral certainty that they cannot. For it must be real affection that brings us together; not interest or compulsion." Such were the feelings, and such the sense of duty, with which Nelson became a husband.

During his stay upon this station, he had ample opportunity of observing the scandalous practices of the contractors, prize-agents, and other persons in the West Indies connected with the naval service. When he was first left with the command, and bills were brought him to sign for money which was owing for goods purchased for the navy, he required the original voucher, that he might examine whether those goods had been really purchased at the market price. But to produce vouchers would not have been convenient, and therefore was not the custom. Upon this Nelson wrote to Sir Charles Middleton,[1] then comptroller of the navy, representing the abuses which were likely to be practised in this manner. The answer which he received seemed to imply that the old forms were thought sufficient: and thus, having no alternative, he was compelled, with his eyes open, to submit to a practice originating in fraudulent intentions. Soon afterwards two Antigua merchants informed him that they were privy to great frauds which had been committed upon government in various departments; at Antigua, to the amount of nearly £500,000; at St. Lucia, £300,000; at Barbados, £250,000; at Jamaica, upwards of a million. The informers were both shrewd, sensible men of business; they did not affect to be actuated by a sense of justice, but required a percentage upon so much as government should actually recover through their means. Nelson examined the books and papers which they produced, and was convinced that government had been most infamously plundered. Vouchers, he found, in that country, were no check whatever. The principle was that " a thing was always worth what it

---

[1] Known to-day as Lord Barham.

would bring "; and the merchants were in the habit of signing vouchers for each other, without even the appearance of looking at the articles. These accounts he sent home to the different departments which had been defrauded. But the peculators were too powerful; and they succeeded not merely in impeding inquiry, but even in raising prejudices against Nelson at the Board of Admiralty, which it was many years before he could subdue.

Owing, probably, to these prejudices, and the influence of the peculators, he was treated, on his return to England, in a manner which had nearly driven him from the service. During the three years that the *Boreas* had remained upon a station which is usually so fatal, not a single officer or man of her whole complement had died. This almost unexampled instance of good health, though mostly, no doubt, imputable to a healthy season, must, in some measure, also be ascribed to the wise conduct of the captain. He never suffered the ships to remain more than three or four weeks at a time at any of the islands; and when the hurricane months confined him to English Harbour, he encouraged all kinds of useful amusements; music, dancing, and cudgelling [1] among the men; theatricals among the officers; anything which could employ their attention, and keep their spirits cheerful.

The *Boreas* arrived in England in June. Nelson, who had many times been supposed to be consumptive when in the West Indies, and perhaps was saved from consumption by that climate, was still in a precarious state of health; and the raw wet weather of one of our ungenial summers brought on cold, and sore throat, and fever. Yet his vessel was kept at the Nore till the end of June from the end of November, serving as a slop and receiving ship.[2]

This unworthy treatment, which more probably proceeded from intention than from neglect, excited in Nelson the strongest indignation. During the whole five months he seldom or never quitted the ship, but carried on the duty with strict and sullen attention. On the morning when orders were received to prepare the *Boreas* for being

[1] A duel or mêlée with wooden weapons, analogous to single-stick.. The rough-and-tumble horseplay which it occasioned made it a favourite diversion of seamen.
[2] A depôt for seamen waiting to be assigned to a ship, and a store for clothes and bedding, which were known in the service as " slops."

paid off, he expressed his joy to the senior officer in the Medway, saying, " It will release me for ever from an ungrateful service, for it is my firm and unalterable determination never again to set my foot on board a king's ship. Immediately after my arrival in town I shall wait on the First Lord of the Admiralty, and resign my commission." The officer to whom he thus communicated his intentions behaved in the wisest and most friendly manner: for finding it in vain to dissuade him in his present state of feeling, he secretly interfered with the First Lord to save him from a step so injurious to himself, little foreseeing how deeply the welfare and honour of England were at that moment at stake. This interference produced a letter from Lord Howe, the day before the ship was paid off, intimating a wish to see Captain Nelson as soon as he arrived in town: when, being pleased with his conversation, and perfectly convinced, by what was then explained to him of the propriety of his conduct, he desired that he might present him to the King on the first levee-day; and the gracious manner in which Nelson was then received effectually removed his resentment.

Prejudices had been, in like manner, excited against his friend, Prince William Henry. " Nothing is wanted, sir," said Nelson, in one of his letters, " to make you the darling of the English nation, but truth. Sorry I am to say, much to the contrary has been dispersed." This was not flattery; for Nelson was no flatterer. The letter in which this passage occurs shows in how wise and noble a manner he dealt with the Prince. One of his Royal Highness's officers had applied for a court martial upon a point in which he was unquestionably wrong.[1] His Royal Highness, however, while he supported his own character and authority, prevented

[1] Lieutenant Isaac Schomberg, first lieutenant of the *Pegasus*, and in after days author of *Naval Chronology* (a valuable work in five volumes, published 1802), on 22nd January, 1787, sent a boat ashore at English Harbour, Antigua, without informing his captain (Prince William Henry). His Royal Highness commented upon the omission in the Public Order Book; and Mr. Schomberg, taking this notification as a personal affront, instantly applied to Nelson for a court martial. Nelson was indignant over the episode, because the arrest of Schomberg, at that individual's own desire, deprived the squadron of a useful officer. A somewhat difficult situation was eventually ended by the graciousness of the Prince in overlooking the subordinate's offence and so rendering the court martial unnecessary. The case, however, was a complicated one, and the misunderstandings and misinterpretations it involved were not cleared up until Nelson and the Prince reached home. All the letters and documents arising out of the controversy are given in Nicolas, Vol. I. pp. 209-51.

the trial, which must have been injurious to a brave and
deserving man. " Now that you [1] are parted," said Nelson,
" pardon me, my prince, when I presume to recommend
that he may stand in your royal favour as if he had never
sailed with you, and that at some future day you will serve
him. There only wants this to place your conduct in the
highest point of view. None of us are without failings.
His, was being rather too hasty: [2] but that, put in com-
petition with his being a good officer, will not, I am bold
to say, be taken in the scale against him. More able friends
than myself your Royal Highness may easily find, and of
more consequence in the state; but one more attached and
affectionate is not so easily met with. Princes seldom,
very seldom, find a disinterested person to communicate
their thoughts to. I do not pretend to be that person. But
of this be assured, by a man who, I trust, never did a dishonourable act, that I am interested only that your Royal
Highness should be the greatest and best man this country
ever produced."

Encouraged by the conduct of Lord Howe, and by his
reception at court, Nelson renewed his attack upon the
peculators with fresh spirit. He had interviews with Mr.
Rose, Mr. Pitt, and Sir Charles Middleton, to all of whom
he satisfactorily proved his charges. In consequence, it
is said, these very extensive public frauds were at length
put in a proper train to be provided against in future. His
representations were attended to; and every step which
he recommended was adopted. The investigation was put
into a proper course, which ended in the detection and
punishment of some of the culprits. An immense saving
was made to government, and thus its attention was directed
to similar peculations in other parts of the colonies. But
it is said also, that no mark of commendation seems to have
been bestowed upon Nelson for his exertion. And it is
justly remarked [3] that the spirit of the navy cannot be
preserved so effectually by the liberal honours bestowed
on officers when they are worn out in the service, as by an
attention to those who, like Nelson at this part of his life,

[1] Prince William and Lieutenant Schomberg. Nelson's letter was written at
Portsmouth when the trouble was ended.
[2] In demanding the court martial.
[3] Clarke and McArthur, Vol. I. p. 107.—SOUTHEY'S NOTE.

have only their integrity and zeal to bring them into notice. A junior officer, who had been left with the command at Jamaica, received an additional allowance, for which Nelson had applied in vain. Double pay was allowed to every artificer and seaman employed in the naval yard. Nelson had superintended the whole business of that yard with the most rigid exactness, and he complained that he was neglected. " It was most true," he said, " that the trouble which he took to detect the fraudulent practices then carried on, was no more than his duty; but he little thought that the expenses attending his frequent journeys to St. John's upon that duty (a distance of twelve miles) would have fallen upon his pay as captain of the *Boreas.*"

Nevertheless, the sense of what he thought unworthy usage did not diminish his zeal. " I," said he, " must still buffet the waves in search of—what? Alas! That they called honour is now thought of no more. My fortune, God knows, has grown worse for the service. So much for serving my country! But the devil, ever willing to tempt the virtuous, has made me offer, if any ships should be sent to destroy his Majesty of Morocco's ports, to be there; and I have some reason to think, that, should any more come of it, my humble services will be accepted. I have invariably laid down, and followed close, a plan of what ought to be uppermost in the breast of an officer,—that it is much better to serve an ungrateful country than to give up his own fame. Posterity will do him justice. A uniform course of honour and integrity seldom fails of bringing a man to the goal of fame at last."

The design against the Barbary pirates, like all other designs against them, was laid aside; and Nelson took his wife to his father's parsonage,[1] meaning only to pay him a visit before they went to France; a project which he had formed for the sake of acquiring a competent knowledge of the French language. But his father could not bear to lose him thus unnecessarily. Mr. Nelson had long been an invalid, suffering under paralytic and asthmatic affections, which, for several hours after he rose in the

[1] At Christmas, 1787. Nelson continued to live at Burnham Thorpe until the outbreak of war against the French Revolution in 1793.

morning, scarcely permitted him to speak.[1] He had been given over by his physicians, for this complaint, nearly forty years before his death; and was, for many of his latter years, obliged to spend all his winters at Bath. The sight of his son, he declared, had given him new life. " But, Horatio," said he, " it would have been better that I had not been thus cheered, if I am so soon to be bereaved of you again. Let me, my good son, see you whilst I can. My age and infirmities increase, and I shall not last long." To such an appeal there could be no reply. Nelson took up his abode at the parsonage, and amused himself with the sports and occupations of the country. Sometimes he busied himself with farming the glebe; sometimes spent the greater part of the day in the garden, where he would dig as if for the mere pleasure of wearying himself. Some-times he went a-birds'-nesting, like a boy: and in these expeditions Mrs. Nelson always, by his express desire, accompanied him. Coursing [2] was his favourite amuse-ment. Shooting, as he practised it, was far too dangerous for his companions: for he carried his gun upon the full cock, as if he were going to board an enemy; and the moment a bird rose, he let fly, without ever putting the fowling-piece to his shoulder. It is not, therefore, extraordinary that his having once shot a partridge should be remembered by his family among the remarkable events of his life.

But his time did not pass away thus without some vex-atious cares to ruffle it. The affair of the American ships was not yet over, and he was again pestered with threats of prosecution. " I have written them word," said he, " that I will have nothing to do with them, and they must act as they think proper. Government, I suppose, will do what is right, and not leave me in the lurch. We have heard enough lately of the consequences of the Navigation Act to this country. They may take my person; but if sixpence would save me from a prosecution, I would not give it."

It was his great ambition at this time to possess a pony;

---

[1] An admirable portrait of Nelson's father is given in *The Nelsons of Burnham Thorpe*, a record compiled from unpublished letters and notebooks by M. Eyre Matcham.

[2] The pack with which Nelson hunted was that of the famous " Coke of Norfolk."

and having resolved to purchase one, he went to a fair for that purpose. During his absence two men abruptly entered the parsonage, and enquired for him. Then they asked for Mrs. Nelson; and, after they had made her repeatedly declare that she was really and truly the captain's wife, presented her with a writ, or notification, on the part of the American captains, who now laid their damages at £20,000, and they charged her to give it to her husband on his return. Nelson having bought his pony, came home with it in high spirits. He called out his wife to admire the purchase, and listen to all its excellences: nor was it till his glee had in some measure subsided that the paper could be presented to him. His indignation was excessive: and in the apprehension that he should be exposed to the anxieties of the suit, and the ruinous consequences which might ensue, he exclaimed " This affront I did not deserve! But I'll be trifled with no longer. I will write immediately to the Treasury; and if government will not support me, I am resolved to leave the country." Accordingly, he informed the Treasury, that if a satisfactory answer were not sent him by return of post, he should take refuge in France. To this he expected he should be driven, and for this he arranged everything with his characteristic rapidity of decision. It was settled that he should depart immediately, and Mrs. Nelson follow under the care of his elder brother, Maurice, ten days after him. But the answer which he received from government quieted his fears. It stated that Captain Nelson was a very good officer, and needed to be under no apprehension, for he would assuredly be supported.

Here his disquietude upon this subject seems to have ended. Still he was not at ease; he wanted employment, and was mortified that his applications for it produced no effect. " Not being a man of fortune," he said, " was a crime which he was unable to get over, and therefore none of the great cared about him." Repeatedly he requested the Admiralty that they would not leave him to rust in indolence. During the armament which was made upon occasion of the dispute concerning Nootka Sound,[1] he

---

[1] In 1789 the Spaniards seized three ships belonging to English settlers in Vancouver Island. War was in consequence narrowly averted. *Cp. Mariner's Mirror*, Vol. VII. pp. 74–9.

renewed his application: and his steady friend, Prince William, who had then been created Duke of Clarence, recommended him to Lord Chatham. The failure of this recommendation wounded him so keenly, that he again thought of retiring from the service in disgust: a resolution from which nothing but the urgent remonstrances of Lord Hood induced him to resist. Hearing that the *Raisonnable,* in which he had commenced his career, was to be commissioned, he asked for her. This also was in vain: and a coolness ensued, on his part, toward Lord Hood, because that excellent officer did not use his influence with Lord Chatham upon this occasion. Lord Hood, however, had certainly sufficient reasons for not interfering; for he ever continued his steady friend.

In the winter of 1792, when we were on the eve of the Revolutionary War, Nelson once more offered his services, earnestly requested a ship, and added, that if their lordships should be pleased to appoint him to a cockle-boat he should feel satisfied. He was answered in the usual official form, " Sir, I have received your letter of the 5th instant, expressing your readiness to serve, and have read the same to my Lords Commissioners of the Admiralty." On the 12th of December he received this dry acknowledgment. The fresh mortification did not, however, affect him long; for, by the joint interest of the Duke and Lord Hood, he was appointed, on the 30th of January following, to the *Agamemnon,* of sixty-four guns.

PART III

THE CRUISE OF THE "AGAMEMNON"

As Southey in this section leaves his reader very much in the dark as to the passage of time, a short chronology is prefixed to each chapter.

CHAPTER I

LORD HOOD BEING COMMANDER-IN-CHIEF IN THE MEDITERRANEAN

1793.	21st January.	Execution of Louis XVI.
	26th January.	Nelson appointed to the *Agamemnon*.
	June.	Sails for Mediterranean.
	16th July.	Arrives at Toulon.
	September.	At Naples.
	22nd October.	Engages *La Melpomène*, one of a squadron of French frigates off the east end of Sardinia.
	November.	At Tunis.
	December.	Corsican campaign begins.
1794.	19th February–19th March.	Siege and capture of Bastia.
	June.	With Lord Hood's fleet Nelson pursues the French, who take refuge in Golfe Juan Bay.
	10th July.	Loses right eye at Calvi.

[*SOUTHEY. CHAPTER III*]

" THERE are three things, young gentleman," said Nelson to one of his midshipmen, " which you are constantly to bear in mind. First, you must always implicitly obey orders, without attempting to form any opinion of your own respecting their propriety. Secondly, you must consider every man your enemy who speaks ill of your king: and, thirdly, you must hate a Frenchman as you do the devil." With these feelings he engaged in the war. Josiah, his son-in-law, went with him as a midshipman.

49

The *Agamemnon* [1] was ordered to the Mediterranean, under Lord Hood. The fleet arrived in those seas at a time when the South of France would willingly have formed itself into a separate republic, under the protection of England. But good principles had been at that time perilously abused by ignorant and profligate men; and, in its fear and hatred of democracy, the English Government abhorred whatever was republican.[2] Lord Hood could not take advantage of the fair occasion which presented itself, and which, if it had been seized with vigour, might have ended in dividing France; but he negotiated with the people of Toulon to take possession provisionally of their port and city, which, fatally for themselves, was done.[3]

Before the British fleet entered, Nelson was sent with dispatches to Sir William Hamilton, our envoy at the court of Naples. Sir William, after his first interview with him, told Lady Hamilton he was about to introduce a little man to her, who could not boast of being very handsome; but such a man as, he believed, would one day astonish the world. " I have never before," he continued, " entertained

---

[1] Nelson's first sail-of-the-line or battleship. She was only a sixty-four (see Note 3, p. 1), but Nelson loved her none the less for that. His ship's company liked all but her name. They did not approve of classical titles. *Bellerophon* they called the " Bully Ruffian," *Polyphemus* the " Polly Infamous," and their own *Agamemnon*, without meaning any disrespect, they corrupted into " Eggs and Bacon."

[2] In his first edition Southey wrote: " the English Government leagued itself with despotism—a miserable error, of which the consequences will long be to be deplored. For had not England in an unhappy hour interfered, the rotten governments of the Continent would then have fallen; and the continental nations, acquiring a revolutionary impulse and strength at the same time as France, would now have been the rivals of France instead of her prey."

Southey meant that the English Government (when it instructed Lord Hood to occupy Toulon in the interests of Louis XVI. and Marie Antoinette) took a step inimical to the best interests of the world. For without English help (he argues) the monarchical principle would have gone down throughout Europe; and the peoples, everywhere made free and enfranchised, would, like Spain in 1813 (when he was writing), have fought against the overweening tyranny of France as exemplified in Napoleon. Contrariwise, if England had patronised the Republican principle in the south of France, the enfranchisement of Europe would have come more quickly, for other states would have followed the example of Spain, and united in one irresistible effort to break the rod of Napoleon's oppression.

This rod, when Southey wrote in 1813, seemed still unbreakable: but when, in the following year, a second edition of the book was called for, Napoleon was vanquished and imprisoned in Elba, and the passage, in consequence, came under the shears.

For Southey's political opinions, see Introduction, pp. xxvii–xxix.

[3] Though the harbour of Toulon was occupied by his fleet, Lord Hood was unable to procure sufficient troops to garrison the town, and when the army of the Revolution recaptured the place in December the most merciless vengeance was meted out to its citizens. Nelson's mission to the King of Naples, mentioned in the next paragraph, had for its object the loan of Neapolitan troops.

an officer at my house; but I am determined to bring him here. Let him be put in the room prepared for Prince Augustus." [1] Thus that acquaintance began which ended in the destruction of Nelson's domestic happiness. It seemed to threaten no such consequences at its commencement.[2] He spoke of Lady Hamilton, in a letter to his wife, as a young woman of amiable manners, who did honour to the station to which she had been raised; and he remarked that she had been exceedingly kind to Josiah. The activity with which the envoy exerted himself in procuring troops from Naples, to assist in garrisoning Toulon, so delighted him, that he is said to have exclaimed: " Sir William, you are a man after my own heart! You do business in my own way ": and then to have added, " I am now only a captain; but I will, if I live, be at the top of the tree." Here, also, that acquaintance with the Neapolitan court commenced, which led to the only blot upon Nelson's public character.[3] The King,[4] who was sincere at that time in his enmity to the French, called the English the saviours of Italy, and of his dominions in particular. He paid the most flattering attentions to Nelson, made him dine with him, and seated him at his right hand.

Having accomplished this mission, Nelson received orders to join Commodore Linzee at Tunis.[5] On the way, five sail of the enemy were discovered off the coast of Sardinia, and he chased them. They proved to be three forty-four gun frigates with a corvette [6] of twenty-four, and

[1] George III.'s ninth son.

[2] " It seemed to threaten no such consequences at its commencement." The reader should not fail to notice that these words make their accompaniment of censorious commentary not only irrelevant but impertinent.

[3] It is a literary trick to intensify the evil side of a wrongdoer by the mention of crimes which he has not yet committed. The reader should be, therefore, on his guard against such a passage as this; and refuse to allow his judgment to be influenced until he has had the actual facts (which are only hinted at) submitted to him in concrete form.

[4] Ferdinand IV. He married Maria Carolina, a sister of Marie Antoinette, and was therefore vitally interested in the anti-Jacobin movement which was stirring the south of France.

[5] The Dey of Tunis was sheltering French ships, including a big man-of-war (compare the *Goeben* and *Breslau* at Constantinople in 1914). Commodore Linzee's task was to capture the enemy's vessels and remove a menace to British trade. Nelson was sent to reinforce Linzee, who with three seventy-fours and a couple of frigates had failed so far in his efforts to intimidate the Dey. The mission in the end was not successful; but it had the effect of taking Nelson away from Toulon, where there was no honour to be gained.

[6] The French equivalent for a small frigate or sloop of war mounting all her ordnance on the upper deck. In Southey's day the word was not to be found in English maritime dictionaries.

a brig [1] of twelve. The *Agamemnon* had only 345 men at
quarters, having landed part of her crew at Toulon, and
others being absent in prizes. He came near enough one
of the frigates to engage her, but at great disadvantage,
the Frenchman manœuvring well, and sailing greatly
better. A running fight of three hours ensued; during
which the other ships, which were at some distance, made
all speed to come up. By this time the enemy was almost

WESTERN MEDITERRANEAN, 1793–96

Explanation

Kingdom of Naples shaded.

   ✗ A. Where Nelson fought the *Melpomène*.
   ✗ B. Where Nelson captured the *Sabina*.
   ✗ H. Hotham's first battle.
   ✗ HH. Hotham's second battle.

silenced, when a favourable change of wind enabled her to
get out of reach of the *Agamemnon's* guns; and that ship
had received so much damage in the rigging, that she
could not follow her. Nelson conceiving that this was but
the forerunner of a far more serious engagement, called his
officers together, and asked them if the ship was fit to go
into action against such a superior force, without some
small refit and refreshment for the men. Their answer was,

[1] See Note 2, p. 18.

that she certainly was not. He then gave these orders,
" Veer the ship,[1] and lay her head to the westward. Let
some of the best men be employed in refitting the rigging,
and the carpenter in getting crows and capstan-bars [2] to
prevent our wounded spars from coming down: and get
the wine up for the people, with some bread, for it may be
half an hour good before we are again in action." But when
the French came up, their comrade made signals of distress,
and they all hoisted out their boats to go to her assistance,
leaving the *Agamemnon* unmolested.[3]

Nelson found Commodore Linzee at Tunis, where he had
been sent to expostulate with the Dey upon the impolicy
of his supporting the revolutionary government of France.
Nelson represented to him the atrocity of that government.
Such arguments were of little avail in Barbary: and when
the Dey was told that the French had put their sovereign
to death, he drily replied that " Nothing could be more
heinous; and yet, if historians told the truth, the English
had once done the same." This answer had doubtless been
suggested by the French about him. They had completely
gained the ascendancy, and all negotiation on our part
proved fruitless.

Shortly afterward Nelson was detached with a small
squadron, to co-operate with General Paoli [4] and the
Anti-Gallican party in Corsica.

[1] (Or wear the ship.) Turn the ship about by going off the wind. The
Agamemnon was not to beat a strategic retreat; but to put her helm up
and retire to a distance where, before re-engaging, she could conduct repairs
uninterrupted.

[2] The upper masts and yards of the *Agamemnon* were much injured. He
therefore ordered that these limbs of his ship should, as it were, be put in splints,
by binding them up with the crowbars or handspikes used for moving the guns
and weighing the anchor.

[3] The points to notice about this engagement are the following:

(*a*) Frigates like those that constituted the French flotilla ought to have been
able easily to elude a battleship like the *Agamemnon*. It argues amazing skill
on Nelson's part that he was able to bring one of them to action.

(*b*) The lucky hits made by Nelson's antagonist (whose name was *l a Melpomène*)
put the *Agamemnon* at a still greater disadvantage in the matter of sailing. The
other four ships of the French flotilla (with 124 guns to his 64) had the chance of
delivering a massed attack, which Nelson cheerfully prepared to repel. However,
they eventually satisfied themselves with binding up the wounds of their
companion.

[4] Pasquale de Paoli, born in 1725, was brought up to believe that the rule
exercised over his island home by Genoa might one day be broken. At thirty
years of age he was appointed by his fellow-countrymen to lead them in their
struggle for freedom, and earned a European renown by the wisdom and moderation of his leadership. Against Genoa alone, he would probably have worked
his way and established the cause of Corsican independence: but in 1768 the

G

LIFE OF NELSON

At this point Southey wanders off into a characteristic digression which has for its subject "The History of Corsica." (See above, p. xxvii). It sadly interrupts the story he is telling; and for that reason should be ruthlessly cut. The reader, most anxious to master all the facts of Nelson's life, will offer no violence to his conscience nor miss one essential detail if he skips the next twelve paragraphs and resumes the narrative at the words "About twenty years Paoli remained in England."

¶ Some thirty years before this time, the heroic patriotism of the Corsicans, and of their leader, Paoli, had been the admiration of England. The history of these brave people is but a melancholy tale. The island which they inhabit has been abundantly blessed by nature. It has many excellent harbours; and though the *mal-aria*, or pestilential atmosphere, which is so deadly in many parts of Italy, and of the Italian islands, prevails on the eastern coast, the greater part of the country is mountainous and healthy. It is about one hundred and fifty miles long, and from forty to fifty broad; in circumference, some three hundred and twenty:—a country large enough, and sufficiently distant from the nearest shores, to have subsisted as an independent state, if the welfare and happiness of the human race had ever been considered as the end and aim of policy.

¶ The Moors, the Pisans, the kings of Aragon, and the Genoese, successively attempted, and each for a time effected, its conquest. The yoke of the Genoese continued longest, and was the heaviest. These petty tyrants ruled with an iron rod: and when at any time a patriot rose to resist their oppressions, if they failed to subdue him by force, they resorted to assassination. At the commencement of the last century they quelled one revolt by the aid of German auxiliaries, whom the Emperor Charles VI. sent against a people who had never offended him, and who were fighting for whatever is most dear to man. In 1734 the war was renewed; and Theodore, a Westphalian baron, then appeared upon the stage.

¶ In that age men were not accustomed to see adventurers play for kingdoms, and Theodore became the common talk

impecunious Genoese sold their insurgent island to France. Paoli still for a year held out against an army of 22,000 Frenchmen; but being at last obliged to make his escape, sailed for England, where he was welcomed effusively. Boswell, who had met him in Corsica, introduced him to Dr. Johnson, and Johnson, forming the most favourable opinion of him, admitted him to terms of the closest friendship.

of Europe. He had served in the French armies: and having afterwards been noticed both by Ripperda and Alberoni, their example, perhaps, inflamed a spirit as ambitious and as unprincipled as their own. He employed the whole of his means in raising money and procuring arms: then wrote to the leaders of the Corsican patriots, to offer them considerable assistance, if they would erect Corsica into an independent kingdom, and elect him king. When he landed among them, they were struck with his stately person, his dignified manners, and imposing talents. They believed the magnificent promises of foreign assistance which he held out, and elected him king accordingly.

¶ Had his means been as he represented them, they could not have acted more wisely than in thus at once fixing the government of their country, and putting an end to those rivalries among the leading families, which had so often proved pernicious to the public weal. He struck money, conferred titles, blocked up the fortified towns which were held by the Genoese, and amused the people with promises of assistance for about eight months. Then, perceiving that they cooled in their affections towards him, in proportion as their expectations were disappointed, he left the island, under the plea of expediting himself the succours which he had so long awaited. Such was his address, that he prevailed upon several rich merchants in Holland, particularly the Jews, to trust him with cannon and warlike stores to a great amount. They shipped these under the charge of a supercargo. Theodore returned with this supercargo to Corsica, and put him to death on his arrival, as the shortest way of settling the account. The remainder of his life was a series of deserved afflictions. He threw in the stores which he had thus fraudulently obtained. But he did not dare to land; for Genoa had now called in the French to their assistance, and a price had been set upon his head. His dreams of royalty were now at an end. He took refuge in London, contracted debts, and was thrown into the King's Bench. After lingering there many years, he was released under an act of insolvency; in consequence of which, he made over the kingdom of Corsica for the use of his creditors, and died shortly after his deliverance.

¶ The French, who have never acted a generous part in the

history of the world, readily entered into the views of the
Genoese, which accorded with their own policy: for such
was their ascendancy at Genoa, that in subduing Corsica
for these allies, they were in fact subduing it for themselves.
They entered into the contest, therefore, with their usual
vigour, and their usual cruelty. It was in vain that the
Corsicans addressed a most affecting memorial to the court
of Versailles. That remorseless government persisted in its
flagitious project. They poured in troops; dressed a part
of them like the people of the country, by which means
they deceived and destroyed many of the patriots; cut
down the standing corn, the vines, and the olives; set fire
to the villages, and hung all the most able and active men
who fell into their hands. A war of this kind may be carried
on with success against a country so small and so thinly
peopled as Corsica. Having reduced the island to perfect
servitude, which they called Peace, the French withdrew
their forces.

¶ As soon as they were gone, men, women, and boys
rose at once against their oppressors. The circumstances
of the times were now favourable to them; and some
British ships, acting as allies of Sardinia, bombarded Bastia
and San Fiorenzo, and delivered them into the hands of the
patriots. This service was long remembered with gratitude.
The impression made upon our own countrymen was less
favourable.   They had witnessed the heart-burnings of
rival chiefs, and the dissensions among the patriots; and
perceiving the state of barbarism to which continual oppression and habits of lawless turbulence had reduced the
nation, did not recollect that the vices of the people were
owing to their unhappy circumstances, but that the virtues
which they displayed arose from their own nature. This
feeling, perhaps, influenced the British court, when, in
1746, Corsica offered to put herself under the protection of
Great Britain. An answer was returned, expressing satisfaction at such a communication, hoping that the Corsicans
would preserve the same sentiments, but signifying also
that the present was not the time for such a measure.

¶ These brave islanders then formed a government for
themselves, under two leaders, Gaffori and Matra, who had
the title of protectors. The latter is represented as a partisan

of Genoa, favouring the views of the oppressors of his country by the most treasonable means. Gaffori was a hero worthy of old times. His eloquence was long remembered with admiration. A band of assassins was once advancing against him. He heard of their approach, went out to meet them; and, with a serene dignity, which overawed them, requested them to hear him. He then spake to them so forcibly of the distresses of their country, her intolerable wrongs, and the hopes and views of their brethren in arms, that the very men who had been hired to murder him, fell at his feet, implored his forgiveness, and joined his banner. While he was besieging the Genoese in Corte, a part of the garrison perceiving the nurse with his eldest son, then an infant in arms, straying at a little distance from the camp, suddenly sallied out and seized them. The use they made of their persons was in conformity to their usual execrable conduct. When Gaffori advanced to batter the walls, they held up the child directly over that part of the wall at which the guns were pointed. The Corsicans stopped: but Gaffori stood at their head, and ordered them to continue the fire. Providentially the child escaped, and lived to relate, with becoming feeling, a fact so honourable to his father. That father conducted the affairs of the island till 1753, when he was assassinated by some wretches, set on (it is believed) by Genoa, but certainly pensioned by that abominable government after the deed. He left the country in such a state that it was enabled to continue the war two years after his death without a leader. The Corsicans then found one worthy of their cause in Pasquale de Paoli.

¶ Paoli's father was one of the patriots who effected their escape from Corsica when the French reduced it to obedience. He retired to Naples, and brought up this his youngest son in the Neapolitan service. The Corsicans heard of young Paoli's abilities, and solicited him to come over to his native country and take the command. He did not hesitate long. His father, who was too far advanced in years to take an active part himself, encouraged him to go; and when they separated, the old man fell on his neck, and kissed him, and gave him his blessing. " My son," said he, " perhaps I may never see you more; but in my mind I shall ever be present with you. Your design is great and noble; and I doubt not but God will bless you in it. I shall devote to your cause the little remainder of my life in offering up my prayers for your success."

¶ When Paoli assumed the command, he found all things in confusion. He formed a democratical government, of which he was chosen chief; restored the authority of the laws; established a university; and took such measures, both for repressing abuses and moulding the rising generation, that, if France had not interfered, upon its wicked and detestable principle of usurpation, Corsica might at this day have been as free and flourishing and happy a commonwealth as any of the Grecian states in the days of their prosperity.

¶ The Genoese were at this time driven out of their fortified towns, and must in a short time have been expelled. France was indebted some millions of livres to Genoa. It was not convenient to pay this money; so the French minister proposed to the Genoese, that she should discharge the debt by sending six battalions to serve in Corsica for four years. The indignation which this conduct excited in all generous hearts was forcibly expressed by Rousseau, who, with all· his errors, was seldom deficient in feeling for the wrongs of humanity. "You Frenchmen," said he, writing to one of that people, "are a thoroughly servile nation, thoroughly sold to tyranny, thoroughly cruel and relentless in persecuting the unhappy. If you knew of a freeman at the other end of the world, I believe you would go thither for the mere pleasure of extirpating him."

¶ The immediate object of the French happened to be purely mercenary. They wanted to clear off their debts to Genoa; and, as the presence of their troops in the island effected this, they aimed at doing the people no further mischief. Would that the conduct of England had been at this time free from reproach! But a proclamation was issued by the English government, after the Peace of Paris, prohibiting any intercourse with the rebels of Corsica. Paoli said he did not expect this from Great Britain. This great man was deservedly proud of his country. "I defy Rome, Sparta, or Thebes," he would say, "to show me thirty years of such patriotism as Corsica can boast!"

Availing himself of the respite which the inactivity of the French and the weakness of the Genoese allowed, he prosecuted his plans of civilising the people. He used to say, that though he had an unspeakable pride in the prospect of the fame to which he aspired; yet, if he could but render his countrymen happy, he could be content to be forgotten. His own importance he never affected to undervalue. " We are now to our country," said he, " like the prophet Elisha, stretched over the dead child of the Shunamite,—eye to eye, nose to nose, mouth to mouth. It begins to recover warmth, and to revive. I hope it will yet regain full health and vigour."

¶ But when the four years were expired, France purchased the sovereignty of Corsica from the Genoese for forty millions of livres; as if the Genoese had been entitled to sell it; as if any bargain and sale could justify one country in taking possession of another against the will of the inhabitants, and butchering all who opposed the usurpation! Among the enormities which France has committed, this action seems but as a speck. Yet the foulest murderer that ever suffered by the hand of the executioner has infinitely less guilt upon his soul than the statesman who concluded this treaty, and the monarch who sanctioned and confirmed it. A desperate and glorious resistance was made; but it was in vain; no power interposed in behalf of these injured islanders, and the French poured in as many troops as were required. They offered to confirm Paoli in the supreme authority, only on condition that he would hold it under their government. His answer was, that " the rocks which surrounded him should melt away before he would betray a cause which he held in common with the poorest Corsican." This people then set a price upon his head. During two campaigns he kept them at bay. They overpowered him at length. He was driven to the shore, and, having escaped on shipboard, took refuge in England. It is said that Lord Shelburne resigned his seat in the cabinet because the ministry looked on, without attempting to prevent France from succeeding in this abominable and important act of aggrandisement. In one respect, however, our country acted as became her. Paoli was welcomed with the honours which he deserved; a pension of £1,200 was immediately

granted him; and provision was liberally made for his elder
brother and his nephew.

Above twenty years Paoli [1] remained in England, enjoying the friendship of the wise, and the admiration of the
good. But when the French Revolution began, it seemed
as if the restoration of Corsica was at hand. The whole
country, as if animated by one spirit, rose and demanded
liberty; and the national assembly passed a decree, recog-
nising the island as a department of France, and therefore
entitled to all the privileges of the new French constitution. This satisfied the Corsicans, [which it ought not
to have done; and Paoli, in whom the ardour of youth was
passed, seeing that his countrymen were contented, and
believing that they were about to enjoy a state of freedom,
naturally wished to return to his native country.] [2] He
resigned his pension in the year 1790, and appeared at the
bar of the assembly with the Corsican deputies, when they
took the oath of fidelity to France. But the course of events
in France soon dispelled those hopes of a new and better
order of things, which Paoli, in common with so many of
the friends of humankind, had indulged: and perceiving,
after the execution of the king, that a civil war was about
to ensue, of which no man could foresee the issue, he prepared
to break the connection between Corsica and the French
republic. The Convention, suspecting such a design, and
perhaps occasioning it by their suspicions, ordered him to
their bar. That way, he well knew, led to the guillotine;
and, returning a respectful answer, he declared that he would
never be found wanting in his duty, but pleaded age and
infirmity as a reason for disobeying the summons. Their
second order was more summary: and the French troops,
who were in Corsica, aided by those of the natives, who
were either influenced by hereditary party feelings, or who
were sincere in Jacobinism, took the field against him.
But the people were with him. He repaired to Corte, the
capital of the island, and was again invested with the
authority which he had held in the noonday of his fame.

---

[1] If the reader has skipped the twelve preceding paragraphs, he should refer
to Note 4, p. 53, for the previous history of Paoli.

[2] In the first edition Southey omitted the words in brackets, saying simply:
" This satisfied the Corsicans and it satisfied Paoli too." The alteration was
made in the second edition of 1814.

The Convention upon this denounced him as a rebel, and
set a price upon his head.   It was not the first time that
France had proscribed Paoli.

Paoli now opened a correspondence with Lord Hood,
promising, if the English would make an attack upon San
Fiorenzo from the sea, he would, at the same time, attack
it by land.   This promise he was unable to perform: and
Commodore Linzee, who, in reliance upon it, was sent
upon this service, was repulsed with some loss.   Lord Hood,
who had now been compelled to evacuate Toulon, suspected
Paoli of intentionally deceiving him.   This was an injurious
suspicion.   Shortly afterwards he dispatched Lieutenant-
Colonel (afterward Sir John) Moore and Major Koehler to
confer with him upon a plan of operations.   Sir Gilbert
Elliot [1] accompanied them: and it was agreed that, in
consideration of the succours both military and naval,
which his Britannic Majesty should afford for the purpose
of expelling the French, the island of Corsica should be
delivered into the immediate possession of his Majesty,
and bind itself to acquiesce in any settlement he might
approve of concerning its government and its future relation
with Great Britain.   While this negotiation was going on,
Nelson cruised off the island with a small squadron, to
prevent the enemy from throwing in supplies.   Close to
San Fiorenzo the French had a storehouse of flour, near
their only mill.   He watched an opportunity, and landed
one hundred and twenty men, who threw the flour into the
sea, burnt the mill, and re-embarked before one thousand
men, who were sent against him, could occasion them the
loss of a single man.   While he exerted himself thus, keeping
out all supplies, intercepting dispatches, attacking their
outposts and forts, and cutting out [2] vessels from the
bay,—a species of warfare which depresses the spirit of an
enemy even more than it injures them, because of the
sense of individual superiority which it indicates in the
assailants,—troops were landed, and San Fiorenzo was

---

[1] Representative of the Foreign Office.   He had already acted as head of the
English Government in Toulon, and on the conquest of Corsica was installed as
Viceroy.   Thrown constantly with Nelson, he became one of his dearest friends,
and a constant correspondent when absence separated them.   He eventually
became first Earl of Minto, and was Governor-General of India from 1807 to 1814.

[2] To attack and capture a ship by armed forces in boats.   Such assaults were
always dangerous and sometimes attended by desperate hazard.

besieged. The French, finding themselves unable to maintain their post, sank one of their frigates, burnt another, and retreated to Bastia. Lord Hood submitted to General Dundas, who commanded the land forces, a plan for the reduction of this place. The general declined co-operating, thinking the attempt impracticable without a reinforcement of two thousand men, which he expected from Gibraltar. Upon this Lord Hood determined to reduce it with the naval force under his command; and leaving part of his fleet off Toulon, he came with the rest to Bastia.

He showed a proper sense of respect for Nelson's services, and of confidence in his talents, by taking care not to bring with him any older captain. A few days before their arrival Nelson had had what he called a brush with the enemy. " If I had had with me five hundred troops," he said, " to a certainty I should have stormed the town; and I believe it might have been carried. Armies go so slow, that seamen think they never mean to get forward: but I dare say they act on a surer principle, although we seldom fail." During this partial action our army appeared upon the heights: and having reconnôitred the place, returned to San Fiorenzo. " What the General could have seen to make a retreat necessary," said Nelson, " I cannot comprehend. A thousand men would certainly take Bastia. With five hundred and *Agamemnon* I would attempt it. My seamen are now what British seamen ought to be—almost invincible. They really mind shot no more than peas."

General Dundas had not the same confidence. " After mature consideration," he said in a letter to Lord Hood, " and a personal inspection for several days of all circumstances, local as well as others, I consider the siege of Bastia with our present means and force to be a most visionary and rash attempt, such as no officer would be justified in undertaking." Lord Hood replied that nothing would be more gratifying to his feelings than to have the whole responsibility upon himself; and that he was ready and willing to undertake the reduction of the place at his own risk, with the force and means at present there. General d'Aubant, who succeeded at this time to the command of the army, coincided in opinion with his predecessor, and did not think it right to furnish his lordship with a single soldier, cannon, or any stores. Lord Hood could only obtain a few artillery-men; and ordering on board that part of the troops who, having been embarked as marines, were borne on the ships' books as part of their respective complements, he began the siege with eleven hundred and eighty-three soldiers, artillery-men, and marines, and two hundred and fifty sailors. " We are but few," said Nelson, " but of the right sort; our General at San Fiorenzo not giving us one of the five regiments he has there lying idle."

These men were landed on the 4th of April, under Lieutenant-Colonel Villettes and Nelson, who had now acquired from the army the title of Brigadier. Guns were dragged by the sailors up heights where it appeared almost impossible to convey them—a work of the greatest difficulty; and which Nelson said could never, in his opinion, have been accomplished by any but British seamen. The soldiers, though less dexterous in such service, because not accustomed like sailors to habitual dexterity, behaved with equal spirit. " Their zeal," said the Brigadier, " is almost unexampled. There is not a man but considers himself as personally interested in the event, and deserted by the General. It has, I am persuaded, made them equal to double their numbers." This is one proof, of many, that for our soldiers to equal our seamen, it is only necessary for them to be equally well commanded. They have the same heart and soul, as well as the same flesh and blood. Too much may, indeed, be exacted from them in a retreat; but set their face toward a foe, and there is nothing within the reach of human achievement which they cannot perform.

The French had improved the leisure which our military commander had allowed them; and before Lord Hood commenced his operations, he had the mortification of seeing that the enemy were every day erecting new works, strengthening old ones, and rendering the attempt more difficult. La Combe St. Michel, the commissioner from the national convention, who was in the city, replied in these terms to the summons of the British Admiral: " I have hot shot for your ships, and bayonets for your troops. When two-thirds of our men are killed, I will then trust to the generosity of the English." The siege, however, was not sustained with the firmness which such a reply seemed to augur. On the 19th of May a treaty of capitulation was begun. That same evening the troops from San Fiorenzo made their appearance on the hills; and, on the following morning, General d'Aubant arrived with the whole army to take possession of Bastia.

The event of the siege had justified the confidence of the sailors; but they themselves excused the opinion of the generals, when they saw what they had done. " I am all astonishment," said Nelson, " when I reflect on what we have achieved. One thousand regulars, fifteen hundred national guards, and a large party of Corsican troops, four thousand in all, laying down their arms to twelve hundred soldiers, marines and seamen! I always was of opinion, have ever acted up to it, and never had any reason to repent it, that one Englishman was equal to three Frenchmen. Had this been an English town, I am sure it would not have been taken by them." When it had been resolved to attack the place, the enemy were supposed to be far inferior in number; and it was not till the whole had been arranged, and the siege publicly undertaken, that Nelson received certain information of the great superiority of the garrison. This intelligence he kept secret, fearing lest, if so fair a pretext were afforded, the attempt would be abandoned. " My own honour," said he to his wife, " Lord Hood's honour, and the honour of our country, must have been sacrificed, had I mentioned what I knew. Therefore you will believe what must have been my feelings during the whole siege, when I had often proposals made to me to write to Lord Hood to raise it." Those very persons, who thus advised him, were rewarded for their conduct at the siege of Bastia. Nelson, by whom it may truly be affirmed that Bastia was taken, received no reward. Lord Hood's thanks to him, both public and private, were, as he himself said, the handsomest which man could give: but his signal merits were not so mentioned in the dispatches as to make them sufficiently known to the nation, nor to obtain for him from government those honours to which they so amply entitled him. This could only have arisen from the haste in which the dispatches were written; certainly not from any deliberate purpose, for Lord Hood was uniformly his steady and sincere friend.[1]

One of the Cartel's ships,[2] which carried the garrison of Bastia to Toulon, brought back intelligence that the French were about to sail from that port; such exertions had they made to repair the damage done at the evacuation, and to fit out a fleet. The intelligence was speedily verified. Lord Hood sailed in quest of them toward the islands of Hyères. The *Agamemnon* was with him. " I pray God," said Nelson, writing to his wife, " that we may meet their fleet. If any accident should happen to me, I am sure my conduct will be such as will entitle you to the royal favour. Not that I have the least idea but I shall return to you, and full of honour. If not, the Lord's will be done. My name shall never be a disgrace to those who may belong to me. The little I have I have given to you, except a small annuity. I wish it was more; but I have never got a farthing dishonestly. It descends from clean hands. Whatever fate awaits me, I pray God to bless you, and preserve you for your son's sake."

With a mind thus prepared, and thus confident, his hopes and wishes seemed on the point of being gratified, when the enemy were discovered close under the land, near St. Tropez. The wind fell, and prevented Lord Hood from getting between them and the shore, as he designed. Boats came out from Antibes and other places to their assistance, and towed them within the shoals in Gourjean Roads,[3] where they were protected by the batteries on isles St. Honoré and St. Marguerite, and on Cape Garoue.[4] Here the English Admiral planned a new mode of attack, meaning to double on five of the nearest ships. But the wind again died away, and it was found that they had anchored in compact order, guarding the only passage for large ships.

---

[1] There is no reason to suppose that Lord Hood wrote his dispatch in undue haste. He desired to avoid even the appearance of friction between navy and army, and so refused, even in Nelson's interest, to make capital out of the unwillingness of General Dundas to undertake the siege. The dispatch is dated 24th May, five days after negotiations for surrender were begun.

[2] A " cartel-ship " was a vessel commissioned in time of war to exchange the prisoners of any two hostile powers or carry a proposal from one to the other. Such being her use, she was expressly forbidden to carry any implements of war other than a single gun for signalling purposes. Southey probably miscopied his phrase from Clarke and McArthur's *Life*.

[3] English corruption of Golfe Juan Roads.

[4] All three places are quite close to Golfe Juan and Antibes.

There was no way of effecting this passage, except by towing or warping [1] the vessels; and this rendered the attempt impracticable. For this time the enemy escaped. But Nelson bore in mind the admirable plan of attack which Lord Hood had devised, and there came a day when they felt its tremendous effects. [2]

The *Agamemnon* was now dispatched to co-operate at the siege of Calvi [3] with General Sir Charles Stuart; an officer who, unfortunately for his country, never had an adequate field allotted him for the display of those eminent talents, which were, to all who knew him, so conspicuous. [4] Nelson had less responsibility here than at Bastia; and was acting with a man after his own heart, who was never sparing of himself, and slept every night in the advanced battery. But the service was not less hard than that of the former siege. " We will fag ourselves to death," said he to Lord Hood, " before any blame shall lie at our doors. I trust it will not be forgotten that twenty-five pieces of heavy ordnance have been dragged to the different batteries, mounted, and, all but three, fought by seamen, except one artillery-man to point the guns.

The climate proved more destructive than the service; for this was during the lion sun, as they there call our season of the dog-days. Of two thousand men, above half were sick, and the rest like so many phantoms. Nelson described himself as the reed among the oaks, bowing before the storm when they were laid low by it. " All the prevailing disorders have attacked me," said he, " but I have not strength enough for them to fasten on." The loss from the enemy was not great; but Nelson received a serious injury. A shot struck the ground near him, and drove the sand and small gravel into one of his eyes. He spoke of it slightly at the time. Writing the same day to Lord Hood,

---

[1] See Note 1, p. 8.

[2] It was an accepted doctrine at this time that a fleet snugly berthed in a chosen anchorage could successfully defy all the attempts of a superior fleet, either by cunning or force, to dislodge it. Indeed, no one had done more to establish the validity of the doctrine than the Admiral who now proposed to disprove it. Lord Hood, however, believed that, if he had the breeze in his favour, he would be able to mass his strength on the hostile vessels nearest to the wind, and leave their companions (who were furthest away from it) helpless spectators of a struggle in which their immobility would forbid them to participate.

[3] In Corsica.

[4] Lord Melville was fully sensible of these talents, and bore testimony to them in the handsomest manner after Sir Charles's death.—SOUTHEY'S NOTE.

he only said that he got a little hurt that morning, not
much; and the next day, he said he should be able to
attend his duty in the evening. In fact, he suffered it to
confine him only one day; but the sight was lost.[1]

After the fall of Calvi, his services were, by a strange
omission, altogether overlooked; and his name was not
even mentioned in the list of wounded. This was no ways
imputable to the Admiral, for he sent home to government
Nelson's journal of the siege, that they might fully understand the nature of his indefatigable and unequalled exertions. If those exertions were not rewarded in the conspicuous manner which they deserved, the fault was in the
administration of the day, not in Lord Hood. Nelson felt
himself neglected. " One hundred and ten days," said he,
" I have been actually engaged at sea and on shore, against
the enemy; three actions against ships, two against Bastia
in my ship, four boat actions, and two villages taken, and
twelve sail of vessels burnt. I do not know that any one
has done more. I have had the comfort to be always
applauded by my commander-in-chief, but never to be
rewarded: and, what is more mortifying, for services in
which I have been wounded, others have been praised, who,
at the same time, were actually in bed, far from the scene
of action. They have not done me justice. But never mind,
I'll have a gazette of my own." How amply was this second-
sight of glory realised!

The health of his ship's company had now, in his own
words, been miserably torn to pieces by as hard service as
a ship's crew ever performed: one hundred and fifty were
in their beds when he left Calvi; of them he lost fifty, and
believed that the constitutions of the rest were entirely
destroyed. He was now sent with dispatches to Mr. Drake,
at Genoa, and had his first interview with the Doge. The
French had, at this time, taken possession of Vado Bay,
in the Genoese territory; and Nelson foresaw that, if their

---

[1] " On the 10th of July, a shot having hit our battery, the splinters and stones
from it struck me with great violence in the face and breast. Although the blow
was so severe as to occasion a great flow of blood from my head, yet I most
fortunately escaped, having only my right eye nearly deprived of its sight. It
was cut down, but is so far recovered as for me to be able to distinguish light from
darkness. As to all the purpose of use, it is gone. However, the blemish is nothing;
not to be perceived, unless told. The pupil is nearly the size of the blue part. . . .
I don't know the name."—NELSON TO HIS WIFE.

thoughts were bent on the invasion of Italy, they would accomplish it the ensuing spring. " The allied powers," he said, " were jealous of each other; and none but England was hearty in the cause." His wish was for peace, on fair terms, because England, he thought, was draining herself, to maintain allies who would not fight for themselves.

CHAPTER II

ADMIRAL HOTHAM BEING COMMANDER-IN-CHIEF IN THE MEDITERRANEAN

1794. 11th October.   Lord Hood returns to England, making over his fleet to Admiral Hotham.
1795. 13th, 14th March. Battle of the Gulf of Genoa.
      1st June.   Nelson made Colonel of Marines.
      5th July.   Sent to co-operate with General de Vins on coast of Genoa.
      6th, 7th July.   On his way to Genoa discovers the main French fleet, and retreating before them draws them into the arms of Hotham.
      13th July.   Battle of Hyères.

[SOUTHEY.   CHAPTER III—continued]

LORD HOOD had now returned to England, and the command devolved on Admiral Hotham.[1] The affairs of the Mediterranean wore at ·this time a gloomy aspect. The arts, as well as the arms of the enemy, were gaining the ascendancy there. Tuscany concluded peace, relying upon the faith of France, which was, in fact, placing itself at her mercy. Corsica was in danger. We had taken that island for ourselves, annexed it formally to the crown of Great Britain, and given it a constitution as free as our own. This was done with the consent of the majority of the inhabitants: and no transaction between two countries was ever more fairly or legitimately conducted.[2] Yet our conduct was unwise. The island is large enough to form an independent state, and such we should have made it, under our protection, as long as protection might be needed.

---

[1] Lord Hood returned to England to discuss the affairs of the Mediterranean with the Board of Admiralty. He did not intend to be long absent, and made over his fleet (temporarily, as it was thought) to his second-in-command. In the conversations at home, however, no agreement could be reached; and Admiral Hotham succeeded to one of the most important naval commands, though he was patently lacking in the vital qualifications requisite for his office.

[2] The arrangement debarred Paoli from the viceroyalty of the island, and in 1796 he returned to England, to die there in exile nine years later—a bitterly disappointed man.

The Corsicans would then have felt as a nation. But, when one party had given up the country to England, the natural consequence was, that the other looked to France. The question proposed to the people was, to which would they belong? Our language and our religion were against us; our unaccommodating manners, it is to be feared, still more so. The French were better politicians. In intrigue they have ever been unrivalled; and it now became apparent, that, in spite of old wrongs, which ought never to have been forgotten nor forgiven, their partisans were daily acquiring strength. It is part of the policy of France, and a wise policy it is, to impress upon other powers the opinion of its strength, by lofty language, and by threatening before it strikes; a system which, while it keeps up the spirit of its allies, and perpetually stimulates their hopes, tends also to dismay its enemies.

Corsica was now loudly threatened. The French, who had not yet been taught to feel their own inferiority upon the seas, braved us, in contempt, upon that element. They had a superior fleet in the Mediterranean, and they sent it out with express orders to seek the English and engage them. Accordingly, the Toulon fleet, consisting of seventeen ships of the line and five smaller vessels, put to sea. Admiral Hotham received this information at Leghorn, and sailed immediately in search of them. He had with him fourteen sail of the line, and one Neapolitan seventy-four;[1] but his ships were only half manned, containing but seven thousand six hundred and fifty men, whereas the enemy had sixteen thousand nine hundred. He soon came in sight of them. A general action was expected; and Nelson, as was his custom on such occasions, wrote a hasty letter to his wife, as that which might possibly contain his last farewell. "The lives of all," said he, "are in the hand of Him who knows best whether to preserve mine or not. My character and good name are in my own keeping."

But however confident the French government might be of their naval superiority, the officers had no such feeling: and after manœuvring for a day in sight of the English fleet, they suffered themselves to be chased. One of their ships, the *Ça Ira*, of eighty-four guns, carried away her main

[1] The *Tancredi*, Captain Caracciolo.

and fore topmasts.   The *Inconstant* frigate fired at the
disabled ship, but received so many shot, that she was
obliged to leave her.   Soon afterwards a French frigate took
the *Ça Ira* in tow; and the *Sans-Culottes*, one hundred and
twenty, and the *Jean Barras*, seventy-four, kept about
gunshot distance on her weather bow.   The *Agamemnon*
stood towards her, having no ship of the line to support her
within several miles.   As she drew near, the *Ça Ira* fired her
stern guns so truly, that not a shot missed some part of the
ship, and, latterly, the masts were struck by every shot.   It
had been Nelson's intention not to fire before he touched her
stern; but seeing how impossible it was that he should be
supported, and how certainly the *Agamemnon* must be
severely cut up if her masts were disabled, he altered his
plan according to the occasion.   As soon, therefore, as he
was within a hundred yards of her stern, he ordered the
helm to be put a-starboard, and the driver and after-sails
to be brailed up and shivered; and, as the ship fell off, gave
the enemy her whole broadside.   They instantly braced up
the after-yards, put the helm a-port, and stood after her
again.   This manœuvre he practised for two hours and a
quarter, never allowing the *Ça Ira* to get a single gun from
either side to bear on him; and when the French fired their
after-guns now, it was no longer with coolness and precision,
for every shot went far ahead.   By this time her sails were
hanging in tatters, her mizzen topmast, mizzen-topsail, and
crossjack-yards shot away.   But the frigate which had
her in tow hove in stays, and got her round.   Both these
French ships now brought their guns to bear, and opened
their fire.   The *Agamemnon* passed them within half pistol-
shot; almost every shot passed over her, for the French had
elevated their guns for the rigging, and for distant firing,
and did not think of altering the elevation.   As soon as the
Agamemnon's after-guns ceased to bear, she hove in stays,
keeping a constant fire as she came round; and being worked,
said Nelson, with as much exactness as if she had been
turning into Spithead.   On getting round, he saw that the
Sans-Culottes, which had wore, with many of the enemy's
ships, was under his lee bow, and standing to leeward.   The
Admiral, at the same time, made the signal for the van ships
to join him.   Upon this Nelson bore away, and prepared to

set all sail; and the enemy, having saved their ship, hauled close to the wind, and opened upon him a distant and ineffectual fire. Only seven of the *Agamemnon's* men were hurt—a thing which Nelson himself remarked as wonderful. Her sails and rigging were very much cut, and she had many shots in her hull, and some between wind and water. The *Ça Ira* lost one hundred and ten men that day, and was so cut up that she could not get a topmast aloft during the night.[1]

At daylight, on the following morning, the English ships were taken aback with a fine breeze at N.W., while the enemy's fleet kept the southerly wind. The body of their

[1] Southey took his story of the *Agamemnon's* fight with the *Ça Ira* almost verbatim from Nelson's account which had already been published from the Admiral's own papers in Clarke and McArthur's *Life*. He did so because he had insufficient acquaintance with seacraft to convert the story into ordinary prose. To-day the work of literal translation is many times more difficult because the naval language of our own era affords no parallels for the terminology of the sailing marine. It must suffice, then, to give in non-technical language a brief abstract of what occurred.

The French ships, refusing battle, were running as fast as they could in the hopes of giving Hotham the slip. The English ships were pursuing on a parallel line, with the *Agamemnon* well ahead. In the prevalent excitement the *Ça Ira* collided with the *Victoire* and was so much injured that she dropped behind. The French admiral ordered one of his greyhounds to take the cripple in tow, and two of his lustiest fighters to stand by and protect her. A swift vessel on the English side immediately ran up to pommel the *Ça Ira*, but, receiving many well-directed blows, very soon discreetly retired. Nelson then seized the occasion to show what he was made of. Altering course, he adroitly placed himself where the immense body of the *Ça Ira* would not only protect him from her own guards, the *Jean Barras* and the *Sans-Culottes*, but from her own murderous artillery that bristled on either flank. In short, he utilised his pigmy stature to snuggle under his adversary's stern.

If there had been no frigate towing the *Ça Ira*, Nelson would have brought his little ship within stone's throw of the Frenchman and slain her by a mortal thrust in her most vulnerable part. But as the *Ça Ira* was moving fairly rapidly through the water; as she had more guns mounted in her stern than any English ship could boast; and as Nelson could not possibly change his position without increasing his danger, he suffered for a while without compensation. But only for a while. Enduring blows while he ran forward, he then slewed round on his heel, delivered a broadside which smashed through the *Ça Ira's* stern-windows, and then working all his sails as easily as a pedestrian would twirl a walking-stick, resumed his offenceless attitude of pursuit while his gunners loaded again. In short, by a quick alternation of kick and carry on, he made the burden of existence intolerable to the Frenchman, who bade the towing-frigate pull her round, so that she also could wield her tiers of guns.

Nine commanders out of ten, sensing the new danger, would immediately have halted. But Nelson purposely ran on so as to close the range, and had the satisfaction of seeing the *Ça Ira's* shot fly harmlessly over his head. But it was time to be gone, because the *Jean Barras* and the *Sans-Culottes* now stood by their friend, with the towing-frigate to help them. Nelson, therefore, sheltered till the last moment from his new opponents under the towering sides of the *Ça Ira*; and then, pouring into the walls that had protected him a Parthian broadside, he turned and made off at full speed. So amazed were the hostile quartette that not one of them touched him.

Such was the state of the battle when Hotham, instead of speeding reinforcements to capture the four vessels that Nelson had stopped, hoisted the signal of recall.

fleet was about five miles distant; the *Ça Ira,* and the *Censeur,* seventy-four, which had her in tow, about three and a half. All sail was made to cut these ships off; and as the French attempted to save them, a partial action was brought on. The *Agamemnon* was again engaged with her yesterday's antagonist; but she had to fight on both sides the ship at the same time. The *Ça Ira* and the *Censeur* fought most gallantly. The first lost nearly three hundred men, in addition to her former loss; the last, three hundred and fifty. Both at length struck: and Lieutenant Andrews, of the *Agamemnon,* brother to the lady to whom Nelson had become attached in France, and, in Nelson's own words, " as gallant an officer as ever stepped a quarter-deck," hoisted English colours on board them both. The rest of the enemy's ships behaved very ill.

As soon as these vessels had struck, Nelson went to Admiral Hotham, and proposed that the two prizes should be left with the *Illustrious* and *Courageux* (which had been crippled in the action) and with four frigates, and that the rest of the fleet should pursue the enemy, and follow up the advantage to the utmost.[1] But his reply was, " We must be contented. We have done very well." " Now," said Nelson, " had we taken ten sail, and allowed the eleventh to escape when it had been possible to have got at her, I could never have called it well done.[2] Goodall [3] backed

[1] On the second day of the battle both fleets were running due west, that is, in the direction of Toulon. The French were showing a clean pair of heels, even the *Ça Ira* with the *Censeur's* help outdistancing pursuit. But both fleets were very close inshore; and a land-breeze suddenly struck the English fleet and drove it down upon the enemy. If this fresh motive-power had reached the French, their escape could still have been effected. But they lay in a pocket of southerly wind, and saw, to their consternation, the whole of Hotham's fleet running with deadly intent at their cripples. Valour prompted them to turn about, and at the risk of a general engagement endeavour to effect a rescue. And thus it came about that the two fleets approached one another from opposite directions. The English line was successful in cutting off the two lame ducks; but, in doing so, put its head in chancery. For while the *Ça Ira* and *Censeur* pounded away on one side, the main body of the French fleet came surging up on the other.

Nelson would like to have singled out special champions to deal independently with the *Ça Ira* and *Censeur,* and reversed the rest of the English line so that the opposing fleets could proceed side by side and fight it out to a finish. But Hotham preferred to use caution, and to bring up the tail of his line in support of its somewhat battered head. By doing so he rendered absolutely certain the subjugation of the two detached French ships, but allowed the rest of the enemy's line to draw clear of his own and escape.

[2] " I can, *entre nous,*" says Sir William Hamilton in a letter to Nelson, " perceive that my old friend, Hotham, is not quite awake enough for such a command as that of the king's fleet in the Mediterranean, although he appears the best creature imaginable."—SOUTHEY'S NOTE, Fourth Edition.

[3] Vice-Admiral of Hotham's fleet.

me. I got him to write to the Admiral. But it would not
do. We should have had such a day as, I believe, the annals
of England never produced." In this letter, the character
of Nelson fully manifests itself. " I wish," said he, " to be
an admiral, and in the command of the English fleet. I
should very soon either do much, or be ruined. My disposition cannot bear tame and slow measures. Sure I am,
had I commanded on the 14th, that either the whole French
fleet would have graced my triumph, or I should have been
in a confounded scrape." What the event would have been,
he knew from his prophetic feelings and his own consciousness of power. And we also know it now, for Aboukir and
Trafalgar have told it.

The *Ça Ira* and *Censeur* probably defended themselves
with more obstinacy in this action from a persuasion that,
if they struck, no quarter would be given; because they
had fired red-hot shot, and had also a preparation, sent,
as they said, by the Convention from Paris, which seems
to have been of the nature of the Greek fire; [1] for it became
liquid when it was discharged, and water would not extinguish its flames. This combustible was concealed with great
care in the captured ships. Like the red-hot shot, it had
been found useless in battle.

Admiral Hotham's action saved Corsica for the time;
but the victory had been incomplete, and the arrival at
Toulon of six sail of the line, two frigates, and two cutters
from Brest, gave the French a superiority which, had they
known how to use it, would materially have endangered
the British Mediterranean fleet. That fleet had been greatly
neglected at the Admiralty during Lord Chatham's administration; and it did not, for some time, feel the beneficial effect of his removal. Lord Hood had gone home to
represent the real state of affairs, and solicit reinforcements
adequate to the exigencies of the time, and the importance
of the scene of action. But that fatal error of under-pro-
portioning the force to the service; that ruinous economy,
which, by sparing a little, renders all that is spent useless,
infected the British councils; and Lord Hood, not being

---

[1] A preparation that ignited when brought into contact with the air, like the
liquid fire used in the Great War against Germany. The secret of Greek Fire was
known to the Byzantine Emperors, who gave it its name and used it with effect
in their wars against the Mohammedans.

able to obtain such reinforcements as he knew were necessary, resigned the command. "Surely," said Nelson, "the people at home have forgotten us." Another Neapolitan seventy-four joined Admiral Hotham, and Nelson observed with sorrow that this was matter of exultation to an English fleet. When the store-ships and victuallers from Gibraltar arrived, their escape from the enemy was thought wonderful; and yet, had they not escaped, "the game," said Nelson, "was up here. At this moment our operations are at a stand for want of ships to support the Austrians in getting possession of the sea-coast of the King of Sardinia;[1] and behold, our Admiral does not feel himself equal to show himself, much less to give assistance in their operations." It was reported that the French were again out with eighteen or twenty sail. The combined British and Neapolitan were but sixteen. Should the enemy be only eighteen, Nelson made no doubt of a complete victory; but if they were twenty, he said, it was not to be expected; and a battle, without complete victory, would have been destruction, because another mast was not to be got on that side Gibraltar.[2] At length Admiral Man arrived with a squadron from England. " What they can mean by sending him with only five sail of the line," said Nelson, " is truly astonishing: but all men are alike, and we in this country do not find any amendment or alteration from the old board of Admiralty. They should know that half the ships in the fleet require to go to England; and that long ago they ought to have reinforced us."

About this time Nelson was made Colonel of Marines—a mark of approbation which he had long wished for rather than expected. It came in good season, for his spirits were oppressed by the thought that his services had not been acknowledged as they deserved;[3] and it abated the resentful feeling which would else have been excited by the answer to an application to the War Office. During his four months'

[1] See map. The principal Sardinian harbour on the mainland of Italy was Nice.
[2] It must be remembered that England had lost Minorca and had not yet gained possession of Malta. The Royal Navy had, therefore, no English-controlled dockyard in the western Mediterranean, and had to put up with what hospitality could be exacted from such states as Naples and Tuscany. Neither of these countries had at their disposal naval stores sufficient for a first-class fleet.
[3] In his dispatch on the battle of the Gulf of Genoa, Admiral Hotham named for special commendation no one but his own flag-captain. " It is difficult," he wrote, " to specify particular desert where emulation was common to all."

land service in Corsica, he had lost all his ship-furniture, owing to the movements of a camp. Upon this he wrote to the Secretary at War, briefly stating what his services on shore had been, and saying, he trusted it was not asking an improper thing to request that the same allowance might be made to him which would be made to a land officer of his rank, which, situated as he was, would be that of a Brigadier-General. If this could not be accorded, he hoped that his additional expenses would be paid him. The answer which he received was, that " no pay had ever been issued under the direction of the War Office to officers of the navy serving with the army on shore."

He now entered upon a new line of service. The Austrian and Sardinian armies, under General de Vins, required a British squadron to co-operate with them in driving the French from the Riviera di Genoa;[1] and as Nelson had been so much in the habit of soldiering, it was immediately fixed that the Brigadier should go. He sailed from San Fiorenzo on this destination; but fell in, off Cape del Mele,[2] with the enemy's fleet, who immediately gave his squadron chase.[3] The chase lasted four-and-twenty hours; and, owing to the fickleness of the wind, the British ships were sometimes hard pressed. But the want of skill on the part of the French gave Nelson many advantages. He bent his way back to San Fiorenzo, where the fleet, which was in the midst of watering and refitting, had, for seven hours, the mortification of seeing him almost in possession of the enemy, before the wind would allow them to put out to his assistance. The French, however, at evening, went off, not choosing to approach nearer the shore.[4]

During the night, Admiral Hotham, by great exertions, got under weigh; and, having sought the enemy four days, came in sight of them on the fifth.[5] Baffling winds, and

[1] The coast of the Republic of Genoa; see map.
[2] Midway between Genoa and Nice; roughly, seventy miles from each.
[3] In addition to the *Agamemnon* (which, it must be remembered, was a very diminutive man-of-war) Nelson had only six smaller vessels. The French were seventeen strong in battleships alone, and compelled him by weight of numbers to retreat.
[4] The French scouting was bad. They supposed that Hotham's fleet was cruising near the Balearic Isles; and when Nelson, keeping just ahead of them, reached the British headquarters at San Fiorenzo, they realised somewhat tardily that he was drawing them into a trap.
[5] Southey's date is wrong. The battle of Hyères took place on 13th July.

vexatious calms, so common in the Mediterranean, rendered it impossible to close with them. Only a partial action could be brought on, and then the firing made a perfect calm. The French, being to windward, drew in-shore; and the English fleet was becalmed six or seven miles to the westward. *L'Alcide*, of seventy-four guns, struck; but before she could be taken possession of, a box of combustibles in her fore-top took fire, and the unhappy crew experienced how far more perilous their inventions were to themselves than to their enemies. So rapid was the conflagration, that the French in their official account say, " The hull, the masts, and sails, all seemed to take fire at the same moment "; and though the English boats were put out to the assistance of the poor wretches on board, not more than two hundred could be saved. The *Agamemnon*, and Captain Rowley, in the *Cumberland*, were just getting into close action a second time, when the Admiral called them off, the wind now blowing directly into the Gulf of Fréjus, where the enemy anchored after the evening closed.[1]

[1] The battle of Hyères, though it might have been one of the decisive battles of the world, hardly deserves more than the few contemptuous words that Southey devotes to it. The French ships (twenty-three in number) were running north hotly chased by the English, who were about equal in strength. The weather favoured the pursuit for a while, and the leading ships (including Nelson's and Troubridge's) clung to the skirts of the fugitives. But then the wind capriciously turned about and allowed the rearguard of the French to concentrate on their tormentors. Notwithstanding the fact that the French *Alcide* surrendered, and the chances of a general engagement were every moment increasing, Admiral Hotham, who refused to accept for a whole fleet risks which he would cheerfully have run in a single ship, hoisted an agitated signal ordering his whole force to retire.

The principal armies fighting against the French Republic at this time were those of Austria and Sardinia, and these could join forces and fight shoulder to shoulder in northern Italy. To reach her opponents France brought pressure to bear on the republic of Genoa, which was technically neutral but open to bribes. If Hotham had only forced a decision in either of his battles with the French fleet, it would not have been necessary to expend all his energy in the blockade of Toulon. And freed from the burden of watching Toulon, he could have paralysed the Genoese coast and have prohibited Napoleon's invasion of Italy. The sending of a small detached squadron under Nelson had no effect other than to emphasise the fact that nothing but the main fleet could achieve what the situation required.

CHAPTER III

A Digression from the Main Theme to the Italian Campaign of 1795

15th July–31st December

SOUTHEY wrote the following section of his work while the great war he described was still in progress and while the generation for whom he wrote were still familiar with its details. He takes for granted that his audience has the requisite knowledge to follow him; and this knowledge few modern readers are likely to possess.[1] Their lack of it is the more unfortunate because, in dealing with the Italian campaign of 1795, Southey is describing a phase of the war

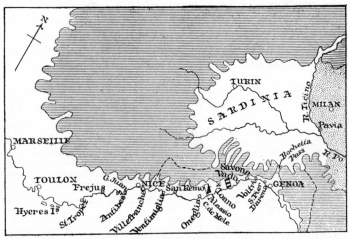

THE ITALIAN CAMPAIGN OF 1795

which has faded into nothing from contrast with Napoleon's brilliant achievements on the same ground in 1796; and he is describing that part of Nelson's career which (for want of backing from his commander-in-chief) afforded little or no opportunity for distinction. As a consequence, the narrative at this point is decidedly difficult. Indeed, it can only be interpreted in terms of physical and political geography.

The accompanying diagram shows the north-west portion of the Italian peninsula. The shaded area represents the main mass of

[1] *Cp.* above, p. xxix.

Alps and Apennines, the Bochetta Pass (immediately north of Genoa) forming a gateway into the Plain of Lombardy between the two. Lombardy in 1795 was divided between Sardinia, Austria, Venice, and lesser states. In the diagram the dotted area east of the Ticino shows the district actually possessed or virtually controlled by Austria, who (as already stated) was at this time allied with Great Britain and Sardinia in opposition to France. The boundaries of the various states (to avoid confusion) have been omitted except in the case of the Genoese Republic, whose border (where the mountain edge does not define it) is marked by a broken line.

It will be seen at once that this coastal state of Genoa formed the key to the whole situation in the western Mediterranean. Not only did it control the only easy gateway into the Plain of Lombardy, but it interposed an almost complete barrier between England and her friends.

This would have mattered little, perhaps, if Genoa had observed a strict neutrality, or if Austria had not had any Italian possessions. But since Genoa was particularly susceptible to bribes, and since France had discovered in the Plain of Lombardy the best region in which to strike a mortal blow at the Hapsburgs, the need of a strong British fleet off the Riviera became a prime necessity.

The map shows clearly that, save for a Hannibal or a Napoleon, the Alpine wall between France and Sardinia is impassable to armies. But without actually robbing Genoa of her independence, or (in other words) taking over the Bochetta Pass, the French hoped, in return for adequate payment, to utilise the coastal road; and, in the neighbourhood of Savona, strike across the narrow mountain chain that separates it from Sardinia. Genoa accepted the bribes of France, and allowed the Jacobin soldiers to use her highroad as much as they liked; but to show that she was (at least nominally) neutral, she extended the same sort of privilege to the Austrians, allowing them also to enter her territory in order to guard the passages that led from it into their own. When, therefore, Nelson took up his station off the Riviera, the French and Austrian armies were already facing one another, the French to the north of Oneglia, and the Austrians to the west of Vado (see map).

The most vulnerable point in the French position was their dependence upon ocean-borne supplies; and this gave Nelson a chance of bringing pressure to bear upon them. But the blockade of the hostile part of the coast, feasible in theory, broke down in practice; because France drew upon neutral shipping even more than on her own, and the multitude of small vessels that swarmed along the Riviera could only have been rounded up by a considerable flotilla, which Nelson asked for but did not receive.

He therefore advocated two alternative measures of great efficacy:

1. The occupation of San Remo so as to cut the French communications with their base.

2. A descent upon Alassio, where they had assembled a vast accumulation of supplies preparatory to an advance.

The first proposal was vetoed by Admiral Hotham, and the second by Hyde Parker who succeeded him.

[*SOUTHEY. CHAPTER III—continued*]

Nelson now proceeded to his station with eight sail of frigates under his command. Arriving at Genoa, he had a conference with Mr. Drake, the British envoy to that state; the result of which was, that the object of the British must be to put an entire stop to all trade between Genoa, France, and the places occupied by the French troops; for, unless this trade were stopped, it would be scarcely possible for the allied armies to hold their situation, and impossible for them to make any progress in driving the enemy out of the Riviera di Genoa.[1] Mr. Drake was of opinion, that even Nice might fall for want of supplies, if the trade with Genoa were cut off.

This sort of blockade Nelson could not carry on without great risk to himself. A captain in the navy, as he represented to the envoy, is liable to prosecution for detention and damages. This danger was increased by an order which had then lately been issued; by which, when a neutral ship was detained, a complete specification of her cargo was directed to be sent to the secretary of the Admiralty, and no legal process instituted against her till the pleasure of that board should be communicated. This was requiring an impossibility. The cargoes of ships detained upon this station, consisting chiefly of corn, would be spoiled long before the orders of the Admiralty could be known; and then, if they should happen to release the vessel, the owners would look to the captain for damages. Even the only precaution which could be taken against this danger involved another danger not less to be apprehended. For, if the captain should direct the cargo to be taken out, the freight paid for, and the vessel released, the agent employed might prove fraudulent, and become bankrupt; and in that case the captain became responsible. Such things had happened. Nelson therefore required, as the only means for carrying on that service, which was judged essential to the common cause, without exposing the officers to ruin, that the British

---

[1] Mr. Drake advocated the blockade of the Genoese coast, so far as it was occupied by the French, in order that the enemy, who depended on seaborne supplies, should be starved out, or at least be thrown back on their own resources, and compelled (like the Allies) to depend exclusively on land communications. "The places occupied by the French troops" is a diplomatic euphemism for "Genoese territory upon which the French army were encamped."

envoy should appoint agents to pay the freight, release the vessels, sell the cargo, and hold the amount till process was had upon it, government thus securing its officers. " I am acting," said Nelson, " not only without the orders of my commander-in-chief, but, in some measure, contrary to him. However, I have not only the support of his Majesty's ministers, both at Turin and Genoa, but a consciousness that I am doing what is right and proper for the service of our King and country. Political courage, in an officer abroad, is as highly necessary as military courage."

This quality, which is as much rarer than military courage as it is more valuable, and without which the soldier's bravery is often of little avail, Nelson possessed in an eminent degree. His representations were attended to as they deserved.[1] Admiral Hotham commended him for what he had done; and the attention of government was awakened to the injury which the cause of the allies con- tinually suffered from the frauds of neutral vessels. " What changes in my life of activity! " said this indefatigable man. " Here I am; having commenced a co-operation with an old Austrian General, almost fancying myself charging at the head of a troop of horse! I do not write less than from ten to twenty letters every day: which, with the Austrian General and aides-de-camp, and my own little squadron, fully employ my time. This I like;—active service, or none." It was Nelson's mind which supported his feeble body through these exertions. He was at this time almost blind, and wrote with very great pain. " Poor *Agamemnon*," he sometimes said, " was as nearly worn out as her Captain: and both must soon be laid up to repair."

When Nelson first saw General de Vins, he thought him an able man, who was willing to act with vigour. The General charged his inactivity upon the Piedmontese and Neapolitans, whom, he said, nothing could induce to act; and he concerted a plan with Nelson for embarking a part of the Austrian army, and landing it in the rear of the French. But the English Commodore soon began to suspect that the Austrian General was little disposed to any active operations. In the hope of spurring him on, he wrote to

---

[1] Hotham issued the instructions, which Nelson had framed, as general orders to the whole fleet.

him, telling him that he had surveyed the coast to the
westward as far as Nice, and would undertake to embark
four or five thousand men with their arms and a few days'
provisions on board the squadron, and land them within
two miles of San Remo, with their field-pieces. Respecting
further provisions for the Austrian army, he would provide
convoys, that they should arrive in safety; and, if a re-
embarkation should be found necessary, he would cover it
with the squadron. The possession of San Remo, as headquarters for magazines of every kind, would enable the
Austrian general to turn his army to the eastward or
westward. The enemy at Oneglia would be cut off from
provisions, and men could be landed to attack that place
whenever it was judged necessary.

San Remo was the only place between Vado [1] and Ville-
franche [2] where the squadron could lie in safety, and
anchor in almost all winds. The bay was not as good as
Vado for large ships; but it had a mole, which Vado had
not, where all small vessels could lie, and load and unload
their cargoes. This bay being in possession of the allies,
Nice could be completely blockaded by sea.

General de Vins affecting, in his reply, to consider that
Nelson's proposal had no other end than that of obtaining
the Bay of San Remo as a station for the ships, told him,
what he well knew, and had expressed before, that Vado
Bay was a better anchorage; nevertheless if *Monsieur le
Commandant Nelson* was well assured that part of the fleet
could winter there, there was no risk to which he would
not expose himself with pleasure, for the sake of procuring
a safe station for the vessels of his Britannic Majesty.

Nelson soon assured the Austrian commander that this
was not the object of his memorial. He now began to suspect
that both the Austrian court and their General had other
ends in view than the cause of the allies. " This army," said
he, " is slow beyond all description; and I begin to think
that the Emperor is anxious to touch another four millions
of English money. As for the German generals, war is their
trade, and peace is ruin to them. Therefore we cannot
expect that they should have any wish to finish the war.

---

[1] The port in which Nelson made contact with the Austrians.
[2] Forming with its neighbour Nice the French coastal headquarters.

The politics of courts are so mean, that private people would be ashamed to act in the same way. All is trick and finesse, to which the common cause is sacrificed. The general wants a loop-hole. It has for some time appeared to me that he means to go no further than his present position, and to lay [1] the miscarriage of the enterprise against Nice (which has always been held out as the great object of his army) to the non-co-operation of the British fleet, and of the Sardinians." [2]

To prevent this plea, Nelson again addressed De Vins, requesting only to know the time, and the number of troops ready to embark; then he would, he said, dispatch a ship to Admiral Hotham, requesting transports, having no doubt of obtaining them, and trusting that the plan would be successful to its fullest extent. Nelson thought at the time, that if the whole fleet were offered him [3] for transports, he [3] would find some other excuse: and Mr. Drake, who was now appointed to reside at the Austrian headquarters, entertained the same idea of the General's sincerity. It was not, however, put so clearly to the proof as it ought to have been. He [3] replied, that as soon as Nelson could declare himself ready with the vessels necessary for conveying ten thousand men with their artillery and baggage, he would put the army in motion. But Nelson was not enabled to do this. Admiral Hotham, who was highly meritorious in leaving such a man so much at his own discretion, pursued a cautious system, ill according with the bold and comprehensive views of Nelson, who continually regretted Lord Hood, saying that the nation had suffered much by his resignation of the Mediterranean command. The plan which had been concerted, he said, would astonish the French, and perhaps the English.

There was no unity in the views of the allied powers, no cordiality in their co-operation, no energy in their councils. The neutral powers assisted France more effectually than the allies assisted each other. The Genoese ports were at this time filled with French privateers, which swarmed out every night, and covered the gulf: and French vessels

[1] Attribute.
[2] Nice was properly a Sardinian port, and its rescue constituted a first claim upon the honour of the Allies.
[3] General de Vins.

were allowed to tow out of the port of Genoa itself, board vessels which were coming in, and then return into the mole. This was allowed without a remonstrance; while, though Nelson abstained most carefully from offering any offence to the Genoese territory or flag, complaints were so repeatedly made against his squadron, that, he says, it seemed a trial who should be tired first; they of complaining, or he of answering their complaints.

But the question of neutrality was soon at an end.[1] An Austrian commissary was travelling from Genoa towards Vado. It was known that he was to sleep at Voltri, and that he had £10,000 with him, a booty which the French minister in that city and the captain of a French frigate in that port considered as far more important than the word of honour of the one, the duties of the other, and the laws of neutrality. The boats of the frigate went out with some privateers, landed, robbed the commissary, and brought back the money to Genoa. The next day men publicly enlisted in that city for the French army. Seven hundred men were embarked, with seven thousand stand of arms, on board the frigates and other vessels, who were to land between Voltri and Savona. There a detachment from the French army was to join them, and the Genoese peasantry were to be invited to insurrection,—a measure for which everything had been prepared.

The night of the 13th was fixed for the sailing of this expedition. The Austrians called loudly for Nelson to prevent it; and he, on the evening of the 13th, arrived at Genoa. His presence checked the plan.[2] The frigate, knowing her deserts, got within the merchant-ships in the inner mole; and the Genoese government did not now even demand of Nelson respect to the neutral port, knowing that they had allowed, if not connived at, a flagrant breach of neutrality, and expecting the answer which he was prepared to return, that it was useless and impossible for him to respect it longer.[3]

---

[1] Nelson arrived off the coast in the middle of July: the events which Southey is about to describe occurred in the middle of November.

[2] Nelson laid the *Agamemnon* across the entrance to the harbour, so that the expedition was debarred from setting out.

[3] In drawing the *Agamemnon* across the harbour mouth, Nelson had, in a technical sense, blockaded Genoa, and so committed a breach of neutrality. Yet the Genoese Government, who had not hesitated to vex him with incessant

But though this movement produced the immediate effect which was designed, it led to ill consequences, which Nelson foresaw, but, for want of sufficient force, was unable to prevent. His squadron was too small for the service which it had to perform.[1] He required two seventy-fours, and eight or ten frigates and sloops; but when he demanded this reinforcement, Admiral Hotham had left the command. Sir Hyde Parker succeeded till the new commander should arrive; and he immediately reduced it almost to nothing, leaving him only one frigate and a brig. This was a fatal error. While the Austrian and Sardinian troops, whether from the imbecility or the treachery of their leaders, remained inactive, the French were [2] preparing for the invasion of Italy. Not many days before Nelson was thus summoned to Genoa, he chased a large convoy into Alassio. Twelve vessels he had formerly destroyed in that port, though two thousand French troops occupied the town. This former attack had made them take new measures of defence; and there were now above one hundred sail of victuallers, gun-boats, and ships of war.[3] Nelson represented to the Admiral how important it was to destroy these vessels; and offered, with his squadron of frigates, and the *Culloden* and *Courageux*, to lead himself in the *Agamemnon*, and take or destroy the whole. The attempt was not permitted: but it was Nelson's belief, that, if it had been made, it would have prevented the attack upon the Austrian army, which took place almost immediately afterwards.

General de Vins demanded satisfaction of the Genoese government for the seizure of his commissary; and then,

protests on much slenderer grounds, were on this occasion silent because their own violation of international law had been so ostentatiously flagrant.

The concluding words of the paragraph are slightly ambiguous. Nelson (Southey means) would certainly have had a very cogent answer ready if the Genoese had been brazen enough to register a formal complaint.

What Nelson, however, actually intended to say (if the Genoese had remonstrated) was diplomatically more adroit and correct: " If the Genoese Government have not the power to prevent these expeditions sailing from their ports, I conceive it to be my obvious duty to stand by and assist them." (Nicolas, Vol. II. p. 101.)

[1] He was kept at Genoa in the very hour when the French were assaulting the Austrian army at Loano, 24th November. Had he possessed a stronger fleet, he might, so to speak, have been in both places at once. As it was, his presence at Genoa had the effect of keeping the Bochetta open for the flying Austrians; see below.

[2] Had been.

[3] Southey's words hardly emphasise sufficiently the fact that Alassio was now the French advanced base, and that the destruction of the stores which they had accumulated there would effectually check their advance.

I

without waiting for their reply, took possession of some empty magazines of the French, and pushed his sentinels to the very gates of Genoa. Had he done so at first, he would have found the magazines full; but, timid as the measure was, and useless as it was to the cause of the allies, it was in character with the whole of the Austrian General's conduct: and it is no small proof of the dexterity with which he served the enemy, that in such circumstances he could so act with Genoa as to contrive to put himself in the wrong.

Nelson was at this time, according to his own expression, placed in a cleft-stick. Mr. Drake, the Austrian minister, and the Austrian General, all joined in requiring him not to leave Genoa. If he left that port unguarded, they said, not only the imperial troops of San Pier d'Arena and Voltri would be lost, but the French plan for taking post between Voltri and Savona would certainly succeed; if the Austrians should be worsted in the advanced posts, the retreat of the Bochetta would be cut off; and, if this happened, the loss of the army would be imputed to him, for having left Genoa. On the other hand, he knew, that if he were not at Pietra,[1] the enemy's gun-boats would harass the left flank of the Austrians, who, if they were defeated, as was to be expected from the spirit of all their operations, would, very probably, lay their defeat to the want of assistance from the *Agamemnon.*

Had the force for which Nelson applied been given him, he could have attended to both objects; and had he been permitted to attack the convoy in Alassio, he would have disconcerted the plans of the French, in spite of the Austrian General. He had foreseen the danger, and pointed out how it might be prevented; but the means of preventing it were withheld. The attack was made as he foresaw; and the gun-boats brought their fire to bear upon the Austrians. It so happened, however, that the left flank, which was exposed to them, was the only part of the army that behaved well. This division stood its ground till the centre and the right wing fled, and then retreated in a soldierlike manner.

General de Vins gave up the command in the middle of the battle,[2] pleading ill-health. "From that moment,"

[1] Loano.
[2] General de Vins was succeeded by General Wallis about the time that Nelson was summoned to Genoa.

says Nelson, " not a soldier stayed at his post. It was the
devil take the hindmost. Many thousands ran away who
had never seen the enemy; some of them thirty miles from
the advanced posts. Had I not, though I own against my
inclination, been kept at Genoa, from eight to ten thousand
men would have been taken prisoners, and, amongst the
number, General de Vins himself: but, by this means, the
pass of the Bochetta was kept open. The purser of the ship,
who was at Vado, ran with the Austrians eighteen miles
without stopping; the men without arms, officers without
soldiers, women without assistance. The oldest officer, say
they, never heard of so complete a defeat, and certainly
without any reason. Thus has ended my campaign. We
have established the French Republic; which, but for us,
I verily believe, would never have been settled by such a
volatile, changeable people. I hate a Frenchman. They are
equally objects of my detestation, whether royalists or
republicans. In some points, I believe, the latter are the
best." Nelson had a lieutenant and two midshipmen taken
at Vado. They told him, in their letter, that few of the
French soldiers were more than three or four and twenty
years old, a great many not more than fourteen, and all
were nearly naked. They were sure, they said, his barge's
crew could have beat a hundred of them; and that, had he
himself seen them, he would not have thought, if the world
had been covered with such people, that they could have
beaten the Austrian army.

The defeat of General de Vins gave the enemy possession
of the Genoese coast from Savona to Voltri; and it deprived
the Austrians of their direct communication with the
English fleet. The *Agamemnon*, therefore, could no longer
be useful on this station, and Nelson sailed for Leghorn to
refit. When his ship went into dock, there was not a mast,
yard, sail, or any part of the rigging, but what stood in need
of repair, having been cut to pieces with shot. The hull
was so damaged, that it had for some time been secured by
cables, which were served or thrapped [1] round it.

---

[1] A mistake for " frapping," the act of crossing and drawing together the
several parts of a tackle or other complication of ropes which have already been
straightened to their utmost extent; compare the bracing up of a drum.

CHAPTER IV

ADMIRAL SIR JOHN JERVIS BEING COMMANDER-IN-CHIEF IN THE MEDITERRANEAN

1795.	29th November.	Jervis reaches San Fiorenzo Bay, Corsica.
1796.	January.	Jervis institutes a strict blockade of Toulon.
	January.	Nelson, after refitting at Leghorn, joins Jervis.
	27th March.	Bonaparte begins his first Italian campaign.
		Jervis appoints Nelson a Commodore, second class.
	28th April.	Sardinia retires from the war.
	31st May.	Nelson captures Bonaparte's maps, plans, and literature.
	11th June.	Nelson shifts from *Agamemnon* into *Captain*.
	28th June.	Bonaparte seizes Leghorn.
	10th July.	Nelson captures Elba to facilitate the blockade of Leghorn.
	11th August.	Jervis appoints him a Commodore, first class.
	18th September.	Nelson captures Capraja.
	5th October.	Spain makes an alliance with France, rendering the western Mediterranean untenable by the British fleet.
	19th October.	Nelson completes the evacuation of Corsica, and
	December.	at Gibraltar shifts his broad pendant from *Captain* to *La Minerve* frigate, to superintend evacuation of Elba.
	19th December.	Captures Spanish frigate *La Sabina* off Carthagena.

[*SOUTHEY. CHAPTER IV*]

SIR JOHN JERVIS had now arrived to take the command of the Mediterranean fleet. The *Agamemnon* having, as her Captain said, been made as fit for sea as a rotten ship could be, Nelson sailed from Leghorn,[1] and joined the admiral in Fiorenzo Bay. " I found him," said he, " anxious to know many things, which I was a good deal surprised to find had not been communicated to him by others in the fleet. And it would appear that he was so well satisfied with my opinion of what is likely to happen and the means

---

[1] Chief port of Tuscany. See above, Note 2, p. 75.

of prevention to be taken, that he had no reserve with me respecting his information and ideas of what is likely to be done." The manner in which Nelson was received is said to have excited some envy. One captain observed to him, " You did just as you pleased in Lord Hood's time, the same in Admiral Hotham's, and now again with Sir John Jervis. It makes no difference to you who is commander-in-chief." A higher compliment could not have been paid to any commander-in-chief than to say of him that he understood the merits of Nelson, and left him, as far as possible, to act upon his own judgment.

Sir John Jervis offered him the *St. George*, ninety, or the *Zealous*, seventy-four, and asked if he should have any objection to serve under him with his flag.[1] He replied, that if the *Agamemnon* were ordered home, and his flag were not arrived, he should, on many accounts, wish to return to England: still, if the war continued, he should be very proud of hoisting his flag under Sir John's command. " We cannot spare you," said Sir John, " either as captain or admiral." Accordingly, he resumed his station in the Gulf of Genoa.

The French had not followed up their successes in that quarter with their usual celerity. Schérer, who commanded there, owed his advancement to any other cause than his merit.[2] He was a favourite of the Directory; but, for the present, through the influence of Barras, he was removed from a command for which his incapacity was afterwards clearly proved, and Bonaparte was appointed to succeed him.[3] Bonaparte had given indications of his military talents at Toulon, and of his remorseless nature at Paris :[4] but the extent, either of his ability or his wickedness, was at this time known to none, and, perhaps, not even suspected by himself.

Nelson supposed, from the information which he had obtained, that one column of the French army would take possession of Spezia; either penetrating through the

---

[1] Jervis asked Nelson if he would obligingly continue to serve with the Mediterranean fleet when he was promoted from captain to admiral.

[2] " Schérer, who commanded there, was one of the few French generals during the Revolution who owed their advancement to other causes than merit."—First Edition.

[3] This substitution was really the work of Carnot.

[4] VENDÉMIAIRE, when he cleared the streets with a " whiff of grape-shot."

Genoese territory, or proceeding coastways in light vessels; our ships of war not being able to approach the coast because of the shallowness of the water. To prevent this, he said, two things were necessary,—the possession of Vado Bay, and the taking of Spezia. If either of these points were secured, Italy would be safe from any attack of the French by sea. General Beaulieu, who had now superseded De Vins in the command of the allied Austrian and Sardinian army, sent his nephew and aide-de-camp to communicate with Nelson, and enquire whether he could anchor in any other place than Vado Bay. Nelson replied that Vado was the only place where the British fleet could lie in safety: but all places would suit his squadron; and wherever the General came down to the sea-coast, there he should find it. The Austrian repeatedly asked, if there was not a risk of losing the squadron; and was constantly answered that if these ships should be lost, the Admiral would find others. But all plans of co-operation with the Austrians were soon frustrated by the battle of Montenotte. Beaulieu ordered an attack to be made upon the post of Voltri. It was made twelve hours before the time which he had fixed, and before he arrived to direct it. In consequence, the French were enabled to effect their retreat, and fall back to Montenotte; thus giving the troops there a decisive superiority in number over the division which attacked them. This drew on the defeat of the Austrians. Bonaparte, with a celerity which had never before been witnessed in modern war, pursued his advantages; and, in the course of a fortnight, dictated to the court of Turin terms of peace, or rather of submission, by which all the strongest places of Piedmont were put into his hands.

On one occasion, and only on one, Nelson was able to impede the progress of this new conqueror. Six vessels, laden with cannon and ordnance-stores for the siege of Mantua, sailed from Toulon for San Pier d'Arena.[1] Assisted by Captain Cockburn, in the *Meleager*, he drove them under a battery, pursued them, silenced the batteries, and captured the whole. Military books, plans, and maps of Italy, with the different points marked upon them where former battles had been fought, sent by the Directory for Bonaparte's

---

[1] A little to the west of Genoa.

use, were found in the convoy. The loss of this artillery
was one of the chief causes which compelled the French
to raise the siege of Mantua. But there was too much
treachery, and too much imbecility, both in the councils
and armies of the allied powers, for Austria to improve this
momentary success. Bonaparte perceived that the conquest of all Italy was within his reach. Treaties, and the
rights of neutral or of friendly powers, were as little regarded
by him as by the government for which he acted. In open
contempt of both, he entered Tuscany and took possession
of Leghorn. In consequence of this movement, Nelson
blockaded that port, and landed a British force in the Isle
of Elba, to secure Porto Ferrajo.[1] Soon afterwards he took
the Island of Capraja, which had formerly belonged to
Corsica, being less than forty miles distant from it; a
distance, however, short as it was, which enabled the
Genoese to retain it, after their infamous sale of Corsica to
France. Genoa had now taken part with France. Its government had long covertly assisted the French, and now
willingly yielded to the first compulsory menace which
required them to exclude the English from their ports.
Capraja was seized, in consequence: but this act of vigour
was not followed up as it ought to have been. England
at that time depended too much upon the feeble governments of the Continent, and too little upon itself. It was
determined by the British cabinet to evacuate Corsica, as
soon as Spain should form an offensive alliance with France.
This event, which, from the moment that Spain had been
compelled to make peace,[2] was clearly foreseen, had now
taken place; and orders for the evacuation of the island
were immediately sent out. It was impolitic to annex this
island to the British dominions; but, having done so, it
was disgraceful thus to abandon it. The disgrace would
have been spared, and every advantage which could have
been derived from the possession of the island secured,

[1] The harbour of Elba.
[2] Spain, a member of the first alliance against the French Revolution, withdrew in July 1795. She did not change sides and sign an offensive and defensive
alliance with France till October 1796; but her inclinations and disposition were
well known beforehand. The numerical strength of her fleet, and the absence in
the western Mediterranean of a British naval dockyard, made her coming union
with the Jacobin forces a signal for recasting British plans. It was obviously
impossible for Jervis to blockade Toulon and cover Corsica if a Spanish fleet
were waiting behind him to stab him in the back.

if the people had at first been left to form a government
for themselves, and protected by us in the enjoyment of
their independence.

The Viceroy, Sir Gilbert Elliot, deeply felt the impolicy
and ignominy of this evacuation. The fleet also was ordered
to leave the Mediterranean. This resolution was so contrary
to the last instructions which had been received, that Nelson
exclaimed: " Do his Majesty's ministers know their own
minds? They at home," said he, " do not know what this
fleet is capable of performing—anything and everything.
Much as I shall rejoice to see England, I lament our present
orders in sackcloth and ashes, so dishonourable to the
dignity of England, whose fleets are equal to meet the world
in arms: and of all the fleets I ever saw, I never beheld one,
in point of officers and men, equal to Sir John Jervis's, who
is a commander-in-chief able to lead them to glory."

Sir Gilbert Elliott believed that the great body of the
Corsicans were perfectly satisfied, as they had good reason
to be, with the British government, sensible of its advantages
and attached to it. However this may have been, when
they found that the English intended to evacuate the
island, they naturally and necessarily sent to make their
peace with the French. The partisans of France found none
to oppose them. A committee of thirty took upon them
the government of Bastia, and sequestrated all the British
property. Armed Corsicans mounted guard at every place,
and a plan was laid for seizing the Viceroy.

Nelson, who was appointed to superintend the evacuation,
frustrated these projects. At a time when everyone else
despaired of saving stores, cannon, provisions, or property
of any kind, and a privateer was moored across the mole-
head to prevent all boats from passing, he sent word to
the committee, that if the slightest opposition were made
to the embarkment and removal of British property, he
would batter the town down. The privateer pointed her
guns at the officer who carried this message, and muskets
were levelled against his boats from the mole-head. Upon
this, Captain Sutton, of the *Egmont*, pulling out his watch,
gave them a quarter of an hour to deliberate upon their
answer. In five minutes after the expiration of that time,
the ships, he said, would open their fire. Upon this the

very sentinels scampered off, and every vessel came out of
the mole. A ship-owner complained to the Commodore
that the municipality refused to let him take his goods out
of the custom house. Nelson directed him to say that,
unless they were instantly delivered, he would open his fire.
The committee turned pale, and, without answering a word,
gave him the keys. Their last attempt was to levy a duty
upon the things that were re-embarked. He sent them
word, that he would pay them a disagreeable visit if there
were any more complaints. The committee then finding
that they had to deal with a man who knew his own power,
and was determined to make the British name respected,
desisted from the insolent conduct which they had assumed;
and it was acknowledged that Bastia never had been so
quiet and orderly since the English were in possession of
it. This was on the 14th of October. During the five following days the work of embarkation was carried on, the private
property was saved, and public stores to the amount of
£200,000. The French, favoured by the Spanish fleet,
which was at that time within twelve leagues of Bastia,
pushed over troops from Leghorn, who landed near Cape
Corse on the 18th; and, on the twentieth, at one in the
morning, entered the citadel, an hour only after the British
had spiked the guns and evacuated it. Nelson embarked
at daybreak, being the last person who left the shore; having
thus, as he said, seen the first and the last of Corsica.
Provoked at the conduct of the municipality, and the disposition which the populace had shown to profit by the
confusion, he turned toward the shore as he stepped into
his boat, and exclaimed, " Now, John Corse, follow the
natural bent of your detestable character—plunder and
revenge." This, however, was not Nelson's deliberate opinion
of the people of Corsica; he knew that their vices were
the natural consequences of internal anarchy and foreign
oppression, such as the same causes would produce in any
people: and when he saw, that of all those who took leave
of the Viceroy, there was not one who parted from him without tears, he acknowledged, that they manifestly acted
not from dislike of the English, but from fear of the French.
England then might, with more reason, reproach her own
rulers for pusillanimity, than the Corsicans for ingratitude.

Having thus ably effected this humiliating service, Nelson [1] was ordered to hoist his broad pendant [2] on board the *Minerve* frigate, Captain George Cockburn, and, with the *Blanche* under his command, proceed to Porto Ferrajo, and superintend the evacuation of that place also. On his way, he fell in with two Spanish frigates, the *Sabina* and the *Ceres*. The *Minerve* engaged the former, which was commanded by Don Jacopo Stuart, a descendant of the Duke of Berwick. After an action of three hours, during which the Spaniards lost one hundred and sixty-four men, the *Sabina* struck. The Spanish captain, who was the only surviving officer, had hardly been conveyed on board the *Minerve*, when another enemy's frigate came up, compelled her to cast off the prize, and brought her a second time to action. After half an hour's trial of strength, this new antagonist wore and hauled off. But a Spanish squadron of two ships of the line and two frigates came in sight. The *Blanche*, from which the *Ceres* had got off, was far to windward, and the *Minerve* escaped only by the anxiety of the enemy to recover their own ship. As soon as Nelson reached Porto Ferrajo, he sent his prisoner in a flag of truce to Carthagena, having returned him his sword. This he did in honour of the gallantry which Don Jacopo had displayed, and not without some feeling of respect for his ancestry. "I felt it," said he, "consonant to the dignity of my country, and I always act as I feel right, without regard to custom. He was reputed the best officer in Spain, and his men were worthy of such a commander." By the same flag of truce he sent back all the Spanish prisoners at Porto Ferrajo; in exchange for whom he received his own men who had been taken in the prize.

General de Burgh, who commanded at the Isle of Elba, did not think himself authorised to abandon the place till he had received specific instructions from England to that effect; professing that he was unable to decide between the contradictory orders of Government, or to guess at what their present intentions might be: but he said his only motive for urging delay in this measure arose from a desire that his own conduct might be properly sanctioned, not

[1] After rejoining Sir John Jervis's fleet, which, in obedience to orders, had fallen back upon Gibraltar.
[2] A swallow-tailed banner, the distinctive mark of a commodore.

from any opinion that Porto Ferrajo ought to be retained. But Naples having made peace, Sir J. Jervis considered his business with Italy as concluded; and the protection of Portugal was the point to which he was now instructed to attend. Nelson, therefore, whose orders were perfectly clear and explicit, withdrew the whole naval establishment from that station, leaving the transports victualled, and so arranged, that all the troops and stores could be embarked in three days. He was now about to leave the Mediterranean, Mr. Drake, who had been our minister at Genoa, expressed to him, on this occasion, the very high opinion which the allies entertained of his conspicuous merit; adding, that it was impossible for any one, who had the honour of co-operating with him, not to admire the activity, talents, and zeal, which he had so eminently and constantly displayed. In fact, during this long course of services in the Mediterranean, the whole of his conduct had exhibited the same zeal, the same indefatigable energy; the same intuitive judgment, the same prompt and unerring decision, which characterised his after-career of glory. His name was as yet hardly known to the English public; but it was feared and respected throughout Italy. A letter came to him, directed " Horatio Nelson, Genoa "; and the writer, when he was asked how he could direct it so vaguely, replied, " Sir, there is but one Horatio Nelson in the world." At Genoa, in particular, where he had so long been stationed, and where the nature of his duty first led him to continual disputes with the government, and afterwards compelled him to stop the trade of the port, he was equally respected by the Doge and by the people: for, while he maintained the rights and interests of Great Britain with becoming firmness, he tempered the exercise of power with courtesy and humanity, wherever duty would permit. " Had all my actions," said he, writing at this time to his wife, " been gazetted, not one fortnight would have passed, during the whole war, without a letter from me. One day or other I will have a long gazette to myself. I feel that such an opportunity will be given me. I cannot, if I am in the field of glory, be kept out of sight: wherever there is anything to be done, there Providence is sure to direct my steps."

These hopes and anticipations were soon to be fulfilled.

PART IV

THE BATTLE OF ST. VINCENT, 14th February, 1797
AND
THE REVERSE AT TENERIFFE, 24th July, 1797

THE Battle of St. Vincent forms one of the most remarkable sea victories in the annals of the world. The historian selecting it for his theme would have to explain:

(a) The trend of events which led up to it, and the new political situation which so decisive an encounter created.

(b) The sea strategy that drew together on the Atlantic coast of Spain two fleets which had in the first instance been mobilised for service in the Mediterranean.

(c) The training and discipline whereby Jervis had converted the ships at his disposal into a fighting fleet of unexampled efficiency.

(d) The reasons that induced him with fifteen sail to accept battle with a force nearly double his strength.

(e) The tactics whereby he routed his opponents.

Southey deals with none of these points except the last, and of the last he knows so little that he would have been better advised to omit it altogether. In brushing aside the larger issues he was justified, no doubt, by the nature of his theme. His task was to write a biography of Nelson, and the Battle of St. Vincent supplied him with brilliantly picturesque material in the capture by his hero of the *San Nicolas* and *San Josef*. To the conquest of these two ships, however, he devotes his narrative with zeal so whole-hearted that the modern reader is apt to overlook the fact that he is deliberately neglecting every other aspect of the struggle and almost every other name but Nelson's own.

[*SOUTHEY. CHAPTER IV.—continued*]

Nelson's mind had long been irritated and depressed by the fear that a general action would take place before he could join the fleet. At length he sailed from Porto Ferrajo with a convoy [1] for Gibraltar: and having reached that place, proceeded to the westward in search of the Admiral. Off the mouth of the Straits he fell in with the Spanish fleet; and on the 13th of February, reaching the station off Cape St. Vincent, communicated this intelligence to Sir John Jervis. He was now directed to shift his broad

[1] Non-combatant ships accepting his protection.

pendant on board the *Captain*, seventy-four (Captain R. W. Miller), and, before sunset, the signal was made to prepare for action, and to keep, during the night, in close order.

At daybreak the enemy were in sight. The British force consisted of two ships of one hundred guns, two of ninety-eight, two of ninety, eight of seventy-four, and one sixty-four: fifteen of the line in all; with four frigates, a sloop, and a cutter. The Spaniards had one four-decker, of one hundred and thirty-six guns ;[1] six three-deckers, of one hundred and twelve; two eighty-fours; eighteen seventy-fours: in all, twenty-seven ships of the line, with ten frigates and a brig. Their admiral, Don Joseph de Cordova, had learnt from an American, on the 5th, that the English had only nine ships, which was indeed the case when his informer had seen them; for a reinforcement of five ships from England under Admiral Parker had not then joined, and the *Culloden* had parted company.   Upon this information, the Spanish commander, instead of going into Cadiz, as was his intention when he sailed from Carthagena, determined to seek an enemy so inferior in force; and relying, with fatal confidence, upon the American account, he suffered his ships to remain too far dispersed, and in some disorder.

When the morning of the 14th broke and discovered the English fleet, a fog for some time concealed their number. That fleet had heard their signal-guns during the night, the weather being fine, though thick and hazy; soon after daylight they were seen very much scattered, while the British ships were in a compact little body. The look-out ship of the Spaniards fancying that her signal was disregarded, because so little notice seemed to be taken of it, made another signal that the English force consisted of forty sail of the line.   The Captain afterwards said he did this to rouse the Admiral: it had the effect of perplexing him, and alarming the whole fleet.[2] The absurdity of such an act

[1] The *Santissima Trinidad*, the only four-decker ever built.
[2] That Don Josef de Cordova met an American captain and gave implicit credence to misleading information received from him, and that his own look-out captain endeavoured to rouse him from his complacent torpor by a signal that did very much more harm than good, are stories which Mahan omitted from his biography perhaps because they seemed almost too lively to be true. They have, however, received complete confirmation from the papers of Earl Spencer, First Lord of the Admiralty, which have recently been edited by Sir Julian Corbett for the Navy Records Society (Vol. XLVI. pp. 356–7).

shows what was the state of the Spanish navy under that
miserable government, by which Spain was so long oppressed
and degraded, and finally betrayed. In reality, the general
incapacity of the naval officers was so well-known, that in
a pasquinade, which about this time appeared at Madrid,
wherein the different orders of the state were advertised
for sale, the greater part of the sea-officers, with all their
equipments, were offered as a gift: and it was added, that
any person who would please to take them should receive
a handsome gratuity.   When the probability that Spain
would take part in the war, as an ally of France, was first
contemplated, Nelson said that their fleet, if it were no
better than when it acted in alliance with us, would " soon
be done for."

   Before the enemy could form a regular order of battle,
Sir J. Jervis, by carrying a press of sail, came up with
them, passed through their fleet, then tacked, and thus
cut off nine of their ships from the main body.[1]   These
ships attempted to form on the larboard tack, either with
a design of passing through the British line, or to leeward
of it, and thus rejoining their friends.[2]   Only one of them

   [1] In his St. Vincent dispatch Jervis wrote: " *By carrying a press of sail,* I was
fortunate in getting in with the enemy's fleet at half past eleven o'clock, *before
it had time to connect and form a regular order of battle.* Such a moment was not
to be lost; and confident in the skill, valour, and discipline of the officers and men
I had the happiness to command, and judging that the honour of His Majesty's
arms, and the circumstances of the war in those seas, required a considerable
degree of enterprise, I felt myself justified in departing from the regular system;
and, *passing through their fleet* in a line formed with the utmost celerity, [I] *tacked
and thereby separated one-third from the main body.*"
   When the enemy were discovered, they were sailing before a westerly wind in
the direction of Cadiz. They were not in the least prepared for a sudden emergency,
and had fallen into two disconnected squadrons, the lesser being farthest from the
wind. Jervis approaching from the north—that is, at right angles to the enemy's
front—ran the risk of annihilation if he continued on his course, because his ships
were bound to expose themselves singly to the concentrated Spanish broadsides.
The " regular system " of which Jervis speaks required that he should re-align
his force on a front extending from west to east so that it might be parallel to the
foe. Jervis, however, accepted a big risk; and, using his battle-fleet like a rapier,
lunged through the main body of the Spaniards at the point of intersection between
their separate squadrons. Once through the gap, his fleet, acting like a fence or
barricade, had nine Spanish ships on its eastern side and eighteen on its western.
   Thus the first round of the battle was won; and as the two dislocated portions
of the foe turned themselves about (the eighteen to avoid collisions, and the nine,
if possible, to rejoin their friends), Jervis signalled the head of his line to curl
itself into the shape of the capital letter J, so as at one and the same time to thwart
the sidling tactics of the smaller Spanish squadron, and to follow hard upon the
heels of the larger (see diagram).
   [2] It is somewhat strange that Southey should have troubled himself over the
smaller Spanish squadron, because, whatever part it played in the actual battle,
its history has little connection with his own narrative. His meaning, however,
is fairly clear. The nine vessels, which had been heading towards Cadiz, now altered

succeeded in this attempt; and that only because she was
so covered with smoke that her intention was not discovered till she had reached the rear.[1] The others were so
warmly received, that
they put about, took
to flight, and did not
appear again in the
action till its close.

The Admiral was
now able to direct his
attention to the
enemy's main body,
which was still superior
in number to his whole
fleet, and greatly so in
weight of metal. He
made signal to tack in
succession.[2] Nelson,
whose station was in
the rear of the British
line, perceived that the
Spaniards were bear
ing up before the wind,
with an intention of
forming their line, go-
ing large, and join-
ing their separated

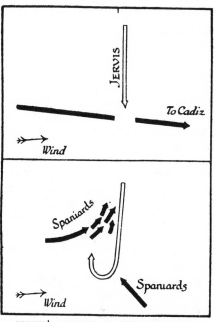

JERVIS'S TACTICS AT THE BATTLE OF
ST. VINCENT

ships; or else, of getting off without an engagement. To
prevent either of these schemes, he disobeyed the signal
without a moment's hesitation, and ordered his ship to be
wore.[3] This at once brought him into action with the

course so that they had the breeze to the left of them. Their obvious intention
was to join their friends, either by clearing a road through Jervis's line (unlikely),
or by passing along his western front to a meeting-place further north.

[1] The tail of the English fleet.

[2] Not a second time. Southey here repeats what he has already said, perhaps
in order to throw into greater relief Nelson's treatment of the signal in question.
This, if obeyed, would have kept him in his original place until the ship next ahead
went about.

[3] Nelson, who was last but two in Jervis's line, saw that the leading ships of the
larger Spanish squadron were preparing to alter course (" bearing up "), so that
they might round the tail of the British fleet, and run before the wind (" going
large ") with the military object of joining their nine ships to leeward, or the
vulgar object of making good their escape. To spoil their little game, he left the
line without permission and flung himself unaided in front of them.

Santissima Trinidad, one hundred and thirty-six, the *San Josef,* one hundred and twelve, the *Salvador del Mundo,* one hundred and twelve, the *San Nicolas,* eighty, the *San Isidro,* seventy-four, another seventy-four, and another first-rate. Troubridge, in the *Culloden,*[1] immediately joined, and most nobly supported him: and for nearly an hour did the *Culloden* and *Captain* maintain what Nelson called " this apparently, but not really, unequal contest." Such was the advantage of skill and discipline, and the confidence which brave men derive from them. The *Blenheim,* then passing between them and the enemy, gave them a respite, and poured in her fire upon the Spaniards.[2] The *Salvador del Mundo* and *San Isidro* dropped astern, and were fired into, in a masterly style, by the *Excellent,* Captain Collingwood.[3] The *San Isidro* struck: and Nelson thought that the *Salvador* struck also. " But Collingwood," says he, " disdaining the parade of taking possession of beaten enemies, most gallantly pushed up, with every sail set, to save his old friend and messmate, who was, to appearance, in a critical situation." For the *Captain* was at this time actually fired upon by three first-rates, by the *San Nicolas,* and by a seventy-four, within about pistol-shot of that vessel. The *Blenheim* was ahead, the *Culloden* crippled and astern. Collingwood ranged up, and hauling up his mainsail just astern, passed within ten feet of the *San Nicolas,* giving her a most tremendous fire, then passed on for the *Santissima Trinidad.* The *San Nicolas* luffing up, the *San Josef* fell on board her, and Nelson resumed his station abreast of them, and close alongside. The *Captain* was now incapable of further service, either in the line or in chase. She had lost her foretop-mast. Not a sail, shroud, or rope was left, and her wheel was shot away. Nelson, therefore, directed Captain Miller [4] to put the helm

---

[1] Troubridge was the leader of the English line. His opportune arrival shows that Jervis's signal to tack in succession had already had the intended effect of bringing the nose of his fleet on the enemy's traces.

[2] The *Blenheim* (Captain T. L. Frederick) was next astern of Troubridge in the *Culloden.*

[3] Collingwood in the *Excellent* had the rearmost ship in the British line. In answer to a signal from Jervis, he also wore round as Nelson had done to carry assistance where it was needed.

[4] As Commodore (first class) Nelson had a captain under him. Miller afterwards commanded the *Theseus* at the Battle of the Nile, and was killed on board his ship by the accidental explosion of a shell when he was assisting Sir Sidney Smith to defend Acre.

a-starboard,[1] and, calling for the boarders, ordered them to board.

Captain Berry, who had lately been Nelson's first lieutenant,[2] was the first man who leaped into the enemy's mizzen chains.[3] Miller, when in the very act of going, was ordered by Nelson to remain. Berry was supported from the spritsail-yard,[4] which locked in the *San Nicolas's* main rigging. A soldier of the Sixty-ninth broke the upper quarter-gallery window, and jumped in, followed by the Commodore himself, and by others as fast as possible. The cabin doors were fastened, and the Spanish officers fired their pistols at them through the window. The doors were soon forced, and the Spanish Brigadier fell while retreating to the quarter-deck. Nelson pushed on, and found Berry in possession of the poop, and the Spanish ensign hauling down.[5] He passed on to the forecastle, where he met two or three Spanish officers, and received their swords. The English were now in full possession of every part of the ship when a fire of pistols and musketry opened upon them from the Admiral's stern-gallery [6] of the *San Josef*. Nelson having placed sentinels at the different ladders, and ordered Captain Miller to send more men into the prize,[7] gave orders for boarding that ship from the *San*

[1] By putting the helm a-starboard, Nelson caused the *Captain* to collide with the *San Nicolas*, which was on his port bow.

[2] And was now a volunteer on board the *Captain*.

[3] The " chains " of a sailing-ship were wooden platforms that projected from her sides like shelves or ledges. Their use was to extend the shrouds or rigging that afforded support to the masts. The name was derived from the links of iron that held them in position.

[4] The spritsail was the canvas set under the bowsprit. The yard that extended it, having fouled the main-rigging of the *San Nicolas*, served as a bridge whereby reinforcements for Berry boarded the Spanish vessel.

[5] The officers' quarters in an old man-of-war were right aft; and, though encumbered by guns and other obstacles to comfort, were nicely lighted by stern and quarter (side) windows. Nelson, following the soldier who had smashed a way through the glass, found himself in the room immediately under the *San Nicolas's* poop. The Spaniards tried to imprison him by closing the door which led to the quarter-deck; but by this delay they allowed Berry to work his will above, while reinforcements joined the Commodore, through the broken window, and enabled him to break down the door.

[6] A balcony built outside the body of the ship, where the admiral could take the air. The position formed a favourable one for Spanish snipers bent on picking off the officers who had boarded the *San Nicolas*.

[7] If the assailants combined speed with an element of surprise it was not so difficult to carry a man-of-war by boarding as it might at first sight appear, for the majority of her company were down below standing to their guns and could only reach the point of danger by the narrow ladders or hatchways. The boarders, in short, had only to master the upper deck, and then overawe the men below. In order to rob the English of their prize, sharpshooters in the *San Josef's* stern-walk were now attempting, by small-arm fire, to expel from the *San Nicolas*

K

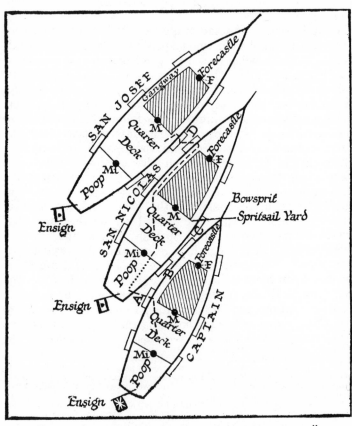

"NELSON'S PATENT BRIDGE FOR BOARDING FIRST-RATES"

Explanation

M Main Mast.
F Fore Mast.
Mi Mizzen Mast.
A Where Nelson boarded the *San Nicolas*.
B Where Berry boarded the *San Nicolas*.
C Where reinforcements for Berry boarded the *San Nicolas*.
D Where Nelson boarded the *San Josef*.

[The broken line shows Nelson's route from the quarter-deck of the *Captain* to the quarter-deck of the *San Josef*.]

Nicolas. It was done in an instant, he himself leading the way, and exclaiming—" Westminster Abbey or victory!" Berry assisted him into the main chains; and at that moment a Spanish officer looked over the quarter-deck-rail, and said they surrendered. It was not long before he was on the quarter-deck, where the Spanish Captain presented to him his sword, and told him the Admiral was below, dying of his wounds. There, on the quarter-deck of an enemy's first-rate, he received the swords of the officers; giving them, as they were delivered, one by one, to William Fearney, one of his old *Agamemnons*, who, with the utmost coolness, put them under his arm [" bundling them up," in the lively expression of Collingwood, " with as much composure as he would have made a faggot, though twenty-two sail of their line were still within gun-shot."] [1] One of his sailors came up, and, with an Englishman's feeling, took him by the hand, saying, he might not soon have such another place to do it in, and he was heartily glad to see him there. Twenty-four of the *Captain's* men were killed, and fifty-six wounded; a fourth part of the loss sustained by the whole squadron falling upon this ship. Nelson received only a few bruises.

The Spaniards had still eighteen or nineteen ships which had suffered little or no injury. That part of the fleet which had been separated from the main body in the morning was now coming up, and Sir John Jervis made signal to bring to.[2] His ships could not have formed without abandoning those which they had captured, and running to leeward. The *Captain* was lying a perfect wreck on board her two prizes; and many of the other vessels were so shattered in their masts and rigging as to be wholly unmanageable.[3] The Spanish Admiral meantime, according

her handful of invaders. Nelson, who was on the forecastle of the *San Nicolas*, detected the danger, and immediately decided to remove it by capturing the *San Josef* herself. For this purpose he required fresh hands from his own ship, so that they might guard the hatchways of the *San Nicolas* while he flew at higher game.

[1] The passage in brackets does not occur in the first, second or third edition. *Cp.* G. L. Newnham Collingwood, *Correspondence and Memoir of Lord Collingwood*, p. 39.

[2] To check the course of a ship by trimming the sails in such a manner that they counteract one another and keep her nearly stationary.

[3] This unintelligible paragraph Southey took almost verbatim from Clarke and McArthur's *Life*, which quotes, as its authority, the *Naval Chronicle* (Vol. IV. p. 37). Tucker's *Memoirs of the Earl of St. Vincent* (Vol. I. p. 261) states the direct

to his official account, being altogether undecided in his own opinion respecting the state of the fleet, enquired of his captains whether it was proper to renew the action. Nine of them answered explicitly, that it was not; others replied, that it was expedient to delay the business. The *Pelayo* and the *Principe Conquistador* [1] were the only ships that were for fighting.

As soon as the action was discontinued, Nelson went on board the Admiral's ship. Sir John Jervis received him on the quarter-deck, took him in his arms, and said he could not sufficiently thank him. For this victory the commander-in-chief was rewarded with the title of Earl St. Vincent. [2] Nelson, who, before the action was known

opposite, affirming emphatically that Jervis " formed " (*i.e.*, the regular line of battle) for the very reasons which Southey gives as motives why he refrained from doing so. The situation is easily visualised. The wind was still west, and the Spanish prizes together with Nelson's damaged ship lay to leeward of Jervis's main body, who were scattered and in no sort of order. At such a moment the smaller squadron of Spanish ships which had hitherto taken no part in the fight appeared to windward of the battlefield. Their main intention no doubt was to join forces with Don Josef de Cordova, but their position gave them the opportunity either of re-engaging Jervis, or of rescuing their captured compatriots, or of wreaking vengeance on the disabled *Captain*. Jervis accordingly, to guard against such eventualities, formed line on the starboard tack, as is proved by the *Victory's* log.

[1] There was a *Principe de Asturias* in the Spanish fleet and a *Conquistador*, but no such vessel as that here named.

[2] In the official letter of Sir John Jervis Nelson was not mentioned. It is said that the admiral had seen an instance of the ill-consequence of such selections after Lord Howe's victory, and therefore would not name any individual, thinking it proper to speak to the public only in terms of general approbation. His private letter to the First Lord of the Admiralty was, with his consent, published, for the first time, in a *Life of Nelson* by Mr. Harrison. Here it is said, that " Commodore Nelson, who was in the rear, on the starboard tack, took the lead on the larboard, and contributed very much to the fortune of the day." It is also said that he boarded the two Spanish ships successively; but the fact that Nelson wore without orders, and thus planned as well as accomplished the victory, is not explicitly stated. Perhaps it was thought proper to pass over this part of his conduct in silence as a splendid fault; but such an example is not dangerous. The author of the work in which this letter was first made public protests against those over-zealous friends " who would make the action rather appear as. Nelson's battle, than that of the illustrious commander-in-chief, who derives from it so deservedly his title. No man," he says, " ever less needed, or less desired, to strip a single leaf from the honoured wreath of any other hero, with the vain hope of augment-ing his own, than the immortal Nelson. No man ever more merited the whole of that which a generous nation unanimously presented to Sir J. Jervis, than the Earl St. Vincent." Certainly Earl St. Vincent well deserved the reward which he received. But it is not detracting from his merit to say that Nelson is fully entitled to as much fame from this action as the Commander-in-Chief; not because the brunt of the action fell upon him; not because he was engaged with all the four ships which were taken, and took two of them (it may almost be said) with his own hand; but because the decisive movement which enabled him to perform all this, and by which the action became a victory, was executed in neglect of orders, upon his own judgment, and at his peril. Earl St. Vincent deserved his earldom: but it is not to the honour of those by whom titles were distributed in those days that Nelson never obtained the rank of earl for either of those victories which he

in England, had been advanced to the rank of Rear-Admiral, had the Order of the Bath given him. The sword of the Spanish Rear-Admiral, which Sir John Jervis insisted upon his keeping, he presented to the mayor and corporation of Norwich, saying that he knew no place where it could give him or his family more pleasure to have it kept than in the capital city of the county where he was born. The freedom of that city was voted him on this occasion. But of all the numerous congratulations which he received, none could have affected him with deeper delight than that which came from his venerable father. " I thank my God," said this excellent man, " with all the power of a grateful soul, for the mercies he has most graciously bestowed on me in preserving you. Not only my few acquaintance here, but the people in general, met me at every corner with such handsome words, that I was obliged to retire from the public eye. The height of glory to which your professional judgment, united with a proper degree of bravery, guarded by Providence, has raised you, few sons, my dear child, attain to, and fewer fathers live to see. Tears of joy have involuntarily trickled down my furrowed cheeks. Who could stand the force of such general congratulation? The name and services of Nelson have sounded through this city of Bath—from the common ballad-singer to the public theatre." The good old man concluded by telling him that the field of glory, in which he had so long been conspicuous, was still open, and by giving him his blessing.

Sir Horatio, who had now hoisted his flag as Rear-Admiral of the Blue,[1] was sent to bring away the troops from Porto Ferrajo;[2] having performed this, he shifted his flag to the

lived to enjoy, though the one was the most complete and glorious in the annals of naval history, and the other the most important in its consequences of any which was achieved during the whole war.—SOUTHEY'S NOTE.

[1] The following was the order of precedence among flag-officers: Admiral of the White; Admiral of the Blue; Vice-Admiral of the Red; Vice-Admiral of the White; Vice-Admiral of the Blue; Rear-Admiral of the Red; Rear-Admiral of the White; Rear-Admiral of the Blue.

An admiral flew his flag at the main-mast, a vice-admiral at the fore, and a rear-admiral at the mizzen. All ships wore an " ensign " similar in colour to the flag of the admiral in whose division they were placed. At Trafalgar Nelson set aside all colour distinctions, and by using the white ensign to the exclusion of others set a fashion which is followed to this day.

[2] On his previous visit to Porto Ferrajo (see above, p. 94), Nelson found the general commanding the garrison unwilling to evacuate the place. As he had no means of compelling him to do so, he had now again to set out for Elba. Fortunately, he was not obliged to journey the whole way. For transports had already taken the troops on board, and he met them sixty miles to the westward of Corsica.

Theseus.[1] That ship had taken part in the mutiny[2] in England, and being just arrived from home, some danger was apprehended from the temper of the men. This was one reason why Nelson was removed to her. He had not been on board many weeks before a paper, signed in the name of all the ship's company, was dropped on the quarter-deck, containing these words: " Success attend Admiral Nelson! God bless Captain Miller! We thank them for the officers they have placed over us. We are happy and comfortable, and will shed every drop of blood in our veins to support them; and the name of the *Theseus* shall be immortalised as high as her captain's." [3] Wherever Nelson commanded, the men soon became attached to him. In ten days' time he would have restored the most mutinous ship in the navy to order. Whenever an officer fails to win the affections of those who are under his command, he may be assured that the fault is chiefly in himself.

While Sir Horatio was in the *Theseus*, he was employed in the command of the inner squadron at the blockade of Cadiz. During this service, the most perilous action occurred in which he was ever engaged.[4] Making a night attack upon the Spanish gun-boats, his barge was attacked by an armed launch, under their commander, Don Miguel Tregoyen, carrying twenty-six men. Nelson had with him only his ten bargemen, Captain Fremantle, and his coxswain John Sykes, an old and faithful follower, who twice saved the life of his Admiral by parrying the blows that were aimed at him, and, at last, actually interposed his own head to receive the blow of a Spanish sabre, which he could not by any other means avert. Thus dearly was Nelson beloved. This was a desperate service—hand to hand with swords; and Nelson always considered that his personal

---

[1] Because the *Captain* was worn out by her exertions at St. Vincent and her voyage towards Elba.

[2] The Great Mutiny of the fleet took place in the spring of 1797.

[3] An odd little mistake on Southey's part. What the ship's company wrote was, " The name óf the *Theseus* shall be immortalised as high as the *Captain's*."

[4] The Spanish ships that escaped from the stricken field of St. Vincent fled for refuge into Cadiz. There Jervis blockaded them. His ships of the line had to keep their distance to avoid the perilous shoals, but a flotilla of small craft kept watch on the harbour-mouth, and these composed the " inner " (inshore) squadron of which Southey speaks. On 3rd July, at Jervis's order, some English mortar vessels bombarded the town, and one of these being disabled was attacked by Spanish gunboats. Nelson sped to the rescue with what craft he could assemble, and risked his life in a hand-to-hand struggle for which his delicate frame unfitted him.

courage was more conspicuous on this occasion than on any other during his whole life. Notwithstanding the great disproportion of numbers, eighteen of the enemy were killed, all the rest wounded, and their launch taken. Nelson would have asked for a lieutenancy for Sykes, if he had served long enough. His manner and conduct, he observed, were so entirely above his situation, that Nature certainly intended him for a gentleman. But though he recovered from the dangerous wound which he received in this act of heroic attachment, he did not live to profit by the gratitude and friendship of his commander.

Twelve days after this rencontre,[1] Nelson sailed at the head of an expedition against Teneriffe.[2] A report had prevailed a few months before that the Viceroy of Mexico, with the treasure ships, had put into that island. This had led Nelson to meditate the plan of an attack upon it, which he communicated to Earl St. Vincent. He was perfectly aware of the difficulties of the attempt. " I do not," said he, " reckon myself equal to Blake:[3] but, if I recollect right, he was more obliged to the wind coming off the land, than to any exertions of his own. The approach by sea to the anchoring-place is under very high land, passing three valleys. Therefore the wind is either in from the sea, or squally with calms from the mountains." And he perceived, that if the Spanish ships were won, the object would still be frustrated, if the wind did not come off shore. The land force, he thought, would render success certain; and there were the troops from Elba, with all necessary stores and artillery, already embarked. " But here," said he, " soldiers must be consulted; and I know, from experience, they have not the same boldness in undertaking a political measure that we have. We look to the benefit of our country, and risk our own fame every day to serve her. A soldier obeys his orders, and no more." Nelson's experience at Corsica justified him in this harsh opinion. He did not live to see the glorious days of the British Army under Wellington. The army from Elba, consisting of three thousand seven hundred men, would do the business, he said, in three days,

---

[1] 15th July, 1797.   One of the Canary Islands.
[3] The crowning event in Blake's career was the destruction of the Spanish galleons in Santa Cruz Bay, Teneriffe, in 1657. See Lord Clarendon, *History of the Great Rebellion*, Bk. XV. §§ 53–7.

probably in much less time; and he would undertake, with a very small squadron, to perform the naval part; for, though the shore was not easy of access, the transports might run in and land the troops in one day.

The report concerning the Viceroy was unfounded. But a homeward-bound Manilla ship put into Santa Cruz at this time, and the expedition was determined upon. It was not fitted out upon the scale which Nelson had proposed. Four ships of the line,[1] three frigates, and the *Fox* cutter, formed the squadron; and he was allowed to choose such ships and officers as he thought proper. No troops were embarked; the seamen and marines of the squadron being thought sufficient. His orders were to make a vigorous attack; but on no account to land in person, unless his presence should be absolutely necessary. The plan was, that the boats should land in the night, between the fort on the N.E. side of Santa Cruz bay and the town, make themselves masters of that fort, and then send a summons to the Governor.

By midnight, the three frigates, having the force on board which was intended for this debarkation, approached within three miles of the place. But owing to a strong gale of wind in the offing, and a strong current against them in-shore, they were not able to get within a mile of the landing-place before daybreak; and then they were seen, and their intention discovered. Troubridge and Bowen, with Captain Oldfield of the marines, went upon this to consult with the Admiral what was to be done; and it was resolved that they should attempt to get possession of the heights above the fort. The frigates accordingly landed their men; and Nelson stood in with the line-of-battle ships, meaning to batter the fort for the purpose of distracting the attention of the garrison. A calm and contrary current hindered him from getting within a league of the shore; and the heights were by this time so secured, and manned with such a force, as to be judged impracticable.

Thus foiled in his plans by circumstances of wind and tide, he still considered it a point of honour that some attempt should be made. This was on the twenty-second of July. He re-embarked his men that night, got the ships on the twenty-fourth to anchor about two miles north of the town,

---

[1] One was a fifty-gun ship and should count as a frigate rather than a battleship.

and made show as if he intended to attack the heights. At six in the evening, signal was made for the boats to prepare to proceed on the service as previously ordered.

When this was done, Nelson addressed a letter to the commander-in-chief—the last which was ever written with his right hand. " I shall not," said he, " enter on the subject, why we are not in possession of Santa Cruz. Your partiality will give credit that all has hitherto been done which was possible; but without effect. This night I, humble as I am, command the whole destined to land under the batteries of the town; and, to-morrow, my head will probably be crowned either with laurel or cypress. I have only to recommend Josiah Nisbet [1] to you and my country. The Duke of Clarence, should I fall, will, I am confident, take a lively interest for my son-in-law, on his name being mentioned." Perfectly aware how desperate a service this was likely to prove, before he left the *Theseus* he called Lieutenant Nisbet, who had the watch on deck,[2] into the cabin, that he might assist in arranging and burning his mother's letters. Perceiving that the young man was armed, he earnestly begged him to remain behind. " Should we both fall, Josiah," said he, " what would become of your poor mother! The care of the *Theseus* falls to you. Stay, therefore, and take charge of her." Nisbet replied: " Sir, the ship must take care of herself. I will go with you to-night, if I never go again."

He met his captains at supper on board the *Seahorse*, Captain Fremantle, whose wife, whom he had lately married in the Mediterranean, presided at table. At eleven o'clock, the boats, containing between six and seven hundred men, with one hundred and eighty on board the *Fox* cutter, and from seventy to eighty in a boat which had been taken the day before, proceeded in six divisions toward the town, conducted by all the captains of the squadron, except Fremantle and Bowen, who attended with Nelson to regulate and lead the way to the attack. They were to land on the mole, and thence hasten, as fast as possible, into the great square; then form, and proceed, as should be found expedient. They were not discovered till about half-past one o'clock, when, being within half gun-shot of the landing-place, Nelson directed the boats to cast off

[1] His stepson. [2] Who for the time being had charge of the ship.

from each other, give a huzza, and push for the shore. But the Spaniards were exceedingly well prepared. The alarm-bells answered the huzza, and a fire of thirty or forty pieces of cannon, with musketry from one end of the town to the other, opened upon the invaders. Nothing however, could check the intrepidity with which they advanced. The night was exceedingly dark. Most of the boats missed the mole, and went on shore through a raging surf, which stove all to the left of it. The Admiral, Fremantle, Thompson, Bowen, and four or five other boats, found the mole. They stormed it instantly, and carried it, though it was defended, as they imagined, by four or five hundred men. Its guns, which were six-and-twenty pounders, were spiked; but such a heavy fire of musketry and grape was kept up from the citadel and the houses at the head of the mole, that the assailants could not advance, and nearly all of them were killed or wounded.

In the act of stepping out of the boat, Nelson received a shot through the right elbow, and fell; but, as he fell, he caught the sword, which he had just drawn, in his left hand, determined never to part with it while he lived, for it had belonged to his uncle, Captain Suckling, and he valued it like a relic. Nisbet, who was close to him, placed him at the bottom of the boat, and laid his hat over the shattered arm, lest the sight of the blood, which gushed out in great abundance, should increase his faintness. He then examined the wound, and taking some silk handkerchiefs from his neck, bound them round tight above the lacerated vessels. Had it not been for this presence of mind in his son-in-law, Nelson must have perished. One of his bargemen, by name Lovel, tore his shirt into shreds, and made a sling with them for the broken limb. They then collected five other seamen, by whose assistance they succeeded, at length, in getting the boat afloat; for it had grounded with the falling tide. Nisbet took one of the oars, and ordered the steersman to go close under the guns of the battery, that they might be safe from its tremendous fire. Hearing his voice, Nelson roused himself, and desired to be lifted up in the boat, that he might look about him. Nisbet raised him up; but nothing could be seen, except the firing of the guns on shore, and what could be discerned by their flashes upon the stormy sea.

In a few minutes, a general shriek was heard from the crew of the *Fox*, which had received a shot under water, and went down. Ninety-seven men were lost in her; eighty-three were saved, many by Nelson himself, whose exertions on this occasion greatly increased the pain and danger of his wound. The first ship which the boat could reach happened to be the *Seahorse*; but nothing could induce him to go on board, though he was assured that if they attempted to row to another ship, it might be at the risk of his life. " I had rather suffer death," he replied, " than alarm Mrs. Fremantle, by letting her see me in this state, when I can give her no tidings whatever of her husband." They pushed on for the *Theseus*. When they came alongside, he peremptorily refused all assistance in getting on board, so impatient was he that the boat should return, in hopes that it might save a few more from the *Fox*. He desired to have only a single rope thrown over the side, which he twisted round his left hand, saying, " Let me alone: I have yet my legs left and one arm. Tell the surgeon to make haste and get his instruments. I know I must lose my right arm, so the sooner it is off the better." [1] The spirit which he displayed in jumping up the ship's side astonished everybody.

Fremantle had been severely wounded in the right arm, soon after the Admiral. He was fortunate enough to find a boat on the beach, and got instantly to his ship. Thompson was wounded: Bowen [2] killed, to the great regret of Nelson; as was also one of his own officers, Lieutenant Weatherhead, who had followed him from the *Agamemnon*, and whom he greatly and deservedly esteemed.

[1] During the Peace of Amiens, when Nelson was passing through Salisbury, and received there with those acclamations which followed him everywhere, he recognised among the crowd a man who had assisted at the amputation, and attended him afterwards. He beckoned him up the stairs at the Council-house, shook hands with him, and made him a present, in remembrance of his services at that time. The man took from his bosom a piece of lace, which he had torn from the sleeve of the amputated limb, saying he had preserved and would preserve it to the last moment, in memory of his old commander.—SOUTHEY'S NOTE.

[2] Captain Bowen's gold seals and chain and sword were preserved in the town-house at Teneriffe; his watch and other valuables had been made booty of by the populace. In 1810, the magistrates of the island sent these memorials of the dead to his brother, Commissioner Bowen, saying that they conceived it would be gratifying to his feelings to receive them, and that as the two nations were now united in a cause which did equal honour to both, they did not wish to retain a trophy which could remind them that they had ever been opposed to each other. —*Naval Chronicle* Vol. XXIV. p. 393. SOUTHEY'S NOTE, Fourth Edition.)

Troubridge, meantime, fortunately for his party, missed the mole in the darkness, but pushed on shore under the batteries, close to the south end of the citadel. Captain Waller of the *Emerald*, and two or three other boats, landed at the same time. The surf was so high that many others put back. The boats were instantly filled with water, and stove against the rocks; and most of the ammunition in the men's pouches was wetted. Having collected a few men, they pushed on to the great square, hoping there to find the Admiral and the rest of the force. The ladders were all lost, so that they could make no immediate attempt on the citadel; but they sent a sergeant with two of the townspeople to summon it. This messenger never returned; and Troubridge having waited about an hour, in painful expectation of his friends, marched to join Captains Hood [1] and Miller, who had effected their landing to the south-west. They then endeavoured to procure some intelligence of the Admiral and the rest of the officers, but without success. By daybreak they had gathered together about eighty marines, eighty pikemen, and one hundred and eighty small-arm seamen; all the survivors of those who had made good their landing. They obtained some ammunition from the prisoners whom they had taken, and marched on, to try what could be done at the citadel without ladders. They found all the streets commanded by field-pieces, and several thousand Spaniards, with about a hundred French, under arms, approaching by every avenue.

Finding himself without provisions, the powder wet, and no possibility of obtaining either stores or reinforcements from the ships, the boats being lost, Troubridge, with great presence of mind, sent Captain Samuel Hood [1] with

[1] A cousin of the great Lord Hood, under whom he had served at Toulon. (See above, pp. 50–68.)

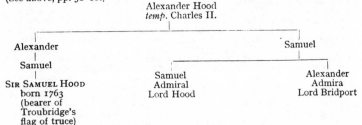

Alexander Hood
temp. Charles II.

Alexander
|
Samuel
|
SIR SAMUEL HOOD
born 1763
(bearer of
Troubridge's
flag of truce)

Samuel
Admiral
Lord Hood

Samuel

Alexander
Admira
Lord Bridport

a flag of truce to the Governor, to say he was prepared to burn the town, and would instantly set fire to it, if the Spaniards approached one inch nearer. This, however, if he were compelled to do it, he should do with regret, for he had no wish to injure the inhabitants: and he was ready to treat upon these terms,—that the British troops should re-embark, with all their arms, of every kind, and take their own boats, if they were saved, or be provided with such others as might be wanting: they, on their part, engaging that the squadron should not molest the town, nor any of the Canary Islands: all prisoners on both sides to be given up. When these terms were proposed, the Governor made answer, that the English ought to surrender as prisoners of war: but Captain Hood replied, he was instructed to say, that if the terms were not accepted in five minutes, Captain Troubridge would set the town on fire, and attack the Spaniards at the point of the bayonet.

Satisfied with his success, which was indeed sufficiently complete, and respecting like a brave and honourable man the gallantry of his enemy, the Spaniard acceded to the proposal, found boats to re-embark them, their own having all been dashed to pieces in landing, and before they parted gave every man a loaf and a pint of wine. " And here," says Nelson in his journal, " it is right we should notice the noble and generous conduct of Don Juan Antonio Gutierrez, the Spanish Governor. The moment the terms were agreed to, he directed our wounded men to be received into the hospitals, and all our people to be supplied with the best provisions that could be procured; and made it known that the ships were at liberty to send on shore, and purchase whatever refreshments they were in want of during the time they might be off the island." A youth, by name Don Bernardo Collagon, stripped himself of his shirt, to make bandages for one of those Englishmen, against whom not an hour before, he had been engaged in battle. Nelson wrote to thank the Governor for the humanity which he had displayed. Presents were interchanged between them. Sir Horatio offered to take charge of his despatches for the Spanish government; and thus actually became the first messenger to Spain of his own defeat.

The total loss of the English, in killed, wounded, and

drowned, amounted to two hundred and fifty. Nelson made no mention of his own wound in his official dispatches. But in a private letter to Lord St. Vincent,—the first which he wrote with his left hand,—he shows himself to have been deeply affected by the failure of this enterprise. " I am become," he said, " a burthen to my friends, and useless to my country: but by my last letter you will perceive my anxiety for the promotion of my son-in-law, Josiah Nisbet. When I leave your command, I become dead to the world: ' I go hence, and am no more seen.' If from poor Bowen's loss you think it proper to oblige me, I rest confident you will do it. The boy is under obligations to me; but he repaid me, by bringing me from the mole of Santa Cruz. I hope you will be able to give me a frigate, to convey the remains of my carcase to England." " A left-handed admiral," he said in a subsequent letter, " will never again be considered as useful. Therefore the sooner I get to a very humble cottage the better, and make room for a sounder man to serve the state." His first letter to Lady Nelson was written under the same opinion, but in a more cheerful strain. " It was the chance of war," said he, " and I have great reason to be thankful: and I know it will add much to your pleasure to find that Josiah, under God's providence, was principally instrumental in saving my life. I shall not be surprised if I am neglected and forgotten: probably I shall no longer be considered as useful: however, I shall feel rich if I continue to enjoy your affection. I beg neither you nor my father will think much of this mishap. My mind has long been made up to such an event."

His son-in-law, according to his wish, was immediately promoted; [1] and honours enough to heal his wounded spirit awaited him in England. Letters were addressed to him by the First Lord of the Admiralty, and by his steady friend, the Duke of Clarence, to congratulate him on his return, covered as he was with glory. He assured the Duke, in his reply, that not a scrap of that ardour, with which he had hitherto served his king, had been shot away. The freedom of the cities of Bristol and London were transmitted to

---

[1] He was given command of the *Dolphin* (hospital ship) with the rank of master, and presently transferred to the *Bonne Citoyenne*, sloop-of-war. At the time of his appointment he was seventeen years of age.

him. He was invested with the Order of the Bath; and received a pension of £1000 a year. The memorial which, as a matter of form, he was called upon to present on this occasion, exhibited an extraordinary catalogue of services performed during the war. It stated, that he had been in four actions with the fleets of the enemy, and in three actions with boats employed in cutting out of harbour, in destroying vessels, and in taking three towns: he had served on shore with the army four months, and commanded the batteries at the sieges of Bastia and Calvi: he had assisted at the capture of seven sail of the line, six frigates, four corvettes, and eleven privateers: taken and destroyed near fifty sail of merchant vessels: and actually been engaged against the enemy upwards of a hundred and twenty times; in which service he had lost his right eye and right arm, and been severely wounded and bruised in his body.

His sufferings from the lost limb were long and painful. A nerve had been taken up in one of the ligatures at the time of the operation; and the ligature, according to the practice of the French surgeons, was of silk, instead of waxed thread; this produced a constant irritation and discharge; and the ends of the ligature being pulled every day, in hopes of bringing it away, occasioned fresh agony. He had scarcely any intermission of pain, day or night, for three months after his return to England. Lady Nelson, at his earnest request, attended the dressing of his arm, till she had acquired sufficient resolution and skill to dress it herself. One night, during this state of suffering, after a day of constant pain, Nelson retired early to bed, in hope of enjoying some respite by means of laudanum. He was at that time lodging in Bond Street; and the family were soon disturbed by a mob knocking loudly and violently at the door. The news of Duncan's victory [1] had been made public, and the house was not illuminated. But when the mob were told that Admiral Nelson lay there in bed, badly wounded, the foremost of them made answer, " You shall hear no more from us to-night; " and in fact, the feeling of respect and sympathy was communicated from one to another with such effect that, under the confusion of such a night, the house was not molested again.

[1] The Battle of Camperdown, 11th October, 1797.

About the end of November, after a night of sound sleep, he found the arm nearly free from pain. The surgeon was immediately sent for to examine it; and the ligature came away with the slightest touch. From that time it began to heal. As soon as he thought his health established, he sent the following form of thanksgiving to the minister of St. George's, Hanover Square: "An officer desires to return thanks to Almighty God for his perfect recovery from a severe wound, and also for the many mercies bestowed on him."

Not having been in England till now, since he lost his eye, he went to receive a year's pay, as smart money; but could not obtain payment, because he had neglected to bring a certificate from a surgeon that the sight was actually destroyed. A little irritated that this form should be insisted upon, because, though the fact was not apparent, he thought it was sufficiently notorious, he procured a certificate, at the same time, for the loss of his arm; saying, they might just as well doubt one as the other. This put him in good humour with himself, and with the clerk who had offended him. On his return to the office, the clerk, finding it was only the annual pay of a captain, observed, he thought it had been more. "Oh!" replied Nelson, "this is only for an eye. In a few days I shall come for an arm; and in a little time longer, God knows, most probably for a leg." Accordingly he soon afterwards went; and with perfect good humour exhibited the certificate of the loss of his arm.

PART V

THE BATTLE OF THE NILE

1st August, 1798

[SOUTHEY. CHAPTER V]

EARLY in the year 1798, Sir Horatio Nelson hoisted his flag in the *Vanguard*, and was ordered to rejoin Earl St. Vincent. Upon his departure, his father addressed him with that affectionate solemnity by which all his letters were distinguished. " I trust in the Lord," said he, " that He will prosper your going out and your coming in. I earnestly desired once more to see you, and that wish has been heard. If I should presume to say, I hope to see you again, the question would be readily asked, ' How old art thou?' *Vale! vale! Domine, vale!*" It is said that a gloomy foreboding hung on the spirits of Lady Nelson at their parting. This could have arisen only from the dread of losing him by the chance of war. Any apprehension of losing his affections could hardly have existed; for all his correspondence to this time shows that he thought himself happy in his marriage; and his private character had hitherto been as spotless as his public conduct.[1] One of the last things he said to her was, that his own ambition was satisfied, but that he went to raise her to that rank in which he had long wished to see her.

Immediately on his rejoining the fleet, he was dispatched to the Mediterranean with a small squadron, in order to ascertain, if possible, the object of the great expedition which at that time was fitting out, under Bonaparte, at Toulon. The defeat of this armament, whatever might be its destination, was deemed by the British government an object paramount to every other; and Earl St. Vincent was directed, if he thought it necessary, to take his whole force into the Mediterranean; to relinquish, for that purpose,

the blockade of the Spanish fleet, as a thing of inferior
moment; but, if he should deem a detachment sufficient,
" I think it almost unnecessary," said the First Lord of the
Admiralty in his secret instructions, " to suggest to you the
propriety of putting it under Sir Horatio Nelson." It is
to the honour of Earl St. Vincent, that he had already made
the same choice.[1] This appointment to a service in which
so much honour might be acquired gave great offence to
the senior admirals of the fleet. Sir William Parker, who
was a very excellent officer and as gallant a man as any in
the navy, and Sir John Orde, who on all occasions of service
had acquitted himself with great honour, each wrote to
Lord Spencer, complaining that so marked a preference
should have been given to a junior of the same fleet. This
resentment is what most men in a like case would feel;
and if the preference thus given to Nelson had not originated
in a clear perception that (as his friend Collingwood said of
him a little while before) " his spirit was equal to all under-
takings and his resources fitted to all occasions," an injustice
would have been done to them by his appointment. But
if the services were conducted with undeviating respect to
seniority, the naval and military character would soon be
brought down to the dead level of mediocrity.[2]

[1] The situation was not quite so simple as Southey would give us to understand.
Pitt was anxious to build up a new coalition against France, and with that end
in view made overtures to Austria. Austria replied that her previous campaigning
against France had been ruined by the English withdrawal from the Mediterranean
(see above, pp. 91–2), and made any further assistance conditional on the navy's
instant return. No one was more anxious for this than Earl St. Vincent, but the
blockade of the Spanish fleet kept him on the wrong side of the Straits. It was
in an endeavour to lure his opponents out to a second and conclusive action that
he sanctioned the bombardment of Cadiz which led to Nelson's hand-to-hand
action with the Spanish gunboat (see above, p. 106), and it was with the same
purpose that he ordered the raid on Santa Cruz in Teneriffe. By the time that
Nelson returned to his flag, the extensive preparations in Toulon (as affecting his
own position outside Cadiz) demanded investigation; and, before the Admiralty
revealed to him what Pitt's new plans required, he dispatched the man he trusted
most to discover what was afoot. Anon came word from London that the navy
must demonstrate in the Mediterranean to secure Austria's adherence to the
Second Coalition; and Earl Spencer, the First Lord, gave him the choice of leaving
someone at Cadiz and going himself, or staying at Cadiz and sending a substitute.
St. Vincent, who of course knew nothing of Bonaparte's dream of conquering
the Orient, thereupon resolved to reinforce Nelson, and so was instrumental in
matching, one against the other, the greatest soldier and sailor of all time.

[2] In the first, second and third editions of his book Southey omitted all reference
to Sir John Orde and Sir William Parker, and after the words " it is to the honour
of Earl St. Vincent that he had already made the same choice," concluded his paragraph thus: " The British government at this time, with a becoming spirit, gave
orders that any port in the Mediterranean should be considered as hostile, where
the governor or chief magistrate should refuse to let our ships of war procure
supplies of provisions, or of any article which they might require."

The armament at Toulon consisted of thirteen ships of the line, seven forty-gun frigates, with twenty-four smaller vessels of war, and nearly two hundred transports. Mr. Udney, our consul at Leghorn, was the first person who procured certain intelligence of the enemy's design against Malta; and, from his own sagacity, foresaw that Egypt must be their after object. Nelson sailed from Gibraltar on the 9th of May, with the *Vanguard, Orion,* and *Alexander,* seventy-fours; the *Caroline, Flora, Emerald,* and *Terpsichore,* frigates; and the *Bonne Citoyenne,* sloop of war; to watch this formidable armament. On the 19th, when they were in the Gulf of Lions, a gale came on from the N.W. It moderated so much on the 20th, as to enable them to get their top-gallant masts and yards aloft. After dark, it again began to blow strong: but the ships had been prepared for a gale, and therefore Nelson's mind was easy. Shortly after [1] midnight, however, his main topmast went over the side, and the mizzen topmast soon afterward. The night was so tempestuous, that it was impossible for any signal either to be seen or heard; and Nelson determined, as soon as it should be daybreak, to wear, and scud before the gale. But at half-past three the foremast went in three pieces, and the bowsprit was found to be sprung in three places. When day broke they succeeded in wearing the ship with a remnant of the spritsail. This was hardly to have been expected. The *Vanguard* was at that time twenty-five leagues south of the islands of Hyères, with her head lying to the N.E. and if she had not wore,[2] the ship must have drifted to Corsica. Captain Ball, in the *Alexander,* took her in tow, to carry her into the Sardinian harbour of San Pietro.[3] Nelson, apprehensive that this attempt might endanger both vessels, ordered him to cast off: but that excellent officer, with a spirit like his commander's, replied he was confident he could save the *Vanguard,* and by God's help he would do it. There had been a previous coolness between these great men; but from this time Nelson became fully sensible of the extraordinary talents of Captain Ball, and a sincere friendship subsisted between them during the

[1] Many modern editions print " before " instead of " after."
[2] If she had not been brought before the wind.
[3] See map, p. 52.

remainder of their lives.[1] " I ought not," said the Admiral,
writing to his wife,—" I ought not to call what has happened
to the *Vanguard* by the cold name of accident. I believe
firmly it was the Almighty's goodness, to check my consummate vanity. I hope it has made me a better officer, as I
feel confident it has made me a better man. Figure to
yourself, on Sunday evening, at sunset, a vain man walking
in his cabin, with a squadron around him, who looked up
to their chief to lead them to glory, and in whom their chief
placed the firmest reliance that the proudest ships of equal
numbers belonging to France would have lowered their
flags. Figure to yourself, on Monday morning, when the
sun rose, this proud man, his ship dismasted, his fleet dispersed, and himself in such distress, that the meanest
frigate out of France would have been an unwelcome guest."
Nelson had indeed more reason to refuse the cold name of
accident to this tempest than he was then aware of; for
on that very day the French fleet sailed from Toulon,[2] and
must have passed within a few leagues of his little squadron, which was thus preserved by the thick weather that
came on.

[The British government at this time, with a becoming
spirit, gave orders that any port in the Mediterranean
should be considered as hostile, where the governor, or
chief magistrate, should refuse to let our ships of war
procure supplies of provisions, or of any article which
they might require.

In these orders the ports of Sardinia were excepted.][3]
The continental possessions of the King of Sardinia were at
this time completely at the mercy of the French, and that
prince was now discovering, when too late, that the terms
to which he had consented, for the purpose of escaping
immediate danger, necessarily involved the loss of the
dominions which they were intended to preserve. The
citadel of Turin was now occupied by French troops; and

[1] The account of the storm, with the injuries it inflicted upon the *Vanguard*,
and the efforts of her company to set the spritsail and put her before the wind,
is taken out of a letter from Nelson to Earl St. Vincent quoted by Clarke and
McArthur, Vol. II. p. 59.

[2] Bonaparte sailed from Toulon on 19th May.

[3] In the first, second and third editions Southey wrote, " In the orders of the
British government to consider all ports as hostile where the British ships should
be refused supplies, the ports of Sardinia were excepted."   See above, Note 2
p. 118.

his wretched court feared to afford the common rights of humanity to British ships, lest it should give the French occasion to seize on the remainder of his dominions—a measure for which it was certain they would soon make a pretext, if they did not find one. Nelson was informed that he could not be permitted to enter the port of St. Pietro. Regardless of this interdict, which, under his circumstances, it would have been an act of suicidal folly to have regarded, he anchored in the harbour: and, by the exertions of Sir James Saumarez,[1] Captain Ball,[2] and Captain Berry,[3] the *Vanguard* was refitted in four days. Months would have been employed in refitting her in England.[4] Nelson, with that proper sense of merit, wherever it was found, which proved at once the goodness and the greatness of his character, especially recommended to Earl St. Vincent the carpenter of the *Alexander*, under whose directions the ship had been repaired; stating that he was an old and faithful servant of the crown, who had been nearly thirty years a warrant Carpenter ;[5] and begging most earnestly that the commander-in-chief would recommend him to the particular notice of the Board of Admiralty. He did not leave the harbour without expressing his sense of the treatment which he had received there, in a letter to the Viceroy of Sardinia. " Sir," it said, " having, by a gale of wind, sustained some trifling damages, I anchored a small part of his Majesty's fleet under my orders off this island, and was surprised to hear, by an officer sent by the governor, that admittance was to be refused to the flag of his Britannic Majesty into this port. When I reflect, that my most gracious sovereign is the oldest, I believe, and certainly the most faithful ally which the King of Sardinia ever had, I could feel the sorrow which it must have been to his Majesty to have given such an order; and also for

[1] Of the *Orion*. From Nelson's letters we learn that it was Saumarez who discovered in an hour of need the anchorage at San Pietro.
[2] Of the *Alexander*.
[3] His flag-captain.
[4] This is not Southey's verdict on the merits of the home dockyards, but a further quotation from Nelson's letter to his wife.
[5] Who had for nearly thirty years held a " Carpenter's " warrant; that is, served as warrant officer responsible for the upkeep of one of His Majesty's ships and the repair of her fabric. To-day the word " Shipwright " replaces the older word, which at the outbreak of the Great War of 1914 had grown obsolete and misleading.

your Excellency, who had to direct its execution. I cannot but look at the African shore, where the followers of Mohammed are performing the part of the good Samaritan, which I look for in vain at St. Peter's, where it is said the Christian religion is professed."

The delay which was thus occasioned was useful to him in many respects. It enabled him to complete his supply of water, and to receive a reinforcement, which Earl St. Vincent, being himself reinforced from England, was enabled to send him.[1] It consisted of the best ships of his fleet: the *Culloden*, seventy-four, Captain T. Troubridge; *Goliath*, seventy-four, Captain T. Foley; *Minotaur*, seventy-four, Captain T. Louis; *Defence*, seventy-four, Captain John Peyton; *Bellerophon*, seventy-four, Captain H. D. E. Darby; *Majestic*, seventy-four, Captain G. B. Westcott; *Zealous*, seventy-four, Captain S. Hood; *Swiftsure*, seventy-four, Captain B. Hallowell; *Theseus*, seventy-four, Captain R. W. Miller; *Audacious*, seventy-four, Captain Davidge Gould. The *Leander*, fifty, Captain T. B. Thompson, was afterward added. These ships were made ready for the service as soon as Earl St. Vincent received advice from England that he was to be reinforced. As soon as the reinforcement was seen from the mast-head of the Admiral's ship, off Cadiz Bay, signal was immediately made to Captain Troubridge to put to sea; and he was out of sight before the ships from home cast anchor in the British station. Troubridge took with him no instructions to Nelson as to the course he was to steer, nor any certain account of the enemy's destination. Everything was left to his own judgment. Unfortunately, the frigates had been separated from him in the tempest, and had not been able to rejoin. They sought him unsuccessfully in the Bay of Naples, where they obtained no tidings of his course; and he sailed without them.[2]

The first news of the enemy's armament was, that it had surprised Malta.[3] Nelson formed a plan for attacking it while at anchor at Gozo; but on the 22nd of June in-

---

[1] This was the contingent, referred to in a previous note, which was intended to win converts to the Second Coalition by demonstrating in the Mediterranean.

[2] As in a literal sense they were the " eyes of the fleet," their absence had the effect of blindfolding Nelson in his task of searching for Bonaparte's fleet.

[3] At that time belonging to the Knights of St. John of Jerusalem, one of the old crusading brotherhoods which had survived under the patronage of one European potentate or another as a bulwark against Turkish aggression.

telligence reached him that the French had left that island on the 16th, the day after their arrival.[1] It was clear that their destination was eastward—he thought for Egypt— and for Egypt, therefore, he made all sail. Had the frigates been with him he could scarcely have failed to gain informa- tion of the enemy. For want of them, he only spoke three vessels on the way. Two came from Alexandria, one from the Archipelago; and neither of them had seen anything of the French. He arrived off Alexandria on the 28th, and the enemy were not there, neither was there any account of them; but the governor was endeavouring to put the city in a state of defence, having received advice from Leghorn that the French expedition was intended against Egypt, after it had taken Malta. Nelson then shaped his course [2] to the northward, for Caramania,[3] and steered from thence along the southern side of Candia,[4] carrying a press of sail, both night and day, with a contrary wind. It would have been his delight, he said, to have tried Bona- parte on a wind.[5] It would have been the delight of Europe, too, and the blessing of the world, if that fleet had been overtaken with its General on board. But of the myriads and millions of human beings who would have been preserved by that day's victory there is not one to whom such essential benefit would have resulted as to Bonaparte himself. It would have spared him his defeat at Acre—his only dis- grace; for to have been defeated by Nelson upon the seas would not have been disgraceful. It would have spared him all his after enormities. Hitherto his career had been glorious; the baneful principles of his heart had never yet

---

[1] This intelligence was false. Bonaparte did not leave Malta until 19th inst., and was only three days' sailing ahead; not a week, as Nelson supposed.

[2] But for the false intelligence commented upon in the previous note, Nelson would probably have waited longer at Alexandria. And had he done so, the arrival of the French would have saved him from all the agony of the ensuing search.

[3] The Turkish name for what St. Paul knew as Pamphylia and Cilicia.

[4] Crete.

[5]

To Lady Nelson

Syracuse, 20th July, 1798.

I have not been able to find the French fleet, to my great mortification, or the event I can scarcely doubt. We have been off Malta, to Alexandria in Egypt, Syria, into Asia, and are returned here without success. However, no person will say that it has been for want of activity. I yet live in hopes of meeting these fellows; but it would have been my delight to have tried Bonaparte on a wind; for he commands the fleet as well as the army. Glory is my object, and that alone. God Almighty bless you.—HORATIO NELSON.

passed his lips. History would have represented him as a soldier of fortune, who had faithfully served the cause in which he engaged: and whose career had been distinguished by a series of successes unexampled in modern times. A romantic obscurity would have hung over the expedition to Egypt, and he would have escaped the perpetration of those crimes which have incarnadined his soul with a deeper dye than that of the purple for which he committed them; those acts of perfidy, midnight murder,[1] usurpation, and remorseless tyranny, which have consigned his name to universal execration, now and for ever.

Conceiving that when an officer is not successful in his plans it is absolutely necessary that he should explain the motives upon which they were founded, Nelson wrote at this time an account and vindication of his conduct for having carried the fleet to Egypt. The objection which he anticipated was that he ought not to have made so long a voyage without more certain information. " My answer," said he, " is ready—Who was I to get it from? The governments of Naples and Sicily either knew not, or chose to keep me in ignorance. Was I to wait patiently until I heard certain accounts? If Egypt were their object, before I could hear of them they would have been in India. To do nothing was disgraceful. Therefore I made use of my understanding. I am before your lordships'[2] judgment; and if, under all circumstances, it is decided that I am wrong, I ought, for the sake of our country, to be superseded; for at this moment, when I know the French are not in Alexandria, I hold the same opinion as off Cape Passaro,[3] —that, under all circumstances, I was right in steering for Alexandria; and by that opinion I must stand or fall." Captain Ball, to whom he showed this paper, told him he should recommend a friend never to begin a defence of his conduct before he was accused of error: he might give the fullest reasons for what he had done, expressed in such terms as would evince that he had acted from the strongest conviction of being right; and of course he must expect that

[1] An allusion to the mock trial and judicial murder of the Duc D'Enghien on the night of 20th March, 1804.

[2] The justification was to have been sent to the Lords of the Admiralty.

[3] Nelson had sighted Cape Passaro, the southernmost point of Sicily (see map, p. 52), on 22nd June.

the public would view it in the same light.[1] Captain Ball
judged rightly of the public, whose first impulses, though
from want of sufficient information they must frequently
be erroneous, are generally founded upon just feelings.
But the public are easily misled, and there are always
persons ready to mislead them. Nelson had not yet attained
that fame which compels envy to be silent; and when it
was known in England that he had returned after an unsuccessful pursuit, it was said that he deserved impeach-
ment: and Earl St. Vincent was severely censured for
having sent so young an officer upon so important a service.

Baffled in his pursuit, he returned to Sicily. The Neapolitan ministry had determined to give his squadron no
assistance, being resolved to do nothing which could possibly endanger their peace with the French Directory. By
means, however, of Lady Hamilton's influence at court,
he procured secret orders to the Sicilian governors; and,
under those orders, obtained everything which he wanted
at Syracuse—a timely supply; without which, he always
said, he could not have recommenced his pursuit with any
hope of success.[2] " It is an old saying," said he, in his letter,
" that the devil's children have the devil's luck. I cannot
to this moment learn, beyond vague conjecture, where the

[1] The actual words of Captain Ball's letter are as follow: " I was particularly
struck with the clear and accurate style, as well as with the candour of the statement in your letter. But *I felt a regret that your too anxious zeal should make you
start an idea that your judgment was impeachable because you have not yet fallen
in with the French fleet ; as it implicates a doubt, and may induce suspicion, that
you are not perfectly satisfied with your own conduct.* I should recommend a friend
never to begin a defence of his conduct before he is accused of error. He may give
the fullest reasons for what he has done, expressed in such terms as will evince that
he acted from the strongest conviction of being right; and of course, he must
expect that the public will view it in the same light." (Clarke and McArthur,
Vol. II., pp. 68–9.)
By omitting the italicised passage Southey somewhat obscures Captain Ball's
argument. " If you appear dissatisfied with your decision, you will give the man
in the street good ground for doubting your capacity."

[2] Some critics have thrown doubt upon the value of Lady Hamilton's services
on this occasion. Nelson, however, was in a better position to realise what he owed
to her than anyone else, and to the end of his life he retained a vivid and ever
present sense of gratitude to one whom he regarded as his partner in the victory
of the Nile. A few hours only before he met his glorious death at Trafalgar he called
Captains Blackwood and Hardy into his cabin to witness a codicil to his will. In
this he set forth as a last request that his country would support Lady Hamilton
in a manner becoming to her rank and dignity, because " the British fleet, under
my command, could never have returned the second time to Egypt, had not Lady
Hamilton's influence with the Queen of Naples caused letters to be wrote to the
Governor of Syracuse, that he was to encourage the fleet's being supplied with
everything, should they put into any port in Sicily. We put into Syracuse, and
received every supply; went to Egypt, and destroyed the French fleet." See
below, p. 304.

French fleet are gone to: and having gone a round of six
hundred leagues at this season of the year, with an expedition [1] incredible, here I am, as ignorant of the situation of
the enemy as I was twenty-seven days ago. Every moment
I have to regret the frigates having left me. Had one-half
of them been with me, I could not have wanted information.
Should the French be so strongly secured in port that I
cannot get at them, I shall immediately shift my flag into
some other ship, and send the *Vanguard* to Naples to be
refitted; for hardly any person but myself would have
continued on service so long in such a wretched state."
Vexed, however, and disappointed as he was, Nelson, with
the true spirit of a hero, was still full of hope. " Thanks
to your exertions," said he, writing to Sir W. and Lady
Hamilton, "we have victualled and watered: and surely,
watering at the fountain of Arethusa,[2] we must have
victory. We shall sail with the first breeze; and be assured
I will return either crowned with laurel, or covered with
cypress." Earl St. Vincent he assured that if the French
were above water he would find them out. He still held
his opinion that they were bound for Egypt: " but," said
he to the First Lord of the Admiralty, " be they bound to
the Antipodes, your lordship may rely that I will not lose
a moment in bringing them to action."

On the 25th of July he sailed from Syracuse for the
Morea.[3] Anxious beyond measure, and irritated that the
enemy should so long have eluded him, the tediousness of
the nights made him impatient; and the officer of the watch
was repeatedly called on to let him know the hour, and
convince him, who measured time by his own eagerness,
that it was not yet daybreak. The squadron made the
Gulf of Koron on the 28th. Troubridge entered the port,
and returned with intelligence that the French had been
seen about four weeks before steering to the S.E. from
Candia. Nelson then determined immediately to return to
Alexandria: and the British fleet accordingly, with every
sail set, stood once more for the coast of Egypt. On the 1st

[1] Speed.
[2] The " Fountain," into which (according to the fable) Artemis converted the
nymph Arethusa, is situated in the island of Ortygia which defines and circum-
scribes the harbour of Syracuse.
[3] Or Peloponnese.

of August, about ten in the morning, they came in sight of Alexandria. The port had been vacant and solitary when they saw it last; it was now crowded with ships; and they perceived, with exultation, that the tricoloured flag was flying upon the walls. At four in the afternoon, Captain Hood, in the *Zealous*, made the signal for the enemy's fleet. For many preceding days Nelson had hardly taken either sleep or food. He now ordered his dinner to be served, while preparations were making for battle; and when his officers rose from table, and went to their separate stations, he said to them, " Before this time to-morrow I shall have gained a peerage, or Westminster Abbey."

The French, steering direct for Candia, had made an angular passage for Alexandria; whereas Nelson, in pursuit of them, made straight for that place, and thus materially shortened the distance. The comparative smallness of his force made it necessary to sail in close order, and it covered a less space than it would have done if the frigates had been with him. The weather also was constantly hazy. These circumstances prevented the English from discovering the enemy on the way to Egypt, though it appeared, upon examining the journals of the French officers taken in the action, that the two fleets must actually have crossed on the night of the twenty-second of June. During the return to Syracuse, the chances of falling in with them were fewer.[1]

Why Bonaparte, having effected his landing, should not have suffered the fleet to return, has never yet been explained.[2]   Thus much is certain, that it was detained by his command; though, with his accustomed falsehood, he accused Admiral Brueys, after that officer's death, of having lingered on the coast, contrary to orders. The French fleet arrived at Alexandria on the 1st of July; and Brueys, not being able to enter the port, which time and neglect had ruined, moored his ships in Aboukir Bay, in a

---

[1] In this paragraph Southey is, of course, referring to Nelson's previous visit to Egypt which at the time had seemed so fruitless.

[2] On 3rd July Bonaparte, who knew of no reason for supposing that the fleet that had brought him to Egypt was in the smallest danger, and who was only too glad in a distant land to have the ships of France at his back, ordered Brueys, if he thought the position defensible, to anchor in Aboukir Bay.   Subsequently he changed his mind and sent Brueys an order to withdraw, but the altered mandate did not reach the admiral before Nelson delivered his attack.

strong and compact line of battle; the headmost vessel,
according to his own account, being as close as possible

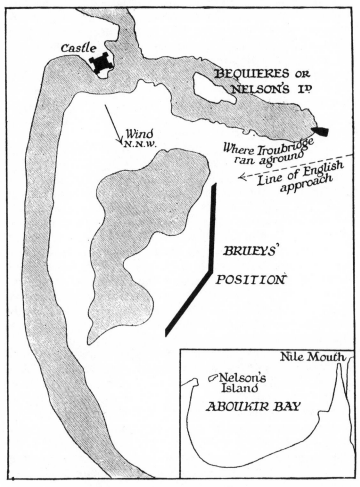

THE FRENCH POSITION IN ABOUKIR BAY

to a shoal on the N.W., and the rest of the fleet forming a
kind of curve along the line of deep water, so as not to be
turned by any means in the S.W. By Bonaparte's desire
he had offered a reward of 10,000 livres to any pilot of the

country who would carry the squadron in; but none could be found who would venture to take charge of a single vessel drawing more than twenty feet. He had therefore made the best of his situation, and chosen the strongest position which he could possibly take in an open road. The commissary of the fleet said they were moored in such a manner as to bid defiance to a force more than double their own. This presumption could not then be thought unreasonable. Admiral Barrington, when moored in a similar manner off St. Lucia, in the year 1778, beat off the Comte d'Estaing in three several attacks, though his force was inferior by almost one third to that which assailed it.[1] Here the advantage in numbers, both in ships, guns and men, was in favour of the French. They had thirteen ships of the line and four frigates, carrying eleven hundred and ninety-six guns, and eleven thousand two hundred and thirty men. The English had the same number of ships of the line, and one fifty-gun ship, carrying ten hundred and twelve guns, and eight thousand and sixty-eight men. The English ships were all seventy-fours: the French had three eighty-gun ships, and one three-decker of one hundred and twenty.

During the whole pursuit, it had been Nelson's practice, whenever circumstances would permit, to have his captains on board the *Vanguard*, and explain to them his own ideas of the different and best modes of attack, and such plans as he proposed to execute on falling in with the enemy, whatever their situation might be. There is no possible position, it is said, which he did not take into calculation. His officers were thus fully acquainted with his principles

[1] Battles at sea in the sailing era were, like battles to-day, fought by fleets in motion. Admiral Barrington, however, during the War of American Independence (see above, pp. 15–16), having captured the French island of St. Lucia, managed to retain it by a kind of tactical immobility. Learning of the approach of a superior French fleet, he anchored himself in the Grand Cul de Sac, with his ships stretching from one side of the bay to the other, his flanks being protected by batteries ashore. D'Estaing attempted to fight in the regulation manner, but found his movements impeded and his assault ineffective. Four years later Hood followed Barrington's example amid surroundings more richly picturesque. There is little doubt that French maritime opinion was deeply impressed by these examples, and that Brueys in consequence prided himself on the strength of the position which he had selected in Aboukir Bay. But Nelson, who had learnt at first hand from Lord Hood what that master of tactics intended in Golfe Juan (see above, Note 2, p. 66), did not intend to fight in motion as D'Estaing had done at St. Lucia and De Grasse had done at St. Kitts. He proposed in overmastering strength to anchor snugly by the side of his foes and fight them standing still.

of tactics; and such was his confidence in their abilities, that the only thing determined upon, in case they should find the French at anchor, was for the ships to form as most convenient for their mutual support,[1] and to anchor by the stern.[2]

"First gain the victory," he said, "and then make the best use of it you can."[3]

The moment he perceived the position of the French, that intuitive genius with which Nelson was endowed displayed itself; and it instantly struck him, that where there was room for an enemy's ship to swing, there was room for one of ours to anchor.[4] The plan which he intended to pursue, therefore, was to keep entirely on the outer side of the French line, and station his ships, as far as he was able, one on the outer bow, and another on the

[1] Nelson had made all his officers fully conversant with his ideas, and left them a wide latitude in executing his wishes. In fact, the only points upon which he insisted beforehand were mutual support, etc.

[2] Ships anchor as a rule by the bows. But Nelson desired that each unit of his fleet, after worsting one antagonist, should move against another. And so he adopted an arrangement whereby every ship could go ahead by the simple device of paying out cable.

[3] This speech is taken from *The Voyage up the Mediterranean* by the Chaplain of the *Swiftsure*. It has no relation to what comes immediately before, or to what follows immediately after. It refers to Nelson's general scheme of operations which required that all his ships should concentrate on the enemy's van until that part was destroyed and victory assured.

[4] Southey makes terribly heavy weather in this paragraph, not having any reliable knowledge as to: (1) What Nelson intended to do; (2) What Nelson actually did; (3) What tactical plans had been employed by his predecessors.

He begins by quoting one of the best accounts of the battle, the *Authentic Narrative* of Sir Edward Berry, an octavo pamphlet (with map) published before the end of 1798. "The position of the enemy," wrote Nelson's flag-captain, "presented the most formidable obstacles (*i.e.* to the plan already projected). But the Admiral viewed these with the eye of a seaman determined on attack, and it instantly struck his eager and penetrating mind that *where there was room for an enemy's ship to swing, there was room for one of ours to anchor.*"

What do these words mean? If the reader will examine the diagram, he will see that the essence of Nelson's plan was to mass his entire fleet upon one half only of the enemy's line. He proposed to match a pair of English ships with every vessel in Brueys' van; and it was therefore necessary for half of his captains to pass to rearward of the French formation. To prevent just such a thing from happening, Brueys had wisely drawn his flanks as near to the shallows as he dared.

Nelson, as Southey learned from Berry's *Narrative*, had coached his captains beforehand in what he intended to do: and it remained for him to decide whether, in view of Brueys' dispositions, it would be necessary or not to modify his scheme. If Brueys had been anchored stern and bow, it is arguable that Nelson would have signalled his ships to fight on the outer side only. But Brueys had anchored in the ordinary way, *i.e.* from the bows; and his vessels were therefore at liberty to swing in a circle round their anchor-buoys. In other words, Nelson saw at a glance that, however near the French might be to the shoals, they had allowed themselves plenty of elbow-room; and he therefore accepted the tremendous risk of keeping to his original resolution, and thrusting half his ships through the perilous defile that separated Brueys' left wing from the shallows.

outer quarter, of each of the enemy's.[1] This plan of doubling
on the enemy's ships was projected by Lord Hood, when

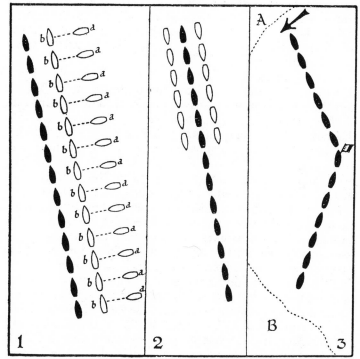

THE TACTICS OF THE NILE

 1. How battles were usually fought in Nelson's day. The white ships, having
the advantage of the wind, are attacking.   (a..a..a) First Position, running
down;   (b..b..b) Second Position, bringing broadsides to bear.
 2. How Nelson (white) proposed to fight the French, if he was so fortunate as
to find them at anchor.
 3. Brueys' position in Aboukir Bay, the shoals A and B (in his belief) rendering
such an attack, as Nelson contemplated, impossible. The broad arrow shows the
perilous defile through which Nelson's ships squeezed a way to victory.

he designed to attack the French fleet at their anchorage in
Gourjean Road.   Lord Hood found it impossible to make
the attempt; but the thought was not lost upon Nelson,

 [1] This sentence flatly contradicts the sentence that goes before. If Nelson
decided to put all to the touch and risk his ships among the shallows, how can he
possibly have meant to limit hostilities to the outer side of the enemy's line?
 There was certainly no confusion in Nelson's arrangements. The confusion
existed only in the mind of Southey, who was puzzled by contradictory evidence
and found himself unable to reconcile conflicting opinions. See below, Note 1,
p. 133.

who acknowledged himself, on this occasion, indebted for
it to his old and excellent commander. Captain Berry, when
he comprehended the scope of the design, exclaimed with
transport, " If we succeed, what will the world say! "
" There is no ' if ' in the case," replied the Admiral. " That
we shall succeed is certain. Who may live to tell the story
is a very different question." [1]

As the squadron advanced, they were assailed by a
shower of shot and shells from the batteries on the island,
and the enemy opened a steady fire from the starboard side
of their whole line, within half gunshot distance, full into
the bows of our van ships.[2]　It was received in silence.
The men on board every ship were employed aloft [3] in furling
sails, and below [3] in tending the braces,[4] and making
ready for anchoring. A miserable sight for the French; who,
with all their skill, and all their courage, and all their advantages of numbers and situation, were upon that element
on which, when the hour of trial comes, a Frenchman has
no hope. Admiral Brueys was a brave and able man; yet
the indelible character of his country broke out in one of his
letters, wherein he delivered it as his private opinion that the
English had missed him, because, not being superior in force,
they did not think it prudent to try their strength with him.[5]
The moment was now come in which he was to be undeceived.

A French brig was instructed to decoy the English, by
manœuvring so as to tempt them toward a shoal lying off
the island of Bequières; but Nelson either knew the danger,
or suspected some deceit; and the lure was unsuccessful.
Captain Foley led the way in the *Goliath,* outsailing the
Zealous,[6] which for some minutes disputed this post of

[1] This story gave great offence to Captain Berry, who stoutly asserted that no
such conversation ever occurred. As Southey did not delete the passage, Sir
Harris Nicolas published a repudiation from Lady Berry in the *Dispatches and
Letters of Lord Nelson,* Vol. III. p. 65.
[2] For the direction of the English approach and the convergence of the French
fire upon the head of Nelson's line, see diagram, p. 128.
[3] The words " aloft " and " below " do not refer to the hull of a ship. What
the passage means is that some hands were lying out on the yards and others
working on deck.
[4] Ropes fastened to either end of a yard to fix or change its position.
[5] This letter, which was written to the Minister of Marine on 12th July, was
among those intercepted by Nelson himself. The phrase to which Southey refers
runs as follows: " *et que ne se trouvant pas en nombre supérieur, ils n'auront pas
jugé à-propos de se mesurer avec nous.*"
[6] The captain of the *Zealous* was Captain Hood, Troubridge's ambassador
at Santa Cruz (see above, pp. 112–13).

honour with him. He had long conceived that if the enemy were moored in line of battle in with the land, the best plan of attack would be to lead between them and the shore, because the French guns on that side were not likely to be manned, nor even ready for action.[1] Intending, therefore, to fix himself on the inner bow of the *Guerrier*, he kept as near the edge of the bank as the depth of water would admit; but his anchor hung, and having opened his fire, he drifted to the second ship, the *Conquérant*, before it was clear; then anchored by the stern, inside of her, and in ten minutes shot away her mast. Hood, in the *Zealous*, perceiving this, took the station which the *Goliath* intended to have occupied, and totally disabled the *Guerrier* in twelve minutes. The third ship which doubled the enemy's van was the *Orion*, Sir J. Saumarez.[2] She passed to windward of the *Zealous*, and opened her larboard guns as long as they bore on the *Guerrier*; then passing inside the *Goliath*, sank a frigate which annoyed her, hauled round toward the

---

[1] In this sentence Southey does grievous wrong to Nelson by giving to Captain Foley the credit for the tactical surprise that won the battle. Foley, it is true, was the first to round the tip of the enemy's left wing, and anchor among the shoals; but in doing so he was only giving visible expression to the idea that Nelson evolved.

The claim put forward on Foley's behalf first appeared in a note to the volume of *The Annual Register* for 1798, and was doubtless extracted thence by Clarke and McArthur, from whom Southey copied it. There is little evidence now available on the point, but it would appear that the claim originated with Foley himself or with his friends. It certainly takes its most explicit shape in Marshall's *Naval Biography* (1823. Vol. I. p. 365), a book best described as a series of memoirs contributed by the subjects thereof or by their families.

The claim rests on the slenderest basis, and is flatly denied by the consentient statements of Nelson's second-in-command, Nelson's own flag-captain, and Sir Samuel Hood of the *Zealous*. The evidence of the first-mentioned officer is almost conclusive by itself, for he tells us that he did not agree with Nelson's fighting device and protested against it in advance. (Ross, *Life of Saumarez*, Vol. I. pp. 228-9.)

Doubtless Foley's claim was honestly made, and if there were a little more testimony it might be possible to prove that Nelson, after ordering his ships to penetrate to the inner side of the enemy's line, left them at liberty to reach their fighting station in any manner they pleased. If Foley was expected to pierce the enemy's array between the first French ship and the second (as the *Audacious* did), and if he preferred the riskier but more effective path between the first French ship and the shoals, then there was sufficient reason on his part for claiming some originality, although it is demonstrably clear, from what Berry says, that there was no course of action adopted in the fight which Nelson had not discussed beforehand. See also above, p. 129.

Nelson's main idea in fighting on the side of the shoals was to put the enemy between two fires; but his resolution was strengthened by a firm belief that the French would be unprepared for battle on their shoreward side. This belief was based on his knowledge of the battle of the Saints (12th April, 1782), when Rodney, accepting battle on one side of the French fleet, broke through and fought them on the other. And this knowledge he derived from his " master of naval tactics," Rodney's second at the Saints—Lord Hood.

[2] Nelson's second-in-command.

M

French line, and anchoring inside, between the fifth and sixth ships from the *Guerrier*, took her station on the larboard bow of the *Franklin*, and the quarter of the *Peuple Souverain*, receiving and returning the fire of both. The

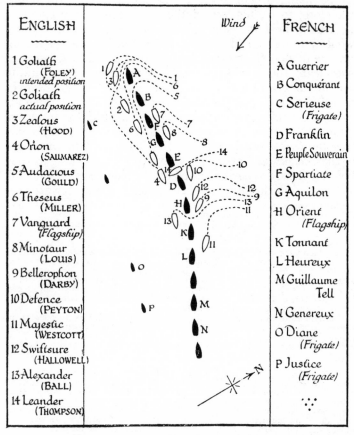

ENGLISH	Wind	FRENCH
1 Goliath (FOLEY) *intended position*		A Guerrier
2 Goliath *actual position*		B Conquérant
3 Zealous (HOOD)		C Serieuse *(Frigate)*
4 Orion (SAUMAREZ)		D Franklin
5 Audacious (GOULD)		E Peuple Souverain
6 Theseus (MILLER)		F Spartiate
7 Vanguard *(Flagship)*		G Aquilon
8 Minotaur (LOUIS)		H Orient *(Flagship)*
9 Bellerophon (DARBY)		K Tonnant
10 Defence (PEYTON)		L Heureux
11 Majestic (WESTCOTT)		M Guillaume Tell
12 Swiftsure (HALLOWELL)		N Genereux
13 Alexander (BALL)		O Diane *(Frigate)*
14 Leander (THOMPSON)		P Justice *(Frigate)*

THE FIGHTING AT THE NILE

sun was now nearly down. The *Audacious,* Captain Gould, pouring a heavy fire into the *Guerrier* and the *Conquérant,* fixed herself on the larboard bow of the latter; and when that ship struck, passed on to the *Peuple Souverain.* The *Theseus,* Captain Miller, followed, brought down the

Guerrier's remaining main and mizzen masts, then anchored inside of the *Spartiate*, the third in the French line.

While these advanced ships doubled the French line, the *Vanguard* was the first that anchored on the outer side of the enemy, within half pistol-shot of their third ship, the *Spartiate*. Nelson had six colours flying in different parts of his rigging, lest they should be shot away;—that they should be struck, no British admiral considers as a possibility. He veered half a cable,[1] and instantly opened a tremendous fire; under cover of which the other four ships of his division, the *Minotaur, Bellerophon, Defence,* and *Majestic,* sailed on ahead of the Admiral. In a few minutes, every man stationed at the first six guns in the forepart of the *Vanguard's* deck was killed or wounded: these guns were three times cleared. Captain Louis, in the *Minotaur,* anchored just ahead, and took off the fire of the *Aquilon,* fourth in the enemy's line. The *Bellerophon* (Captain Darby) passed ahead, and dropped her stern anchor on the starboard bow of the *Orient,* seventh in the line, Brueys' own ship, of one hundred and twenty guns, whose difference of force was in proportion of more than seven to three, and whose weight of ball, from the lower deck alone, exceeded that from the whole broadside of the *Bellerophon.* Captain Peyton, in the *Defence,* took his station ahead of the *Minotaur,* and engaged the *Franklin,* the sixth in the line; by which judicious movement the British line remained unbroken.[2] The *Majestic* (Captain Westcott) got entangled with the main rigging of one of the French ships astern of the *Orient,* and suffered dreadfully from that three-decker's fire. But she swung clear, and closely engaging the *Heureux,* the ninth ship on the starboard bow, received also the fire of the *Tonnant,* which was the eighth in the line. The other four ships of the British squadron, having been detached previous to the discovery of the French, were at a considerable distance when the action began. It commenced at half after six. About seven night closed, and there was no other light than that from the fire of the contending fleets.

[1] Nelson dropped anchor, and then paid out cable astern until the *Vanguard* assumed the position he required. Half a cable equals 100 yards.

[2] This phrase, which Southey took direct from Clarke and McArthur, is not particularly illuminating.

Troubridge, in the *Culloden*, then foremost of the remaining ships, was two leagues astern. He came on sounding, as the others had done. As he advanced, the increasing darkness increased the difficulty of the navigation; and suddenly, after having found eleven fathoms water, before the lead could be hove again he was fast aground; nor could all his own exertions, joined to those of the *Leander* and the *Mutine* brig, which came to his assistance, get him off in time to bear a part in the action. His ship, however, served as a beacon to the *Alexander* and *Swiftsure*, which would else, from the course which they were holding, have gone considerably farther on the reef, and must inevitably have been lost. These ships entered the bay, and took their stations, in the darkness, in a manner still spoken of with admiration by all who remember it.

Captain Hallowell, in the *Swiftsure*, as he was bearing down, fell in with what seemed to be a strange sail. Nelson had directed his ships to hoist four lights horizontally at the mizzen-peak [1] as soon as it became dark; and this vessel had no such distinction. Hallowell, however, with great judgment, ordered his men not to fire. If she was an enemy, he said, she was in too disabled a state to escape; but, from her sails being loose, and the way in which her head was, it was probable she might be an English ship. It was the *Bellerophon*, overpowered by the huge *Orient*. Her lights had gone overboard. Nearly two hundred of her crew were killed or wounded. All her masts and cables had been shot away, and she was drifting out of the line, toward the lee side of the bay.[2] Her station, at this important time, was occupied by the *Swiftsure*, which opened a steady fire on the quarter of the *Franklin* and the bows of the French Admiral. At the same instant Captain Ball, with the *Alexander*, passed under his stern,[3] and anchored within side on his larboard quarter, raking him, and keeping up a severe fire of musketry upon his decks. The last ship which arrived to complete the destruction of the enemy was the *Leander*. Captain Thompson, finding that nothing

---

[1] Unlike the mainsail and foresail, which were square, the mizzen was set fore and aft. Its yard pointed upward abaft the mast, and the outer end or summit was known as the " peak." From its eminence it was an ideal place for visibility, and had been utilised for signals from time immemorial.

[2] Or the eastern side of the bay, the wind being slightly to the west of north.

[3] Under the stern of Admiral Brueys' flagship.

could be done that night to get off the *Culloden*, advanced with the intention of anchoring athwarthawse of the *Orient*. The *Franklin* was so near her ahead, that there was not room for him to pass clear of the two. He therefore took his station athwarthawse [1] of the latter, in such a position as to rake [2] both.

The two first ships of the French line had been dismasted within a quarter of an hour after the commencement of the action; and the others had in that time suffered so severely that victory was already certain. The third, fourth, and fifth were taken possession of at half-past eight. Meantime Nelson received a severe wound on the head from a piece of langridge shot.[3] Captain Berry caught him in his arms as he was falling. The great effusion of blood occasioned an apprehension that the wound was mortal. Nelson himself thought so. A large flap of the skin of the forehead, cut from the bone, had fallen over one eye: and the other being blind, he was in total darkness. When he was carried down, the surgeon,—in the midst of a scene scarcely to be conceived by those who have never seen a cockpit in time of action, and the heroism which is displayed amid its horrors,—with a natural and pardonable eagerness, quitted the poor fellow then under his hands, that he might instantly attend the Admiral. "No!" said Nelson, "I will take my turn with my brave fellows." Nor would he suffer his own wound to be examined till every man who had been previously wounded was properly attended to. Fully believing that the wound was mortal, and that he was about to die, as he had ever desired, in battle and in victory, he called the Chaplain, and desired him to deliver what he supposed to be his dying remembrance to Lady Nelson. He then sent for Captain Louis on board from the *Minotaur*, that he might thank him personally for the great assistance which he had rendered to the *Vanguard*: and ever mindful of those who deserved to be his friends, appointed Captain Hardy from the brig to the command of his own ship, Captain Berry having to go home with the news of the victory.

[1] Across the bows of.

[2] To cannonade a ship so that the shots, instead of striking her upon the broadside where her guns can reply, range along her decks from end to end, with devastating effect.

[3] Scrap iron used instead of shot. It was much affected by the French, with whom the destruction of sails was always a prime object.

When the surgeon came in due time to examine his wound (for it was in vain to entreat him to let it be examined sooner), the most anxious silence prevailed; and the joy of the wounded men, and of the whole crew, when they heard that the hurt was merely superficial, gave Nelson deeper pleasure than the unexpected assurance that his life was in no danger. The surgeon requested, and as far as he could, ordered him to remain quiet. But Nelson could not rest. He called for his secretary, Mr. Campbell, to write the dispatches. Campbell had himself been wounded; and was so affected at the blind and suffering state of the Admiral that he was unable to write. The Chaplain was then sent for; but, before he came, Nelson, with his characteristic eagerness, took the pen, and contrived to trace a few words, marking his devout sense of the success which had already been obtained. He was now left alone; when suddenly a cry was heard on the deck, that the *Orient* was on fire. In the confusion he found his way up, unassisted and un-noticed; and, to the astonishment of every one, appeared on the quarter-deck, where he immediately gave order that the boats should be sent to the relief of the enemy.

It was soon after nine that the fire on board the *Orient* broke out. Brueys was dead. He had received three wounds, yet would not leave his post. A fourth cut him almost in two. He desired not to be carried below, but to be left to die upon deck. The flames soon mastered his ship. Her sides had just been painted; and the oil-jars, and paint-bucket, were lying on the poop. By the prodigious light of this conflagration, the situation of the two fleets could now be perceived, the colours of both being clearly dis-tinguishable. About ten o'clock the ship blew up, with a shock which was felt to the very bottom of every vessel. Many of her officers and men jumped overboard, some clinging to the spars and pieces of wreck with which the sea was strewn, others swimming to escape from the destruction which they momently dreaded. Some were picked up by our boats; and some even in the heat and fury of the action were dragged into the lower ports of the nearest British ships by the British sailors. The greater part of her crew, however, stood the danger till the last, and continued to fire from the lower deck. This tremendous explosion was

followed by a silence not less awful. The firing immediately
ceased on both sides; and the first sound which broke the
silence was the dash of her shattered masts and yards
falling into the water from the vast height to which they
had been exploded. It is upon record, that a battle between
two armies was once broken off by an earthquake. Such an
event would be felt like a miracle. But no incident in war,
produced by human means, has ever equalled the sublimity
of this co-instantaneous pause, and all its circumstances.

About seventy of the *Orient's* crew were saved by the
English boats. Among the many hundreds who perished,
were the Commodore, Casabianca, and his son, a brave
boy only ten years old. [1] They were seen floating on a
shattered mast when the ship blew up. She had money on
board (the plunder of Malta) to the amount of £600,000
sterling. The masses of burning wreck, which were scattered
by the explosion, excited for some moments apprehensions
in the English which they had never felt from any other
danger. Two large pieces fell into the main and fore-tops
of the *Swiftsure* without injuring any person. A port-fire [2]
also fell into the main royal [3] of the *Alexander;* the fire
which it occasioned was speedily extinguished. Captain
Ball had provided, as far as human foresight could provide,
against any such danger. All the shrouds and sails of his
ship, not absolutely necessary for its immediate management, were thoroughly wetted, and so rolled up, that they
were as hard and as little inflammable as so many solid
cylinders. [4]

The firing recommenced with the ships to leeward of the
centre, and continued till about three. At daybreak, the
Guillaume Tell and the *Généreux,* [5] the two rear ships of the
enemy, were the only French ships of the line which had
their colours flying. They cut their cables in the forenoon,

[1] The poem by Felicia Hemans, so oft derided, is fictitious in every particular
save that both father and son met their death.

[2] A paper tube, about sixteen inches long, filled with a composition of mealed
powder, sulphur, and nitre, rammed moderately hard, and used instead of match
to fire the guns.

[3] The uppermost sail set upon the mainmast. Below it were the main course,
the main topsail, and main topgallant.

[4] "At ten, the enemy's ship that was on fire blew up. With the explosion our
jib and main royal were set on fire. But cutting away the jib-boom and heaving
the royal overboard, the fire was luckily extinguished."—Log of the *Alexander.*

[5] The *Généreux* was the last ship but one in the enemy's line, and the *Guillaume
Tell* (with the flag of Admiral Villeneuve) was last but two.

not having been engaged, and stood out to sea, and two frigates [1] with them. The *Zealous* pursued; but as there was no other ship in a condition to support Captain Hood, he was recalled. It was generally believed by the officers, that if Nelson had not been wounded, not one of these ships could have escaped. The four certainly could not, if the *Culloden* had got into action: and if the frigates belonging to the squadron had been present, not one of the enemy's fleet would have left Aboukir Bay. These four vessels, however, were all that escaped; and the victory was the most complete and glorious in the annals of naval history. "Victory," said Nelson, "is not a name strong enough for such a scene"; he called it "a conquest." Of thirteen sail of the line nine were taken and two burned. Of the four frigates, one was sunk. Another, the *Artémise*, was burned in a villainous manner by her captain, M. Estandlet, who, having fired a broadside at the *Theseus*, struck his colours, then set fire to the ship, and escaped with most of his crew to shore. The British loss, in killed and wounded, amounted to eight hundred and ninety-five. Westcott was the only captain who fell. Three thousand one hundred and five of the French, including the wounded, were sent on shore by cartel, and five thousand two hundred and twenty-five perished.

As soon as the conquest was completed, Nelson sent orders through the fleet to return thanksgiving in every ship for the victory with which Almighty God had blessed his Majesty's arms. The French at Rosetta, who with miserable fear beheld the engagement, were at a loss to understand the stillness of the fleet during the performance of this solemn duty; but it seemed to affect many of the prisoners, officers as well as men: and graceless and godless as the officers were, some of them remarked, that it was no wonder such order was preserved in the British navy, when the minds of our men could be impressed with such sentiments after so great a victory, and at a moment of such confusion. The French at Rosetta, seeing their four ships sail out of the bay unmolested, endeavoured to persuade themselves that they were in possession of the place of battle. But it was in vain thus to attempt, against their own secret and

[1] The *Diane* and *Justice* (see plan, p. 134).

certain conviction, to deceive themselves: and even if they could have succeeded in this, the bonfires which the Arabs kindled along the whole coast, and over the country, for the three following nights, would soon have undeceived them. Thousands of Arabs and Egyptians lined the shore, and covered the house-tops, during the action, rejoicing in the destruction which had overtaken their invaders. Long after the battle, innumerable bodies were seen floating about the bay, in spite of all the exertions which were made to sink them, as well from fear of pestilence as from the loathing and horror which the sight occasioned. [Great numbers were cast up upon the Isle of Bequières (Nelson's Island, as it has since been called), and our sailors raised mounds of sand over them. Even after an interval of nearly three years Dr. Clarke saw them, and assisted in interring heaps of human bodies, which, having been thrown up by the sea, where there were no jackals to devour them, presented a sight loathsome to humanity.] [1] The shore, for an extent of four leagues, was covered with wreck; and the Arabs found employment for many days in burning on the beach the fragments which were cast up, for the sake of the iron.[2] Part of the *Orient's* main-mast was picked up by the *Swiftsure.* Captain Hallowell ordered his carpenter to make a coffin of it; the iron, as well as the wood, was taken from the wreck of the same ship. It was finished as well and handsomely as the workman's skill and materials would permit; and Hallowell then sent it to the Admiral with the following letter:—"Sir, I have taken the liberty of presenting you a coffin made from the main-mast of *l'Orient*, that when you have finished your military career in this world, you may be buried in one of your trophies. But that that period may be far distant is the earnest wish of your sincere friend, Benjamin Hallowell." An offering so strange, and yet so suited to the occasion, was received by Nelson in the spirit with which it was sent. As if he felt it good for him, now that he was at the summit of his wishes, to have death before his eyes, he ordered the coffin to be placed upright

[1] The passage within brackets is not found in the first, second and third editions.
[2] During his long subsequent cruise off Alexandria, Captain Hallowell kept his crew employed and amused in fishing up the small anchors in the road, which, with the iron found on the masts, was afterwards sold at Rhodes, and the produce applied to purchase vegetables and tobacco for the ship's company.—SOUTHEY'S NOTE, Fourth Edition.

in his cabin. Such a piece of furniture, however, was more suitable to his own feelings than to those of his guests and attendants; and an old favourite servant entreated him so earnestly to let it be removed, that at length he consented to have the coffin carried below; but he gave strict orders that it should be safely stowed, and reserved for the purpose for which its brave and worthy donor had designed it.

The victory was complete; but Nelson could not pursue it as he would have done, for want of means. Had he been provided with small craft, nothing could have prevented the destruction of the storeships and transports in the port of Alexandria. Four bomb-vessels would at that time have burned the whole in a few hours. " Were I to die this moment," said he in his dispatches to the Admiralty, "*want of frigates* would be found stamped on my heart! No words of mine can express what I have suffered, and am suffering, for want of them." He had also to bear up against great bodily suffering. The blow had so shaken his head, that from its constant and violent aching, and the perpetual sickness which accompanied the pain, he could scarcely persuade himself that the skull was not fractured. Had it not been for Troubridge, Ball, Hood, and Hallowell, he declared that he should have sunk under the fatigue of refitting the squadron. " All," he said, " had done well; but these officers were his supporters."

But, amidst his sufferings and exertions, Nelson could yet think of all the consequences of his victory; and that no advantage from it might be lost, he dispatched an officer overland to India, with letters to the governor of Bombay, informing him of the arrival of the French in Egypt, the total destruction of their fleet, and the consequent pre-servation of India from any attempt against it on the part of this formidable armament. " He knew that Bombay," he said, " was their first object, if they could get there; but he trusted that Almighty God would overthrow in Egypt these pests of the human race. Bonaparte had never yet had to contend with an English officer, and he would endeavour to make him respect us." This dispatch he sent upon his own responsibility, with letters of credit upon the East India Company, addressed to the British consuls, vice-consuls, and merchants on his route; Nelson saying, "that if he had done wrong, he hoped the bills would be paid, and he would repay the Company: for, as an Englishman, he should be proud that it had been in his power to put our settlements on their guard." The information which by this means reached India was of great importance. Orders had just been received for defensive preparations upon a scale proportionate to the apprehended danger; and the extraordinary expenses which would otherwise have been incurred were thus prevented.

Nelson was now at the summit of glory. Congratulations, rewards, and honours were showered upon him by all the states, and princes, and powers to whom his victory gave a respite. The first communication of this nature which he received was from the Turkish Sultan; who, as soon as the invasion of Egypt was known, had called upon "all true believers to take arms against those swinish infidels the French, that they might deliver these blessed habitations from their accursed hands"; and who had ordered his "pashas to turn night into day in their efforts to take vengeance." The present of "his Imperial Majesty, the powerful, formidable, and most magnificent Grand Seignior," was a pelisse of sables with broad sleeves valued at five thousand dollars; and a diamond aigrette [1] valued at eighteen thousand, the most honourable badge among the Turks, and in this instance more especially honourable, because it was taken from one of the royal turbans. "If it were worth a million," said Nelson to his wife, "my pleasure would be to see it in your possession." The Sultan also sent, in a spirit worthy of imitation, a purse of two thousand sequins, to be distributed among the wounded. The mother of the Sultan sent him a box, set with diamonds, valued at one thousand pounds. The Czar Paul, in whom the better part of his strangely compounded nature at this time predominated, presented him with his portrait, set in diamonds, in a gold box, accompanied with a letter of congratulation, written by his own hand. The King of Sardinia also wrote to him, and sent a gold box, set with

[1] Called the Chelingk. This most interesting trophy, which Nelson ever afterwards wore in his hat, is still preserved in the Royal United Service Museum, Whitehall, Exhibit No. 3041. Here also are to be found the diamond-hilted sword presented by the City of London, Exhibit No. 3031 (see below, p. 145); and the main royal mast-head of the *Orient*, Exhibit No. 2199.

diamonds. Honours in profusion were awaiting him at
Naples. In his own country the king granted these honourable augmentations to his armorial ensign: a chief undulated
argent; thereon waves of the sea; from which a palm tree
issuant, between a disabled ship on the dexter, and a ruinous
battery on the sinister, all proper: and for his crest, on a
naval crown, *or*, the chelingk, or plume, presented to him
by the Turk, with the motto, *Palmam qui meruit ferat*.[1]
And to his supporters, being a sailor on the dexter, and a
lion on the sinister, were given these honourable augmentations: a palm branch in the sailor's hand, and another
in the paw of the lion, both proper; with a tricoloured flag
and staff in the lion's mouth. He was created Baron Nelson
of the Nile, and of Burnham Thorpe, with a pension of
£2000 for his own life, and those of his two immediate
successors. When the grant was moved in the House of
Commons, General Walpole expressed an opinion that a
higher degree of rank ought to be conferred.[2] Mr. Pitt made
answer, that he thought it needless to enter into that question. " Admiral Nelson's fame," he said, " would be co-
equal with the British name; and it would be remembered
that he had obtained the greatest naval victory on record,
when no man would think of asking whether he had been
created a baron, a viscount, or an earl." It was strange
that, in the very act of conferring a title, the minister should

[1] It has been erroneously said that the motto was selected by the King. It was
fixed on by Lord Grenville, and taken from an ode of Jortin's. The application
was singularly fortunate; and the ode itself breathes a spirit, in which no man
ever more truly sympathised than Nelson:

> *Concurrant paribus cum ratibus rates,*
> *Spectent numina ponti, et*
> *Palmam qui meruit ferat.*

SOUTHEY'S NOTE.

> If ships compete
>   With ships of equal rate,
> If Water Gods preside
>   To arbitrate,
> Then he who best deserves it wins the palm.

[2] This opinion was universal; and much ingenuity was exercised by the public
in an effort to discover an adequate reason why nothing higher than a barony
was conferred. Captain Berry, the bearer of Nelson's dispatches, has left it on
record that, when he reached London, he found Mr. Pitt imbued with the notion
that the victory was to be ascribed not to any skill on the Admiral's part, but to
the accidental destruction of the enemy's flagship. This, however, was not the
reason for the Government's lack of generosity. Nelson was not Commander-
in-Chief in the Mediterranean, but only detached by St. Vincent in charge of a
squadron; and the Admiralty could find no precedent for exalting to a higher
grade in the peerage one who did not exercise an independent command.

have excused himself for not having conferred a higher one, by representing all titles, on such an occasion, as nugatory and superfluous. True, indeed, whatever title had been bestowed, whether viscount, earl, marquis, duke, or prince if our laws had so permitted, he who received it would have been Nelson still. That name he had ennobled beyond all addition of nobility. It was the name by which England loved him, France feared him, Italy, Egypt, and Turkey celebrated him: and by which he will continue to be known while the present kingdoms and languages of the world endure, and as long as their history after them shall be held in remembrance. It depended upon the degree of rank what should be the fashion of his coronet, in what page of the red book his name was to be inserted, and what precedency should be allowed his lady in the drawing-room and at the ball. That Nelson's honours were affected thus far, and no further, might be conceded to Mr. Pitt and his colleagues in administration. But the degree of rank which they thought proper to allot was the measure of their gratitude,[1] though not of his services. This Nelson felt; and this he expressed, with indignation, among his friends.

Whatever may have been the motives of the ministry, and whatever the formalities with which they excused their conduct to themselves, the importance and magnitude of the victory were universally acknowledged. A grant of £10,000 was voted to Nelson by the East India Company; the Turkish Company presented him with a piece of plate; the City of London presented a sword to him, and to each of his captains; gold medals were distributed to the captains : and the first lieutenants of all the ships were promoted, as had been done after Lord Howe's victory.[2] Nelson was exceedingly anxious that the Captain and First

[1] Mr. Windham must be exempted from this well-deserved censure. He, whose fate it seems to have been almost always to think and feel more generously than those with whom he acted, declared, when he contended against his own party for Lord Wellington's peerage, that he always thought Lord Nelson had been inadequately rewarded. The case was the more flagrant, because an earldom had so lately been granted for the battle of St. Vincent; an action which could never be compared with the battle of the Nile, if the very different manner in which it was rewarded did not necessarily force a comparison; especially when the part which Nelson bore in it was considered.—Lords Duncan and St. Vincent had each a pension of £1,000 from the Irish Government. This was not granted to Nelson, in consequence of the Union; though, surely, it would be more becoming to increase the British grant, than to save a thousand a year by the Union in such cases.—SOUTHEY's NOTE.
[2] The glorious First of June, 1794.

Lieutenant of the *Culloden* should not be passed over because of their misfortune. To Troubridge himself he said, " Let us rejoice that the ship which got on shore was commanded by an officer whose character is so thoroughly established." To the Admiralty he stated that Captain Troubridge's conduct was as fully entitled to praise as that of any one officer in the squadron, and as highly deserving of reward. " It was Troubridge," said he, " who equipped the squadron so soon at Syracuse: it was Troubridge who exerted himself for me after the action: it was Troubridge who saved the *Culloden*, when none that I know in the service would have attempted it." The gold medal, therefore, by the king's express desire, was given to Captain Troubridge " for his services both before and since, and for the great and wonderful exertion which he made at the time of the action, in saving and getting off his ship." The private letter from the Admiralty to Nelson informed him, that the first lieutenants of all the ships *engaged* were to be promoted. Nelson instantly wrote to the commander-in-chief. " I sincerely hope," said he, " this is not intended to exclude the first lieutenant of the *Culloden*.—For Heaven's sake,—for my sake,—if it be so, get it altered. Our dear friend Troubridge has endured enough. His sufferings were, in every respect, more than any of us." To the Admiralty he wrote in terms equally warm. " I hope, and believe, the word *engaged* is not intended to exclude the *Culloden*. The merit of that ship, and her gallant captain, are too well-known to benefit by anything I could say. Her misfortune was great in getting aground, while her more fortunate companions were in the full tide of happiness. No: I am confident that my good Lord Spencer will never add misery to misfortune. Captain Troubridge on shore is superior to captains afloat. In the midst of his great misfortunes he made those signals which prevented certainly the *Alexander* and *Swiftsure* from running on the shoals. I beg your pardon for writing on a subject which, I verily believe, has never entered your lordship's head; but my heart, as it ought to be, is warm to my gallant friends." Thus feelingly alive was Nelson to the claims, and interests, and feelings of others. The Admiralty replied, that the exception was necessary, as the ship had not been in action: but they desired the commander-in-chief to promote the lieutenant upon the first vacancy which should occur.

Nelson, in remembrance of an old and uninterrupted friendship, appointed Alexander Davison sole prize agent for the captured ships: upon which Davison ordered medals to be struck in gold, for the captains; in silver, for the lieutenants and warrant officers; in gilt metal, for the petty officers; and in copper, for the seamen and marines. The cost of this act of liberality amounted nearly to £2000. It is worthy of record on another account; for some of the gallant men, who received no other honorary badge of their conduct on that memorable day than this copper medal from a private individual, years afterwards, when they died upon a foreign station, made it their last request, that the medals might carefully be sent home to their respective friends. So sensible are brave men of honour, in whatever rank they may be placed.

Three of the frigates, whose presence would have been so essential a few weeks sooner, joined the squadron on the twelfth day after the action. The fourth joined a few days after them. Nelson thus received dispatches, which rendered it necessary for him to return to Naples. Before he left Egypt he burned three of the prizes. They could not have been fitted for a passage to Gibraltar in less than a month, and that at a great expense, and with the loss of the service of at least two sail of the line. " I rest assured," he said to the Admiralty, " that they will be paid for, and have held out that assurance to the squadron. For if an admiral, after a victory, is to look after the captured ships, and not to the distressing of the enemy, very dearly, indeed, must the nation pay for the prizes. I trust that £60,000 will be deemed a very moderate sum for them: and when the services, time, and men, with the expense of fitting the three ships for a voyage to England, are considered, government will save nearly as much as they are valued at. Paying for prizes," he continued, " is no new idea of mine, and would often prove an amazing saving to the state, even without taking into calculation what the nation loses by the attention of admirals to the property of the captors; an attention absolutely necessary, as a recompense for the exertions of the officers and men. An admiral may be amply rewarded by his own feelings, and by the approbation of his superiors; but what reward have the inferior officers and men, but the value of the prizes? If an admiral takes that from them, on any consideration, he cannot expect to be well supported." To Earl St. Vincent he said, " If he could have been sure that government would have paid a reasonable value for them, he would have ordered two of the other prizes to be burnt; for they would cost more in refitting, and by the loss of ships attending them, than they were worth."

Having sent the six remaining prizes forward, under Sir James Saumarez, Nelson left Captain Hood (in the *Zealous*) off Alexandria, with the *Swiftsure, Goliath, Alcmene, Zealous,* and *Emerald,* and stood out to sea himself on the seventeenth day after the battle.[1]

[1] " Some French officers, during the blockade of Alexandria, were sent off to Captain Hallowell to offer a supply of vegetables, and observe, of course, the state of the blockading squadron. They were received with all possible civility. In the course of conversation after dinner one of them remarked that we had made use of unfair weapons during the action, by which probably the *Orient* was burnt; and that General Bonaparte had expressed great indignation at it. In proof of this assertion he stated that in the late gunboat attacks, their camp had twice been set on fire by balls of unextinguishable matter which were fired from one of the English boats. Captain Hallowell instantly ordered the gunner to bring up some of those balls, and asked him from whence he had them. To the confusion of the accusers he related that they were found on board of the *Spartiate*, one of the ships captured on the 1st of August. As these balls were distinguished by particular marks, though in other respects alike, the Captain ordered an experiment to be made, in order to ascertain the nature of them. The next morning," says Mr. Willyams, " I accompanied Mr. Parr, the gunner, to the island; the first we tried proved to be a fire-ball, but of what materials composed we could not ascertain. As it did not explode (which at first we apprehended), we rolled it into the sea, where it continued to burn under water; a black pitchy substance exuding from it till only an iron skeleton of a shell remained. The whole had been carefully crusted over with a substance that gave it the appearance of a perfect shell. On setting fire to the fusee of the other, which was differently marked, it burst into many pieces. Though somewhat alarmed, fortunately none of us were hurt. People account differently for the fire that happened on board of the French admiral, but why may it not have arisen from some of these fire-balls left, perhaps carelessly, on the poop, or cabin, when it first broke out? and what confirms my opinion on this head is, that several pieces of such shells were found sticking in the *Bellerophon,* which she most probably received from the first fire of *L'Orient.*" Willyams's *Voyages in the Mediterranean,* p. 145.—SOUTHEY's NOTE, Fourth Edition,

PART VI

NAPLES

In the following division of his work Southey, because he did not trouble to sift existing evidence, committed himself to falsehoods, believing them to be the truth. He acted with transparent and fearless honesty of purpose, but as a versatile man of letters rather than as a workmanlike historian. Unhappily his groundless aspersions have blackened Nelson's character, and spattered the Admiral's reputation with foul spots that time has not yet erased. Before examining his narrative, therefore, we shall do well to take a brief survey of what research has since revealed: for only by so doing can we inoculate ourselves against contamination from his virulent perversion of facts.

After the Battle of the Nile Nelson, who needed refreshment both for himself and his fleet, resorted again to the Kingdom of Naples, where he was received no longer with half-hearted hospitality, but with triumphant and boisterous exhibitions of joy. He did not expect to make a long visit; but history had already made a habit of centring round him, and for the next twelve-month Naples drew the eyes of the world.

Since Napoleon's irruption into Italy in 1796, the peninsula had yielded more and more to the forces of the French Revolution. Trees of Liberty had been planted in the northern states before Nelson lost his arm at Teneriffe; and six months before the victory of Aboukir the Jacobins, entering Rome, had established a republic, and carried off to France the aged and decrepit Pope Pius VI. to die in miserable captivity. Naples alone upheld the cause of kings; and into Naples there spread from the Roman Republic the doctrines that had sent to the guillotine Louis XVI. and Marie Antoinette.

On the other hand, Pitt's new coalition against France was nearly complete. Not only was Austria buckling on her armour again; but the Russians were preparing to enter the arena, and the Turks as well. It was inevitable that Naples should join this combination for the defence of royalism; and to organise her army she borrowed from Vienna the services of Mack, who to-day is chiefly remembered for having surrendered to Napoleon at Ulm, but who was at the time believed to be a capable officer. It was a difficult task, however, for the Neapolitans to decide what military wisdom required. The more cautious line of conduct inclined them to wait until the Austro-Russian armies moved south to their assistance. But a bolder initiative might carry them into Rome itself, and enable them to extend their territorial possessions. If they struck too soon, they might be worsted before their allies took the field; if they waited too long, the Frenchmen might attempt to subdue them

N

before their friends could intervene. The situation was one in which weak men temporise; and no immediate decision was reached.

Nelson, returning from Egypt, infused new spirit into the Neapolitan court. He exhorted the king and queen not to sit still until the evil hour approached, but to grapple the red menace while it was still afar off and drive it wholly from their doors. He had no means of judging the quality of the Neapolitan troops. He counted their numbers and, finding them sufficient, formulated a simple plan that promised complete success. King Ferdinand's soldiers under General Mack were to advance northward against the Jacobin front, while the British Navy was to capture Leghorn and cut the enemy's communications.

His fleet achieved its purpose at Leghorn, but the Neapolitan troops showed no aptitude at all except for running away. They retreated precipitately before an army of inferior strength; and, racing in panic to their own borders, drew the Frenchmen after them. The home-bred Jacobins rose in a body to welcome the republican invaders, and the throne of Naples in that hour tottered to its fall. For King Ferdinand and Queen Maria Carolina the only hope lay in flight; and as all land avenues were blocked against them, they turned in despair to the sea. The Jacobins watched them with suspicious eyes, but Nelson was too clever for the Jacobins. Magnificently seconded ashore by Sir William and Lady Hamilton, he rescued the inmates of the royal palace, and carried them, together with their goods and chattels, in safety to Palermo. A new court and a new capital were there set up, while the Neapolitan insurgents and their French allies converted Naples, now vacated by royalty, into the "Parthenopeian" or (as Nelson loved to call it) the "Vesuvian" Republic.

The best hopes for an eventual "Restoration" of monarchy were based by the exiled king and queen on the might of the British fleet. But Nelson, though his desire to help them further was endorsed by instructions to that effect from home, could not at once devote himself whole-heartedly to their cause. As Admiral, his sphere was not a single realm, but the whole of the Mediterranean. Napoleon's fleet had been destroyed at the Nile: but Napoleon's army and Napoleon's self still stood at bay in the Levant; and it was morally certain that at an early date new French and Spanish fleets would combine in an attempt to put themselves into touch with him. Meanwhile between Toulon and Alexandria lay Napoleon's garrison in the island of Malta commanding at its narrowest point the ocean highway to Egypt.

Here then, apart from the downfall of Naples and the helpless cries from Sicily, was a situation perplexing enough. At any moment it might be necessary for the victor of the Nile to wrestle again in diminished strength with the navies of the Jacobin powers. Nelson took a comprehensive view of his responsibilities. He assumed a central position at Palermo where he could keep his fingers on the pulse of things, or (in other words) collect the little grains of intelligence that slowly drifted there; and from Palermo he exercised what may best be described as a double process of "blockade." One squadron he detached, under Captain Ball, with threats of famine to force Malta to capitulate; and a second, under

Troubridge, he ordered to the Bay of Naples to starve the Jacobins into submission. With both these squadrons he kept closely in touch, so that he could at the approach of the Franco-Spanish fleet reassemble them at the point of danger.

Blockade, especially when uninterrupted, is a very compelling method of warfare. But if it operates surely, it operates slowly; and the King and Queen of Naples grew weary of waiting, and turned their hands to another instrument which seemed to promise them a quicker recovery of their kingdom. The Neapolitans in the mass, though indolently accepting the Jacobin upheaval, were at heart devotedly attached to the Church, and almost as devotedly attached to the Crown. It was resolved, therefore, to appeal through an eminent ecclesiastic to their deep-rooted sentiments; and, at Ferdinand's request, his Eminence Cardinal Ruffo crossed the Straits of Messina into Italy, and inaugurated an anti-Jacobin campaign. His success was instantaneous; thousands of warriors flocked to his banner, and the "Army of the Faith" moved northwards from Calabria, driving the "infidels" before them. A contingent of Russians and a handful of Turks crossed the Adriatic in timely fashion and swelled the flowing tide.

While these events were in progress, a French fleet, under Bruix, numbering no less than twenty-six of the line, set out from Brest, eluded pursuit, and entered the Mediterranean; almost immediately afterwards there followed a Spanish fleet, under Masaredo, numbering as many as seventeen sail; and these powerful squadrons succeeded in their preliminary aim by uniting at Carthagena. Nelson, who had no more than a dozen big ships, immediately called up his reserves—Ball from Malta, and Troubridge from Naples. In view, however, of Ruffo's success, he replaced Troubridge's fleet by a group of little ships, part English and part Neapolitan, which he entrusted to Captain Foote of the frigate *Seahorse*. This flotilla, which continued to co-operate with the Cardinal, could show a clean pair of heels to the heavy Franco-Spanish ships if, instead of sailing as expected for Egypt, they moved directly into the Bay of Naples in support of the Vesuvian Republic.

Had the Franco-Spanish fleet come boldly on, it is impossible to doubt but that Nelson, in spite of his marked inferiority, would have reaped a glorious harvest of laurels. But the armada, finding a lion in its path, deemed discretion the better part of valour and retired. Indeed, the utter barrenness of its futile cruising has passed into a proverb. The danger that had loomed so darkly thus passed away like a thunder-cloud, leaving Nelson at liberty, if he would, to listen to fresh entreaties from the court at Palermo.

The land campaign by now had reached a critical stage. The "Army of the Faith," surging forwards irresistibly, had driven their foe in rout from the field, and then penned him into the city of Naples. But at such a moment Cardinal Ruffo, who knew that his sovereigns reserved for themselves the right of making peace, took the liberty of exceeding his instructions by admitting the Jacobin leaders to a parley. The court of Palermo, greatly perturbed, therefore implored Lord Nelson to throw his sword into the scale, and from a commanding position in Naples Bay compel the enemy to surrender.

Nelson set out at once, and learnt on his way that the rebels had obtained an armistice or cessation of hostilities. He argued that this could only mean that the Cardinal was already discussing terms of peace. He urged his fleet forward, and as he entered Naples Bay saw flags of truce flying, not only ashore, but in his own flotilla under Captain Foote. He could discern no reason why, at the particular moment when they had forced the enemy into a corner, the "Army of the Faith" should cease to fight. But the reasons for the blunder did not interest him greatly; his sole concern was how the error could be remedied. Now he knew that, by the laws of warfare, an armistice is terminable on either side when due notice to that effect has been given; and flying into the heart of things with his customary zeal, he annulled by signal the flag of truce, and gave notice that hostilities would at once be resumed.

At this point Captain Foote came aboard, and informed him more exactly of the state of affairs. The enemy, he said, had taken their last stand in three strong fortresses. The French, at the heart of the city, held the castle of St. Elmo, and the native insurgents were in the sea-washed forts of Uovo and Nuovo. Cardinal Ruffo, though he held a master position on the land side, presided over a force which he could ill control, and whose murderous propensities made him anxious to bring his duties to a close. Not only had he entertained a flag of truce and granted an armistice, but upon a promise of the rebels to evacuate the two sea-forts he had run counter to the stringent injunctions of his sovereigns and agreed to a treaty of peace. This capitulation, to which Foote among others had already affixed his name, treated the insurgents as if they were on the same footing as belligerents. They were to march out with all the honours of war, flags flying, drums beating, and weapons bared; they were to carry with them all their property, and they were to be transported in vessels over sea to harbours that would welcome them. Not without reason had the king and queen forbidden Ruffo to listen to a parley! His terms were absurdly generous, and no one was more impressed by the fact than the rebels themselves. They had asked for an armistice, not (as Ruffo feared) to make stouter their defences; but in the hopes that the Franco-Spanish fleet, which Nelson by now had scared away, would at the twelfth hour come and rescue them. In the treaty of peace or capitulation they asked on principle for more than they hoped to obtain; and they insisted on transport oversea because they knew that their fellow-countrymen would tear them to pieces if they committed themselves to the streets. When the Cardinal granted all their desires they felt in their bones (like true Neapolitans) that his moderation covered a calculated treachery, and therefore they were not waiting to receive the honours of war, but were already stealing away in boats under cover of the flag of truce.

It was the sea alone that gave Forts Uovo and Nuovo any status as bargainers. The appearance, that is to say, of the Franco-Spanish fleet would undoubtedly have relieved them of all their fears, and the likelihood of the Franco-Spanish fleet's appearance is the only excuse that can legitimately be offered for Ruffo's treaty of peace. But the arrival of Nelson completely destroyed the hopes of the insurgents, and showing Ruffo the folly of his own haste, reminded him of his sovereign's injunction not to attempt to make terms by himself.

The new intelligence received from Foote made no difference to Nelson's resolution. He informed both parties to the treaty of peace that its terms could only be carried into effect when they had been confirmed by the court of Palermo. He also announced that at the expiry of his ultimatum hostilities would at once be recommenced. If Ruffo's army refused to co-operate, the British bluejackets would come ashore and act as soldiers. Now as the whole gist of the capitulation lay in the clause that allowed insurgents to escape by sea, it was ridiculous for anyone to question Nelson's right to have the treaty of peace made regular. But the resumption of hostilities was another thing. The Cardinal's heart sank when he thought of the scenes of butchery and carnage which he had already witnessed. He implored the British Admiral to let the armistice run its course; and Nelson, believing that the very presence of his ships would bring the Neapolitans to a humbler frame of mind, agreed to defer the employment of his broadsides. Ruffo then, behind the Admiral's back, gave the rebels permission to escape by land; an offer which, from the perils ashore, they regarded as an idle taunt. Their only hope was to get away by sea; and when Nelson told them that he held them in the hollow of his hand, and that he expected them without a second's loss of time to surrender unconditionally, they proceeded to do so as meekly as lambs, and came on board his ships without a protest.

There were one or two, however, who did not come; desperate men who preferred to face murder in the mountains rather than meet again at sea their former friends. Among these was Francesco Caracciolo, who as Captain of the *Tancredi* had fought beside Nelson in the days of Hotham's command. He had risen to high rank through the favour of his sovereigns; and, when the court fled for refuge to Palermo, had attended them in the rôle of prince and with the rank of commodore. When, however, the fortunes of royalty seemed to him to sink to their lowest ebb, he had excused himself from further attendance, and with Ferdinand's permission repaired to Naples to safeguard his own interests. He had made up his mind that the cause of kings was dead; and, though a thousand claims upon his gratitude should have kept his loyalty from decay, he had thrown in his lot with the Jacobins, and been put in charge of the revolutionary flotilla. In this capacity he had fired into the Neapolitan ship *La Minerva*, killing and wounding his old comrades in arms. On the arrival of the British he had succeeded in escaping to the hills; but was caught by the royalists and brought before Ruffo, who handed him over to Nelson, now acting as Commander-in-Chief of the Neapolitan fleet.

Those who would criticise what follows should first acquaint themselves (and Southey did not) with legal procedure at sea; for a naval court-martial differs not only from civil jurisdiction, but from military practice as well.

The first thing necessary is that there should be some officer of high standing to whom the sovereign has delegated the power of sanctioning a trial. It is the duty of this officer, when he has satisfied himself that the evidence is truly found and likely to convict, to summon a court martial, appointing a president thereof, together with a judge advocate to instruct the court in procedure, and a provost-marshal to guard the prisoner's person.   The president will select not less than four and not more than eight additional members who, with himself, will try the case.   There will be no counsel for the defence, and no counsel for the prosecution; the members of the court will act both as judge and jury. The judge advocate will see that all necessary documents are at hand, and will produce such witnesses as the court may require. The prisoner can object to the constitution of the court, but cannot enforce his objections. He can also object to the nature of the evidence and the witnesses called, but on both heads must submit himself to the president's decisions. Proceedings are public until a judgment has been given, whereupon the court is cleared. If the charge is proved, then the members determine how the prisoner shall be punished, being guided in their award by precedent. The judgment of the court is final, and needs no confirmation. It is not even necessary to send to the convening authority any intimation of judgment or award; but this is almost invariably done, because the convening authority is generally the admiral whose staff will see that the sentence is put into effect. In the case of corporal punishment, detention, or loss of status, the convening authority can mitigate or even annul the sentence; but if the award is death, he cannot interfere. The amount of time intervening between judgment and execution will depend on circumstances; in a death sentence, for example, on the recommendation to mercy. If such a recommendation be preferred, then the convening authority will forward it to the sovereign and stay execution till an answer is returned.

When Caracciolo, as a naval officer in the employment of King Ferdinand, was sent afloat by the Cardinal's order, Nelson, as in duty bound, sanctioned a trial by court martial. This was his routine duty as convening authority, and would not have been referred to him if he had not been appointed by Ferdinand Neapolitan Commander-in-Chief. Count Thurn, a Neapolitan captain, was nominated president of the court, and as the law forbade him to institute proceedings ashore, but allowed any ship to serve as tribunal, he chose the *Foudroyant* (Nelson's flagship) because it wore an air of neutrality. Caracciolo raised no demur at the constitution of the court, but requested that he might be tried by British officers rather than Neapolitans. The court considered the request, but rejected it.

Evidence was adduced to show that the prisoner had deserted to the enemy, and with mutinous intent persuaded others to take up arms against their lawful sovereign. Caracciolo pleaded not guilty, and endeavoured to prove that in what he had done he had been acting under compulsion, the Jacobins constraining him to adopt an attitude foreign to all that he felt. It was a reasonable line of argument, but one extremely difficult to substantiate. All available evidence tended to show that the prisoner had been given a free hand by the Jacobins, and could at any time have returned to his allegiance. The court consisted of five members. Each in turn was asked to give his verdict orally, beginning with the youngest. Two out of five were merciful, but three condemned; and, by immemorial usage, judgment went by the majority. The court was then cleared, and all English spectators withdrew. The prisoner was condemned on both counts. He was found guilty of desertion, for which the punishment at that time was death by hanging; and he was found guilty of armed rebellion, for which the punishment was the same. Caracciolo bore himself pluckily, but the members of the court had no option left them, and sentenced him to an ignominious death.

Nelson was informed of the verdict. Although he was the convening authority he had no power to revise the finding of the court, or change the method of execution. If the sentence had been accompanied by a recommendation to mercy, it would have been his duty to forward the recommendation to King Ferdinand. But as there was no such recommendation, there was nothing further that he or any other man could do.

Caracciolo was informed that he would die at nightfall, execution being delayed for half a day so that the necessary preparations might be made. According to immemorial custom, the condemned man was taken on board the ship where his crime had been committed; and at the appointed hour the signal was hoisted on board the *Foudroyant* that all hands should assemble throughout the fleet to witness punishment. At two bells a gun was fired, the drums rolled, and the company of *La Minerva* drew to the yard-arm the body of the conspirator who had fired into their ship.

There still remained between Ferdinand and his throne the French in the Castle of St. Elmo, and in addition to these there were isolated garrisons at Capua and Gaeta. Nelson forthwith landed his seamen under Troubridge and very quickly disposed of the last elements of opposition. Thus Jacobinism was uprooted and rebellion suppressed, and the king came to his own again.

This consummation was, of course, very differently regarded by the two parties to the conflict. The Neapolitan sovereigns showed their gratitude by conferring upon Nelson a dukedom, together with a rich landed estate in Sicily. The First Lord wrote to the Admiral, "the intentions and motives by which all your measures have been governed have been as pure and good as their success has been complete." [1]

But among the Jacobins there was weeping and gnashing of teeth; mournful sounds which still re-echo through the pages of Miss Helen Maria Williams. This obscure authoress, an Englishwoman by birth, migrated to France at the age of twenty-six to live with a sister who had married a Huguenot. Within a few months of her arrival in her new home the States General assembled at Versailles, and the French Revolution broke out. Miss Williams gained the friendship of Madame Roland and forthwith became an ardent republican. Her education had been imperfect, her private life was not without blemish, and the excesses of sansculottism worked like madness in her brain. She may have been honest and warmhearted, but she gathered her information from tainted sources, and wrote fervent narratives and frenzied memoirs which it would be temperate to describe as mere travesties of truth. To her way of thinking, every opponent of Jacobinism was an enemy of the human race; and her account of Nelson's behaviour at Naples is

[1] Sir Harris Nicolas, *Dispatches and Letters of Lord Nelson*, Vol. IV. p. 115, etc.

instructive only as showing how wide of the mark partisanship may carry a reckless writer.

A copy of the book in which she described the Neapolitan proceedings [1] is treasured in the British Museum [2] on account of the annotations made therein by the Admiral whom she so vilely calumniated.

For sheer wanton acerbity even Miss Williams must yield to Captain Foote, of the *Seahorse*. Captain Foote, as we have seen, commanded Nelson's flotilla in Naples Bay, and by an error of judgment affixed his name to Ruffo's treaty with the rebels. His wrong-headedness was freely forgiven by Nelson, who charitably believed that his subordinate had been tricked by the Cardinal's duplicity. Foote appears to have appreciated the indulgence shown to him, and in the period immediately following his trespass wrote to Nelson in terms of affectionate gratitude. But seven years later, when the saviour of the State had laid down his life at Trafalgar, Foote read an early Nelsonian biography (the wretched compilation of Harrison) which disclosed the fact that Nelson in a hasty moment had described Ruffo's treaty as "infamous." Foote accepted this epithet as applicable to himself, and in 1807 published a *Vindication* of his conduct, which nobody had ever impugned. In this worthless and egotistical pamphlet he threw restraint to the winds, and seared the name and fame of his benefactor with vitriolic diatribes.

It is abundantly clear, then, that for a true view of Nelson's conduct at Naples we must look at things otherwise than through the jaundiced eyes of Captain Foote and Miss Williams. And yet these are the main authorities on whom Southey relied for his own account of what occurred.

And Southey's account, it is not too much to say, has been accepted either in whole or in part by all successive writers.

Some of their libellous insinuations have been already met in the foregoing narrative. It will be sufficient merely to summarise the more important of the charges that remain.

(*a*) *Accusation.* Nelson had no power to override Cardinal Ruffo, and never produced any document which entitled him to interfere.

Answer. Nelson was sent direct from the court of Palermo to take matters out of Ruffo's hands. If he exercised wider powers than the Neapolitan sovereigns intended, why did they create him a duke?

(*b*) *Accusation.* Cardinal Ruffo, Captain Foote and others on the one side, and the insurgents in Forts Uovo and Nuovo on the other, had signed and sealed a treaty of peace, which was inviolable and sacrosanct.

Answer. Neither Cardinal Ruffo nor any one else had the power to make a treaty of peace. That prerogative was reserved to themselves by the Neapolitan sovereigns, to whom Nelson insisted that the capitulation should be referred. The insurgents had cause for disappointment; but this would have been avoided if they had insisted on examining the Cardinal's credentials.

(*c*) *Accusation.* Even if Ruffo was unauthorised as a peacemaker, his treaty became effective as soon as its terms had been carried

---

[1] *Sketches of the State of Manners and Opinions in the French Republic* (1801).
[2] Additional MSS. 34391.

out; and as these were in process of execution before the British fleet arrived, Nelson very clearly came too late to suspend their complete fulfilment.

Answer. This is in legal parlance a "nice point." The treaty or capitulation amounted to a bargain whereby Ruffo was to receive the two marine forts and the rebels were to receive safe-conduct over-sea. When Nelson arrived some of the rebels were already embarked in boats, so that at first glance it looks as if the treaty had been made effective. But the insurgents who had embarked were (on Ruffo's own showing) dishonest fellows who stole out of the forts before the pourparlers were complete.[1]

There is, of course, all the difference in the world between an armistice (cessation of hostilities) and a capitulation (terms of surrender). Ruffo had agreed to both before Nelson arrived; and, as we have seen, succeeded in coaxing Nelson to accept the armistice, *i.e.* postpone resumption of hostilities. He brought trouble on his head by concluding a capitulation in direct disobedience to his sovereign's commands, and to clear himself endeavoured to make it appear that it was the capitulation and not the armistice which Nelson promised to observe. In this disingenuous line of conduct he achieved some success owing to an almost universal ignorance or unfamiliarity with the exact meaning of these technical terms.[2]

(*d*) *Accusation.* Nothing will ever exonerate Nelson for withdrawing mercy from Caracciolo, an aged man, whose back was bent with years and infirmity.

Answer. Caracciolo at the time of his death was forty-seven years of age and in the prime of life.

(*e*) *Accusation.* In permitting Caracciolo to be put to death within a few hours of his condemnation, Nelson showed an implacable and unpardonable ferocity.

Answer. If Caracciolo had been guilty of any other crime, and had committed his offence in time of peace, Nelson's whole attitude would be quite inexplicable. But a traitor and mutineer caught red-handed in the act, by immemorial usage, dies in time of war when sentence has been delivered.[3]

"The intentions and motives by which your measures have been governed have been as pure and good as their success has been complete." These words of Earl Spencer, deliberately chosen, when events were fresh in his mind, acquire new meaning when all the evidence since available has been dissected and re-examined. And yet when the mud thrown at Nelson's name has been dutifully scraped away, there are seen to be stains below the mud that are ineffaceable. Why is it that Englishmen who approach the story with unbiased minds do not take up the cudgels in righteous heat

[1] " Ella in buono fede aspettava l'effeto di detta capitolazione, quantunque per precipitazione nell' uscire dal castello non furono gli articoli puntualmente osservati."

[2] Domenico Sacchinelli, *Memorie storiche sulla vita del Cardinale Fabrizio Ruffo.* A full bibliography of Italian sources will be found at the close of *Naples in 1799,* by Constance H. D. Giglioli.

[3] For the opposite point of view quite recently put by the Vere Harmsworth Professor of Naval History at Cambridge, see *Cambridge Modern History,* Vol. VIII. p. 658. *Cp.* also Admiral Sir Cyprian Bridge's reply, *United Service Magazine,* October 1905.

on behalf of their greatest admiral? Three explanations suggest themselves.

In the first place, though Nelson's public life at Naples was free from blame, his private life was marred by sin. It was at this time that he fell passionately in love with Lady Hamilton, the wife of the British Ambassador. Much may be said in extenuation of his fault; but so long as sin is reckoned sinful, his absolution in this world must remain incomplete.

In the second place the shadowy Franco-Spanish fleet, that remained unseen and yet amplified the drama by its "alarums and excursions," provided additional occasion for stumbling. Allowance for its proximity had to enter every calculation, and no reckoner, of course, was more nearly concerned than the *British* Commander-in-Chief. Now Nelson was in charge of only a detachment of Earl St. Vincent's fleet ; and when at this time Earl St. Vincent went home, the Admiralty made choice of Lord Keith as his successor. Lord Keith, puzzled to know what plans were actuating a Franco-Spanish navy of nearly fifty ships, reached the conclusion that Minorca was in peril, and summoned Nelson from Naples to defend it. Nelson decided that Minorca was in no sort of danger, and refused to conform to the summons. Much may be said in extenuation of his fault ; but he was guilty of deliberate and direct disobedience, and the Admiralty in consequence sharply reprimanded him.

Now mankind in the mass is censorious, but censorious without bothering about canons of criticism. Let it be granted that during the Neapolitan business Nelson was cherishing an infatuation for Lady Hamilton; and let it be granted that at the close of the Neapolitan business he was reprimanded by the Admiralty. Then those who love to leap to sudden conclusions put two and two together and make whatever total they please. Nelson, they argue, refused to obey Lord Keith because he could not tear himself from Lady Hamilton's side. Nelson was reprimanded by the Admiralty because he broke the treaty that Ruffo had sanctioned. Nelson put Caracciolo to death because Lady Hamilton, like a second Salome, gained his favour by the way she danced the tarantella.

There is no end to nonsense of this kind and no possible manner of answering it. Nelson was devoted heart and soul to Lady Hamilton. She had helped him to water the fleet that thwarted Bonaparte; she had nursed him back to health when he came back wounded from the Nile. She had enabled him to complete his plans for carrying the royal family to Palermo; and in all his efforts to restore the throne she had acted as interpreter, intermediary, and amanuensis. But there is not so much as a vestige of evidence to prove that she ever influenced his public conduct in thought, or word, or deed. When Nelson was engaged in state affairs, he allowed nothing (not even those he loved best) to come between him and his goal.

A strategic problem quite suddenly arose. Lord Keith *believed* that Minorca was in peril. Nelson *knew* that it was not. Lord Keith was wrong, and Nelson was right. What the occasion required was correctness of judgment; and for that Nelson was reprimanded. The Lords of the Admiralty pulled the mote from his eye, but failed to discern the beam in their own. Their decision to subordinate the greater man to the less was more reprehensible than an act of technical disobedience from the victor of the Nile.

But there is a third reason why the great admiral's conduct at Naples still meets with disapproval. When the present editor's *Life of Nelson* was published in 1912, it evoked in the outspoken pages of the *English Review* an article objecting to its treatment of Caracciolo. The article was entitled "Blind Guides," a term of reproach for those who dress in the garb of patriotism and lead their disciples into the ditch of error. Its argument may be epitomised not unfairly as follows.

The history of the nineteenth century contains no more glorious page than that which recounts the overthrow of the ancient kingdom of Naples. The Bourbon dynasty was the most corrupt in the world; its government was rendered abominable by every loathsome shape that lust, oppression, outrage and atrocity can assume. "The negation of God," Mr. Gladstone called it. So foul a thing should have earned the contempt of every free-born lover of justice. Yet what do we find? Not only is this unspeakable infamy restored and blessed by Nelson, but the British Admiral draws a noose round the neck of the saviour who would have wrought his people deliverance.

Such a line of reasoning serves at least to remind us how difficult it is in examining past ages to tear from one's eyes the veil of the age to which oneself belongs. Nelson died years before Englishmen learnt to pray for the regeneration of Italy. The need of his day was to stem the flood of Jacobinism; and in fighting for the cause of England's allies, he was fighting for the cause which England championed. To condemn Nelson for supporting King "Bomba's" predecessors is to condemn England and condemn ourselves.

A really great Italian like Savanarola, who brought his death upon himself by intermeddling with politics, earns sympathy, pity and admiration, because he had spent all his life in the bold denunciation of spiritual wickedness in high places. But no process of reasoning can make Caracciolo a martyr. If the King and Queen of Naples were wicked tyrants, he supported their despotism his whole life through, until the hour when their fortunes declined. In the days of sunshine he shared their prosperity, and when the dark clouds gathered he deserted them. He fired into the ships which carried the flag that had made him what he was; and, for a paltry handful of this world's goods, betrayed his master and killed his friends.

TIME TABLE

1798. 1st August. Battle of the Nile.
22nd September. Nelson arrives at Naples.
October. Minorca surrenders to Admiral Duckworth.
22nd November. Nelson sails against Leghorn, which surrenders on 28th.
21st–23rd December. Embarks the Neapolitan royal family and transfers them to Palermo.

1799.	April.	Admiral Bruix sails from Brest for the Mediterranean. Nelson promoted to be Rear-Admiral of the Red.
	8th June.	Transfers his flag from *Vanguard* to *Foudroyant*.
	15th June.	Lord Keith succeeds Earl St. Vincent in the Mediterranean command.
	21st June.	Nelson embarks Sir William and Lady Hamilton and proceeds to Naples.
	24th June.	Arrives in the Bay and cancels the flag of truce. Receives news of the "Capitulation."
	25th June.	Receives a visit from Cardinal Ruffo, and refuses to ratify the Capitulation.
	26th June.	Nelson agrees to observe the armistice; Cardinal Ruffo forwards Nelson's terms to Forts Uovo and Nuovo, which surrender unconditionally.
	30th June.	Caracciolo court-martialled and executed.
	10th July.	Ferdinand IV. restored to his throne.
	12th July.	The French in St. Elmo castle surrender.
	13th July.	Nelson summoned by Lord Keith to defend Corsica.
	31st July.	Capua and Gaeta surrender to Troubridge.
	31st August.	Nelson created Duke of Bronte by the King of Naples.
1800.	20th January.	Joins Lord Keith at Leghorn.
	18th February.	Captures *Le Généreux*.
	30th March.	*Foudroyant* captures *Guillaume Tell*.
	10th June.	Nelson sails for Leghorn with Queen of Naples and Sir William and Lady Hamilton.
	17th July.	Leaves Leghorn *en route* for Vienna.
	15th September.	Malta surrenders to Captain Ball.
	6th November.	Nelson lands at Yarmouth.
	10th November.	Attends the Lord Mayor's banquet and receives a presentation sword.
	20th November.	Takes his seat in the House of Peers.

[*SOUTHEY. CHAPTER VI*]

NELSON'S health had suffered greatly while he was in the *Agamemnon*. "My complaint," he said, "is as if a girth were buckled taut over my breast; and my endeavour in the night is to get it loose." After the battle of Cape St. Vincent he felt a little rest to be so essential to his recovery, that he declared he would not continue to serve longer than the ensuing summer, unless it should be absolutely necessary: for, in his own strong language, he had then

been four years and nine months without one moment's
repose for body or mind. A few months' intermission of
labour he had obtained—not of rest, for it was purchased
with the loss of a limb; and the greater part of the time had
been a season of constant pain. As soon as his shattered
frame had sufficiently recovered for him to resume his
duties, he was called to services of greater importance than
any on which he had hitherto been employed, and they
brought with them commensurate fatigue and care. The
anxiety which he endured during his long pursuit of the
enemy was rather changed in its direction, than abated by
their defeat; and this constant wakefulness of thought,
added to the effect of his wound, and the exertions from
which it was not possible for one of so ardent and wide-
reaching a mind to spare himself, nearly proved fatal. On
his way back to Italy he was seized with fever. For eighteen
hours his life was despaired of; and even when the disorder
took a favourable turn and he was so far recovered as again
to appear on deck, he himself thought that his end was
approaching—such was the weakness to which the fever
and cough had reduced him. Writing to Earl St. Vincent,
on the passage, he said to him, " I never expect, my dear
lord, to see your face again. It may please God that this
will be the finish to that fever of anxiety which I have
endured from the middle of June. But be that as it pleases
His goodness. I am resigned to His will."

The kindest attentions of the warmest friendship were
awaiting him at Naples. " Come here," said Sir William
Hamilton, " for God's sake, my dear friend, as soon as the
service will permit you. A pleasant apartment is ready
for you in my house, and Emma is looking out for the
softest pillows to repose the few wearied limbs you have
left." Happy would it have been for Nelson if warm and
careful friendship had been all that awaited him there! He
himself saw at that time the character of the Neapolitan
court, as it first struck an Englishman, in its true light;
and, when he was on the way, he declared that he detested
the voyage to Naples, and that nothing but necessity could
have forced him to it. But never was any hero, on his
return from victory, welcomed with more heartfelt joy.
Before the battle of Aboukir the court of Naples had been

trembling for its existence. The language which the Directory held towards it was well described by Sir William Hamilton, as being exactly the language of a highwayman. The Neapolitans were told that Benevento [1] might be added to their dominions, provided they would pay a large sum sufficient to satisfy the Directory; and they were warned, that if the proposal was refused or even if there were any delay in accepting it, the French would revolutionise all Italy. The joy, therefore, of the court at Nelson's success was in proportion to the dismay from which that success relieved them. The Queen was a daughter of Maria Theresa, and sister of Marie Antoinette. Had she been the wisest and gentlest of her sex, it would not have been possible for her to have regarded the French without hatred and horror; and the progress of revolutionary opinions, while it perpetually reminded her of her sister's fate, excited no unreasonable apprehensions for her own. Her feelings, naturally ardent, and little accustomed to restraint, were excited to the highest pitch when the news of the victory arrived. Lady Hamilton, her constant friend and favourite, who was present, says, " It is not possible to describe her transports. She wept, she kissed her husband, her children, walked frantically about the room, burst into tears again, and again kissed and embraced every person near her; exclaiming, ' O brave Nelson! O God! bless and protect our brave deliverer! O Nelson! Nelson! what do we not owe you! O conqueror—saviour of Italy! O that my swollen heart could now tell him personally what we owe to him.' " She herself wrote to the Neapolitan ambassador at London upon the occasion in terms which show the fulness of her joy and the height of the hopes which it had excited. " I wish I could give wings," said she, " to the bearer of the news, and, at the same time, to our most sincere gratitude. The whole of the sea-coast of Italy is saved; and this is owing alone to the generous English. This battle, or, to speak more correctly, this total defeat of the regicide squadron, was obtained by the valour of this brave admiral, seconded by a navy which is the terror of its enemies. The victory is so complete, that I can still scarcely believe it; and if it were not the brave English

[1] A small alien principality in the very heart of their possessions.

nation, which is accustomed to perform prodigies by sea, I could not persuade myself that it had happened. It would have moved you to have seen all my children, boys and girls, hanging on my neck, and crying for joy at the happy news. Recommend the hero to his master. He has filled the whole of Italy with admiration of the English. Great hopes were entertained of some advantages being gained by his bravery, but no one could look for so total a destruction. All here are drunk with joy."

Such being the feelings of the royal family, it may well be supposed with what delight, and with what honours, Nelson would be welcomed. Early on the 22nd of September, " the poor wretched *Vanguard*," as he called his shattered vessel,[1] appeared in sight of Naples. The *Culloden* and *Alexander* had preceded her by some days, and given notice of her approach. Many hundred boats and barges were ready to go forth and meet him, with music and streamers, and every demonstration of joy and triumph. Sir William and Lady Hamilton led the way in their state barge. They had seen Nelson only for a few days, four years ago, but they then perceived in him that heroic spirit which was now so fully and gloriously manifested to the world. Emma Lady Hamilton, who from this time so greatly influenced his future life, was a woman whose personal accomplishments have seldom been equalled, and whose powers of mind were not less fascinating than her person. She was passionately attached to the Queen: and by her influence the British fleet had obtained those supplies at Syracuse, without which, Nelson always asserted, the battle of Aboukir could not have been fought. During the long interval which passed before any tidings were received, her anxiety had been hardly less than that of Nelson himself, while pursuing an enemy of whom he could obtain no information: and when the tidings were brought her by a joyful bearer, open-mouthed, its effect was such that she fell like one who had been shot. She and Sir William had literally been made ill by their hopes and fears and joy at a catastrophe so far exceeding all that they had dared to hope for. Their admiration for the hero necessarily produced a degree of proportionate gratitude and affection; and

---

[1] Sir Harris Nicolas, *Dispatches and Letters of Lord Nelson*, Vol. III. p. 130.

when their barge came alongside the *Vanguard*, at the sight of Nelson, Lady Hamilton sprang up the ship's side, and exclaiming, " O God! is it possible! " fell into his arms, more, he says, like one dead than alive. He described the meeting as " terribly affecting." [1] These friends had scarcely recovered from their tears, when the King, who went out to meet him three leagues in the royal barge, came on board and took him by the hand, calling him his deliverer and preserver. From all the boats around he was saluted with the same appellations. The multitude who surrounded him when he landed repeated the same enthusiastic cries; and the lazzaroni [2] displayed their joy by holding up birds in cages, and giving them their liberty as he passed.

His birthday, which occurred a week after his arrival, was celebrated with one of the most splendid fêtes ever beheld at Naples. But, notwithstanding the splendour with which he was encircled, and the flattering honours with which all ranks welcomed him, Nelson was fully sensible of the depravity, as well as weakness, of those by whom he was surrounded. " What precious moments," said he, " the courts of Naples and Vienna are losing! Three months would liberate Italy! But this court is so enervated that the happy moment will be lost. I am very unwell; and their miserable conduct is not likely to cool my irritable temper. It is a country of fiddlers and poets, whores and scoundrels." This sense of their ruinous weakness he always retained; nor was he ever blind to the mingled folly and treachery of the Neapolitan ministers, and the complication of iniquities under which the country groaned. But he insensibly, under the influence of Lady Hamilton, formed an affection for the court, to whose misgovernment the miserable condition of the country was so greatly to be imputed. [By the kindness of her nature, as well as by her attractions, she had won his heart. Earl St. Vincent, writing to her at this time, says, " Ten thousand most grateful thanks are due to your ladyship for restoring the health of our invaluable friend Nelson, on whose life the fate of

[1] " Alongside came my honoured friends. The scene in the boat was terribly affecting. Up flew her ladyship, and exclaiming, ' O God, is it possible?' she fell into my *arm* more dead than alive."—*Dispatches and Letters*, Vol. III. p. 130. It will be noticed that Nelson uses the word " arm " in the singular. Southey for the moment had forgotten Teneriffe.

[2] Beggars.

the remaining governments in Europe, whose system has
not been deranged by these devils, depends. Pray do not
let your fascinating Neapolitan dames approach too near
him, for he is made of flesh and blood, and cannot resist
their temptations." But this was addressed to the very
person from whom he was in danger.] [1]

The state of Naples may be described in few words. The
King was one of the Spanish Bourbons. As the Cæsars
have shown us to what wickedness the moral nature of
princes may be perverted, so in this family the degradation to which their intellectual nature can be reduced has
been not less conspicuously evinced. Ferdinand,[2] like the
rest of his race, was passionately fond of field sports,[3] and
cared for nothing else. His queen had all the vices of the
house of Austria, with little to mitigate, and nothing to
ennoble them. Provided she could have her pleasures, and
the King his sports, they cared not in what manner the
revenue was raised or administered. Of course a system
of favouritism existed at court, and the vilest and most
impudent corruption prevailed in every department of
state, and in every branch of administration, from the
highest to the lowest. It is only the institutions of Christianity, and the vicinity of better regulated states, which

---

[1] The passage in brackets does not occur in the first, second, and third editions.

[2] Ferdinand IV., great-grandson of Philip V., first Bourbon King of Spain.

[3] Sir William Hamilton's letters give the history of one of this sovereign's
campaigns against the wolves and boars. " Our first *chase* has not succeeded. The
king would direct how we should beat the wood, and began at the wrong end,
by which the wolves and boars escaped. The king's face is very long at this
moment, but, I dare say, to-morrow's good sport will shorten it again."—" No
sport again! He has no other comfort to-day, than having killed a wild cat, and
his face is a yard long. However, his Majesty has vowed vengeance on the boars
to-morrow, and will go according to his own fancy; and I dare say there will be
a terrible slaughter."—" To-day has been so thoroughly bad that we have not
been able to stir out, and the king, of course, in bad humour."—" The king has
killed twenty-one boars to-day, and is quite happy."—" We have had a miserable
cold day, but good sport. I killed two boars and a doe; the king nineteen boars,
two stags, two does, and a porcupine. He is happy beyond expression."—" Only
think of his not being satisfied with killing more than thirty yesterday! He said
if the wind had favoured him, he should have killed sixty at least."—" The king
has killed eighty-one animals of one sort or other to-day, and amongst them a
wolf and some stags. He fell asleep in the coach: and waking, told me he had
been dreaming of shooting. One would have thought he had shed blood enough."
—" It is a long-faced day with the king. We went far: the weather was bad;
and, after all, met with little or no game. Yesterday, when we brought home
all we killed, it filled the house completely, and to-day they are obliged to white-
wash the walls to take away the blood. There were more than four hundred boars,
deer, stags and all. To-morrow we are to have another slaughter; and not a word
of reason or common sense do I meet with the whole day, till I retire to my volumes
of the old *Gentleman's Magazine*, which just keeps my mind from starving."
—Southey's Note, Fourth Edition.

O

prevent kingdoms, under such circumstances of misrule, from sinking into a barbarism like that of Turkey. A sense of better things was kept alive in some of the Neapolitans by literature, and by their intercourse with happier countries. These persons naturally looked to France at the commencement of the revolution, and, during all the horrors of that revolution, still cherished a hope, that by the aid of France they might be enabled to establish a new order of things in Naples. They were grievously mistaken in supposing that the principles of liberty would ever be supported by France, but they were not mistaken in believing that no government could be worse than their own; and, therefore, they considered any change as desirable. In this opinion men of the most different characters agreed. Many of the nobles, who were not in favour, wished for a revolution, that they might obtain the ascendancy to which they thought themselves entitled; men of desperate fortunes desired it in the hope of enriching themselves; knaves and intriguers sold themselves to the French, to promote it; and a few enlightened men and true lovers of their country joined in the same cause, from the purest and noblest motives. All these were confounded under the common name of Jacobins; and the Jacobins of the continental kingdoms were regarded by the English with more hatred than they deserved. They were classed with Philippe Egalité, Marat, and Hébert;—whereas they deserved rather to be ranked, if not with Locke, and Sidney, and Russell, at least with Argyle and Monmouth, and those who, having the same object as the prime movers of our own revolution, failed in their premature, but not unworthy attempt.

No circumstances could be more unfavourable to the best interests of Europe than those which placed England in strict alliance with the superannuated and abominable governments of the continent. The subjects of those governments who wished for freedom thus became enemies to England, and dupes and agents of France. They looked to their own grinding grievances, and did not see the danger with which the liberties of the world were threatened. England, on the other hand, saw the danger in its true magnitude, but was blind to these grievances, and found herself compelled to support systems which had formerly been equally the object of her abhorrence and her contempt. This was the state of Nelson's mind. He knew that there could be no peace for Europe till the pride of France was humbled, and her strength broken; and he regarded all those who were the friends of France as traitors to the common cause as well as to their own individual sovereigns. There are situations in which the most opposite and hostile parties may mean equally well, and yet act equally wrong. The court of Naples, unconscious of committing any crime by continuing the system of misrule to which they had succeeded, conceived that, in maintaining things as they were, they were maintaining their own rights, and preserving the people from such horrors as had been perpetrated in France. The Neapolitan revolutionists thought that, without a total change of system, any relief from the present evils was impossible, and they believed themselves justified in bringing about that change by any means. Both parties knew that it was the fixed intention of the French to revolutionise Naples. The revolutionists supposed that it was for the purpose of establishing a free government. The court, and all disinterested persons, were perfectly aware that the enemy had no other object than conquest and plunder.

The battle of the Nile shook the power of France. Her most successful general, and her finest army, were blocked up in Egypt—hopeless, as it appeared, of return; and the government was in the hands of men without talents, without character, and divided among themselves. Austria, whom Bonaparte had terrified into a peace,[1] at a time when constancy on her part would probably have led to his destruction, took advantage of the crisis to renew the war. Russia also was preparing to enter the field with unbroken forces; led by a general[2] whose extraordinary military genius would have entitled him to a high and honourable rank in history, if it had not been sullied by all the ferocity of a barbarian. Naples, seeing its destruction at hand, and thinking that the only means of averting it was by meeting the danger, after long vacillations, which were produced by the fears and weakness and treachery of its council, agreed at last to join this new coalition with a

---

[1] Campo Formio, 17th October, 1797. [2] Suvaroff.

numerical force of eighty thousand men. Nelson told the
King, in plain terms, that he had his choice: either to
advance, trusting to God for his blessing on a just cause,
and prepared to die sword in hand—or to remain quiet, and
be kicked out of his kingdom: one of these things must
happen. The King made answer, he would go on, and trust
in God and Nelson; and Nelson, who would else have
returned to Egypt for the purpose of destroying the French
shipping in Alexandria, gave up his intention at the desire
of the Neapolitan court, and resolved to remain on that
station, in the hope that he might be useful to the movements of the army. He suspected also, with reason, that
the continuance of his fleet was so earnestly requested because
the royal family thought their persons would be safer, in case
of any mishap, under the British flag than under their own.

His first object was the recovery of Malta; an island
which the King of Naples pretended to claim. The Maltese,
whom the villainous knights of their order had betrayed
to France, had taken up arms against their rapacious invaders with a spirit and unanimity worthy the highest
praise. They blockaded the French garrison by land, and
a small squadron, under Captain Ball, began to blockade
them by sea, on the 12th of October. Twelve days afterwards Nelson arrived. " It is as I suspected," he says;
" the ministers at Naples know nothing of the situation
of the island. Not a house or bastion of the town is in
possession of the islanders: and the Marquess de Niza tells
us they want arms, victuals, and support. He does not
know that any Neapolitan officers are in the island; perhaps,
although I have their names, none are arrived; and it is
very certain, by the marquess's account, that no supplies
have been sent by the governors of Syracuse or Messina."
The little island of Gozo, dependent upon Malta, which had
also been seized and garrisoned by the French, capitulated
soon after his arrival, and was taken possession of by the
British, in the name of his Sicilian Majesty,—a power
who had no better claim to it than France. Having seen
this effected, and reinforced Captain Ball, he left that
able officer to perform a most arduous and important
part, and returned himself to co-operate with the intended
movements of the Neapolitans.

General Mack was at the head of the Neapolitan troops. All that is now doubtful concerning this man is, whether he was a coward or a traitor. At that time he was assiduously extolled as a most consummate commander, to whom Europe might look for deliverance: and when he was introduced by the King and Queen to the British Admiral, the Queen said to him, " Be to us by land, General, what my hero Nelson has been by sea." Mack, on his part, did not fail to praise the force which he was appointed to command. " It was," he said, " the finest army in Europe." Nelson agreed with him that there could not be finer men: but when the General, at a review, so directed the operations of a mock fight, that, by an unhappy blunder, his own troops were surrounded instead of those of the enemy, he turned to his friends and exclaimed, with bitterness, that the fellow did not understand his business. Another circumstance, not less characteristic, confirmed Nelson in his judgment. " General Mack," said he, in one of his letters, " cannot move without five carriages! I have formed my opinion. I heartily pray I may be mistaken."

While Mack, at the head of thirty-two thousand men, marched into the Roman state, five thousand Neapolitans were embarked on board the British and Portuguese squadron, to take possession of Leghorn. This was effected without opposition; and the Grand Duke of Tuscany, whose neutrality had been so outrageously violated by the French,[1] was better satisfied with the measure than some of the Neapolitans themselves. Naselli, their general, refused to seize the French vessels at Leghorn, because he, and the Duke di Sangro who was ambassador at the Tuscan court, maintained that the King of Naples was not at war with France. " What!" said Nelson, " has not the King received, as a conquest made by him, the republican flag taken at Gozo? Is not his own flag flying there, and at Malta, not only by his permission, but by his order? Is not his flag shot at every day by the French, and their shot returned from batteries which bear that flag? Are not two frigates and a corvette placed under my orders ready to fight the French, meet them where they may? Has not the King sent publicly from Naples, guns, mortars, etc., with officers

[1] See above, p. 91.

and artillery, against the French in Malta? If these acts are not tantamount to any written paper, I give up all knowledge of what is war."

This reasoning was of less avail than argument [1] addressed to the General's fears. Nelson told him that if he permitted the many hundred French who were then in the mole to remain neutral till they had a fair opportunity of being active, they had one sure resource, if all other schemes failed, which was to set one vessel on fire; the mole would be destroyed, probably the town also; and the port ruined for twenty years. This representation made Naselli agree to the half measure of laying an embargo on the vessels. Among them were a great number of French privateers, some of which were of such force as to threaten the greatest mischief to our commerce, and about seventy sail of vessels belonging to the Ligurian republic (as Genoa was now called) laden with corn and ready to sail for Genoa and France, where their arrival would have expedited the entrance of more French troops into Italy.

"The General," said Nelson, "saw, I believe, the consequence of permitting these vessels to depart in the same light as myself. But there is this difference between us. He prudently, and certainly safely, waits the orders of his court, taking no responsibility upon himself. I act from the circumstances of the moment, as I feel may be most advantageous for the cause which I serve, taking all responsibility on myself."

It was in vain to hope for anything vigorous or manly from such men as Nelson was compelled to act with. The crews of the French ships and their allies were ordered to depart in two days. Four days elapsed, and nobody obeyed the order, nor, in spite of the representations of the British minister, Mr. Windham, were any means taken to enforce it. "The true Neapolitan shuffle," as Nelson called it, took place on all occasions. After an absence of ten days he returned to Naples; and receiving intelligence there from Mr. Windham that the privateers were at last to be disarmed, the corn landed, and the crews sent away, he expressed his satisfaction at the news in characteristic language, saying, "So far I am content. The enemy will be distressed;

[1] "An argument," first edition.

and, thank God, I shall get no money. The world, I know, think that money is our god; and now they will be undeceived as far as relates to us. Down, down with the French! is my constant prayer."

Odes, sonnets, and congratulatory poems of every description were poured in upon Nelson, on his arrival at Naples. An Irish Franciscan, who was one of the poets, not being content with panegyric upon this occasion, ventured upon a flight of prophecy, and predicted that Lord Nelson would take Rome with his ships. His lordship reminded Father M'Cormick that ships could not ascend the Tiber: but the father, who had probably forgotten this circumstance, met the objection with a bold front, and declared he saw that it would come to pass notwithstanding.

Rejoicings of this kind were of short duration. The King of Naples was with the army, which had entered Rome; but the castle of St. Angelo was held by the French, and thirteen thousand French were strongly posted in the Roman states at Castallana. Mack had marched against them with twenty thousand men. Nelson saw that the event was doubtful; or rather that there could be very little hope of the result. But the immediate fate of Naples, as he well knew, hung upon the issue. "If Mack is defeated," said he, "in fourteen days this country is lost. For the Emperor has not yet moved his army, and Naples has not the power of resisting the enemy. It was not a case of choice, but of necessity, which induced the King to march out of his kingdom, and not wait till the French had collected a force sufficient to drive him out of it in a week." He had no reliance upon the Neapolitan officers, who, as he described them, seemed frightened at a drawn sword or a loaded gun; and he was perfectly aware of the consequences which the sluggish movements and deceitful policy of the Austrians were likely to bring down upon themselves and all their continental allies.

"A delayed war on the part of the Emperor," said he, writing to the British minister at Vienna, "will be destructive to this monarchy of Naples; and, of course, to the newly-acquired dominions of the Emperor in Italy.[1] Had

[1] By the peace of Campo Formio Austria had received from Napoleon the possessions of Venice.

the war commenced in September or October, all Italy would, at this moment, have been liberated. This month [1] is worse than the last: the next will render the contest doubtful; and, in six months, when the Neapolitan republic will be organised, armed, and with its numerous resources called forth, the Emperor will not only be defeated in Italy, [2] but will totter on his throne at Vienna. " *Down, down with the French!* " ought to be written in the council-room of every country in the world: and may Almighty God give right thoughts to every sovereign, is my constant prayer! "

His perfect foresight of the immediate event was clearly shown in this letter, when he desired the Ambassador to assure the Empress (who was a daughter of the house of Naples) that, notwithstanding the councils which had shaken the throne of her father and mother, he would remain there, ready to save their persons, and her brothers and sisters; and that he had also left ships at Leghorn to save the lives of the Grand Duke and her sister. " For all," said he, "must be a republic, if the Emperor does not act with expedition and vigour."

His fears were soon verified. " The Neapolitan officers," said Nelson, " did not lose much honour, for, God knows, they had not much to lose. But they lost all they had." General St. Philip commanded the right wing of nineteen thousand men. He fell in with three thousand of the enemy; and, as soon as he came near enough, deserted to them. One of his men had virtue enough to level a musket at him, and shot him through the arm; but the wound was not sufficient to prevent him from joining with the French in pursuit of his own countrymen. Cannon, tents, baggage, and military chest, were all forsaken by the runaways, though they lost only forty men: for the French having put them to flight, and got possession of everything, did not pursue an army of more than three times their own number. The main body of the Neapolitans, under Mack, did not behave better. The King returned to Naples, where every day brought with it tidings of some new disgrace from the army, and the discovery of some new treachery at home; till, four days after his return, the General sent him advice

[1] December, 1798.
[2] What Nelson actually wrote was: " I will suffer to have my head cut off, if the Emperor is not only defeated in Italy, but," etc. (Nicolas, Vol. III. p. 194.)

that there was no prospect of stopping the progress of the enemy, and that the royal family must look to their own personal safety.

The state of the public mind at Naples was such, at this time, that neither the British minister, nor the British Admiral, thought it prudent to appear at court. Their motions were watched; and the revolutionists had even formed a plan for seizing and detaining them as hostages, to prevent any attack on the city after the French should have taken possession of it. A letter, which Nelson addressed at this time to the First Lord of the Admiralty, shows in what manner he contemplated the possible issue of the storm. It was in these words, " My dear lord, there is an old saying, that when things are at the worst they must mend. Now the mind of man cannot fancy things worse than they are here. But, thank God! my health is better, my mind never firmer, and my heart in the right trim to comfort, relieve, and protect those whom it is my duty to afford assistance to. Pray, my lord, assure our gracious sovereign, that while I live, I will support his glory; and that, if I fall, it shall be in a manner worthy of your lordship's faithful and obliged NELSON. I must not write more. Every word may be a text for a long letter."

Meantime Lady Hamilton arranged everything for the removal of the royal family. This was conducted, on her part, with the greatest address, and without suspicion, because she had been in habits of constant correspondence with the Queen. It was known that the removal could not be effected without danger; for the mob, and especially the lazzaroni, were attached to the King: and as, at this time, they felt a natural presumption in their own numbers and strength, they insisted that he should not leave Naples. Several persons fell victims to their fury. Among others was a messenger from Vienna, whose body was dragged under the windows of the palace in the King's sight. The King and Queen spoke to the mob, and pacified them; but it would not have been safe, while they were in this agitated state, to have embarked the effects of the royal family openly. Lady Hamilton, like a heroine of modern romance, explored, with no little danger, a subterraneous passage, leading from the palace to the seaside. Through this passage the royal treasure, the choicest pieces of painting and sculpture, and other property, to the amount of two millions and a half, were conveyed to the shore, and stowed safely on board the English ships. On the night of the 21st,[1] at half-past eight, Nelson landed, brought out the whole royal family, embarked them in three barges, and carried them safely, through a tremendous sea, to the *Vanguard*. Notice was then immediately given to the British merchants, that they should be received on board any ship in the squadron. Their property had previously been embarked in transports. Two days were passed in the bay, for the purpose of taking such persons on board as required an asylum; and, on the night of the 23rd, the fleet sailed. The next day a more violent storm arose than Nelson had ever before encountered. On the 25th the youngest of the princes was taken ill, and died in Lady Hamilton's arms. During this whole trying season Lady Hamilton waited upon the royal family with the zeal of the most devoted servant, at a time when, except one man, no person belonging to the court assisted them.

On the morning of the 26th the royal family were landed at Palermo. It was soon seen that their flight had not been premature. Prince Pignatelli, who had been left as Vicar-General and Viceroy, with orders to defend the kingdom to the last rock in Calabria, sent plenipotentiaries to the French camp before Capua; and they, for the sake of saving the capital, signed an armistice, by which the greater part of the kingdom was given up to the enemy: a cession that necessarily led to the loss of the whole. This was on the 10th of January. The French advanced towards Naples. Mack, under pretext of taking shelter from the fury of the lazzaroni, fled to the French general Championnet, who sent him under an escort to Milan; but, as France hoped for further services from this wretched traitor, it was thought prudent to treat him apparently as a prisoner of war. The Neapolitan army disappeared in a few days. Of the men, some following their officers, deserted to the enemy; the greater part took the opportunity of disbanding themselves. The lazzaroni proved true to their country. They attacked the enemy's advanced posts, drove them in, and were not

---

[1] 21st December, 1798.

dispirited by the murderous defeat which they suffered from the main body. Flying into the city, they continued to defend it, even after the French had planted their artillery in the principal streets. Had there been a man of genius to have directed their enthusiasm, or had there been any correspondent feelings in the higher ranks, Naples might have set a glorious example to Europe, and have proved the grave of every Frenchman who entered it.

But the vices of the government had extinguished all other patriotism than that of a rabble, who had no other virtue than that sort of loyalty which was like the fidelity of a dog to its master. This fidelity the French and their adherents counteracted by another kind of devotion. The priests affirmed that St. Januarius had declared in favour of the revolution.[1] The miracle of his blood was performed with the usual success and more than usual effect, on the very evening when, after two days of desperate fighting, the French obtained possession of Naples. A French guard of honour was stationed at his church. Championnet gave " Respect for St. Januarius! " as the word for the army; and the next day *Te Deum* was sung by the archbishop in the cathedral; and the inhabitants were invited to attend the ceremony, and join in thanksgiving for the glorious entry of the French; who, it was said, being under the peculiar protection of Providence, had regenerated the Neapolitans, and were come to establish and consolidate their happiness.

It seems to have been Nelson's opinion that the Austrian cabinet regarded the conquest of Naples with complacency, and that its measures were directed so as designedly not to prevent the French from overrunning it. That cabinet was assuredly capable of any folly and of any baseness; and it is not improbable that, at this time, calculating upon the success of the new coalition,[2] it indulged in a dream of adding extensively to its former Italian possessions, and therefore left the few remaining powers of Italy to be overthrown, as a means which would facilitate its own ambitious views.

[1] The blood of St. Januarius, patron saint of Naples, preserved in phials, was held by the Neapolitans in great veneration. In critical moments it was consulted like the Delphic oracle; and, if found to have passed from a solid to a liquid state, was accepted as a portent fraught with tremendous consequence.
[2] The " Second Coalition " against France, formed at the beginning of 1799, comprised Great Britain, Austria, Russia, Turkey and Portugal.

The King of Sardinia, finding it impossible longer to endure the exactions of France and the insults of the French commissary, went to Leghorn, embarked on board a Danish frigate, and sailed under British protection to Sardinia, that part of his dominions which the maritime supremacy of England rendered a secure asylum. On his arrival he published a protest against the conduct of France, declaring upon the faith and word of a king that he had never infringed, even in the slightest degree, the treaties which he had made with the French Republic. Tuscany was soon occupied by French troops, a fate which bolder policy might, perhaps, have failed to avert, but which its weak and timid neutrality rendered inevitable. Nelson began to fear even for Sicily. " Oh, my dear sir," said he, writing to Commodore Duckworth, " one thousand English troops would save Messina, and I fear General Stuart cannot give me men to save this most important island!" But his representations were not lost upon Sir Charles Stuart. This officer hastened immediately from Minorca with a thousand men, assisted in the measures of defence which were taken, and did not return before he had satisfied himself that, if the Neapolitans were excluded from the management of affairs and the spirit of the peasantry properly directed, Sicily was safe. Before his coming, Nelson had offered the King, if no resources should arrive, to defend Messina with the ship's company of an English man-of-war.

Russia had now entered into the war. Corfu surrendered to a Russian and Turkish fleet, acting now, for the first time, in strange confederacy; yet against a power which was certainly the common and worst enemy of both. Troubridge having given up the blockade of Alexandria to Sir Sidney Smith, joined Nelson, bringing with him a considerable addition of strength; and in himself, what Nelson valued more, a man, upon whose sagacity, indefatigable zeal, and inexhaustible resources, he could place full reliance. Troubridge was entrusted to commence the operations against the French in the Bay of Naples.

Meantime Cardinal Ruffo, a man of questionable character but of a temper fitted for such times, having landed in Calabria, raised what he called a Christian army, composed of the best and the vilest materials: loyal peasants, enthusiastic priests and friars, galley slaves, the emptying of the jails, and banditti. The islands in the Bay of Naples were joyfully delivered up by the inhabitants, who were in a state of famine already from the effect of this baleful revolution. Troubridge distributed among them all his flour; and Nelson pressed the Sicilian court incessantly for supplies; telling them, that £10,000 given away in provisions would, at this time, purchase a kingdom. Money, he was told, they had not to give; and the wisdom and integrity which might have supplied its want were not to be found. " There is nothing," said he, " which I propose, that is not, as far as orders go, implicitly complied with; but the execution is dreadful, and almost makes me mad. My desire to serve their Majesties faithfully, as is my duty, has been such that I am almost blind and worn out; and cannot, in my present state, hold much longer."

Before any government can be overthrown by the consent of the people, the government must be intolerably oppressive, or the people thoroughly corrupted. Bad as the misrule at Naples had been, its consequences had been felt far less there than in Sicily; and the peasantry had that attachment to the soil which gives birth to so many of the noblest as well as of the happiest feelings. In all the islands the people were perfectly frantic with joy when they saw the Neapolitan colours hoisted. At Procida, Troubridge could not procure even a rag of the tricoloured flag to lay at the King's feet. It was rent into ten thousand pieces by the inhabitants and entirely destroyed. " The horrid treatment of the French," he said, " had made them mad." It exasperated the ferocity of a character which neither the laws nor the religion under which they lived tended to mitigate. Their hatred was especially directed against the Neapolitan revolutionists; and the fishermen, in concert among themselves, chose each his own victim, whom he would stiletto when the day of vengeance should arrive. The head of one was sent off one morning to Troubridge, with his basket of grapes for breakfast; and a note from the Italian who had, what he called, the glory of presenting it, saying, he had killed the man as he was running away, and begging his Excellency to accept the head, and consider it as a proof of the writer's attachment to the crown.

With the first successes of the court, the work of punishment began. The judge at Ischia said it was necessary to have a bishop to degrade the traitorous priests before he could execute them: upon which Troubridge advised him to hang them first, and send them to him afterwards, if he did not think that degradation sufficient. This was said with the straightforward feeling of a sailor, who cared as little for canon-law as he knew about it: but when he discovered that the judge's orders were to go through the business in a summary manner, under his sanction, he told him at once, that could not be, for the prisoners were not British subjects; and he declined having anything to do with it. There were manifestly persons about the court, who, while they thirsted for the pleasure of vengeance, were devising how to throw the odium of it upon the English. They wanted to employ an English man-of-war to carry the priests to Palermo for degradation, and then bring them back for execution; and they applied to Troubridge for a hangman, which he indignantly refused. He, meantime, was almost heart-broken by the situation in which he found himself. He had promised relief to the islanders, relying upon the Queen's promise to him. He had distributed the whole of his private stock. There was plenty of grain at Palermo and in its neighbourhood, and yet none was sent to him. The enemy, he complained, had more interest there than the King; and the distress for bread, which he witnessed, was such, he said, that it would move even a Frenchman to pity.

Nelson's [heart, too, was at this time ashore. "To tell you," he says, writing to Lady Hamilton, "how dreary and uncomfortable the *Vanguard* appears, is only telling you what it is to go from the pleasantest society to a solitary cell; or from the dearest friends to no friends. I am now perfectly the *great man*,—not a creature near me. From my heart I wish myself the little man again. You and good Sir William have spoiled me for any place but with you."

His] [1] mind was not in a happier state respecting public affairs. "As to politics," said he, "at this time they are my abomination. The ministers of kings and princes are

---

[1] The passage within brackets does not occur in the first edition.

as great scoundrels as ever lived. The brother of the Emperor is just going to marry the great Something of Russia,[1] and it is more than expected that a kingdom is to be found for him in Italy, and that the King of Naples will be sacrificed." Had there been a wise and manly spirit in the Italian states, or had the conduct of Austria been directed by anything like a principle of honour, a more favourable opportunity could not have been desired for restoring order and prosperity in Europe than the misconduct of the French Directory at this time afforded. But Nelson perceived selfishness and knavery wherever he looked; and even the pleasure of seeing a cause prosper, in which he was so zealously engaged, was poisoned by his sense of the rascality of those with whom he was compelled to act.

At this juncture intelligence arrived that the French fleet had escaped from Brest, under cover of a fog, passed Cadiz unseen by Lord Keith's squadron, in hazy weather, and entered the Mediterranean. It was said to consist of twenty-four sail of the line, six frigates, and three sloops. The object of the French was to liberate the Spanish fleet, form a junction with them, act against Minorca[2] and Sicily, and overpower our naval force in the Mediterranean, by falling in with detached squadrons, and thus destroying it in detail. When they arrived off Carthagena, they requested the Spanish ships to make sail and join; but the Spaniards replied, they had not men to man them. To this it was answered, that the French had men enough on board for that purpose. But the Spaniards seem to have been apprehensive of delivering up their ships thus entirely into the power of such allies, and refused to come out. The fleet from Cadiz, however, consisting of from seventeen to twenty sail of the line, got out, under Masaredo, a man who then bore an honourable name, which he has since rendered infamous by betraying his country.[3] They met with a violent storm off the coast of Oran, which dismasted many of their ships, and so effectually disabled them

---

[1] Joseph, brother of Francis II., in October 1799 married Alexandra, daughter of Czar Paul.

[2] Minorca had surrendered to Duckworth in October 1798. See Table of Events, p. 159.

[3] Southey calls Masaredo a traitor because in 1808, when the Spaniards were rising against their oppressors, he accepted the office of Minister of Marine under Joseph Bonaparte.

as to prevent the junction, and frustrate a well-planned expedition.[1]

Before this occurred, and while the junction was as probable as it would have been formidable, Nelson was in a state of the greatest anxiety. " What a state am I in! " said he to Earl St. Vincent. " If I go, I risk, and more than risk, Sicily; for we know, from experience, that more depends upon opinion than upon acts themselves; and as I stay, my heart is breaking." His first business was to summon Troubridge to join him with all the ships of the line under his command, and a frigate, if possible. Then hearing that the French had entered the Mediterranean, and expecting them at Palermo, where he had only his own ship;—with that single ship he prepared to make all the resistance possible. Troubridge having joined him, he left Captain E. J. Foote, of the *Seahorse*, to command the smaller vessels in the Bay of Naples, and sailed with six ships; one a Portuguese, and a Portuguese corvette; telling Earl St. Vincent that the squadron should never fall into the hands of the enemy. " And before we are destroyed," said he, " I have little doubt but they will have their wings so completely clipped, that they may be easily overtaken."

It was just at this time that he received from Captain Hallowell the present of the coffin. Such a present was regarded by the men with natural astonishment. One of his old shipmates in the *Agamemnon* said, " We shall have hot work of it indeed! You see the Admiral intends to fight till he is killed: and there he is to be buried." Nelson placed it upright against the bulkhead of his cabin, behind his chair, where he sat at dinner. The gift suited him at this time. It is said that he was disappointed in the son-in-law whom he had loved so dearly from his childhood, and who had saved his life at Teneriffe: [2] and it is certain that he had now formed an infatuated attachment for Lady Hamilton, which totally weaned his affections from his wife.[3] Further than this, there is no reason to believe that this most unfortunate attachment was criminal: but this was crim-

[1] Southey's account of Bruix's abortive cruise is incorrect in details, and gives the reader the impression that its movements were well known at a time when they were puzzling both friends and foes.

[2] See Nelson's letter to Earl St. Vincent of 5th June, 1799 (*Dispatches and Letters*, Vol. III. p. 375).

[3] Not until his return to England in the following year. See below, p. 259.

inality enough, and it brought with it its punishment. Nelson was dissatisfied with himself; and, therefore, weary of the world. This feeling he now frequently expressed. " There is no true happiness in this life," said he, " and in my present state I could quit it with a smile." And in a letter to his old friend Davison he said, " Believe me, my only wish is to sink with honour into the grave; and when that shall please God, I shall meet death with a smile. Not that I am insensible to the honours and riches my king and country have heaped upon me,—so much more than any officer could deserve. Yet am I ready to quit this world of trouble, and envy none but those of the estate six feet by two."

  Well had it been for Nelson if he had made no other sacrifices to this unhappy attachment than his peace of mind; but it led to the only blot upon his public character.[1] While he sailed from Palermo, with the intention of collecting his whole force, and keeping off Maritimo,[2] either to receive reinforcements there, if the French were bound upwards, or to hasten to Minorca, if that should be their destination, Captain Foote, in the *Seahorse*, with the Neapolitan frigates and some small vessels under his command, was left to act with a land force consisting of a few regular troops, of four different nations, and with the armed rabble which Cardinal Ruffo called the Christian Army. His directions were to co-operate to the utmost of his power with the royalists, at whose head Ruffo had been placed, and he had no other instructions whatever. Ruffo advancing, without any plan, but relying upon the enemy's want of numbers (which prevented them from attempting to act upon the offensive) and ready to take advantage of any accident which might occur, approached Naples. Fort St. Elmo, which commands the town, was wholly garrisoned by the French troops; the castles of Uovo and Nuovo, which commanded the anchorage, were chiefly defended by Neapolitan revolutionists, the powerful men among them having taken shelter there. If these castles were taken, the reduction of Fort St. Elmo would be greatly expedited. They were strong places, and there was reason to apprehend that the French fleet might arrive to relieve them. Ruffo

  [1] For this unfair and mischievous imputation there remains not so much as a shred of evidence.
  [2] See above, map, p. 52.

  P

proposed to the garrison to capitulate, on condition that their persons and property should be guaranteed, and that they should, at their own option, either be sent to Toulon, or remain at Naples, without being molested either in their persons or families. This capitulation was accepted. It was signed by the Cardinal, and the Russian and Turkish commanders; and, lastly, by Captain Foote, as commander of the British force. About six-and-thirty hours afterwards, Nelson arrived in the bay, with a force which had joined him during his cruise, consisting of seventeen sail of the line, with seventeen hundred troops on board, and the Prince Royal of Naples in the Admiral's ship. A flag of truce was flying on the castles, and on board the *Seahorse.* Nelson made a signal to annul the treaty;[1] declaring that he would grant rebels no other terms than those of unconditional submission.[2] The Cardinal objected to this: nor could all the arguments of Nelson, Sir W. Hamilton, and Lady Hamilton, who took an active part in the conference,[3] convince him that a treaty of such a nature, solemnly concluded, could honourably be set aside.[4] He retired at last, silenced by Nelson's authority,[5] but not convinced.

[1] Nelson did nothing of the kind. The flag of truce informed him that his own side had agreed to a cessation of hostilities, and he signalled the customary intimation that he intended in due course " to break the armistice."
For further details, see Introduction to this chapter.
[2] When he had been informed by Foote how matters stood, Nelson insisted that Ruffo's unauthorised capitulation must be confirmed by the sovereign before it was put into effect. The insurgents had still the option of seeking confirmation or of resuming hostilities. Neither alternative afforded them, however, the smallest measure of hope. It was wholly improbable that the king would confirm the treaty; and they were little likely to succeed in battle against Nelson when they had failed against Cardinal Ruffo. Ashore there awaited them a hideous fate at the hands of their murderous compatriots. Oversea at Palermo the treatment accorded them might possibly be kinder. All they could obtain from Nelson was the curt advice to submit to their rightful king; and bowing to his demand for " unconditional surrender " they accepted a temporary asylum in his ships.
[3] The negotiations at Naples required an intimate knowledge of Italian, idiomatic and vernacular. Nelson had no acquaintance with the language himself; and gratefully accepted the assistance of Sir William and Lady Hamilton, who relieved one another in the arduous duties of interpreter and scribe.
[4] It should be noticed that in this sentence Southey supports a wily Italian of whose character he knew absolutely nothing in preference to England's representative, who in every public transaction of his life showed himself the very soul of honour.
[5] He was not silenced. When Nelson found that he was no match for the cardinal in conversation, he excused himself from further talk and put his own " opinion " in writing as follows: " Rear-Admiral Lord Nelson arrived with the British fleet, the 24th of June, in the Bay of Naples, and found a treaty entered into with the rebels which, in his opinion, cannot be carried into execution without the approbation of his Sicilian Majesty. *Foudroyant,* 26th of June, 1799." (*Dispatches and Letters,* Vol. III. p. 388.)

Captain Foote was sent out of the bay ;[1] and the garrisons, taken out of the castles under pretence of carrying the treaty into effect, were delivered over as rebels to the vengeance of the Sicilian court.—A deplorable transaction![2] A stain upon the memory of Nelson, and the honour of England! To palliate it would be in vain; to justify it would be wicked; there is no alternative, for one who will not make himself a participator in guilt, but to record the disgraceful story [3] with sorrow and with shame.

Prince Francesco Caraccioli,[4] a younger branch of one of the noblest Neapolitan families, escaped from one of these castles before it capitulated. He was at the head of the marine, and was nearly seventy years of age, bearing a high character both for professional and personal merit.

---

[1] Foote, being in command of Nelson's fastest frigate, was sent to Palermo with dispatches. Southey's insinuation is unworthy of his theme.

[2] Southey here accuses Nelson of Machiavellian devilry, utterly oblivious to the fact that such an accusation directly contradicts his previous statement that the Admiral insisted on " unconditional surrender." The insurgents were addressed from the *Foudroyant* as follows:

" 25th June, 1799.

" Rear-Admiral Lord Nelson, K.B., commander of his Britannic Majesty's fleet in the Bay of Naples, acquaints the rebellious subjects of his Sicilian Majesty in the castles of Uovo and Nuovo that he will not permit them to embark or quit those places. They must surrender themselves to his Majesty's royal mercy." (*Dispatches and Letters*, Vol. III. p. 386.)

In the face of this document and the " opinion " delivered in writing to Ruffo, how vile it is to say that Nelson cheated the insurgents out of sanctuary by a dishonest pretence of carrying the capitulation into effect!

On Southey's part truly a " deplorable transaction "!

[3] In one of his letters to Lady Hamilton, written a few months before this fatal transaction, Nelson says, speaking of the Queen, " I declare to God, my whole study is how best to meet her approbation."—SOUTHEY'S NOTE, Fourth Edition.

This note is of deep interest as illustrating Southey's bias in all that concerns the relations of Nelson and Lady Hamilton. He insinuates that the Admiral, forgetting what the honour of England demanded, enslaved himself first to a beautiful woman and then at her bidding obsequiously put himself at the disposal of the Queen of Naples. " A few months before," Southey carelessly remarks. What are the actual dates?

Nelson returned to Naples from the Battle of the Nile at the end of September 1798. After a rest he set out in October to put things in train for the conquest of Malta, and it was while he was reconnoitring the island that he wrote to Lady Hamilton the words here quoted (24th October, 1798). Not only were they uttered eight solid months before the events with which Southey groups them, but they were uttered before Nelson had fallen under the spell of Lady Hamilton's charm.

The letter in question, which is too long to quote in full, sets forth the Admiral's excuses for not leaving his post and coming to Naples (where the royal family then were), and gives his reasons for thinking that the British fleet, if centrally placed, would serve most efficaciously the purposes of the Queen as well as the interests of the rest of Europe (Nicolas, Vol. III. pp. 154–5).

In twisting a single sentence out of its context to lend substance to his insinuations, Southey is not merely tampering with, but deliberately falsifying the evidence.

[4] His name was Caracciolo.

He had accompanied the court to Sicily; but when the revolutionary government, or Parthenopæan Republic as it was called, issued an edict, ordering all absent Neapolitans to return on pain of confiscation of their property, he solicited and obtained permission of the King to return, his estates being very great. It is said that the King, when he granted him this permission, warned him not to take any part in politics; expressing at the same time his own persuasion that he should recover his kingdom. But neither the King, nor he himself, ought to have imagined that, in such times, a man of such reputation would be permitted to remain inactive; and it soon appeared that Caraccioli was again in command of the navy, and serving under the republic against his late sovereign. The sailors reported that he was forced to act thus: and this was believed, till it was seen that he directed ably the offensive operations of the revolutionists, and did not avail himself of opportunities for escaping when they offered. When the recovery of Naples was evidently near, he applied to Cardinal Ruffo, and to the Duke of Calvirrano, for protection; expressing his hope that the few days during which he had been forced to obey the French would not outweigh forty years of faithful services. But, perhaps not receiving such assurances as he wished, and knowing too well the temper of the Sicilian court, he endeavoured to secrete himself, and a price was set upon his head. More unfortunately for others than for himself, he was brought in alive, having been discovered in the disguise of a peasant, and carried one morning on board Lord Nelson's ship, with his hands tied behind him.

Caraccioli was well known to the British officers, and had been ever highly esteemed by all who knew him. Captain Hardy ordered him immediately to be unbound, and to be treated with all those attentions which he felt due to a man who, when last on board the *Foudroyant*,[1] had been received as an admiral and a prince. Sir William and Lady Hamilton were in the ship; but Nelson, it is affirmed, saw no one except his own officers during the

[1] The *Foudroyant*, which was brought out to reinforce Nelson, did not join his flag until 6th June. By that time Caracciolo had deserted Palermo and gone over to the enemy. The prisoner cannot possibly, therefore, have been on board the ship before.

tragedy which ensued.[1] His own determination was made; and he issued an order to the Neapolitan commodore, Count Thurn, to assemble a court martial of Neapolitan officers, on board the British flagship, proceed immediately to try the prisoner, and report to him, if the charges were proved, what punishment he ought to suffer. These proceedings were as rapid as possible. Caraccioli was brought on board at nine in the forenoon, and the trial begun at ten. It lasted two hours. He averred in his defence that he had acted under compulsion, having been compelled to serve as a common soldier, till he consented to take command of the fleet. This, the apologists of Lord Nelson say, he failed in proving. They forget that the possibility of proving it was not allowed him; for he was brought to trial within an hour after he was legally in arrest; and how, in that time, was he to collect his witnesses? [2] He was found guilty, and sentenced to death; and Nelson gave orders that the sentence should be carried into effect that evening, at five o'clock, on board the Sicilian frigate, *La Minerva*, by hanging him at the fore yard-arm till sunset; when the body was to be cut down and thrown into the sea.[3] Caraccioli requested Lieutenant Parkinson, under whose custody he was placed, to intercede with Lord Nelson for a second trial,—for this, among other reasons, that Count Thurn,

[1] As Nelson saw no one except his own officers from the time that Caracciolo came on board until the hour of the execution, how wilful of Southey to drag in by the hair the person of Lady Hamilton! She was carried by the *Foudroyant* in an official capacity, and could hardly be dropped overboard, as Jonah was, simply because a Neapolitan prisoner was being tried.

Southey, it must be remembered, was attempting to persuade his readers that Nelson and Lady Hamilton were re-enacting on a ship's deck the tragedy of Antipas and Herod Philip's wife.

[2] Southey is judging the case by what he knew of legal procedure before civilian tribunals. In a naval court-martial there was no reason why the inquiry (for such it was) should be postponed or delayed. The prisoner could call for what papers or witnesses he required, and the court (open to the public) was bound to produce them. Proceedings continued so long as examiners or examinee had anything left to say. Professional men bred to the law are copious in their talk, if not actually long-winded; professional men bred to the sea are exactly the reverse. The salient points of the case were already well known; and it did not take the court very long to adjudicate on Caracciolo's plea that he had acted under compulsion.

[3] By describing the nature of Caracciolo's punishment immediately after the words " Nelson gave orders," Southey helps his reader to forget that the sentence was passed by the Neapolitan court-martial; and makes it appear that the severity of the award was due to the English Admiral. For Southey's version read: " He was found guilty, and sentenced to be hanged at the fore yard-arm of the Sicilian frigate *La Minerva*. Nelson gave orders that the sentence should be carried into effect at five o'clock that evening, and that at sunset the body should be cut down and thrown into the sea."

who presided at the court martial, was notoriously his personal enemy.[1] Nelson made answer, that the prisoner had been fairly tried by the officers of his own country, and he could not interfere: forgetting that, if he felt himself justified in ordering the trial and the execution, no human being could ever have questioned the propriety of his interfering on the side of mercy.[2] Caraccioli then entreated that he might be shot. " I am an old man, sir," said he. " I leave no family to lament me, and therefore cannot be supposed to be very anxious about prolonging my life. But the disgrace of being hanged is dreadful to me." When this was repeated to Nelson, he only told the lieutenant, with much agitation, to go and attend his duty.[3] As a last hope, Caraccioli asked the lieutenant if he thought an application to Lady Hamilton would be beneficial? Parkinson went to seek her. She was not to be seen on this occasion. But she was present at the execution. She had the most devoted attachment to the Neapolitan court; and the hatred which she felt against those whom she regarded as its enemies made her at this time forget what was due to the character of her sex as well as of her country.[4]

Here also, a faithful historian is called upon to pronounce a severe and unqualified condemnation of Nelson's conduct. Had he the authority of his Sicilian Majesty for proceeding

[1] It was customary in naval courts martial for the captain of the ship in which the crime was committed to preside at the trial, unless he was deemed of rank too exalted for the status of the prisoner or was required to give evidence before the court. The prisoner was entitled to challenge the suitability of any of his judges, but the eventual decision lay with the bench, whose general sense of fair play went from generation to generation unimpugned. Caracciolo, through the weakness of his human nature, was snatching at any straw that might prolong his earthly life.

[2] The sweet reasonableness of this sentiment is dispelled when we remember that, as Commander-in-Chief of the British and Neapolitan fleets, Nelson was obliged to summon a court martial, and see that its judgment was carried into effect, but was forbidden to interfere with a death-sentence unless it was accompanied by a recommendation to mercy.

[3] Here again it must be remembered that hanging was the prescribed punishment for the crimes of which Caracciolo had been found guilty. There was no precedent for departing from the customary code; no reason or excuse for tampering with it.

[4] These vile insinuations are absolutely groundless. Lady Hamilton had no part or lot in the apprehension, trial, or judgment of Caracciolo. She was a passenger in the Foudroyant, but (as Southey admits) remained inaccessible while proceedings lasted. Caracciolo was conveyed to La Minerva for execution; and there is neither jot nor tittle of evidence to suggest that Lady Hamilton witnessed his death. Even by those who disliked her, and they were very few, she was admitted to be tender-hearted to a fault; and if there is any crime in supporting enthusiastically the cause of England's allies, it had not been discovered by English hearts in 1799.

as he did? If so, why was not that authority produced?
If not, why were the proceedings hurried on without it?
Why was the trial precipitated, so that it was impossible
for the prisoner, if he had been innocent, to provide the
witnesses who might have proved him so? Why was a
second trial refused, when the known animosity of the
president of the court against the prisoner was considered?
Why was the execution hastened, so as to preclude any
appeal for mercy, and render the prerogative of mercy
useless?—Doubtless, the British Admiral seemed to himself
to be acting under a rigid sense of justice; but, to all other
persons, it was obvious that he was influenced by an infatuated attachment [1]—a baneful passion which destroyed
his domestic happiness, and now, in a second instance,[2]
stained ineffaceably his public character.[3]

The body was carried out to a considerable distance, and

[1] The sting of all this rhetorical questioning resides in its tail. Nelson (so runs
Southey's argument) was in love with Lady Hamilton; and therefore *presumably*
allowed all his actions to be governed by her whim. The affection of the pair
was a guilty affection; and therefore *presumably* all that sprang from it must
have been culpable. Lady Hamilton was a passenger on board the *Foudroyant*,
and therefore Caracciolo was wrongfully executed.

It seems strange that anyone should ever have been misled by such puerile
reasoning.

[2] The first was his insistence that the rebel forts should make unconditional
surrender.

[3] It has already been stated (above, p. xxii.) that McArthur, one of the joint
authors whom Southey as a rule followed so closely, was himself the most eminent
living authority on naval court martial procedure. All that McArthur says on the
subject of Caracciolo's trial and execution should, therefore, be most carefully
weighed by the fair-minded (Vol. II. pp. 184-7). A few sentences will serve to show
how widely Southey parted from his guide. " During the trial, which lasted from
ten o'clock to twelve, the Ward Room of the *Foudroyant* was open, as is customary,
to everyone who chose to enter. Some account of what passed has therefore been
preserved. Everything appeared to be fairly and honourably conducted to such
of the English officers who understood Italian. Caraccioli was repeatedly asked
questions best calculated to clear those aspersions that had been attached to his
character. . . .

" Caraccioli in vain attempted to prove his innocence. His answers were vague
and supported by no evidence whatever—the last efforts of a man striving to save
his life. The court was then cleared, and sentence of death passed on the prisoner.
On its being transmitted by the president to Lord Nelson, his lordship immediately
issued the following order for its being carried into execution on the same
evening. . . .

" It has been objected to the fairness of the whole proceedings against Caraccioli,
and to the justice of Lord Nelson in sanctioning their execution, that Count Thurn
(who presided at the trial) was an inveterate enemy of the Sicilian commodore,
and was not generally considered as possessing sufficient magnanimity to cause
his private feelings to give way to public duty. But if it could be made to appear
that Lord Nelson was aware of the private and secret politics of the Sicilian Navy,
they who urge this objection should recollect that he, who was incapable of possessing the feelings imputed to Count Thurn, would be the last man to suspect
another, particularly a loyal officer, of dishonourable conduct in the discharge
of public duty, and that he had sent Caraccioli to the only competent tribunal
to which he could be committed.'

sunk in the bay, with three double-headed shot, weighing two hundred and fifty pounds,[1] tied to its legs. Between two and three weeks afterwards, when the King was on board the *Foudroyant*, a Neapolitan fisherman came to the ship, and solemnly declared that Caraccioli had risen from the bottom of the sea, and was coming, as fast as he could, to Naples, swimming half out of the water. Such an account was listened to like a tale of idle credulity. The day being fair, Nelson, to please the King, stood out to sea; but the ship had not proceeded far before a body was distinctly seen, upright in the water, and approaching them. It was soon recognised to be, indeed, the corpse of Caraccioli, which had risen, and floated, while the great weights attached to the legs kept the body in position like that of a living man. A fact so extraordinary astonished the King, and perhaps excited some feeling of superstitious fear, akin to regret. He gave permission for the body to be taken on shore, and receive Christian burial. It produced no better effect. Naples exhibited more dreadful scenes than it had witnessed in the days of Masaniello.[2] After the mob had had their fill of blood and plunder, the reins were given to justice—if that can be called justice which annuls its own stipulations, looks to the naked facts alone, disregarding all motives and all circumstances; and without considering character, or science, or sex, or youth, sacrifices its victims, not for the public weal, but for the gratification of greedy vengeance.

The castles of St. Elmo, Gaeta, and Capua, remained to be subdued. On the land side there was no danger that the French in these garrisons should be relieved, for Suvarof was now beginning to drive the enemy before him. But Nelson thought his presence necessary in the Bay of Naples: and when Lord Keith, having received intelligence that the French and Spanish fleets had formed a junction and sailed for Carthagena, ordered him to repair to Minorca with the whole or the greater part of his force, he sent Admiral Duckworth with a small part only. This was a dilemma which he had foreseen. " Should such an order come at

---

[1] " One hundred and fifty pounds."—CLARKE AND McARTHUR.
[2] Leader of a famous Neapolitan uprising, which took place in the year 1647, and was marked by scenes of appalling bloodshed and ferocity.

this moment," he said in a letter previously written to the
Admiralty, " it would be a case for some consideration,
whether Minorca is to be risked, or the two kingdoms of
Naples and Sicily. I rather think my decision would be
to risk the former." And, after he had acted upon this
opinion, he wrote in these terms to the Duke of Clarence,
with whose high notions of obedience he was well acquainted,
" I am well aware of the consequences of disobeying my
orders; but as I have often before risked my life for the
good cause, so I, with cheerfulness, did my commission:
for, although a military tribunal may think me criminal,
the world will approve of my conduct. And I regard not my
own safety, when the honour of my King is at stake."

Nelson was right in his judgment. No attempt was made
upon Minorca: and the expulsion of the French from
Naples may rather be said to have been effected, than
accelerated, by the English and Portuguese of the allied
fleet, acting upon shore, under Troubridge. The French
commandant at St. Elmo, relying upon the strength of the
place and the nature of the force which attacked it, had
insulted Captain Foote in the grossest terms; but *citoyen*
Méjean was soon taught better manners, when Troubridge,
in spite of every obstacle, opened five batteries upon the
fort. He was informed, that none of his letters, with the
insolent printed words at the top, " *Liberté, Egalité, Guerre
aux Tyrans*, etc.," would be received; but that, if he wrote
like a soldier and a gentleman, he should be answered in
the same style. The Frenchman then began to flatter his
antagonist upon the *bienfaisance* and *humanité*, which, he
said, were the least of the many virtues which distinguished
Monsieur Troubridge. Monsieur Troubridge's *bienfaisance*
was, at this time, thinking of mining the fort. " If we
can accomplish that," said he, " I am a strong advocate to
send them, hostages and all, to Old Nick, and surprise him
with a group of nobility and republicans. Meantime,"
he added, " it was some satisfaction to perceive that the
shells fell well, and broke some of their shins." Finally,
to complete his character, Méjean offered to surrender for
150,000 ducats. Great Britain, perhaps, has made but
too little use of this kind of artillery, which France has
found so effectual towards subjugating the continent. But

Troubridge had the prey within his reach; and in the course of a few days his last battery, "after much trouble and palaver," as he said, "brought the vagabonds to their senses."

Troubridge had more difficulties to overcome in this siege from the character of the Neapolitans who pretended to assist him and whom he made useful, than even from the strength of the place and the skill of the French. " Such damned cowards and villains," he declared, " he had never seen before." The men at the advanced posts carried on what he called " a diabolical good understanding " with the enemy, and the workmen would sometimes take fright and run away. " I make the best I can," said he, " of the degenerate race I have to deal with. The whole means of guns, ammunition, pioneers, etc., with all materials, rest with them. With fair promises to the men, and threats of instant death if I find any one erring, a little spur has been given." Nelson said of him, with truth, upon this occasion, that he was a first-rate general. " I find, sir," said he afterwards in a letter to the Duke of Clarence, " that General Koehler [1] does not approve of such irregular proceedings as naval officers attacking and defending fortifications. ˙We have but one idea,—to get close alongside. None but a sailor would have placed a battery only one hundred and eighty yards from the castle of St. Elmo; a soldier must have gone according to art, and the ∿ way. My brave Troubridge went straight on, for we had no time to spare."

Troubridge then proceeded to Capua, and took the command of the motley besieging force. One thousand of the best men in the fleet were sent to assist in the siege. Just at this time Nelson received a peremptory order from Lord Keith to sail with the whole of his force for the protection of Minorca; or, at least, to retain no more than was absolutely necessary at Sicily. " You will easily conceive my feelings," said he, in communicating this to Earl St. Vincent; " but my mind, as your lordship knows, was perfectly prepared for this order; and it is now, more than ever, made up. At this moment I will not part with a single ship. As I cannot do that without drawing a hundred and twenty

¹ See above, p. 61.

men from each ship now at the siege of Capua. I am fully aware of the act I have committed; but I am prepared for any fate which may await my disobedience. Capua and Gaeta will soon fall; and the moment the scoundrels of French are out of this kingdom I shall send eight or nine ships of the line to Minorca. I have done what I thought right. Others may think differently. But it will be my consolation that I have gained a kingdom, seated a faithful ally of his Majesty firmly on his throne, and restored happiness to millions."

At Capua Troubridge had the same difficulties as at St. Elmo; and being farther from Naples, and from the fleet, was less able to overcome them. The powder was so bad that he suspected treachery: and when he asked Nelson to spare him forty casks from the ships, he told him it would be necessary that some Englishmen should accompany it, or they would steal one-half, and change the other. " All the men you see," said he, " gentle and simple, are such notorious villains, that it is misery to be with them." Capua, however, soon fell. Gaeta immediately afterwards surrendered to Captain Louis of the *Minotaur*. Here the commanding officer acted more unlike a Frenchman, Captain Louis said, than any one he had ever met; meaning that he acted like a man of honour. He required, however, that the garrison should carry away their horses, and other pillaged property: to which Nelson replied, " That no property which they did not bring with them into the country could be theirs; and that the greatest care should be taken to prevent them from carrying it away." " I am sorry," said he to Captain Louis, " that you have entered into any altercation. There is no way of dealing with a Frenchman but to knock him down. To be civil to them is only to be laughed at, when they are enemies."

The whole kingdom of Naples was thus delivered by Nelson from the French. The Admiralty, however, thought it expedient to censure him for disobeying Lord Keith's orders, and thus hazarding Minorca, without, as it appeared to them, any sufficient reason; and also for having landed seamen for the siege of Capua, to form part of an army employed in operations at a distance from the coast: where, in case of defeat, they might have been prevented from returning to their ships; and they enjoined him "not to employ the seamen in like manner in future." This reprimand was issued before the event was known; though, indeed, the event would not affect the principle upon which it proceeded. When Nelson communicated the tidings of his complete success, he said, in his public letter, "that it would not be the less acceptable for having been principally brought about by British sailors." His judgment in thus employing them had been justified by the result: and his joy was evidently heightened by the gratification of a professional and becoming pride. To the First Lord he said, at the same time, "I certainly, from having only a left hand, cannot enter into details which may explain the motives that actuated my conduct. My principle is, to assist in driving the French to the devil, and in restoring peace and happiness to mankind. I feel that I am fitter to do the action than to describe it." He then added, that he would take care of Minorca.

In expelling the French from Naples, Nelson had, with characteristic zeal and ability, discharged his duty. But he deceived himself when he imagined that he had seated Ferdinand firmly on his throne, and that he had restored happiness to ·millions. These objects might have been accomplished if it had been possible to inspire virtue and wisdom into a vicious and infatuated court. And if Nelson's eyes had not been, as it were, spell-bound by that unhappy attachment, which had now completely mastered him, he would have seen things as they were; and might, perhaps, have awakened the Sicilian court to a sense of their interest, if not of their duty. That court employed itself in a miserable round of folly and festivity, while the prisons of Naples were filled with groans, and the scaffolds streamed with blood. St. Januarius was solemnly removed from his rank as patron saint of the kingdom, having been convicted of Jacobinism; and St. Antonio as solemnly installed in his place. The King, instead of re-establishing order at Naples by his presence, speedily returned to Palermo, to indulge in his favourite amusements.

Nelson, and the ambassador's family, accompanied the court; and Troubridge remained, groaning over the villainy and frivolity of those with whom he was compelled to deal.

A party of officers applied to him for a passage to Palermo, to see the procession of St. Rosalia. He recommended them to exercise their troops, and not behave like children. It was grief enough for him that the court should be busied in these follies, and Nelson involved in them. " I dread, my lord," said he, " all the feasting, etc., at Palermo. I am sure your health will be hurt. If so, all their saints will be damned by the navy. The King would be better employed digesting a good government. Everything gives way to their pleasures. The money spent at Palermo gives discontent here. Fifty thousand people are unemployed, trade discouraged, manufactures at a stand. It is the interest of many here to keep the King away. They all dread reform. Their villainies are so deeply rooted, that if some method is not taken to dig them out, this government cannot hold together. Out of twenty millions of ducats, collected as the revenue, only thirteen millions reach the treasury; and the King pays four ducats where he should pay one. He is surrounded by thieves; and none of them have honour or honesty enough to tell him the real and true state of things." In another letter he expressed his sense of the miserable state of Naples. " There are upwards of forty thousand families," said he, " who have relations confined. If some act of oblivion is not passed, there will be no end of persecution; for the people of this country have no idea of anything but revenge, and to gain a point would swear ten thousand false oaths. Constant efforts are made to get a man taken up, in order to rob him. The confiscated property does not reach the King's treasury.—All thieves! It is selling for nothing. His own people, whom he employs, are buying it up, and the vagabonds pocket the whole. I should not be surprised to hear that they brought a bill of expenses against him for the sale."

The Sicilian court, however, were at this time duly sensible of the services which had been rendered them by the British fleet, and their gratitude to Nelson was shown with proper and princely munificence. They gave him the dukedom and domain of Bronte, worth about £3000 a year. It was some days before he could be persuaded to accept it. The argument which finally prevailed is said to have been suggested by the Queen, and urged, at her request, by Lady Hamilton upon her knees. "He considered his own honour too much," she said, "if he persisted in refusing what the King and Queen felt to be absolutely necessary for the preservation of theirs." The King himself, also, is said to have addressed him in words which show that the sense of rank will sometimes confer virtue upon those who seem to be most unworthy of the lot to which they have been born. "Lord Nelson, do you wish that your name alone should pass with honour to posterity; and that I, Ferdinand Bourbon, should appear ungrateful?" He gave him also, when the dukedom was accepted, a diamond-hilted sword, which his father, Charles III. of Spain, had given him on his accession to the throne of the two Sicilies. Nelson said, "The reward was magnificent, and worthy of a king, and he was determined that the inhabitants on the domain should be the happiest in all his Sicilian Majesty's dominions.—Yet," said he, speaking of these and the other remunerations which were made him for his services, "these presents, rich as they are, do not elevate me. My pride is that, at Constantinople, from the Grand Seignior to the lowest Turk, the name of Nelson is familiar in their mouths; and in this country I am everything which a grateful monarch and people can call me." Nelson, however, had a pardonable pride in the outward and visible signs of honour, which he had so fairly won. He was fond of his Sicilian title. The signification, perhaps, pleased him. Duke of Thunder was what in Dahomey would be called a *strong name*. It was to a sailor's taste; and certainly to no man could it ever be more applicable. But a simple offering, which he received not long afterwards, from the island of Zante, affected him with a deeper and finer feeling. The Greeks of that little community sent him a golden-headed sword and a truncheon, set round with all the diamonds that the island could furnish, in a single row. They thanked him "for having, by his victory, preserved that part of Greece from the horrors of anarchy; and prayed that his exploits might accelerate the day, in which, amidst the glory and peace of thrones, the miseries of the human race would cease." This unexpected tribute touched Nelson to the heart. "No officer," he said, "had ever received from any country a higher acknowledgment of his services."

The French still occupied the Roman states; from which, according to their own admission, they had extorted in jewels, plate, specie, and requisitions of every kind, to the enormous amount of eight millions sterling. Yet they affected to appear as deliverers among the people whom they were thus cruelly plundering; and they distributed portraits of Bonaparte, with the blasphemous inscription —" This is the true likeness of the holy saviour of the world! " The people, detesting the impiety, and groaning beneath the exactions of these perfidious robbers, were ready to join any regular force that should come to their assistance. But they dreaded Cardinal Ruffo's rabble, and declared they would resist him as a banditti, who came only for the purpose of pillage. Nelson perceived that no object was now so essential for the tranquillity of Naples as the recovery of Rome; which in the present state of things, when Suvarof was driving the French before him, would complete the deliverance of Italy. He applied, therefore, to Sir James St. Clair Erskine, who in the absence of General Fox commanded at Minorca, to assist in this great object with twelve hundred men. " The field of glory," said he, " is a large one, and was never more open to any one than at this moment to you. Rome would throw open her gates and receive you as her deliverer; and the Pope would owe his restoration to a heretic." But Sir James Erskine looked only at the difficulties of the undertaking. " Twelve hundred men," he thought, " would be too small a force to be committed in such an enterprise; for Civita Vecchia was a regular fortress; the local situation and climate also were such, that even if this force were adequate, it would be proper to delay the expedition till October. General Fox, too, was soon expected; and during his absence, and under existing circumstances, he did not feel justified in sending away such a detachment."

What this General thought it imprudent to attempt, Nelson and Troubridge effected without his assistance, by a small detachment from the fleet. Troubridge first sent Captain Hallowell to Civita Vecchia, to offer the garrison there, and at Castle St. Angelo, the same terms which had been granted to Gaeta. Hallowell perceived, by the overstrained civility of the officers who came off to him and the compliments which they paid to the English nation, that they were sensible of their own weakness, and their inability to offer any effectual resistance. But the French know that, while they are in a condition to serve their government, they can rely upon it for every possible exertion in their support; and this reliance gives them hope and confidence to the last. Upon Hallowell's report, Troubridge, who had now been made Sir Thomas for his services, sent Captain Louis with a squadron, to enforce the terms which he had offered; and, as soon as he could leave Naples, he himself followed. The French, who had no longer any hope from the fate of arms, relied upon their skill in negotiation, and proposed terms to Troubridge with that effrontery which characterises their public proceedings; but which is as often successful as it is impudent. They had a man of the right stamp to deal with. Their ambassador at Rome began by saying that the Roman territory was the property of the French by right of conquest. The British Commodore settled that point by replying, " It is mine by reconquest." A capitulation was soon concluded for all the Roman states, and Captain Louis rowed up the Tiber in his barge, hoisted English colours on the Capitol, and acted, for the time, as governor of Rome. The prophecy of the Irish poet was thus accomplished, and the friar reaped the fruits: for Nelson, who was struck with the oddity of the circumstance, and not a little pleased with it, obtained preferment for him from the King of Sicily, and recommended him to the Pope.

Having thus completed his work upon the continent of Italy, Nelson's whole attention was directed towards Malta; where Captain Ball, with most inadequate means, was besieging the French garrison. Never was any officer engaged in a more anxious and painful service. The smallest reinforcement from France would, at any moment, have turned the scale against him; and had it not been for his consummate ability, and the love and veneration with which the Maltese regarded him, Malta must have remained in the hands of the enemy. Men, money, food; all things were wanting. The garrison consisted of five thousand troops; the besieging force of five hundred English and Portuguese marines and about fifteen hundred armed

peasants. Long and repeatedly did Nelson solicit troops
to effect the reduction of this important place. " It has
been no fault of the navy," said he, " that Malta has not
been attacked by land. But we have neither the means
ourselves, nor influence with those who have." The same
causes of demurral existed which prevented British troops
from assisting in the expulsion of the French from Rome.
Sir James Erskine was expecting General Fox. He could
not act without orders; and not having, like Nelson, that
lively spring of hope within him, which partakes enough
of the nature of faith to work miracles in war, he thought
it " evident that unless a respectable land force, in numbers
sufficient to undertake the siege of such a garrison, in one
of the strongest places of Europe, and supplied with proportionate artillery and stores, were sent against it, no
reasonable hope could be entertained of its surrender."

Nelson groaned over the spirit of over-reasoning caution,
and unreasoning obedience. " My heart," said he, " is
almost broken. If the enemy gets supplies in, we may bid
adieu to Malta. All the force we can collect would then be
of little use against the strongest place in Europe. To say
that an officer is never, for any object, to alter his orders,
is what I cannot comprehend. The circumstances of this
war so often vary, that an officer has almost every moment
to consider, ' What would my superiors direct, did they know
what is passing under my nose?' But, sir," said he, writing
to the Duke of Clarence, " I find few think as I do. To
obey orders is all perfection. To serve my king and to
destroy the French, I consider as the great order of all,
from which little ones spring: and if one of these militate
against it (for who can tell exactly at a distance?) I go
back, and obey the great order and object, to down,—down
with the damned French villains!—My blood boils at the
name of Frenchman!"

At length, General Fox arrived at Minorca, and, at
length, permitted Colonel Graham to go to Malta, but with
means miserably limited. In fact, the expedition was at
a stand for want of money; when Troubridge, arriving
at Messina, to co-operate in it, and finding this fresh delay,
immediately offered all that he could command of his own.
" I procured him, my lord," said he to Nelson, " fifteen

Q

thousand of my cobs. Every farthing and every atom of me shall be devoted to the cause."—" What can this mean ? " said Nelson, when he learned that Colonel Graham was ordered not to incur any expense for stores, or any articles except provisions! " The cause cannot stand still for want of a little money. If nobody will pay it, I will sell Bronte, and the Emperor of Russia's box." And he actually pledged Bronte for £6600 if there should be any difficulty about paying the bills. The long-delayed expedition was thus, at last, sent forth. But Troubridge little imagined in what scenes of misery he was to bear his part. He looked to Sicily for supplies. It was the interest, as well as the duty, of the Sicilian government to use every exertion for furnishing them; and Nelson and the British Ambassador were on the spot to press upon them the necessity of exertion. But, though Nelson saw with what a knavish crew the Sicilian court was surrounded, he was blind to the vices of the court itself; and resigning himself wholly to Lady Hamilton's influence, never even suspected the crooked policy which it was remorselessly pursuing. The Maltese and the British in Malta severely felt it. Troubridge, who had the truest affection for Nelson, knew his infatuation and feared that it might prove injurious to his character, as well as fatal to an enterprise which had begun so well, and had been carried on so patiently. " My lord," said he, writing to him from the siege, " we are dying off fast for want. I learn that Sir William Hamilton says Prince Luzzi refused corn some time ago, and Sir William does not think it worth while making another application. If that be the case, I wish he commanded this distressing scene instead of me. Puglia had an immense harvest; near thirty sail left Messina, before I did, to load corn. Will they let us have any? If not, a short time will decide the business. The German interest prevails. I wish I was at your lordship's elbow for an hour. *All, all* will be thrown on you! I will parry the blow as much as in my power. I foresee much mischief brewing. God bless your lordship! I am miserable I cannot assist your operations more. Many happy returns of the day to you—it was the first of the New Year—I never spent so miserable a one. I am not very tender-hearted; but really the distress here would even move a

Neapolitan." Soon afterwards he wrote, " I have this day saved thirty thousand people from starving; but with this day my ability ceases. As the government are bent on starving us, I see no alternative but to leave these poor unhappy people to perish, without our being witnesses of their distress. I curse the day I ever served the Neapolitan government. We have characters, my lord, to lose; these people have none. Do not suffer their infamous conduct to fall on us. Our country is just, but severe. Such is the fever of my brain this minute, that I assure you, on my honour, if the Palermo traitors were here, I would shoot them first, and then myself. Girgenti is full of corn. The money is ready to pay for it. We do not ask it as a gift. Oh! could you see the horrid distress I daily experience, something would be done. Some engine is at work against us at Naples; and I believe I hit on the proper person. If you complain, he will be immediately promoted, agreeably to the Neapolitan custom. All I write to you is known at the Queen's. For my own part, I look upon the Neapolitans as the worst of intriguing enemies. Every hour shows me their infamy and duplicity. I pray your lordship be cautious; your honest, open manner of acting will be made a handle of. When I see you, and tell of their infamous tricks, you will be as much surprised as I am. The whole will fall on you."

Nelson was not, and could not be, insensible to the distress which his friend so earnestly represented. He begged, almost on his knees, he said, small supplies of money and corn, to keep the Maltese from starving. And when the court granted a small supply, protesting their poverty, he believed their protestations, and was satisfied with their professions, instead of insisting that the restrictions upon the exportation of corn should be withdrawn. The anxiety, however, which he endured, affected him so deeply that he said it had broken his spirit for ever. Happily all that Troubridge, with so much reason, foreboded, did not come to pass. For Captain Ball, with more decision than Nelson himself would have shown at that time and upon that occasion, ventured upon a resolute measure, for which his name would deserve always to be held in veneration by the Maltese, even if it had no other claims to the love and reverence of a grateful people. Finding it hopeless longer to look for succour or common humanity from the deceitful and infatuated court of Sicily, which persisted in prohibiting by sanguinary edicts the exportation of supplies, at his own risk he sent his first lieutenant to the port of Girgenti, with orders to seize and bring with him to Malta the ships which were there lying laden with corn; of the number of which he had received accurate information. These orders were executed, to the great delight and advantage of the ship-owners and proprietors; the necessity of raising the siege was removed, and Captain Ball waited, in calmness, for the consequences to himself. The Neapolitan government complained to the English ambassador, and the complaint was communicated to Nelson, who, in return, requested Sir William Hamilton would fully and plainly state that the act ought not to be considered as any intended disrespect to his Sicilian Majesty, but as of the most absolute and imperious necessity; the alternative being either of abandoning Malta to the French, or of anticipating the King's orders for carrying the corn in those vessels to Malta. " I trust," he added, " that the government of the country will never again force any of our royal master's servants to so unpleasant an alternative." Thus ended the complaint of the Neapolitan court. " The sole result was," says Mr. Coleridge,[1] " that the governor of Malta became an especial object of its hatred, its fear, and its respect."

Nelson himself, at the beginning of February,[2] sailed for that island. On the way he fell in with a French squadron bound for its relief, and consisting of the *Généreux*, seventy-four, three frigates, and a corvette. One of these frigates and the line of-battle ship were taken: the others escaped, but failed in their purpose of reaching La Valette.[3] This success was peculiarly gratifying to Nelson for many reasons. During some months he had acted as commander-in-chief in the Mediterranean, while Lord Keith was in England. Lord Keith was now returned; and Nelson had, upon his own plan, and at his own risk, left him, to sail for Malta, " for which," said he, " if I had not succeeded, I might have been broke; and if I had not acted thus,

---

[1] See above, Introduction, p. xi.   [2] 1800.   [3] Valetta.

the *Généreux* never would have been taken." [1] This ship was one of those which had escaped from Aboukir. Two frigates, and the *Guillaume Tell*, eighty-six, were all that now remained of the fleet which Bonaparte had conducted to Egypt. The *Guillaume Tell* was at this time closely watched in the harbour of La Valette: and shortly afterwards, attempting to make her escape from thence, was taken after an action, in which greater skill was never displayed by British ships, nor greater gallantry by an enemy. She was taken by the *Foudroyant*, *Lion* and *Penelope* frigates. Nelson, rejoicing at what he called this glorious finish to the whole French Mediterranean fleet, rejoiced also that he was not present to have taken a sprig of these brave men's laurels. " They are," said he, " and I glory in them, my children. They served in my school; and all of us caught our professional zeal and fire from the great and good Earl St. Vincent. What a pleasure, what happiness, to have the Nile fleet all taken, under my orders and regulations! " The two frigates still remained in La Valette. Before its surrender they stole out. One was taken in the attempt; the other was the only ship of the whole fleet which escaped capture or destruction.

Letters were found on board the *Guillaume Tell* showing that the French were now become hopeless of preserving the conquest which they had so foully acquired. Troubridge and his brother officers were anxious that Nelson should have the honour of signing the capitulation. They told him, that they absolutely, as far as they dared, insisted on his staying to do this; but their earnest and affectionate entreaties were vain. Sir William Hamilton had just been superseded: Nelson had no feeling of cordiality towards Lord Keith; and thinking that, after Earl St. Vincent, no man had so good a claim to the command in the Mediterranean as himself, he applied for permission to return to England; telling the First Lord of the Admiralty that his

[1] Once more Southey gets his facts all wrong. Lord Keith left the Mediterranean in the summer of 1799 and returned at the beginning of the new year. On 16th January Nelson joined him at Leghorn, and sailed under his command to Malta. On arrival there, Keith blockaded the capital and sent Nelson with specific instructions to intercept the relieving force that was expected any moment from France. Nelson ignored Keith's instructions, took the steps that seemed best to him, and captured the *Généreux* as the text relates. A more detailed account most amusingly told will be found in *Nelsonian Reminiscences*, by Lieutenant G. S. Parsons, R.N.

spirit could not submit patiently, and that he was a broken-hearted man.[1]

From the time of his return from Egypt, amid all the honours which were showered upon him, he had suffered many mortifications. Sir Sidney Smith had been sent to Egypt, with orders to take under his command the squadron which Nelson had left there. Sir Sidney appears to have thought that this command was to be independent of Nelson: and Nelson himself thinking so, determined to return, saying to Earl St. Vincent, " I do feel, for I am a man, that it is impossible for me to serve in these seas with a squadron under a junior officer." Earl St. Vincent seems to have dissuaded him from this resolution. Some heart-burnings, however, still remained, and some incautious expressions of Sir Sidney's were noticed by him in terms of evident displeasure. But this did not continue long, as no man bore more willing testimony than Nelson to the admirable defence of Acre. He differed from Sir Sidney as to the policy which ought to be pursued towards the French in Egypt;[2] and strictly commanded him, in the strongest language, not, on any pretence, to permit a single French-man to leave the country, saying, that he considered it nothing short of madness to permit that band of thieves to return to Europe. " No," said he, " to Egypt they went with their own consent, and there they shall remain, while Nelson commands this squadron. For never, never, will he consent to the return of one ship or Frenchman. I wish them to perish in Egypt, and give an awful lesson to the world of the justice of the Almighty."

If Nelson had not thoroughly understood the character of the enemy against whom he was engaged, their conduct in Egypt would have disclosed it. After the battle of the Nile he had landed all his prisoners, upon a solemn engage-ment, made between Troubridge on one side and Captain Barré on the other, that none of them should serve till regularly exchanged. They were no sooner on shore, than part of them were drafted into the different regiments, and the remainder formed into a corps, called the nautic legion.

---

[1] *Dispatches and Letters*, Vol. IV. pp. 224–5.
[2] Smith had issued passports allowing certain of Napoleon's following to return to Europe, and these passports Nelson refused to recognise.

This occasioned Captain Hallowell to say that the French had forfeited all claim to respect from us. " The army of Bonaparte," said he, " are entirely destitute of every principle of honour. They have always acted like licentious thieves." Bonaparte's escape [1] was the more regretted by Nelson, because, if he had had sufficient force, he thought it would certainly have been prevented. He wished to keep ships upon the watch to intercept anything coming from Egypt. But the Admiralty calculated upon the assistance of the Russian fleet, which failed when it was most wanted. The ships which should have been thus employed were then required for more pressing services; and the bloody Corsican was thus enabled to reach Europe in safety; there to become the guilty instrument of a wider-spreading destruction than any with which the world had ever before been visited.

Nelson had other causes of chagrin. Earl St. Vincent, for whom he felt such high respect, and whom Sir John Orde had challenged for having nominated Nelson instead of himself to the command of the Nile squadron,[2] laid claim to prize-money, as commander-in-chief, after he had quitted the station. The point was contested, and decided against him. Nelson, perhaps, felt this the more, because his own feelings, with regard to money, were so different. An opinion had been given by Dr. Lawrence, which would have excluded the junior Flag Officers from prize-money. When this was made known to him, his reply was in these words, " Notwithstanding Dr. Lawrence's opinion, I do not believe I have any right to exclude the junior Flag Officers. And if I have, I desire that no such claim may be made: no, not if it were sixty times the sum,—and, poor as I am, I were never to see prize-money."

A ship could not be spared to convey him to England.

[1] After spreading false reports about his plans, Napoleon, on 22nd August, 1799, embarked in a frigate; and, leaving behind him his army in Egypt, set out with some of his marshals for France. The voyage lasted no less than six weeks; but the frigate, providentially evading all British craft, at length reached Fréjus on 9th October, and set the adventurous Corsican ashore.

[2] Sir John Orde commented upon Nelson's appointment at the time with so much vigour and freedom that St. Vincent, with customary truculence, sent his subordinate home. On arriving in London, Orde demanded a court-martial, which the Admiralty refused. He waited until St. Vincent's return, and then called his superior out. By the King's command the two duellists were kept apart, and in sums of £5000 were bound over to keep the peace. See also above, Part. V. p. 118 and note.

He therefore travelled through Germany to Hamburg, in company with his inseparable friends, Sir William and Lady Hamilton. The Queen of Naples went with them to Vienna. While they were at Leghorn, upon a report that the French were approaching (for through the folly of weak courts and the treachery of venal cabinets, they had now recovered their ascendancy in Italy) the people rose tumultuously, and would fain have persuaded Nelson to lead them against the enemy. Public honours, and yet more gratifying testimonials of public admiration, awaited Nelson wherever he went. The Prince of Esterhazy entertained him in a style of Hungarian magnificence—a hundred grenadiers, each six feet in height, constantly waiting at table. At Magdeburg, the master of the hotel where he was entertained contrived to show him for money; admitting the curious to mount a ladder, and peep at him through a small window. A wine merchant at Hamburg, who was about seventy years of age, requested to speak with Lady Hamilton, and told her he had some Rhenish wine of the vintage of 1625, which had been in his own possession more than half a century. He had preserved it for some extraordinary occasion; and that which had now arrived was far beyond any that he could ever have expected. His request was that her ladyship would prevail upon Lord Nelson to accept six dozen of this incomparable wine. Part of it would then have the honour to flow into the heart's blood of that immortal hero; and this thought would make him happy during the remainder of his life. Nelson, when this singular request was reported to him, went into the room, and taking the worthy old gentleman kindly by the hand, consented to receive six bottles, provided the donor would dine with him next day. Twelve were sent; and Nelson, saying that he hoped yet to win half a dozen more great victories, promised to lay by six bottles of his Hamburg friend's wine, for the purpose of drinking one after each. A German pastor, between seventy and eighty years of age, travelled forty miles, with the Bible of his parish church, to request that Nelson would write his name on the first leaf of it. He called him the saviour of the Christian world. The old man's hope deceived him. There was no Nelson upon shore, or Europe would have been saved; but, in his foresight of the horrors with which all Germany and all Christendom were threatened by France, the pastor could not possibly have apprehended more than has actually taken place.

[*SOUTHEY. CHAPTER VII*]

NELSON was welcomed in England with every mark of popular honour. At Yarmouth, where he landed, every ship in the harbour hoisted her colours. The mayor and corporation waited upon him with the freedom of the town, and accompanied him in procession to church, with all the naval officers on shore and the principal inhabitants. Bonfires and illuminations concluded the day; and, on the morrow, the volunteer cavalry drew up and saluted him as he departed, and followed the carriage to the borders of the county. At Ipswich, the people came out to meet him, drew him a mile into the town, and three miles out. When he was in the *Agamemnon,* he wished to represent this place in parliament, and some of his friends had consulted the leading men of the corporation. The result was not successful; and Nelson, observing that he would endeavour to find out a preferable path into parliament, said there might come a time when the people of Ipswich would think it an honour to have had him for their representative. In London, he was feasted by the city, drawn by the populace from Ludgate Hill to Guildhall, and received the thanks of the Common Council for his great victory, and a golden-hilted sword studded with diamonds.

Nelson had every earthly blessing, except domestic happiness. He had forfeited that for ever. Before he had been three months in England he separated from Lady Nelson. Some of his last words to her were, " I call God to witness, there is nothing in you, or your conduct, that I wish otherwise." This was the consequence of his infatuated attachment to Lady Hamilton. It had before caused a quarrel with his son-in-law, and occasioned remonstrances from his truest friends; which produced no other effect than that of making him displeased with them, and more dissatisfied with himself.[1]

[1] The discussion of this highly contentious paragraph, held over for the time being, will be found in Part VIII., Note 3, p. 259.

PART VII

THE BALTIC CAMPAIGN OF 1801

CHAPTER I

THE BATTLE OF COPENHAGEN

2nd April, 1801

[*SOUTHEY. CHAPTER VII—continued*]

THE Addington administration was just at this time [1] formed; and Nelson, who had solicited employment,[2] and been made Vice-Admiral of the Blue, was sent to the Baltic, as second in command, under Sir Hyde Parker, by Earl St. Vincent, the new First Lord of the Admiralty. The three northern courts had formed a confederacy for making England resign her naval rights.[3] Of these courts, Russia was guided by the passions of its Emperor, Paul, a man not without fits of generosity, and some natural goodness, but subject to the wildest humours of caprice, and crazed by the possession of greater power than can ever be safely, or perhaps innocently, possessed by weak humanity. Denmark was French at heart, ready to co-operate in all the views of France, to recognise all her usurpations, and obey all

---

[1] March 1801.

[2] Nelson, who happily for himself and his country never allowed himself to be drawn into the game of politics, showed a strange lack of discernment in judging party men. Addington, he always admitted, was his favourite minister; and to the new premier he wrote, " I am *your* admiral."
It was not, however, from any preference for Addington over Pitt that he at this time offered his services. What had brought him home from the Mediterranean was a combination of ill-health with a rooted dislike for serving under Lord Keith. The air of England quickly drove away all ailments, bodily and mental; and he at once professed himself ready to go anywhere, and do anything, in any capacity whatsoever.

[3] The Armed Neutrality of the North (formed December 1800) comprised Russia, Prussia (whom Southey omits), Sweden, and Denmark (which included Norway). The object of the alliance, as in 1780 (see above, p. 15), was to resist Britain's interference with neutral trade in time of war. The best weapon in Britain's armoury was " Blockade," but this could only be made effective by the harassing necessities of the " Right of Search." The foundation of the league may be attributed less to the grievances of neutrals than to the importunity of Bonaparte and the pressure he brought to bear on the northern powers.

her injunctions. Sweden, under a king whose principles were right, and whose feelings were generous, but who had a taint of hereditary insanity, acted in acquiescence with the dictates of two powers whom it feared to offend.

The Danish navy, at this time, consisted of twenty-three ships of the line, with about thirty-one frigates and smaller vessels, exclusive of guard-ships. The Swedes had eighteen ships of the line, fourteen frigates and sloops, seventy-four galleys and smaller vessels, besides gun-boats; and this force was in a far better state of equipment than the Danish. The Russians had eighty-two sail of the line and forty frigates. Of these there were forty-seven sail of the line at Kronstadt, Revel, Petersburg, and Archangel: but the Russian fleet was ill manned, ill officered, and ill equipped. Such a combination under the influence of France would soon have been formidable: and never did the British cabinet display more decision than in instantly preparing to crush it. They erred, however, in permitting any petty consideration to prevent them from appointing Nelson to the command. The public properly murmured at seeing it entrusted to another: and he himself said to Earl St. Vincent, that, circumstanced as he was, this expedition would probably be the last service that he should ever perform. The Earl in reply, besought him, for God's sake, not to suffer himself to be carried away by any sudden impulse.[1]

The season happened to be unusually favourable. So mild a winter had not been known in the Baltic for many years. When Nelson joined the fleet at Yarmouth, he found the Admiral "a little nervous about dark nights and fields of ice." "But we must brace up," said he. "These are not times for nervous systems. I hope[2] we shall give our northern enemies that hailstorm of bullets, which gives our dear country the dominion of the sea. We have it, and all the devils in the north cannot take it from us, if

[1] The ministry desired, if possible, to avoid warlike measures, and therefore sent Parker to employ peaceful persuasion. Nelson was included in the fleet's equipment, so that a thunderbolt could be hurled upon the recalcitrant Danes if Parker's mission failed.

[2] Southey here quotes from two different letters, and amalgamates the quotations. To St. Vincent, on 1st March, Nelson wrote, " . . . Our friend here is a little nervous about dark nights and fields of ice. But we must brace up; these are not times for nervous systems . . .;" and to Sir Edward Berry, on 9th March, " I hope we shall be able as usua to get so close to our enemies that our shot cannot miss their object, and that we shall again give our northern enemies, etc.'

our wooden walls have fair play." Before the fleet left Yarmouth, it was sufficiently known that its destination was against Denmark. Some Danes, who belonged to the *Amazon* frigate, went to Captain Riou, and telling him what they had heard, begged that he would get them exchanged into a ship bound on some other destination. " They had no wish," they said, " to quit the British service; but they entreated that they might not be forced to fight against their own country." There ·was not in our whole navy a man who had a higher and more chivalrous sense of duty than Riou. Tears came into his eyes while the men were speaking. Without making any reply, he instantly ordered his boat, and did not return to the *Amazon* till he could tell them that their wish was effected.

The fleet sailed on the 12th of March. Mr. Vansittart sailed in it, the British cabinet still hoping to obtain its end by negotiation.[1] It was well for England that Sir Hyde Parker placed a fuller confidence in Nelson than the government seems to have done at this most important crisis. Her enemies might well have been astonished at learning that any other man should for a moment have been thought of for the command. But so little deference was paid, even at this time, to his intuitive and all-commanding genius, that when the fleet had reached its first rendezvous, at the entrance of the Cattegat, he had received no official communication whatever of the intended operations. His own mind had been made up upon them with its accustomed· decision. " All I have gathered of our first plans," said he, " I disapprove most exceedingly. Honour may arise from them; good cannot. I hear we are likely to anchor outside of Kronborg Castle, instead of Copenhagen, which would give weight to our negotiation. A Danish minister would think twice before he would put his name to war with England, when the next moment he would probably see his master's fleet in flames, and his capital in ruins. The Dane should see our flag every moment he lifted up his head."

Mr. Vansittart left the fleet at the Scaw [2] and preceded it in a frigate,[3] with a flag of truce. Precious time was lost

---

[1] Nicholas Vansittart, afterwards Lord Bexley. His instructions were to give Denmark forty-eight hours in which to withdraw from the Armed Neutrality.
[2] The most northerly point of Jutland.
[3] The *Blanche*.

by this delay, which was to be purchased by the dearest blood of Britain and Denmark. According to the Danes themselves, the intelligence that a British fleet was seen off the Sound produced a much more general alarm in Copenhagen than its actual arrival in the Roads; for their means of defence were, at that time, in such a state, that they could hardly hope to resist, still less to repel, an enemy. On the 21st [1] Nelson had a long conference with Sir Hyde; and the next day addressed a letter to him, worthy of himself and of the occasion. Mr. Vansittart's report had then been received. It represented the Danish government as in the highest degree hostile; and their state of preparation as exceeding what our cabinet had supposed possible: for Denmark had profited, with all activity, of the leisure which had so impoliticly been given her. " The more I have reflected," said Nelson to his commander, " the more I am confirmed in opinion, that not a moment should be lost in attacking the enemy. They will every day and every hour be stronger. We shall never be so good a match for them as at this moment. The only consideration is how to get at them with the least risk to our ships. Here you are, with almost the safety, certainly with the honour, of England, more entrusted to you than ever yet fell to the lot of any British officer. On your decision depends whether our country shall be degraded in the eyes of Europe, or whether she shall rear her head higher than ever. Again, I do repeat, never did our country depend so much upon the success of any fleet as on this. How best to honour her and abate the pride of her enemies, must be the subject of your deepest consideration."

Supposing him to force the passage of the Sound, Nelson thought some damage might be done among the masts and yards; though, perhaps, not one of them but would be serviceable again. " If the wind be fair," said he, " and you determine to attack the ships and Crown Islands,[2] you must expect the natural issue of such a battle—ships crippled, and, perhaps, one or two lost; for the wind which carries you in, will most probably not bring out a crippled ship. This mode I call taking the bull by the horns. It,

[1] Of March.
[2] The Trekroner (" three crowns ") battery at the entrance to Copenhagen.

however, will not prevent the Revel ships, or the Swedes, from joining the Danes; and to prevent this is, in my humble opinion, a measure absolutely necessary; and still to attack Copenhagen. "[1] For this he proposed two modes. One was, to pass Kronborg, taking the risk of danger; take the deepest and straightest channel along the Middle Grounds; and then coming down the Garbar, or King's Channel, attack the Danish line of floating batteries and ships, as might be found convenient.[2] This would prevent a junction,[3] and might give an opportunity of bombarding Copenhagen. Or to take the passage of the Belt,[4] which might be accomplished in four or five days; and then the attack by Dragor[5] might be made, and the junction of the Russians prevented. Supposing them through the Belt, he proposed that a detachment of the fleet should be sent to destroy the Russian squadron at Revel; and that the business at Copenhagen should be attempted with the remainder. "The measure," he said, "might be thought bold: but the boldest measures are the safest."

The pilots, as men who had nothing but safety to think of, were terrified by the formidable report of the batteries of Elsinore, and the tremendous preparations which our negotiators, who were now returned from their fruitless mission, had witnessed. They, therefore, persuaded Sir Hyde to prefer the passage of the Belt. " Let it be by the Sound, by the Belt, or anyhow," cried Nelson, " only lose

---

[1] *I.e.*—" The approach to Copenhagen through the Sound is defended not only by ships of war, but by the ' Three Crowns ' battery. If we make use of a northerly wind and grapple these defences, we may perhaps prevail; but we shall be badly mauled in the process, and lie at the mercy of Swedes and Russians when they come to the succour of their ally. Copenhagen must, of course, be assaulted, but it should be assaulted in a manner which will secure us from a flank attack, and enable us to withdraw from the jaws of death when our purpose has been achieved."

[2] The city of Copenhagen is built partly on the large island of Zealand, partly on the small island of Amag. Opposite the island of Amag lies the island of Salt-holm; and the channel that divides the one from the other is bifurcated by a sandbank called the Middle Ground. Nelson proposed to pass to the eastward of the Middle Ground, and then return, with a south wind, to the west of it. In the eastward channel (Outer Deep) the British fleet, as it manœuvred for position, would be secure from the enemy's fire; and in the westward channel (King's Deep), where the Danish ships were moored, the same wind that gave it the impetus to attack would lend new strength to its wings when the battle was over. (See map.)

[3] Of a Russo-Swedish fleet with that of the Danes: for the British ships would straddle the route by which the allies of Denmark would approach Copenhagen.

[4] The Great Belt.

[5] See map.

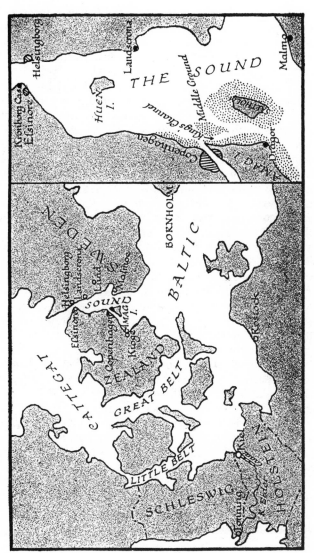

THE APPROACHES TO COPENHAGEN

not an hour!" On the 26th, they sailed for the Belt.[1]
Such was the habitual reserve of Sir Hyde, that his own
captain, the captain of the fleet, did not know which course
he had resolved to take till the fleet were getting under
way. When Captain Domett was thus apprised of it, he
felt it his duty to represent to the Admiral his belief that
if that course were persevered in, the ultimate object would
be totally defeated: it was liable to long delays and to
accidents of ships grounding; in the whole fleet there were
only one captain and one pilot who knew anything of this
formidable passage (as it was then deemed) and their knowledge was very slight; their instructions did not authorise
them to attempt it; supposing them safe through the Belts,
the heavy ships could not come over the *Grounds* to attack
Copenhagen; and light vessels would have no effect on such
a line of defence as had been prepared against them. Domett
urged these reasons so forcibly that Sir Hyde's opinion was
shaken, and he consented to bring the fleet to, and send for
Nelson on board. There can be little doubt but that the
expedition would have failed, if Captain Domett had not
thus timely and earnestly given his advice. Nelson entirely
agreed with him ; and it was finally determined to take
the passage of the Sound,—and the fleet returned to its
former anchorage.[2]

The next day was more idly expended in dispatching
a flag of truce to the governor of Kronborg Castle, to ask
whether he had received orders to fire at the British fleet;
as the Admiral must consider the first gun to be a declaration of war on the part of Denmark. A soldier-like and
becoming answer was returned to this formality. The
governor said that the British minister had not been sent
away from Copenhagen, but had obtained a passport at
his own demand. He himself, as a soldier, could not meddle
with politics; but he was not at liberty to suffer a fleet, of

---

[1] In the first edition this paragraph concluded as follows: " On the 26th they
sailed for the Belt, but after a few hours, this resolution was changed, and the
fleet returned to its former anchorage. The difficulty of the course is said to have
been one reason; Nelson's advice another." The alteration was made in the
second edition.

[2] Parker's flag flew in the *London*. The captain of the *London* was Otway,
afterward Admiral Sir Robert Walter Otway, Bart., G.C.B. Domett was "Captain
of the Fleet," or Chief of Staff. In Ralfe's *Naval Biography* (1828) it is stated that
it was Otway who prevailed upon Hyde Parker to change his plans. Nicolas
(Vol. IV. p. 301, note) confirms this.

which the intention was not yet known, to approach the guns of the castle which he had the honour to command: and he requested, if the British Admiral should think proper to make any proposals to the King of Denmark, that he might be apprised of it before the fleet approached nearer. During this intercourse, a Dane, who came on board the commander's ship, having occasion to express his business in writing, found the pen[1] blunt ; and holding it up, sarcastically said, " If your guns are not better pointed than your pens, you will make little impression on Copenhagen! "

On that day intelligence reached the Admiral of the loss of one of his fleet, the *Invincible*, seventy-four, wrecked on a sandbank, as she was coming out of Yarmouth: four hundred of her men perished in her. Nelson, who was now appointed to lead the van, shifted his flag to the *Elephant* (Captain Foley), a lighter ship than the *St. George*, and, therefore, fitter for the expected operations. The two following days were calm. Orders had been given to pass the Sound as soon as the wind would permit; and, on the afternoon of the 29th, the ships were cleared for action with an alacrity characteristic of British seamen. At daybreak, on the 30th, it blew a topsail breeze [2] from N.W. The signal was made, and the fleet moved on in order of battle; Nelson's division in the van, Sir Hyde's in the centre, and Admiral Graves's in the rear.

Great actions, whether military or naval, have generally given celebrity to the scenes from whence they are denominated; and thus petty villages and capes and bays, known only to the coasting trader, become associated with mighty deeds, and their names are made conspicuous in the history of the world. Here, however, the scene was every way worthy of the drama. The political importance of the Sound is such, that grand objects are not needed there to impress the imagination. Yet is the channel full of grand and interesting objects, both of art and nature. This passage, which Denmark had so long considered as the key of the Baltic, is, in its narrowest part, about three miles wide; and here the city of Elsinore is situated, except

---

[1] No pens except quills were used at this time.
[2] In light breezes a sailing-ship set all the canvas possible—top-gallants, royals, staysails, and studding-sails. But when the wind increased, canvas was shortened; and in a stiffish breeze nothing was set above the topsails.

R

Copenhagen the most flourishing of the Danish towns. Every vessel which passes lowers her top-gallant sails, and pays toll at Elsinore; a toll which is believed to have had its origin in the consent of the traders to that sea, Denmark taking upon itself the charge of constructing lighthouses and erecting signals, to mark the shoals and rocks from the Cattegat to the Baltic: and they, on their part, agreeing that all ships should pass this way, in order that all might pay their shares; none from that time using the passage of the Belt, because it was not fitting that they, who enjoyed the benefit of the beacons in dark and stormy weather, should evade contributing to them in fair seasons and summer nights. Of late years about ten thousand vessels had annually paid this contribution in time of peace. Adjoining Elsinore, and at the edge of the peninsular promontory upon the nearest point of land to the Swedish coast, stands Kronborg Castle, built after Tycho Brahe's [1] design; a magnificent pile—at once a palace, and fortress, and state-prison, with its spires and towers, and battlements, and batteries. On the left of the strait is the old Swedish city of Helsingborg; at the foot, and on the side of a hill. To the north of Helsingborg the shores are steep and rocky; they lower to the south; and the distant spires of Landscrona, Lund, and Malmoe are seen in the flat country. The Danish shores consist partly of ridges of sand; but more frequently they are diversified with corn-fields, meadows, slopes, and are covered with rich wood, and villages, and villas, and summer palaces belonging to the king and the nobility, and denoting the vicinity of a great capital. The isles of Huen, Saltholm, and Amag appear in the widening channel; and at the distance of twenty miles from Elsinore stands Copenhagen in full view; the best city of the north, and one of the finest capitals of Europe; visible, with its stately spires, far off. Amid these magnificent objects there are some which possess a peculiar interest for the recollections which they call forth. The isle of Huen, a lovely domain, about six miles in circumference, had been the munificent gift of Frederick II. to Tycho Brahe. It has higher shores than the near coast of Zealand,

---

[1] One of the world's greatest astronomers. He built on the island of Huen a magnificent castle and observatory called Uranienborg. He died in 1601.

or than the Swedish coast in that part. Here most of his discoveries were made; and here the ruins are to be seen of his observatory, and of the mansion where he was visited by princes; and where, with a princely spirit, he received and entertained all comers from all parts, and promoted science by his liberality, as well as by his labours. Elsinore is a name familiar to English ears, being inseparably associated with Hamlet, and one of the noblest works of human genius. Kronborg had been the scene of deeper tragedy. Here Queen Matilda was confined, the victim of a foul and murderous court intrigue. Here, amid heart-breaking griefs, she found consolation in nursing her infant. Here she took her everlasting leave of that infant, when, by the interference of England, her own deliverance was obtained; and as the ship bore her away from a country where the venial indiscretions of youth and unsuspicious gaiety had been so cruelly punished, upon those towers she fixed her eyes, and stood upon the deck, obstinately gazing toward them till the last speck had disappeared.[1]

The Sound being the only frequented entrance to the Baltic, the great Mediterranean of the North, few parts of the sea display so frequent a navigation. In the height of the season not fewer than a hundred vessels pass every four-and-twenty hours, for many weeks in succession. But never had so busy or so splendid a scene been exhibited there as on this day, when the British fleet prepared to force that passage, where, till now, all ships had vailed [2] their topsails to the flag of Denmark. The whole force consisted of fifty-one sail of various descriptions; of which sixteen were of the line. The greater part of the bomb and gun vessels [3] took their stations off Kronborg Castle, to cover the fleet; while others on the larboard were ready to engage the Swedish shore. The Danes, having improved every moment which ill-timed negotiation and baffling weather gave them, had lined their shores with batteries; and as soon as the *Monarch*, which was the leading ship, came abreast of them,

---

[1] Sister of George III. She married Christian VII. of Denmark in 1766, was imprisoned at Kronborg in 1772, and in the same year was released on the intervention of Great Britain.

[2] An old-fashioned word for let fall or bend, as in submission. To lower topsails was the approved method of saluting a superior power at sea.

[3] These vessels, mounting weapons of the howitzer type, were particularly suitable for dealing with land defences.

a fire was opened from about a hundred pieces of cannon and mortars. Our light vessels immediately, in return, opened their fire upon the castle. Here was all the pompous circumstance, and exciting reality of war, without its effects; for this ostentatious display was but a bloodless prelude to the wide and sweeping destruction which was soon to follow. The enemies' shot fell near enough to splash the water on board our ships. Not relying upon any forbearance of the Swedes, they meant to have kept the mid channel; but, when they perceived that not a shot was fired from Helsingborg, and that no batteries were to be seen on the Swedish shore, they inclined to that side, so as completely to get out of reach of the Danish guns. The uninterrupted blaze which was kept up from them till the fleet had passed, served only to exhilarate our sailors, and afford them matter for jest, as the shot fell in showers a full cable's length short of its destined aim. A few rounds were returned from some of our leading ships, till they perceived its inutility. This, however, occasioned the only bloodshed of the day, some of our men being killed and wounded by the bursting of a gun. As soon as the main body had passed, the gun vessels followed, desisting from their bombardment, which had been as innocent as that of the enemy; and, about mid-day, the whole fleet anchored between the Island of Huen and Copenhagen. Sir Hyde, with Nelson, Admiral Graves, some of the senior captains, and the commanding officers of the artillery and the troops, then proceeded in a lugger,[1] to reconnoitre the enemy's means of defence; a formidable line of ships, radeaus, pontoons, galleys, fire-ships, and gun-boats,[2] flanked and supported by extensive batteries, and occupying, from one extreme point to the other, an extent of nearly four miles.

A council of war was held in the afternoon. It was apparent that the Danes could not be attacked without great difficulty and risk; and some of the members of the council

[1] A light vessel with square sails; very easy to manage, and very speedy; most useful for reconnoitring work.

[2] The meaning of these words must not be unduly pressed. Radeau (Anglice raft) was not a word used in the British marine; and though the nautical dictionaries of the period give a definition of " pontoon " and compare it to a barge or lighter, they dismiss it as a Mediterranean craft little seen in the north of Europe. What the Danes relied on were dismasted vessels or hulks, which they treated less like ships than like floating forts, akin to the batteries whose line of fire they prolonged.

spoke of the number of the Swedes and the Russians whom they should afterwards have to engage, as a consideration which ought to be borne in mind. Nelson, who kept pacing the cabin, impatient as he ever was of anything which savoured of irresolution, repeatedly said, " The more numerous the better. I wish they were twice as many. The easier the victory, depend on it." The plan upon which he had determined, if ever it should be his fortune to bring a Baltic fleet to action, was, to attack the head of their line, and confuse their movements. " Close with a French-man," he used to say, " but outmanœuvre a Russian." He offered his services for the attack, requiring ten sail of the line, and the whole of the smaller craft. Sir Hyde gave him two more line of battle ships than he asked, and left every-thing to his judgment.

The enemy's force was not the only, nor the greatest, obstacle with which the British fleet had to contend. There was another to be overcome before they could come in contact with it. The channel was little known, and ex-tremely intricate; all the buoys had been removed; and the Danes considered this difficulty as almost insuperable, thinking the channel impracticable for so large a fleet. Nelson himself saw the soundings made, and the buoys laid down, boating it upon this exhausting service, day and night, till it was effected. When this was done, he thanked God for having enabled him to get through this difficult part of his duty. " It had worn him down," he said, " and was infinitely more grievous to him than any resistance which he could experience from the enemy."

At the first council of war, opinions inclined to an attack from the eastward.[1] But the next day, the wind being southerly, after a second examination of the Danish posi-tion, it was determined to attack from the south, approach-ing in the manner which Nelson had suggested in his first thoughts. On the morning of the 1st of April the whole fleet removed to an anchorage within two leagues of the town, and off the N.W. end of the Middle Ground; a shoal lying exactly before the town, at about three-quarters of a

[1] For " eastward " read " northward." The entrance to the harbour does face roughly east; but what the Council of War had to decide was whether to go straight ahead from their position to the north of the town, or, adopting Nelson's plan, and moving from the south, to take the Danish defences in reverse.

mile's distance, and extending along its whole sea-front. The King's Channel, where there is deep water, is between this shoal and the town; and here the Danes had arranged their line of defence, as near the shore as possible; nineteen ships and floating batteries, flanked, at the end nearest the town, by the Crown Batteries, which were two artificial islands at the mouth of the harbour, most formidable works; the larger one having by the Danish account sixty-six guns, but, as Nelson believed, eighty-eight. The fleet having anchored, Nelson, with Riou, in the *Amazon*, made his last examination of the ground; and, about one o'clock, returning to his own ship, threw out the signal to weigh. It was received with a shout throughout the whole division. They weighed with a light and favourable wind. The narrow channel between the Island of Saltholm and the Middle Ground had been accurately buoyed. The small craft pointed out the course distinctly. Riou led the way. The whole division coasted along the outer edge of the shoal, doubled its farther extremity, and anchored there off Dragor Point,[1] just as the darkness closed—the headmost of the enemy's line not being more than two miles distant. The signal to prepare for action had been made early in the evening: and as his own anchor dropped, Nelson called out, " I will fight them the moment I have a fair wind." It had been agreed that Sir Hyde, with the remaining ships, should weigh on the following morning at the same time as Nelson, to menace the Crown Batteries (on his side) and the four ships of the line which lay at the entrance of the arsenal; and to cover our own disabled ships as they came out of action.

The Danes, meantime, had not been idle. No sooner did the guns of Kronburg make it known to the whole city that all negotiation was at an end, that the British fleet was passing the Sound, and that the dispute between the two crowns must now be decided by arms, than a spirit displayed itself most honourable to the Danish character. All ranks offered themselves to the service of their country; the university furnished a corps of twelve hundred youths, the flower of Denmark. It was one of those emergencies in which little drilling or discipline is necessary to render

---

[1] Not quite so far south.

courage available; they had nothing to learn but how to
manage the guns, and day and night were employed in
practising them. When the movements of Nelson's squadron
were perceived, it was known when and where the attack
was to be expected, and the line of defence was manned
indiscriminately by soldiers, sailors, and citizens. Had not
the whole attention of the Danes been directed to strengthen
their own means of defence, they might most materially
have annoyed the invading squadron, and, perhaps, frustrated the impending attack. For the British ships were
crowded in an anchoring ground of little extent; it was
calm, so that mortar-boats might have acted against them
to the utmost advantage; and they were within range of
shells from Amag Island. A few fell among them; but the
enemy soon ceased to fire. It was learned afterwards that,
fortunately for the fleet, the bed of the mortar had given
way; and the Danes either could not get it replaced, or,
in the darkness, lost the direction.

This was an awful night for Copenhagen, far more so than
for the British fleet, where the men were accustomed to
battle and victory, and had none of those objects before
their eyes which render death terrible. Nelson sat down to
table with a large party of his officers. He was, as he was
ever wont to be when on the eve of action, in high spirits,
and drank to a leading wind, and to the success of the
morrow. After supper they returned to their respective
ships, except Riou, who remained to arrange the order of
battle with Nelson and Foley, and to draw up instructions.
Hardy, meantime, went in a small boat to examine the
channel between them and the enemy, approaching so
near, that he sounded round their leading ship with a pole,
lest the noise of throwing the lead should discover him.
The incessant fatigue of body, as well as mind, which Nelson
had undergone during the last three days, had so exhausted
him, that he was earnestly urged to go to his cot; and his
old servant, Allen, using that kind of authority which long
and affectionate services entitled and enabled him to assume
on such occasions, insisted upon his complying. The cot
was placed on the floor, and he continued to dictate from it.
About eleven Hardy returned, and reported the practi-
cability of the channel and the depth of water up to the

enemy's line. About one, the orders were completed; and half-a-dozen clerks, in the foremost cabin, proceeded to transcribe them; Nelson frequently calling out to them from his cot to hasten their work, for the wind was becoming fair. Instead of attempting to get a few hours' sleep, he was constantly receiving reports on this important point. At daybreak it was announced as becoming perfectly fair. The clerks finished their work about six. Nelson, who was already up, breakfasted, and made signal for all captains. The land forces, and five hundred seamen under Captain Fremantle and the Hon. Colonel Stewart,[1] were to storm the Crown Battery as soon as its fire should be silenced: and Riou [2]—whom Nelson had never seen till this expedition, but whose worth he had instantly perceived and appreciated as it deserved—had the *Blanche* and *Alcmene* frigates, the *Dart* and *Arrow* sloops, and the *Zephyr* and *Otter* fire-ships, given him, with a special command to act as circumstances might require. Every other ship had its station appointed.

Between eight and nine, the pilots and masters were ordered on board the Admiral's ship. The pilots were mostly men who had been mates in Baltic traders; and their hesitation about the bearing of the east end of the shoal, and the exact line of deep water, gave ominous warning of how little their knowledge was to be trusted. The signal for action had been made. The wind was fair. Not a moment to be lost. Nelson urged them to be steady,—to be resolute, and to decide: but they wanted the only ground for steadiness and decision in such cases; and Nelson had reason to regret that he had not trusted to Hardy's single report. This was one of the most painful moments of his life; and he always spoke of it with bitterness. " I experienced in the Sound," said he, " the misery of having the honour of our country entrusted to a set of pilots, who have no other thought than to keep the ships clear of danger, and their own silly heads clear of shot. Everybody knows what I

[1] This gallant officer throughout the Battle of Copenhagen was present on the quarter-deck of the *Elephant*. He was subsequently asked by Messrs. Clarke and McArthur to contribute to their life of Nelson, and in response to the invitation wrote what must certainly be considered the best contemporary narrative extant. Southey quite rightly admired the composition and transferred it almost bodily to his own work thinly draped in the veil of paraphrase.

[2] Of the *Amazon* frigate.

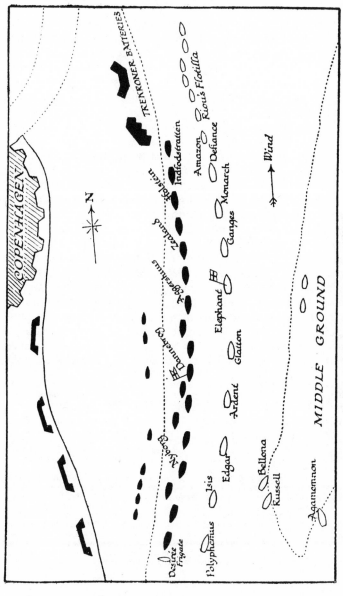

THE FIGHTING AT COPENHAGEN
(The dotted lines indicate the area of the shoals.)

must have suffered: and if any merit attaches itself to me, it was for combating the dangers of the shallows in defiance of them." At length Mr. Briarly,[1] the master of the *Bellona,* declared that he was prepared to lead the fleet. His judgment was acceded to by the rest. They returned to their ships; and, at half-past nine, the signal was made to weigh in succession.

Captain Murray, in the *Edgar,* led the way.[2] The *Agamemnon* was next in order; but on the first attempt to leave her anchorage, she could not weather the edge of the shoal; and Nelson had the grief to see his old ship, in which he had performed so many years' gallant services, immovably aground, at a moment when her help was so greatly required. Signal was then made for the *Polyphemus* :[3] and this change in the order of sailing was executed with the utmost promptitude. Yet so much delay had thus been unavoidably occasioned, that the *Edgar* was for some time unsupported :[4] and the *Polyphemus,* whose place should have been at the end of the enemy's line, where their strength was the greatest, could get no further than the beginning, owing to the difficulty of the channel: there she occupied, indeed, an efficient station, but one where her presence was less required.[5] The *Isis* followed, with better fortune, and took her own berth. The *Bellona* (Sir Thomas Boulden

---

[1] Alexander Briarly, Master of the *Bellona.*

[2] Nelson's proposed order of sailing was as follows: *Edgar, Agamemnon, Ardent, Glatton, Isis, Bellona, Elephant* (flag), *Ganges, Monarch, Defiance, Russell, Polyphemus.*

The *Edgar* was to anchor opposite number five in the enemy's line, and the remainder (with the exception of the *Isis* and *Agamemnon*) were to pass on the disengaged side of the *Edgar* and of those that took station ahead of her.

The first four ships of the enemy's line were to be engaged by the first three English in passing, and afterwards hammered into surrender by the *Isis* and *Agamemnon.*

[3] Last in the prescribed order, to take the *Agamemnon's* place and second the efforts of the *Isis* to subdue the first four of the Danish ships.

[4] There does not seem any real warrant for this remark. The Danes opened fire on the *Edgar* at 10.50; and the *Ardent,* according to her log, came to her sister's help and replied to the Danes at 11 o'clock. See below, Note 3, p. 223.

[5] By " end " of the line Southey means " northern end," where the fire of the ships was heavily reinforced by the immense ordnance of the Trekroner batteries. As, however, the *Polyphemus* was ordered into the *Agamemnon's* place, it is clear that she was not balked by the narrowness of the channel, but took station as required. Her log-book registers the occurrence quite clearly:

H.M. . . .	. 10.48 a.m.
Signal . . .	. 269
By whom made .	. *Elephant*
To whom addressed .	. *Polyphemus*
Signification . .	. Take station astern of the *Isis*

Thompson) kept too close on the starboard shoal,[1] and grounded abreast of the outer ship of the enemy.[2] This was the more vexatious, inasmuch as the wind was fair, the room ample, and three ships[3] had led the way. The *Russell*, following the *Bellona*, grounded in like manner.[4] Both were within reach of shot ;[5] but their absence from their intended stations was severely felt. Each ship had been ordered to pass her leader on the starboard side, because the water was supposed to shoal on the larboard shore.[6] Nelson, who came next after these two ships, thought they had kept too far on the starboard direction, and made signal for them to close with the enemy, not knowing that they were aground. But, when he perceived that they did not obey the signal, he ordered the *Elephant's* helm to starboard, and went within[7] these ships; thus quitting the appointed order of sailing, and guiding those which were to follow. The greater part of the fleet were probably, by this act of promptitude on his part, saved from going on shore. Each ship, as she arrived nearly opposite to her appointed station, let her anchor go by the stern,

[1] The Middle Ground.

[2] By " outer " ship Southey means the " southernmost." The comment, however, as the plan will show, is not quite accurate.

[3] Five! Southey has forgotten the *Ardent* and *Glatton*, both of whom took station without mishap. For this reason they are not mentioned in the earlier part of Colonel Stewart's narrative, which Southey uncritically follows. " After engaging from the south end of the enemy's line," says the log of the *Glatton*, " we anchored precisely in our station abreast of the Danish Commodore." See also above, Note 4, p. 222.

[4] The *Russell*, according to the prescribed arrangement, was last but one in the order of sailing. Her log shows clearly what happened. " At 10.15 weighed and made sail per signal after the *Defiance*. At 10.30 *made more sail*, our headmost ships being engaged with the enemy. At 10.40 the Admiral made the signal for the fleet to engage closer. At 11 o'clock our leader opened fire on the enemy. At five minutes after opened ours on the two southernmost floating batteries. Lost sight of our leader in the smoke, but soon after, seeing a ship's masthead in the same direction which we were coming up with, lowered our topsails on the cap. At a quarter past eleven ceased firing (one of our own ships passing us), and when the smoke cleared away found ourselves directly in the *Bellona's* wake." The *Russell*, in short, had, from sheer keenness, set canvas enough to develop a speed that took her ahead not only of her own leader (the *Defiance*), but of the *Monarch*, *Ganges*, and *Elephant*.

[5] " They were, however, within range of shot, and continued to fire with much spirit upon such of the enemy's ships as they could reach." (Colonel Stewart's narrative.)

[6] This is flat nonsense. On the larboard (left) side of the channel were the Danish ships; on the starboard side were the shoals of the Middle Ground. Every ship passed on the disengaged side of those already in action for obvious reasons. The *Isis* was busy anchoring under a heavy fire when the *Bellona* drew level with her, and it is conceivable that under such circumstances the *Bellona* allowed her sister too much elbow-room.

[7] To larboard of.

and presented her broadside to the Danes. The distance
between each was about half a cable.[1] The action was
fought nearly at the distance of a cable's length from the
enemy.[2] This, which rendered its continuance so long,
was owing to the ignorance and consequent indecision of
the pilots. In pursuance of the same error which had led
the *Bellona* and the *Russell* aground, they, when the lead
was at a quarter less five,[3] refused to approach nearer, in
dread of shoaling their water on the larboard shore: a fear
altogether erroneous, for the water deepened up to the
very side of the enemy's line.[4]

At five minutes after ten the action began. The first
half of our fleet was engaged in about half-an-hour ;[5] and,
by half-past eleven, the battle became general. The plan
of the attack had been complete: but seldom has any plan
been more disconcerted by untoward accidents. Of twelve
ships of the line, one was entirely useless, and two others
in a situation where they could not render half the service
which was required of them. Of the squadron of gun-brigs,
only one could get into action; the rest were prevented, by
baffling currents, from weathering the eastern end of the

[1] One hundred yards.
[2] The English captains loved to fight at the closest possible range. Collingwood
and Troubridge used to instruct their men not to discharge a gun until they could
see the whites of their enemies' eyes.
[3] The lead-line had a piece of black leather to indicate three fathoms, and a
piece of white rag to indicate five, but nothing to indicate four. The seaman
heaving the lead from the main-chains would chant aloud confidently, "By the
mark three," or "By the mark five"; but between these depths he would have
to make an estimate thus:

Estimate		Sing Out
3¼ fathoms	. . . .	"And a quarter three!"
3½ ,,	. . . .	"And a half three!"
3¾ ,,	. . . .	"A quarter less four!"
4 ,,	. . . .	"By the dip four!"
4¼ ,,	. . . .	"And a quarter four!"
4½ ,,	. . . .	"And a half four!"
4¾ ,,	. . . .	"A quarter less five!"

[4] The nervousness of the pilots (*i.e.*, lest the ship for which they were responsible
should come to grief) may possibly account for the range, which could, however,
be closed by the signal "Engage the enemy more closely!"
But the nervousness of the pilots does not explain why the *Bellona* grounded
on the starboard side of the channel. Southey is confusing two points which are
really quite separate. A quotation from the *Russell's* log has shown how that
ship lost her bearings in the screen of smoke: and it may well have been that the
Bellona felt the need of her Master (Mr. Briarly), whom she had lent to the *Edgar*
to pilot the fleet.
[5] This does not quite agree with the *Edgar's* log. "At ten, weighed with the
squadron and led through the King's Channel. At a quarter before eleven the
Danes opened a very heavy fire on us. At eleven came to anchor in seven fathom
water and opened fire on the enemy."

shoal; and only two of the bomb-vessels could reach their station on the Middle Ground, and open their mortars on the arsenal, firing over both fleets. Riou took the vacant station against the Crown Battery with his frigates; attempting, with that unequal force, a service in which three sail of the line had been directed to assist.[1]

Nelson's agitation had been extreme when he saw himself, before the action began, deprived of a fourth part of his ships of the line; but no sooner was he in battle, where his squadron was received with the fire of more than a thousand guns, than, as if that artillery like music had driven away all care and painful thoughts, his countenance brightened; and, as a bystander describes him, his conversation became joyous, animated, elevated, and delightful. The commander-in-chief, meantime, near enough to the scene of action to know the unfavourable accidents which had so materially weakened Nelson, and yet too distant to know the real state of the contending parties, suffered the most dreadful anxiety. To get to his assistance was impossible; both wind and current were against him. Fear for the event, in such circumstances, would naturally preponderate in the bravest mind; and at one o'clock, perceiving that, after three hours' endurance, the enemy's fire was unslackened, he began to despair of success.[2]

" I will make the signal of recall," said he to his captain, " for Nelson's sake. If he is in a condition to continue the action successfully, he will disregard it; if he is not, it will be an excuse for his retreat, and no blame can be imputed to him." Captain Domett urged him at least to delay the signal, till he could communicate with Nelson; but, in Sir Hyde's opinion, the danger was too pressing for delay. " The fire," he said, " was too hot for Nelson to oppose. A retreat he thought must be made. He was aware of the consequences to his own personal reputation, but it would be cowardly in him to leave Nelson to bear the whole shame of the failure, if shame it should be deemed." Under

[1] Nelson had given Riou a free hand; and Riou very pluckily opposed his small craft to the Trekroner batteries, which owing to the accidents to *Agamemnon, Bellona* and *Russell*, would otherwise have gone unmarked.
[2] In the first edition this paragraph concluded, " And at one o'clock, perceiving that, after three hours' endurance, the enemy's fire was unslackened, he began to despair of success; and thinking it became him to save what he could from the hopeless contest, he made signal for retreat."

a mistaken judgment, therefore, but with this disinterested and generous feeling, he made the signal for retreat.[1]

Nelson was at this time,[2] in all the excitement of action, pacing the quarter-deck. A shot through the mainmast knocked the splinters about; and he observed to one of his officers, with a smile, " It is warm work; and this day may be the last to any of us at a moment ": and then stopping short at the gangway, added, with emotion, " But mark you! I would not be elsewhere for thousands." About this time the signal lieutenant called out, that Number Thirty-nine (the signal for discontinuing the action) was thrown out by the commander-in-chief. He continued to walk the deck, and appeared to take no notice of it. The signal officer met him at the next turn, and asked if he should repeat it. " No," he replied; " acknowledge it. "[3] Presently he called after him to know if the signal for close action was still hoisted ;[4] and being answered in the affirmative, said, " Mind you keep it so." He now paced the deck, moving the stump of his lost arm in a manner which always indicated great emotion.[5] " Do you know," said he to Mr. Ferguson, " what is shown on board the

[1] This paragraph, which first occurs in the second edition, was accompanied by the following note (Vol. II. p. 125): " I have great pleasure in rendering this justice to Sir Hyde Parker's reasoning. The fact is here stated upon the highest and most unquestionable authority."

Mr. David Hannay has pointed out in an interesting article that Southey's " unquestionable authority " was his own brother Thomas, who was present at the battle and a close friend of Domett, Sir Hyde Parker's captain of the fleet.

[2] " Now," first edition.

[3] To " acknowledge " a signal is to hoist a flag showing that you have received the message and understood its meaning; to " repeat " it is to re-hoist the signal itself, thereby transmitting it as an order to those who are serving under you.

[4] No. 16.

[5] " The Admiral is working his fin (the stump of his right arm). Do not cross his hawse, I advise you! " (Nelsonian Reminiscences, Lieutenant G. S. Parsons.) Compare also Robert Browning:

Here's to Nelson's memory!
'Tis the second time that I, at sea,
Right off Cape Trafalgar here,
Have drunk it deep in British beer.
Nelson for ever—any time
Am I his to command in prose or rhyme!
Give of Nelson only a touch,
And I save it, be it little or much:
Here's one our Captain gives, and so
Down at the word, by George, shall it go!
He says that at Greenwich they point the beholder
To Nelson's coat, " still with tar on the shoulder:
For he used to lean with one shoulder digging,
Jigging, as it were, and zig-zag-zigging
Up against the mizzen-rigging! "

THE BALTIC CAMPAIGN

227

commander-in-chief? Number thirty-nine!" Mr. Ferguson
asked what that meant. "Why, to leave off action!" Then,
shrugging up his shoulders, he repeated the words, "Leave
off action! Now, damn me if I do! You know, Foley,"
turning to the captain, "I have only one eye,—I have a
right to be blind sometimes: "—and then, putting the glass
to his blind eye, in that mood of mind which sports with
bitterness, he exclaimed, "I really do not see the signal!"
Presently he exclaimed, "Damn the signal! Keep mine
for closer battle flying! That's the way I answer such
signals! Nail mine to the mast!"[1] Admiral Graves, who
was so situated that he could not discern what was done
on board the *Elephant,* disobeyed Sir Hyde's signal in like
manner: whether by fortunate mistake, or by a like brave
intention, has not been made known.[2] The other ships of
the line, looking only to Nelson, continued the action. The
signal, however, saved Riou's little squadron, but did not
save its heroic leader. This squadron, which was nearest

[1] Sir John Laughton, R.N., in his *Life of Nelson* (published 1895), extracted
all the point from this well-known story by an attempt to prove that there was
a preconcerted understanding between Parker and Nelson, so as to facilitate
withdrawal if the Danes proved too strong. Nelson "judged it right to continue;
and the little pantomime was only a joke, which Foley probably understood as
well as he did." (See also the article "Nelson" in the *Dictionary of National
Biography*.)

It is not to be doubted, as Sir John Laughton maintains, that Otway (Parker's
flag-captain) set out from the *London* to tell Nelson that the signal was permissive
in character. But as is clearly shown in Otway's life (Ralfe's *Naval Biography*),
he arrived too late. "Captain Otway fortunately reached his destination in
safety; but, before he got on board, the signal to leave off action was made. It
was, however, disregarded by Nelson."

In addition to this circumstantial evidence, we have the testimony of Colonel
Stewart on which Southey's narrative is based; and more recently (1900) an
interesting letter from Admiral Graves to his brother has been published by the
Navy Records Society (Vol. XVIII. pp. 101-3). This last sets the matter at rest
for ever. "Sir Hyde," writes Nelson's second, "made the signal to discontinue
the action before we had been at it two hours. But our little Hero gloriously said,
'I will not move till we are crowned with victory, or that the Commander-in-Chief
sends an officer to order me away!' And he was right, for if we had discontinued
the action before the enemy struck, we should all have got aground and have been
destroyed."

[2] Southey's narrative differs here in one or two respects from Colonel Stewart's,
which is perhaps worth quoting. "After a turn or two he said to me in a quick
manner, 'Do you know what's shown on board of the commander-in-chief?
No. 39!' On asking him what that meant, he answered, 'Why, to leave off
action!' 'Leave off action!' he repeated, and then added with a shrug, 'Now,
damn me if I do.' He also observed, I believe to Captain Foley, 'You know,
Foley, I have only one eye—I have a right to be blind sometimes'; and then,
with an archness peculiar to his character, he exclaimed, 'I really do not see the
signal.' This remarkable signal was, therefore, only acknowledged on board the
Elephant, not repeated. Admiral Graves did the latter, not being able to distinguish the *Elephant's* conduct. (But) either by a fortunate accident, or
intentionally No. 16 was not displaced."

the commander-in-chief, obeyed, and hauled off. It had suffered severely in its most unequal contest. For a long time the *Amazon* had been firing, enveloped in smoke, when Riou desired his men to stand fast, and let the smoke clear off, that they might see what they were about. A fatal order; for the Danes then got clear sight of her from the batteries, and pointed their guns with such tremendous effect, that nothing but the signal for retreat saved this frigate from destruction. " What will Nelson think of us? " was Riou's mournful exclamation, when he unwillingly drew off. He had been wounded in the head by a splinter, and was sitting on a gun, encouraging his men, when, just as the *Amazon* showed her stern to the Trekroner Battery, his clerk was killed by his side; and another shot swept away several marines, who were hauling in the main-brace. " Come, then, my boys! " cried Riou; " let us die all together! " The words had scarcely been uttered, before a raking shot cut him in two. Except it had been Nelson himself, the British navy could not have suffered a severer loss.[1]

The action continued along the line with unabated vigour on our side, and with the most determined resolution on the part of the Danes. They fought to great advantage, because most of the vessels in their line of defence were without masts. The few which had any standing had their topmasts struck, and the hulls could not be seen at intervals. The *Isis* must have been destroyed by the superior weight of her enemy's fire, if Captain Inman, in the *Desirée* frigate, had not judiciously taken a situation which enabled him to rake the Dane, and if the *Polyphemus* had not also relieved her. Both in the *Bellona* and the *Isis* many men were lost by the bursting of their guns. The former ship was about forty years old, and these guns were believed to be the same which she had first taken to sea. They were, probably, originally faulty, for the fragments were full of little air-holes. The *Bellona* lost seventy-five men; the *Isis*, one

[1] Brave hearts! to Britain's pride
Once so faithful and so true,
On the deck of fame that died
With the gallant good Riou:
Soft sigh the winds of heaven o'er their grave!
While the billow mournful rolls
And the mermaid's song condoles,
Singing glory to the souls
    Of the brave!   CAMPBELL.

hundred and ten; the *Monarch*, two hundred and ten. She was, more than any other line of battle ship, exposed to the great battery: and supporting at the same time the united fire of the *Holstein* and the *Zealand*, her loss this day exceeded that of any single ship during the whole war.[1] Amid the tremendous carnage in this vessel, some of the men displayed a singular instance of coolness; the pork and peas happened to be in the kettle; a shot knocked its contents about; they picked up the pieces, and ate and fought at the same time.

The Prince Royal had taken his station upon one of the batteries, from whence he beheld the action, and issued his orders. Denmark had never been engaged in so arduous a contest, and never did the Danes more nobly display their national courage, a courage not more unhappily than impoliticly exerted in subserviency to the interest of France. Captain Thura, of the *Indfodstratten*, fell early in the action; and all his officers, except one lieutenant and one marine officer, were either killed or wounded. In the confusion, the colours were either struck or shot away; but she was moored athwart one of the batteries in such a situation, that the British made no attempt to board her; and a boat was dispatched to the Prince, to inform him of her situation. He turned to those about him, and said, " Gentlemen, Thura is killed; which of you will take the command? " Schroedersee, a captain who had lately resigned on account of extreme ill-health, answered in a feeble voice, " I will! " and hastened on board. The crew, perceiving a new commander coming alongside, hoisted their colours again, and fired a broadside. Schroedersee, when he came on deck, found himself surrounded by the dead and wounded, and called to those in the boat to get quickly on board. A ball struck him at that moment. A lieutenant, who had accompanied him, then took the command, and continued to fight the ship. A youth of seventeen, by name Villemoes, particularly distinguished himself on this memorable day. He had volunteered to take the command of a floating battery; which was a raft, consisting merely of a number of beams nailed together, with a flooring to support the guns. It was

---

[1] This is too sweeping a statement. At Trafalgar the *Redoutable* lost 522 out of 643.

S

square, with a breastwork full of port-holes, and without masts, carrying twenty-four guns, and one hundred and twenty men. With this he got under the stern of the *Elephant*, below the reach of the stern-chasers; and, under a heavy fire of small arms from the marines, fought his raft, till the truce was announced, with such skill, as well as courage, as to excite Nelson's warmest admiration.

Between one and two the fire of the Danes slackened. About two it ceased from the greater part of their line, and some of their lighter ships were adrift. It was, however, difficult to take possession of those which struck, because the batteries on Amag Island protected them; and because an irregular fire was kept up from the ships themselves as the boats approached. This arose from the nature of the action. The crews were continually reinforced from the shore; and fresh men coming on board, did not inquire whether the flag had been struck, or, perhaps, did not heed it; many or most of them never having been engaged in war before, knowing nothing, therefore, of its laws, and thinking only of defending their country to the last extremity. The *Dannebrog* fired upon the *Elephant's* boats in this manner, though her commodore had removed her pendant and deserted her; though she had struck; and though she was in flames. After she had been abandoned by the commodore, Braun fought her till he lost his right hand, and then Captain Lemming took the command. This unexpected renewal of her fire made the *Elephant* and *Glatton* renew theirs, till she was not only silenced, but nearly every man in the praams,[1] ahead and astern of her, was killed. When the smoke of their guns died away, she was seen drifting in flames before the wind; those of her crew who remained alive and able to exert themselves throwing themselves out at her port-holes. Captain Bertie of the *Ardent* sent his launch to their assistance, and saved three-and-twenty of them.

Captain Rothe commanded the *Nyborg* praam; and, perceiving that she could not much longer be kept afloat, made for the inner road. As he passed the line, he found the *Aggershuus* praam in a more miserable condition than

---

[1] A cavalry transport. There were three such in the Danish fleet, but none of them took station ahead or astern of the *Dannebrog*.

his own; her masts had all gone by the board, and she was on the point of sinking. Rothe made fast a cable to her stern, and towed her off. But he could get her no farther than a shoal called Stubben, when she sank; and soon after he had worked the *Nyborg* up to the landing-place, that vessel also sank to her gunwale. Never did any vessel come out of action in a more dreadful plight. The stump of her foremast was the only stick standing; her cabin had been stove in; every gun, except a single one, was dismounted; and her deck was covered with shattered limbs and dead bodies.

By half-past two the action had ceased along that part of the line which was astern of the *Elephant*, but not with the ships ahead and the Crown Batteries. Nelson, seeing the manner in which his boats were fired upon, when they went to take possession of the prizes, became angry, and said he must either send on shore to have this irregular proceeding stopped, or send a fire-ship and burn them. Half the shot from the Trekroner, and from the batteries at Amag, at this time, struck the surrendered ships, four of which had got close together; and the fire of the English, in return, was equally or even more destructive to these poor devoted Danes. Nelson, who was as humane as he was brave, was shocked at this massacre—for such he called it: and with a presence of mind peculiar to himself, and never more signally displayed than now, he retired into the stern-gallery and wrote thus to the Crown Prince, " Vice-Admiral Lord Nelson has been commanded to spare Denmark when she no longer resists. The line of defence which covered her shores has struck to the British flag: but if the firing is continued on the part of Denmark, he must set on fire all the prizes that he has taken, without having the power of saving the men who have so nobly defended them. The brave Danes are the brothers, and should never be the enemies, of the English. "[1]   A wafer

---

[1] The actual letter which still survives in the Danish archives runs as follows:
" To the brothers of Englishmen, the Danes.
" Lord Nelson has directions to spare Denmark when no longer resisting, but if the firing is continued on the part of Denmark Lord Nelson will be obliged to set on fire all the floating batteries he has taken, without having the power of saving the brave Danes who have defended them.
" Dated on board His Britannic Majesty's ship *Elephant*, Copenhagen Roads, April 2nd, 1801.
" NELSON AND BRONTE, vice-admiral under the command of Admiral Sir Hyde Parker."

was given him; but he ordered a candle to be brought
from the cockpit, and sealed the letter with wax, affixing
a larger seal than he ordinarily used. " This," said he, " is
no time to appear hurried and informal." Captain Sir
Frederic Thesiger,[1] who acted as his aide-de-camp, carried
this letter with a flag of truce. Meantime the fire of the
ships ahead, and the approach of the *Ramillies* and *Defence*
from Sir Hyde's division, which had now worked near enough
to alarm the enemy, though not to injure them, silenced
the remainder of the Danish line to the eastward of the
Trekroner.[2]   That battery, however, continued its fire.
This formidable work, owing to the want of the ships which
had been destined to attack it, and the inadequate force
of Riou's little squadron, was comparatively uninjured.
Towards the close of the action it had been manned with
nearly fifteen hundred men; and the intention of storming
it, for which every preparation had been made, was abandoned as impracticable.

During Thesiger's absence, Nelson sent for Fremantle
from the *Ganges*, and consulted with him and Foley, whether
it was advisable to advance, with those ships which had
sustained least damage, against the yet uninjured part of
the Danish line.[3] They were decidedly of opinion, that the
best thing which could be done was, while the wind continued fair, to remove the fleet out of the intricate channel,
from which it had to retreat. In somewhat more than half
an hour after Thesiger had been dispatched, the Danish
Adjutant-General Lindholm came, bearing a flag of truce;
upon which the Trekroner ceased to fire, and the action
closed, after four hours' continuance. He brought an inquiry from the Prince, " What was the object of Nelson's
note?" The British Admiral wrote in reply, " Lord Nelson's
object in sending the flag of truce was humanity: he therefore consents that hostilities shall cease, and that the
wounded Danes may be taken on shore. And Lord Nelson
will take his prisoners out of the vessels, and burn or carry
off his prizes as he shall think fit. Lord Nelson, with humble

---

[1] Thesiger had a good knowledge of the Danish language.
[2] It would be better to say " ahead of the *Elephant*."
[3] A separate squadron of the Danish fleet numbering seven ships (*Elephanten,
Mars, Dannemark, Trekroner, Iris, Sarpen, Nidelven*) had been detached to assist
the Crown Batteries on their northern side in defending the fairway that led
into Copenhagen.

duty to his Royal Highness the Prince, will consider this the greatest victory he has ever gained, if it may be the cause of a happy reconciliation and union between his own most gracious sovereign and his Majesty the King of Denmark." [1] Sir Frederic Thesiger was dispatched a second time with the reply; and the Danish adjutant-general was referred to the commander-in-chief for a conference upon this overture. Lindholm, assenting to this, proceeded to the *London*, which was riding at anchor full four miles off; and Nelson, losing not one of the critical moments which he had thus gained, made signal for his leading ships to weigh in succession. They had the shoal to clear, they were much crippled, and their course was immediately under the guns of the Trekroner.

The *Monarch* led the way. This ship had received six-and-twenty shot between wind and water. She had not a shroud standing. There was a double-headed shot in the heart of her foremast, and the slightest wind would have sent every mast over her side.[2] The imminent danger from which Nelson had extricated himself soon became apparent. The *Monarch* touched immediately upon a shoal, over which she was pushed by the *Ganges* taking her amidships. The *Glatton* went clear; but the other two, the *Defiance* and the *Elephant*, grounded about a mile from the Trekroner, and there remained fixed, for many hours, in spite of all the

[1] " Lord Nelson's object in sending on shore a flag of truce is humanity, there-ore consents that hostilities shall cease till Lord Nelson can take his prisoners out of the prizes; and he consents to land all the wounded Danes and to burn or remove his prizes. Lord Nelson with humble duty to His Royal Highness begs leave to say that he will ever esteem it the greatest Victory he has ever gain'd if this flag of truce may be the happy forerunner of a lasting and happy Union between my most Gracious Sovereign and His Majesty the King of Denmark.

"Nelson and Bronte,
"*Elephant*, April 2nd, 1801."
(From the original in the Danish Archives.)

It was the custom for the purser to take the Admiral's rough draft and convert it into grammatical English. Mr. Thomas Wallis, purser of the *Elephant*, who stood by Nelson as the scribbling was done on the casing of the rubber head, by force of habit corrected the Admiral's style; and it was Wallis's corrected version that Southey printed. But it was his own hasty holograph, and not a fair copy, that Nelson sent ashore.

[2] It would have been well if the fleet, before they went under the batteries, had left their spare spars moored out of reach of shot. Many would have been saved which were destroyed lying on the booms, and the hurt done by their splinters would have been saved also. Small craft could have towed them up when they were required: and, after such an action, so many must necessarily be wanted, that, if those which were not in use were wounded, it might have rendered it impossible to refit the ships.—SOUTHEY'S NOTE.

exertions of their wearied crews. The *Desirée* frigate also, at the other end of the line, having gone toward the close of the action to assist the *Bellona*, became fast on the same shoal.

Nelson left the *Elephant*, soon after she took the ground, to follow Lindholm. The heat of action was over, and that kind of feeling, which the surrounding scene of havoc was so well fitted to produce, pressed heavily upon his exhausted spirits. The sky had suddenly become overcast. White flags were waving from the mastheads of so many shattered ships. The slaughter had ceased; but the grief was to come; for the account of the dead was not yet made up, and no man could tell for what friends he might have to mourn. The very silence which follows the cessation of such a battle becomes a weight upon the heart at first, rather than a relief; and though the work of mutual destruction was at an end, the *Dannebrog* was, at this time, drifting about in flames. Presently she blew up; while our boats, which had put off in all directions to assist her, were endeavouring to pick up her devoted crew, few of whom could be saved. The fate of these men, after the gallantry which they had displayed, particularly affected Nelson; for there was nothing in this action of that indignation against the enemy, and that impression of retributive justice, which at the Nile had given a sterner temper to his mind, and a sense of austere delight, in beholding the vengeance of which he was the appointed minister. The Danes were an honourable foe. They were of English mould as well as English blood; and now that the battle had ceased, he regarded them rather as brethren than as enemies. There was another reflection also, which mingled with these melancholy thoughts, and predisposed him to receive them. He was not here master of his own movements, as at Egypt. He had won the day by disobeying his orders; and in so far as he had been successful, had convicted the commander-in-chief of an error in judgment. "Well," said he, as he left the *Elephant*, "I have fought contrary to orders, and I shall perhaps be hanged. Never mind: let them!"

This was the language of a man who, while he is giving utterance to an uneasy thought, clothes it half in jest, because he half repents that it has been disclosed. His services had been too eminent on that day, his judgment too conspicuous, his success too signal, for any commander, however jealous of his own authority, or envious of another's merits, to express anything but satisfaction and gratitude: which Sir Hyde heartily felt, and sincerely expressed. It was speedily agreed that there should be a suspension of hostilities for four-and-twenty hours; that all the prizes should be surrendered, and the wounded Danes carried on shore. There was a pressing necessity for this: for the Danes, either from too much confidence in the strength of their position, and the difficulty of the channel; or supposing that the wounded might be carried on shore during the action, which was found totally impracticable; or, perhaps, from the confusion which the attack excited—had provided no surgeons: so that, when our men boarded the captured ships, they found many of the mangled and mutilated Danes bleeding to death for want of proper assistance—a scene, of all others, the most shocking to a brave man's feelings.[1]

[1] The outstanding problem of the Battle of Copenhagen is concerned with Nelson's employment of a flag of truce. Hardly was the last shot of the conflict fired before Niebuhr, the famous historian, impugned the British Admiral's conduct; and from that hour to this there have been doubting Thomases who have questioned Nelson's own estimate that the victory of the Baltic was greater than that of the Nile. The arguments of hostile critics, which have really arisen out of a confusion of thought, may be epitomised as follows:

(1) When Nelson attempted to conduct his fleet out of the King's Deep some of its prime factors ran aground.

(2) These would undoubtedly have been destroyed if the Trekroner had not been silenced by a flag of truce.

(3) Therefore, Nelson's object in sending a flag of truce ashore was to silence the Danish batteries while he removed his vessels from a death-trap.

Now it is undoubtedly true that some of Nelson's best ships (including the *Elephant*) ran aground in retiring from the King's Deep; and it is undoubtedly true that, if the Trekroner had been firing, these ships would have been destroyed. But because the Trekroner had ceased to fire, they could move about with safety; and the Trekroner had ceased to fire, because the Danes of their free will had agreed to Nelson's demand, that without further let or hindrance on their part he should carry away, not his ships, but their own.

How had they been induced to make this concession?

After more than three hours of battle their ships had signified in the usual fashion that they could sustain the struggle no longer.

Nelson thereupon would have boarded them as prizes; but was unable to do so because the Amag batteries, or fresh recruits from shore (it is uncertain which), reopened fire upon his boarding-parties.

Nelson might, on his part, legitimately have poured in fresh broadsides; but, as the ships opposed to him had hauled down their colours, such a course of action was utterly repugnant to him. There was, however, another alternative.

He could send down fireships, which would speak in a language common to all men; but which, before completing the victory, would warn able-bodied defenders to escape in boats to the shore. His own fleet could then join in a massed attack upon the Trekroner.

Now as the Danes could sustain the struggle no longer, it might seem to them preferable that their ships should perish on the battlefield rather than be carried off to adorn a victor's triumph. On the other hand, to Nelson it seemed infinitely better to seize rather than destroy the fruits of conquest. In other words, the threat of fireships was as much a menace to himself as to his enemies.

But he found an argument to his purpose none the less. Though the able-bodied could escape from the Danish hulks, the wounded would certainly fail to do so. In a flash of thought, therefore, he saw that he could take possession of his prizes by putting upon Denmark the care of its own wounded. If resistance continues, so ran his message, the Danes will be responsible for the lives of those who are burnt to death in the coming holocaust.

The Danes accepted the responsibility, and ordered firing to cease.

Now it has been urged by eminent historians that in this line of action Nelson was employing an unworthy *ruse de guerre*. He could not, it has been urged, have burnt the Danish fleet, because its removal would have exposed him to the fire of the Amag batteries. But this is to misapprehend the whole situation. The Danish fleet had been stationed in the King's Deep to cover the city from the terror of bombardment. When the fleet was removed, the English bomb-vessels could move inshore and pour their hail of projectiles into the city.

But putting this aside, we are told that Nelson would never have given effect to his menace, because the laws of humanity would have held him back. This is a more forcible argument. But does his unwillingness to burn the Danish fleet constitute an adequate reason why he should not threaten to do so? The accidental destruction of the Danish flagship by fire lent terror to the mere suggestion. And if, by a timely use of bluff, he restrained his adversaries from violating the laws of warfare, he was surely more than justified in the course which he pursued.

CHAPTER II

AFTER THE BATTLE

[SOUTHEY. CHAPTER VII—continued]

THE boats of Sir Hyde's division were actively employed all night in bringing out the prizes, and in getting afloat the ships which were on shore. At daybreak, Nelson, who had slept in his own ship, the *St. George*, rowed to the *Elephant*; and his delight at finding her afloat seemed to give him new life. There he took a hasty breakfast, praising the men for their exertions, and then pushed off to the prizes which had not yet been removed. The *Zealand*, seventy-four, the last which struck, had drifted on the shoal under the Trekroner; and relying, as it seems, upon the protection which that battery might have afforded, refused to acknowledge herself captured; saying, that though it was true her flag was not to be seen, her pendant was still flying. Nelson ordered one of our brigs and three long-boats to approach her, and rowed up himself to one of the enemy's ships, to communicate with the commodore. This officer proved to be an old acquaintance, whom he had known in the West Indies: so he invited himself on board; and, with that urbanity, as well as decision, which always characterised him, urged his claim to the *Zealand* so well, that it was admitted. The men from the boats lashed a cable round her bowsprit, and the gun-vessel towed her away. It is affirmed, and probably with truth, that the Danes felt more pain at beholding this, than at all their misfortunes on the preceding day: and one of the officers, Commodore Stein Bille,[1] went to the Trekroner battery, and asked the commander why he had not sunk the *Zealand*, rather than suffer her thus to be carried off by the enemy?

This was, indeed, a mournful day for Copenhagen! It was Good Friday; but the general agitation, and the mourning which was in every house, made all distinction of days

---

[1] Captain of the *Dannemark*; *cp.* Note 3, p. 232.

be forgotten. There were, at that hour, thousands in that city, who felt, and more, perhaps, who needed, the consolations of Christianity; but few or none who could be calm enough to think of its observances. The English were actively employed in refitting their own ships, securing the prizes, and distributing the prisoners; the Danes, in carrying on shore and disposing of the wounded and the dead. It had been a murderous action. Our loss, in killed and wounded, was nine hundred and fifty-three. Part of this slaughter might have been spared. The commanding officer of the troops on board one of our ships asked where his men should be stationed? He was told that they could be of no use; that they were not near enough for musketry; and were not wanted at the guns; they had, therefore, better go below. This, he said, was impossible. It would be a disgrace that could never be wiped away. They were, therefore, drawn up upon the gangway, to satisfy this cruel point of honour; and there, without the possibility of annoying the enemy, they were mowed down! The loss of the Danes, including prisoners, amounted to about six thousand.[1] The negotiations, meantime, went on; and it was agreed that Nelson should have an interview with the Prince the following day. Hardy and Fremantle landed with him. This was a thing as unexampled as the other circumstances of the battle. A strong guard was appointed to escort him to the palace, as much for the purpose of security as of honour. The populace, according to the British account, showed a mixture of admiration, curiosity, and displeasure, at beholding that man in the midst of them who had inflicted such wounds upon Denmark. But there were neither acclamations nor murmurs. " The people," says a Dane, " did not degrade themselves with the former, nor disgrace themselves with the latter. The Admiral was received as one brave enemy ever ought to receive another. He was received with respect." The preliminaries of the negotiation were adjusted at this interview. During the repast which followed, Nelson, with all the sincerity of his character, bore willing testimony to the valour of his foes. He told the Prince that he had been in a hundred and five

---

[1] Mr. Jon Stefansson in a letter to *The Times* (18th January, 1917) put the figures at 375 killed, 670 wounded, and 1779 prisoners.

engagements, but that this was the most tremendous of all.
" The French," he said, " fought bravely; but they could
not have stood for one hour the fight which the Danes had
supported for four." He requested that Villemoes might
be introduced to him; and, shaking hands with the youth,
told the Prince that he ought to be made an admiral. The
Prince replied, " If, my lord, I am to make all my brave
officers admirals, I should have no captains or lieutenants
in my service."

The sympathy of the Danes for their countrymen, who
had bled in their defence, was not weakened by distance of
time or place in this instance. Things needful for the service,
or the comfort of the wounded, were sent in profusion to
the hospitals, till the superintendents gave public notice
that they could receive no more. On the third day after
the action, the dead were buried in the naval churchyard.
The ceremony was made as public and as solemn as the
occasion required. Such a procession had never before
been seen in that, or, perhaps, in any other city. A public
monument was erected upon the spot where the slain were
gathered together. A subscription was opened on the day
of the funeral for the relief of the sufferers, and collections
in aid of it made throughout all the churches in the kingdom. This appeal to the feelings of the people was made
with circumstances which gave it full effect. A monument
was raised in the midst of the church, surmounted by the
Danish colours. Young maidens, dressed in white, stood
round it, with either one who had been wounded in the
battle, or the widow and orphans of some one who had fallen.
A suitable oration was delivered from the pulpit, and patriotic hymns and songs were afterwards performed. Medals
were distributed to all the officers, and to the men who had
distinguished themselves. Poets and painters vied with
each other in celebrating a battle which, disastrous as it
was, had yet been honourable to their country. Some,
with pardonable sophistry, represented the advantage of
the day as on their own side. One writer discovered a more
curious, but less disputable ground of satisfaction, in the
reflection, that Nelson, as may be inferred from his name,
was of Danish descent, and his actions, therefore, the Dane
argued, were attributable to Danish valour.

The negotiation was continued during the five following days; and, in that interval, the prizes were disposed of in a manner which was little approved by Nelson. Six line-of-battle ships and eight praams had been taken. Of these the *Holstein*, sixty-four, was the only one which was sent home. The *Zealand* was a finer ship: but the *Zealand*, and all the others, were burned, and their brass cannon sunk with the hulls in such shoal water, that, when the fleet returned from Revel, they found the Danes, with craft over the wrecks, employed in getting the guns up again. Nelson, though he forbore from any public expression of displeasure at seeing the proofs and trophies of his victory destroyed, did not forget to represent to the Admiralty the case of those who were thus deprived of their prize-money. " Whether," said he to Earl St. Vincent, " Sir Hyde Parker may mention the subject to you, I know not; for he is rich and does not want it: nor is it, you will believe me, any desire to get a few hundred pounds that actuates me to address this letter to you; but justice to the brave officers and men who fought on that day. It is true our opponents were in hulks and floats, only adapted for the position they were in; but that made our battle so much the harder, and victory so much the more difficult to obtain. Believe me, I have weighed all circumstances; and, in my conscience, I think that the King should send a gracious message to the House of Commons for a gift to this fleet: for what must be the natural feelings of the officers and men belonging to it, to see their rich commander-in-chief burn all the fruits of their victory,—which if fitted up and sent to England (as many of them might have been by dismantling part of our fleet) would have sold for a good round sum."

On the 9th Nelson landed again, to conclude the terms of the armistice. During its continuance the armed ships and vessels of Denmark were to remain in their then actual situation, as to armament, equipment, and hostile position; and the treaty of Armed Neutrality, as far as related to the co-operation of Denmark, was suspended. The prisoners were to be sent on shore; an acknowledgment being given for them, and for the wounded also, that they might be carried to Great Britain's credit in the account of war, in case hostilities should be renewed. The British fleet was

allowed to provide itself with all things requisite for the
health and comfort of its men. A difficulty arose respecting
the duration of the armistice. The Danish commissioners
fairly stated their fears of Russia; and Nelson, with that
frankness which sound policy and the sense of power seem
often to require as well as justify in diplomacy, told them,
his reason for demanding a long term was, that he might
have time to act against the Russian fleet, and then return
to Copenhagen. Neither party would yield upon this point;
and one of the Danes hinted at the renewal of hostilities.
" Renew hostilities ! " cried Nelson to one of his friends,
—for he understood French enough to comprehend what
was said, though not to answer it in the same language;
—" tell him we are ready at a moment! Ready to bombard
this very night ! " The conference, however, proceeded
amicably on both sides; and as the commissioners could
not agree upon this head, they broke up, leaving Nelson to
settle it with the Prince. A levee was held forthwith in one
of the state rooms; a scene well suited for such a consultation: for all these rooms had been stripped of their furniture
in fear of a bombardment. To a bombardment also Nelson
was looking at this time. Fatigue and anxiety and vexation
at the dilatory measures of the Commander-in-Chief combined to make him irritable; and as he was on the way to
the Prince's dining-room, he whispered to the officer on whose
arm he was leaning, " Though I have only one eye, I can
see that all this will burn well." After dinner he was closeted
with the Prince; and they agreed that the armistice should
continue fourteen weeks; and that, at its termination,
fourteen days' notice should be given before the recom-
mencement of hostilities.

An official account of the battle was published by Olfert
Fischer, the Danish Commander-in-Chief, in which it was
asserted that our force was greatly superior; nevertheless,
that two of our ships of the line had struck; that the others
were so weakened, and especially Lord Nelson's own ship,
as to fire only single shots for an hour before the end of the
action; and that this hero himself, in the middle and very
heat of the conflict, sent a flag of truce on shore, to propose
a cessation of hostilities. For the truth of this account the
Dane appealed to the Prince, and all those who, like him,

had been eye-witnesses of the scene. Nelson was exceedingly indignant at such a statement, and addressed a letter,
in confutation of it, to the Adjutant-General Lindholm;
thinking this incumbent upon him, for the information of
the Prince, since his Royal Highness had been appealed to
as a witness: "Otherwise," said he, "had Commodore
Fischer confined himself to his own veracity, I should have
treated his official letter with the contempt it deserved
and allowed the world to appreciate the merits of the two
contending officers." After pointing out and detecting
some of the misstatements in the account, he proceeds,
"As to his nonsense about victory, his Royal Highness will
not much credit him. I sank, burnt, captured, or drove into
the harbour, the whole line of defence to the southward of
the Crown Islands. He says he is told that two British ships
struck. Why did he not take possession of them? I took
possession of his as fast as they struck. The reason is clear,
that he did not believe it. He must have known the falsity
of the report. He states, that the ship in which I had the
honour to hoist my flag fired latterly only single guns. It is
true: for steady and cool were my brave fellows, and did
not wish to throw away a single shot. He seems to exult
that I sent on shore a flag of truce. You know, and his
Royal Highness knows, that the guns fired from the shore
could only fire through the Danish ships which had surrendered; and that, if I fired at the shore, it could only be
in the same manner. God forbid that I should destroy an
unresisting Dane! When they became my prisoners, I
became their protector."

This letter was written in terms of great asperity against
the Danish commander. Lindholm replied in a manner
every way honourable to himself. He vindicated the
commodore in some points, and excused him in others;
reminding Nelson that every commander-in-chief was liable
to receive incorrect reports. With a natural desire to represent the action in the most favourable light to Denmark,
he took into the comparative strength of the two parties
the ships which were aground, and which could not get into
action; and omitted the Trekroner and the batteries upon
Amag Island. He disclaimed all idea of claiming as a
victory, "what, to every intent and purpose," said he,

" was a defeat,—but not an inglorious one. As to your
lordship's motive for sending a flag of truce, it never can
be misconstrued; and your subsequent conduct has sufficiently shown that humanity is always the companion of
true valour. You have done more; you have shown yourself
a friend to the re-establishment of peace and good harmony
between this country and Great Britain. It is, therefore,
with the sincerest esteem I shall always feel myself attached
to your lordship." Thus handsomely winding up his reply,
he soothed and contented Nelson; who, drawing up a
memorandum of the comparative force of the two parties,
for his own satisfaction, assured Lindholm, that if the
commodore's statement had been in the same manly and
honourable strain, he would have been the last man to have
noticed any little inaccuracies which might get into a
commander-in-chief's public letter.[1]

For the battle of Copenhagen, Nelson was raised to the
rank of viscount—an inadequate mark of reward for
services so splendid and of such paramount importance to
the dearest interests of England. There was, however,
some prudence in dealing out honours to him step by
step: had he lived long enough, he would have fought his
way up to a dukedom.

[SOUTHEY. CHAPTER VIII]

WHEN Nelson informed Earl St. Vincent that the armistice
had been concluded, he told him also, without reserve,
his own discontent at the dilatoriness and indecision which
he witnessed, and could not remedy. " No man," said he,
" but those who are on the spot, can tell what I have gone
through, and do suffer. I make no scruple in saying, that
I would have been at Revel [2] fourteen days ago! that,
without this armistice, the fleet would never have gone,

---

[1] Nelson wrote his rather intemperate letter not to the offending Fischer,
but to Lindholm, whom he had known before the battle, and whose acquaintance
he had renewed under the flag of truce. The protest was intended primarily
for the Crown Prince and probably reached its destination; but it was carefully
kept by him from the cognisance of the Danish Commander-in-Chief; and with
Lindholm's gracefully worded reply Nelson's anger was appeased, and the incident
ended. Fischer, of course, was only attempting to save his credit in the eyes of
his countrymen.

[2] At the entrance to the Gulf of Finland.

but by order of the Admiralty: and with it, I dare say, we shall not go this week. I wanted Sir Hyde to let me, at least, go and cruise off Carlscrona,[1] to prevent the Revel ships from getting in. I said I would not go to Revel to take any of those laurels which I was sure he would reap there. Think of me, my dear lord;—and if I have deserved well, let me return: if ill, for Heaven's sake supersede me,—for I cannot exist in this state."

Fatigue, incessant anxiety, and a climate little suited to one of a tender constitution, which had now for many years been accustomed to more genial latitudes, made him at this time seriously determine upon returning home. " If the northern business were not settled," he said, " they must send more admirals; for the keen air of the north had cut him to the heart." He felt the want of activity and decision in the Commander-in-Chief more keenly; and this affected his spirits, and, consequently, his health, more than the inclemency of the Baltic. Soon after the armistice was signed, Sir Hyde proceeded to the eastward, with such ships as were fit for service, leaving Nelson to follow, with the rest, as soon as those which had received slight damages should be repaired, and the rest sent to England. In passing between the Isles of Amag and Saltholm, most of the ships touched the ground, and some of them stuck fast for a while. No serious injury, however, was sustained. It was intended to act against the Russians first, before the breaking up of the frost should enable them to leave Revel; but learning on the way that the Swedes had put to sea to effect a junction with them, Sir Hyde altered his course, in hopes of intercepting this part of the enemy's force. Nelson had, at this time, provided for the more pressing emergencies of the service, and prepared, on the 18th, to follow the fleet. The *St. George* drew too much water to pass the channel between the isles without being lightened. The guns were therefore taken out, and put on board an American vessel. A contrary wind, however, prevented Nelson from moving; and on that same evening while he was thus delayed, information reached him of the relative situation of the Swedish and British fleets, and the probability of an

---

[1] On the mainland north of Bornholm (see map) and in the latitude of Helsingborg.

action. The fleet was nearly ten leagues distant, and both wind and current contrary; but it was not possible that Nelson could wait for a favourable season under such an expectation. He ordered his boat immediately, and stepped into it. Night was setting in,—one of the cold, spring nights of the north, and it was discovered, soon after they had left the ship, that in their haste they had forgotten to provide him with a boat-cloak. He, however, forbade them to return for one; and when one of his companions offered his own great-coat, and urged him to make use of it, he replied, " I thank you very much,—but, to tell you the truth, my anxiety keeps me sufficiently warm at present."

" Do you think," said he presently, " that our fleet has quitted Bornholm? If it has, we must follow it to Carls-crona." About midnight he reached it, and once more got on board the *Elephant*. On the following morning the Swedes were discovered. As soon, however, as they perceived the English approaching, they retired, and took shelter in Carls-crona, behind the batteries of the island, at the entrance of that port. Sir Hyde sent in a flag of truce, stating that Denmark had concluded an armistice, and requiring an explicit declaration from the court of Sweden, " Whether it would adhere to, or abandon the hostile measures which it had taken against the rights and interests of Great Britain? " The commander, Vice-Admiral Cronstadt, replied that he could not answer a question which did not come within the particular circle of his duty; but that the King was then at Malmoe,[1] and would soon be at Carls-crona. Gustavus shortly afterwards arrived, and an answer was then returned to this effect: that his Swedish Majesty would not, for a moment, fail to fulfil, with fidelity and sincerity, the engagements he had entered into with his allies; but he would not refuse to listen to equitable pro-posals made by deputies furnished with proper authority by the King of Great Britain to the united northern powers. Satisfied with this answer, and with the known disposition of the Swedish court, Sir Hyde sailed for the Gulf of Fin-land. But he had not proceeded far before a dispatch boat from the Russian ambassador at Copenhagen arrived, bringing intelligence of the death of the Emperor Paul; and

[1] See map, p. 211.

T

that his successor Alexander had accepted the offer made by England to his father, of terminating the dispute by a convention. The British Admiral was therefore required to desist from all further hostilities.

It was Nelson's maxim, that, to negotiate with effect, force should be at hand and in a situation to act. The fleet, having been reinforced from England, amounted to eighteen sail of the line; and the wind was fair for Revel. There he would have sailed immediately to place himself between that division of the Russian fleet and the squadron at Kronstadt, in case this offer should prove insincere. Sir Hyde, on the other hand, believed that the death of Paul had effected all which was necessary. The manner of that death,[1] indeed, rendered it apparent that a change of policy would take place in the cabinet of Petersburg. But Nelson never trusted anything to the uncertain events of time, which could possibly be secured by promptitude or resolution. It was not, therefore, without severe mortification, that he saw the commander-in-chief return to the coast of Zealand, and anchor in Kioge Bay, there to wait patiently for what might happen.

There the fleet remained, till dispatches arrived from home, on the 5th of May, recalling Sir Hyde, and appointing Nelson commander-in-chief.

Nelson wrote to Earl St. Vincent that he was unable to hold this honourable station. Admiral Graves also was so ill, as to be confined to his bed; and he entreated that some person might come out and take the command. " I will endeavour," said he, " to do my best while I remain: but, my dear lord, I shall either soon go to Heaven, I hope, or must rest quiet for a time. If Sir Hyde were gone, I would now be under sail." On the day when this was written, he received news of his appointment. Not a moment was now lost. His first signal, as commander-in-chief, was to hoist in all launches, and prepare to weigh: and on the seventh he sailed from Kioge. Part of his fleet was left at Bornholm to watch the Swedes, from whom he required and obtained an assurance that the British trade in the Cattegat and in the Baltic should not be molested; and saying how

---

[1] Paul was strangled on 23rd March by a band of conspirators, who made his son Alexander king in his stead.

unpleasant it would be to him if anything should happen which might, for a moment, disturb the returning harmony between Sweden and Great Britain, he apprised them that he was not directed to abstain from hostilities should he meet with the Swedish fleet at sea. Meantime, he himself, with ten sail of the line, two frigates, a brig, and a schooner, made for the Gulf of Finland.

Paul, in one of the freaks of his tyranny, had seized upon all the British effects in Russia, and even considered British subjects as his prisoners. " I will have all the English shipping and property restored," said Nelson, " but I will do nothing violently,—neither commit the affairs of my country, nor suffer Russia to mix the affairs of Denmark or Sweden with the detention of our ships." The wind was fair, and carried him in four days to Revel Roads. But the Bay had been clear of firm ice on the 29th of April, while the English were lying idly at Kioge. The Russians had cut through the ice in the mole six feet thick, and their whole squadron had sailed for Kronstadt on the third. Before that time it had lain at the mercy of the English. " Nothing," Nelson said, " if it had been right to make the attack, could have saved one ship of them in two hours after our entering the bay."

It so happened that there was no cause to regret the opportunity which had been lost, and Nelson immediately put the intentions of Russia to the proof. He sent on shore to say that he came with friendly views, and was ready to return a salute. On their part the salute was delayed, till a message was sent to them to inquire for what reason, and the officer, whose neglect had occasioned the delay, was put under arrest. Nelson wrote to the Emperor, proposing to wait on him personally, and congratulate him on his accession, and urged the immediate release of British subjects and restoration of British property.

The answer arrived on the 16th. Nelson, meantime, had exchanged visits with the governor, and the most friendly intercourse had subsisted between the ships and the shore. Alexander's ministers, in their reply, expressed their surprise at the arrival of a British fleet in a Russian port and their wish that it should return. They professed, on the part of Russia, the most friendly disposition towards

Great Britain; but declined the personal visit of Lord Nelson, unless he came in a single ship. There was a suspicion implied in this which stung Nelson: and he said the Russian ministers would never have written thus if their fleet had been at Revel. He wrote an immediate reply, expressing what he felt. He told the court of Petersburg that the word of a British admiral, when given in explanation of any part of his conduct, was as sacred as that of any sovereign's in Europe. And he repeated, " that, under other circumstances, it would have been his anxious wish to have paid his personal respects to the Emperor, and signed with his own hand the act of amity between the two countries." Having dispatched this, he stood out to sea immediately, leaving a brig to bring off the provisions which had been contracted for, and to settle the accounts. " I hope all is right," said he, writing to our ambassador at Berlin. " But seamen are bad negotiators; for we put to issue in five minutes what diplomatic forms would be five months doing."

On his way down the Baltic, however, he met the Russian Admiral Tchitchagof, whom the Emperor, in reply to Sir Hyde's overtures, had sent to communicate personally with the British Commander-in-Chief. The reply was such as had been wished and expected: and these negotiators going, seaman-like, straight to their object, satisfied each other of the friendly intentions of their respective governments. Nelson then anchored off Rostock :[1] and there he received an answer to his last dispatch from Revel, in which the Russian court expressed their regret that there should have been any misconception between them; informed him that the British vessels which Paul had detained were ordered to be liberated, and invited him to Petersburg in whatever mode might be most agreeable to himself. Other honours awaited him. The Duke of Mecklenburg Strelitz, the Queen's brother,[2] came to visit him on board his ship; and towns of the inland parts of Mecklenburg sent deputations, with their public books of record, that they might have the name of Nelson in them written by his own hand.

From Rostock the fleet returned to Kioge Bay. Nelson

[1] See map.
[2] Charlotte, Queen-Consort of George III., was the daughter of Karl I., Grand-Duke of Mecklenburg.

saw that the temper of the Danes towards England was such as naturally arose from the chastisement which they had so recently received. "In this nation," said he, "we shall not be forgiven for having the upper hand of them. I only thank God we have, or they would try to humble us to the dust." He saw also that the Danish cabinet was completely subservient to France. A French officer was at this time the companion and counsellor of the Crown Prince; and things were done in such open violation of the armistice that Nelson thought a second infliction of vengeance would soon be necessary. He wrote to the Admiralty, requesting a clear and explicit reply to his inquiry, "Whether the commander-in-chief was at liberty to hold the language becoming a British admiral?"—"Which, very probably," said he, "if I am here, will break the armistice, and set Copenhagen in a blaze. I see everything which is dirty and mean going on, and the Prince Royal at the head of it. Ships have been masted, guns taken on board, floating batteries prepared, and, except hauling out and completing their rigging, everything is done in defiance of the treaty. My heart burns at seeing the word of a Prince, nearly allied to our good King, so falsified. But his conduct is such, that he will lose his kingdom if he goes on; for Jacobins rule in Denmark. I have made no representations yet, as it would be useless to do so until I have the power of correction. All I beg, in the name of the future commander-in-chief is, that the orders may be clear; for enough is done to break twenty treaties, if it should be wished, or to make the Prince Royal humble himself before British generosity."

Nelson was not deceived in his judgment of the Danish cabinet, but the battle of Copenhagen had crippled its power. The death of the Czar Paul had broken the confederacy: and that cabinet, therefore, was compelled to defer, till a more convenient season, the indulgence of its enmity towards Great Britain. Soon afterwards Admiral Sir Charles Maurice Pole arrived to take the command. The business, military and political, had by that time been so far completed, that the presence of the British fleet soon became no longer necessary. Sir Charles, however, made the short time of his command memorable, by passing the Great Belt, for the first time, with line-of-battle ships;

working through the channel against adverse winds. When Nelson left the fleet, this speedy termination of the expedition, though confidently expected, was not certain; and he, in his unwillingness to weaken the British force, thought at one time of traversing Jutland in his boat, by the canal, to Tönning on the Eider, and finding his way home from thence.[1] This intention was not executed. But he returned in a brig, declining to accept a frigate; which few admirals would have done; especially if, like him, they suffered from sea-sickness in a small vessel. On his arrival at Yarmouth, the first thing he did was to visit the hospital, and see the men who had been wounded in the late battle—that victory, which had added new glory to the name of Nelson, and which was of more importance even than the battle of the Nile to the honour, the strength, and security of England.

[1] In Nelson's day a short canal brought Kiel Bay into connection with the River Eider, which reached the North Sea at Tönning (see map). When Southey speaks of Jutland, he, of course, includes the duchies of Schleswig and Holstein, which were not ravished from Denmark till the war with Germany in 1864.

PART VIII

AT HOME

1st July, 1801—18th May, 1803

[SOUTHEY. CHAPTER VIII.—continued]

THE feelings of Nelson's friends, upon the news of his great victory of Copenhagen, were highly described by Sir William Hamilton in a letter to him. " We can only expect," he says, " what we know well, and often said before, that Nelson *was, is,* and to the *last will ever be, the first.* Emma did not know whether she was on her head or heels,—in such a hurry to tell your great news, that she could utter nothing but tears of joy and tenderness. I went to Davison, and found him still in bed, having had a severe fit of the gout, and with your letter, which he had just received and he cried like a child: but what was very extraordinary, assured me that, from the instant he had read your letter, all pain had left him, and that he felt himself able to get up and walk about. Your brother, Mrs. Nelson, and Horace dined with us. Your brother was more extraordinary than ever. He would get up suddenly and cut a caper; rubbing his hands every time that the thought of your fresh laurels came into his head. In short, except myself (and your lordship knows that I have some phlegm) all the company, which was considerable after dinner, were mad with joy. But I am sure that no one really rejoiced more at heart than I did. I have lived too long to have ecstasies! But with calm reflection, I felt for my friend having got to the very summit of glory! the *ne plus ultra*! that he has had another opportunity of rendering his country the most important service, and manifesting again his judgment, his intrepidity, and his humanity." [1]

---

[1] This first paragraph of Part VIII. does not occur in the first, second and third editions.

He had not been many weeks on shore before he was called upon to undertake a service, for which no Nelson was required. Bonaparte, who was now First Consul, and in reality sole ruler, of France, was making preparations, upon a great scale, for invading England. But his schemes in the Baltic had been baffled; fleets could not be created as they were wanted; and his armies, therefore, were to come over in gun-boats and such small craft as could be rapidly built or collected for the occasion. From the former governments of France such threats have only been matter of insult and policy. In Bonaparte they were sincere; for this adventurer, intoxicated with success, already began to imagine that all things were to be submitted to his fortune. We had not at that time proved the superiority of our soldiers over the French; and the unreflecting multitude were not to be persuaded that an invasion could only be effected by numerous and powerful fleets.[1] A general alarm was excited; and, in condescension to this unworthy feeling, Nelson was appointed to a command,[2] extending from Orfordness [3] to Beachy Head, on both shores;—a sort of service, he said, for which he felt no other ability than what might be found in his zeal.

To this service, however, such as it was, he applied with his wonted alacrity; [though in no cheerful frame of mind. To Lady Hamilton, his only female correspondent, he says at this time, " I am not in very good spirits; and except that our country demands all our services and abilities to bring about an honourable peace, nothing should prevent my being the bearer of my own letter. But, my dear friend, I know you are so true and loyal an Englishwoman, that you would hate those who would not stand forth in defence of our King, laws, religion, and all that is dear to us. It is your sex that makes us go forth, and seem to tell us, ' None but the brave deserve the fair ';—and if we fall, we still live in the hearts of those females. It is your sex that rewards us, it is your sex who cherish our memories; and

---

[1] *I.e.* " And the unreflecting multitude were easily persuaded that an invasion could be effected without the aid of numerous and powerful fleets."

[2] On his return from the Baltic he landed (1st July) at Yarmouth, and after visiting the hospitals proceeded to London. On the 24th he received this special command; and three days later hoisted his flag in the *Unité* frigate, transferring it to the *Medusa* in August.

[3] On the coast of Suffolk.

you, my dear honoured friend, are, believe me, the *first*,
the best of your sex. I have been the world around, and
in every corner of it, and never yet saw your equal, or even
one who could be put in comparison with you. You know
how to reward virtue, honour, and courage, and never
ask if it is placed in a prince, duke, lord, or peasant."] [1]
Having hoisted his flag in the *Medusa* frigate, he went to
reconnoitre Boulogne; the point from which it was supposed
the great attempt would be made, and which the French,
in fear of an attack themselves, were fortifying with all
care. He approached near enough to sink two of their
floating batteries, and to destroy a few gun-boats which
were without the pier. What damage was done within
could not be ascertained. "Boulogne," he said, "was
certainly not a very pleasant place that morning:—but,"
he added, "it is not my wish to injure the poor inhabitants;
and the town is spared as much as the nature of the service
will admit." Enough was done to show the enemy that
they could not, with impunity, come outside their own
ports. Nelson was satisfied by what he saw, that they
meant to make an attempt from this place, but that it was
impracticable; for the least wind at W.N.W. and they
were lost. The ports of Flushing and Flanders were better
points. There we could not tell by our eyes what means
of transport were provided. From thence, therefore, if it
came forth at all, the expedition would come. "And what
a forlorn undertaking!" said he. "Consider cross-tides,
etc. As for rowing, that is impossible. It is perfectly right
to be prepared for a *mad* government; but with the active
force which has been given me, I may pronounce it almost
impracticable." [2]

That force had been got together with an alacrity which
has seldom been equalled. On the twenty-eighth of July,
we were, in Nelson's own words, literally at the foundation
of our fabric of defence: and twelve days afterwards we
were so prepared on the enemy's coast, that he did not

[1] The passage within brackets does not occur in the first, second, and third
editions.
[2] Nelson seems at the time of his appointment to have taken the invasion
threat seriously. He estimated that 40,000 men would be employed and that
about 500 light craft would be required for their transport. After a brief study of
the problem he discovered that the craft at Boulogne numbered no more than
sixty; and from this moment he pronounced the enemy's scheme ridiculous.

believe they could get three miles from their ports. The *Medusa*, returning to our own shores, anchored in the rolling ground off Harwich; and, when Nelson wished to get to the Nore in her, the wind rendered it impossible to proceed there by the usual channel. In haste to be at the Nore, remembering that he had been a tolerable pilot for the mouth of the Thames in his younger days, and thinking it necessary that he should know all that could be known of the navigation, he requested the maritime surveyor of the coast, Mr. Spence, to get him into the Swin, by any channel: for neither the pilots which he had on board, nor the Harwich ones, would take charge of the ship. No vessel drawing more than fourteen feet had ever before ventured over the Naze. Mr. Spence, however, who had surveyed the channel, carried her safely through. The channel has since been called Nelson's, though he himself wished it to be named after the *Medusa*. His name needed no new memorial.[1]

Nelson's eye was upon Flushing.[2] " To take possession of that place," he said, " would be a week's expedition for four or five thousand troops." This, however, required a consultation with the Admiralty; and that something might be done meantime, he resolved upon attacking the flotilla in the mouth of Boulogne harbour. This resolution was made in deference to the opinion of others, and to the public feeling which was so preposterously excited. He himself scrupled not to assert that the French army would never embark at Boulogne for the invasion of England; and he owned that this boat-warfare was not exactly congenial to his feelings. Into Helvoetsluys or Flushing he should be happy to lead, if government turned their thoughts that way. " While I serve," said he, " I will do it actively, and to the very best of my abilities. I require nursing like a child," he added. " My mind carries me beyond my strength, and will do me up. But such is my nature."

The attack was made [3] by the boats of the squadron in

---

[1] An easterly wind kept Nelson imprisoned at Harwich; and to the south of him the flats that extend seaward from the Naze cut him off from the entrance to the Thames. With the wind where it was, he could make head to the southward, and so he took his frigate boldly over the Sands, picking a hazardous course which from that day to this has been called the " Medusa Channel."

[2] No sooner had Nelson decided that the French invasion scheme was impracticable than he desired to punish its originators for their insolence in forming it.

[3] 16th August, 1801.

five divisions, under Captains Somerville, Parker, Cotgrave, Jones and Conn. The previous essay had taught the French the weak parts of their position; and they omitted no means of strengthening it, and of guarding against the expected attempt. The boats put off about half-an-hour before midnight; but, owing to the darkness, and tide and half-tide,[1] which must always make night attacks so uncertain on the coasts of the Channel, the divisions separated. One could not arrive at all; another not till near daybreak. The others made their attack gallantly; but the enemy were fully prepared. Every vessel was defended by long poles, headed with iron spikes projecting from their sides; strong nettings were braced up to their lower yards; they were moored by the bottom to the shore;[2] they were strongly manned with soldiers and protected by land batteries; and the shore was lined with troops. Many were taken possession of; and, though they could not have been brought out, would have been burned, had not the French resorted to a mode of offence, which they have often used, but which no other people have ever been wicked enough to employ. The moment the firing ceased on board one of their own vessels they fired upon it from the shore, perfectly regardless of their own men.

The commander of one of the French divisions acted like a generous enemy. He hailed the boats as they approached, and cried out in English, " Let me advise you, my brave Englishmen, to keep your distance. You can do nothing here; and it is only uselessly shedding the blood of brave men to make the attempt." The French official account boasted of the victory. " The combat," it said, " took place in sight of both countries; it was the first of the kind, and the historian would have cause to make this remark."

[1] Where the tide ebbs and flows in a normal way a seaman can make the necessary allowances; but where roadsteads are affected by the interaction of water-volumes retained by river estuaries and extra channels, calculations are always liable to go astray.

[2] In the former editions I had stated, upon what appeared authentic information, that the boats were chained one to another. Nelson himself believed this. But I have been assured that it was not the case, by M. de Bercet, who, when I had the pleasure of seeing him in 1825, was (and I hope still is) Commandant of Boulogne. The word of this brave and loyal soldier is as little to be doubted as his worth. He is the last survivor of Charette's band; and his own memoirs, could he be persuaded to write them (a duty which he owes to his country as well as to himself) would form a redeeming episode in the history of the French Revolution. —SOUTHEY'S NOTE, Fourth Edition.

They guessed our loss at four or five hundred. It amounted to one hundred and seventy-two. In his private letters to the Admiralty Nelson affirmed that, had our force arrived as he intended, it was not all the chains in France which could have prevented our men from bringing off the whole of the vessels. There had been no error committed, and never did Englishmen display more courage. Upon this point Nelson was fully satisfied; but he said he should never bring himself again to allow any attack, wherein he was not personally concerned;[1] and that his mind suffered more than if he had had a leg shot off in the affair. He grieved particularly for Captain Parker, an excellent officer, to whom he was greatly attached, and who had an aged father looking to him for assistance. His thigh was shattered in the action; and the wound proved mortal, after some weeks of suffering and manly resignation. During this interval, Nelson's anxiety was very great. " Dear Parker is my child," said he; " for I found him in distress." And when he received the tidings of his death, he replied, " You will judge of my feelings. God's will be done. I beg that his hair may be cut off and given me. It shall be buried in my grave. Poor Mr. Parker! What a son has he lost! If I were to say I was content, I should lie; but I shall endeavour to submit with all the fortitude in my power. His loss has made a wound in my heart, which time will hardly heal."

[" You ask me, my dear friend," he says to Lady Hamilton, " if I am going on more expeditions. And even if I was to forfeit your friendship, which is dearer to me than all the world, I can tell you nothing. For, I go out.[2] I see the enemy, and can get at them, it is my duty: and you would naturally hate me, if I kept back one moment. I long to pay them, for their tricks t'other day, the debt of a drubbing, which surely I'll pay: but *when, where,* or *how,* it is impossible, your own good sense must tell you, for me or mortal man to say."—Yet][3] he now wished to be relieved from this service. The country, he said, had attached

---

[1] " He should never bring himself to accept responsibility for an attack without leading it himself in person."

[2] Sir Harris Nicolas inserts an " If " at this point (Vol. IV. p. 473).

[3] The passage within brackets does not occur in the first, second, and third editions.

a confidence to his name, which he had submitted to, and therefore had cheerfully repaired to the station. But this boat business, though it might be part of a great plan of invasion, could never be the only one, and he did not think it was a command for a vice-admiral.[1] It was not that he wanted a more lucrative situation; for, seriously indisposed as he was, and low-spirited from private considerations, he did not know, if the Mediterranean were vacant, that he should be equal to undertake it.

[He was offended with the Admiralty for refusing him leave to go to town when he had solicited. In reply to a friendly letter from Troubridge he says, " I am at this moment as firmly of opinion as ever that Lord St. Vincent and yourself should have allowed of my coming to town for my own affairs, for every one knows I left it without a thought for myself." His letters at this time breathe an angry feeling toward Troubridge, who was now become, he said, one of his lords and masters. " I have a letter from him," he says, " recommending me to wear flannel shirts. Does he care for me? NO: but never mind. They shall work hard to get me again. The cold has settled in my bowels. I wish the Admiralty had my complaint: but they have no bowels, at least for me. I dare say Master Troubridge has grown fat. I know I am grown lean with my complaint, which, but for their indifference about my health, could never have happened; or, at least, I should have got well long ago in a warm room with a good fire and sincere friend." In the same tone of bitterness, he complained that he was not able to promote those whom he thought deserving. " Troubridge," he says, " has so completely prevented my ever mentioning anybody's service, that I am become a cipher, and he has gained a victory over Nelson's spirit. I am kept here, for what? He may be able to tell, I cannot. But long it cannot, shall not be." An end was put to this uncomfortable state of mind when, fortunately (on that account) for him as well as happily

---

[1] Nelson felt the repulse of his captains at Boulogne, because the attack he had projected was in a sense unnecessary. So long as the English flotilla held the narrow seas, no troopships could ever hope to cross. Therefore, in his opinion the French activity was merely a blind, or part of a larger scheme in which a fleet of big ships was intended to come and scatter the English flotilla. If this latter surmise was correct, then he desired to hoist his flag in a ship of the line and seek the big fleet and annihilate it.

for the nation,] [1] the peace [2] of Amiens [3] was, just at this time, signed.

Nelson rejoiced that the experiment was made, but was well aware that it was an experiment. He saw what he called the misery of peace, unless the utmost vigilance and prudence were exerted: and he expressed, in bitter terms, his proper indignation at the manner in which the mob of London welcomed the French general, who brought the ratification: saying, "that they made him ashamed of his country."

He had purchased a house and estate at Merton,[4] in Surrey; meaning to pass his days there in the society of Sir William and Lady Hamilton.

[He had indulged in pleasant dreams when looking on to this as his place of residence and rest. " To be sure," he says, " we shall employ the tradespeople of our village in preference to any others, in what we want for common use, and give them every encouragement to be kind and attentive to us."—" Have we a nice church at Merton? We will set an example of goodness to the under-parishioners. I admire the pigs and poultry. Sheep are certainly most beneficial to eat off the grass. Do you get paid for them, and take care that they are kept on the premises all night, for that is the time they do good to the land. They should be folded. Is your head man a good person, and true to our interest? I intend to have a farming-book. I expect that all animals will increase where you are, for I never expect that you will suffer any to be killed. No person can take amiss our not visiting. The answer from me will always be very civil thanks, but that I wish to live retired. We shall have our sea-friends; and I know Sir William thinks they are the best."] [5]

[1] The paragraph within brackets does not occur in the first, second, and third editions.

[2] " Just at this time the peace," first, second, and third editions.

[3] The final treaty of peace was not signed until 25th March, 1802; but preliminaries were agreed to, and hostilities ceased, in October 1801.

[4] The house, which Nelson visited for the first time on 22nd October, 1801, has long since been pulled down and its site built over. The place has been absorbed into and may virtually be considered a part of Wimbledon. To judge from engravings, " Merton" itself must have been a rather hideous stucco building; but it stood in well-wooded grounds, watered by a tributary of the Wandle, which Lady Hamilton playfully rechristened " The Nile." There was certainly no place on earth where the Admiral was ever so happy, and during his last years at sea his thoughts perpetually flew back to it.

[5] The passage within brackets does not occur in the first, second, and third editions.

This place he had never seen till he was now welcomed there by the friends to whom he had so passionately devoted himself, and who were not less sincerely attached to him. The place, and everything which Lady Hamilton had done to it, delighted him; and he declared that the longest liver should possess it all. [Here he amused himself with angling in the Wandle, having been a good fly-fisher in former days, and learning now to practise with his left hand,[1] what he could no longer pursue as a solitary diversion.] [2] [His pensions for his victories, and for the loss of his eye and arm, amounted with his half-pay to about £3,400 a year. From this he gave £1,800 to Lady Nelson, £200 to a brother's widow and £150 for the education of his children; and he paid £500 interest for borrowed money; so that Nelson was comparatively a poor man; and though much of the pecuniary embarrassment which he endured was occasioned by the *separation from his wife* [3]—even if that cause had not existed, his income would not have been sufficient

[1] This is mentioned on the authority and by the desire of Sir Humphrey Davy (*Salmonia*, p. 6), whose name I write with the respect to which it is so justly entitled; and calling to mind the time when we were in habits of daily and intimate intercourse with affectionate regret.—SOUTHEY's NOTE, Third Edition.

[2] The passage within brackets does not occur in the first, second, and third editions.

[3] The real tragedy of Nelson's life was not so much his meeting with Lady Hamilton at Naples, as his marriage in haste with Frances Nisbet. Lady Nelson was a kind, affectionate soul, nice-looking, genteel, and always beautifully dressed. She was wrapped up in her son by her first marriage, the Josiah Nisbet who behaved so well at Teneriffe; and she got on excellently with Nelson's father, whose companion she was when her husband went to the wars. But there is enough correspondence extant to show that she did not easily make friends, and rather repelled the other members of the Nelson family. She was not lacking in sympathy; but was far more interested in herself than in anyone else. She liked fine clothes and comfortable quarters, and she exacted, perhaps a little too persistently, respect for her position and consideration for her rank. She had unhappily the faults of a self-centred woman without the counter-attractions either of wistfulness or charm. Nelson treated her with homage, veneration and respect, and she bore herself as if she were the partner of his life, rather than the queen of his heart. When those lightning-strokes of genius which men call St. Vincent and the Nile sent the world into ecstasies, Lady Nelson with complete composure kept her head. " I sincerely hope, my dear husband," she wrote to him after his first triumph, "that all these wonderful and desperate actions—such as boarding ships—you will leave to others. With the protection of a Supreme Being you have acquired a character or name which all hands agree cannot be greater. Therefore rest satisfied."

Contrast with these sentiments the letter of a comparative stranger after the battle of the Nile. " Joy, joy, joy to you, brave, gallant, immortalised Nelson! May that great God Whose cause you so valiantly support, protect and bless you to the end of your brilliant career! Such a race surely never was run. My heart is absolutely bursting with different sensations of joy, of gratitude, of pride, of every emotion that ever warmed the bosom of a British woman on hearing of her country's glory, and all produced by my dear, my good friend. . . . This moment the guns are firing, illuminations are preparing, your gallant name is echoed from street to street, and every Briton feels his obligations to you weighing him

for the rank which he held, and the claims which would necessarily be made upon his bounty.] [1]

The depression of spirits under which he had long laboured arose from the state of his circumstances, and partly from the other disquietudes in which his connection with Lady Hamilton had involved him; a connection which it was not possible his father could behold without sorrow and

---

[1] The passage within brackets does not occur in the first edition.

---

down. I am half mad, and I feel I have written you a strange letter. But you'll excuse it."

Thus wrote Lady Spencer, the wife of the noble Earl who presided with dignity and decorum over the Board of Admiralty.

Now it may be urged that Lady Spencer and Lady Nelson felt exactly the same electric thrill, but that Lady Spencer could turn her emotion into words and Lady Nelson could not. If this is true, and it may be so, no dishonour attaches to Lady Nelson. But sound reasoning will not deter the doom of tragedy. What Lady Nelson utterly lacked, the victor of the Nile most required. He loved appreciation, he adored flattery; he worshipped those who sang his praise. So infectious was his own enthusiasm that he lit as with a torch the answering spark in others. But his " Fanny " looked on his enthusiasms with something almost like jealousy, and in comparison with others was cold, restrained, undemonstrative, and irresponsive.

The drifting apart of an ill-mated pair was unhappily hastened by Josiah. It has already been seen how Nelson after Teneriffe secured for his stepson an independent command. The custom of the service then allowed such early promotion; but it was bad for all but the steadiest youths, and in Josiah's case it proved fatal. The young man got into serious trouble, and roused the wrath of Earl St. Vincent. Nelson, who was inclined to be over-indulgent for more reasons than one, was at last unable to overlook the boy's delinquencies and took him to task. Josiah became insolent and revengeful. It was always difficult for Nelson with only one arm to climb up the side of a ship, and Josiah expressed the hope that he would slip and break his neck. (Letter in the possession of Lieut.-Commander P. K. Kekewich, R.N.) He then wrote his mother slanderous letters in which he traduced his stepfather's character and put the worst construction on his intimacy with Lady Hamilton. Lady Nelson had to choose between her husband and her son, and decided to put implicit credence in all Josiah said. When Nelson reached home in the summer of 1800, and all England turned out to greet the victor of the Nile, Lady Nelson was conspicuous by her absence.

In after days when Sir Harris Nicolas was compiling his monumental collection of Nelson's *Dispatches and Letters*, he wrote to Mr. Haslewood (the Admiral's solicitor), asking him if he could throw any light on the final severance. Mr. Haslewood replied, " In the winter of 1800-1 I was breakfasting with Lord and Lady Nelson at their lodgings in Arlington Street, and a cheerful conversation was passing on indifferent subjects when Lord Nelson spoke of something that had been done or said by ' dear Lady Hamilton.' Upon which Lady Nelson rose from her chair and exclaimed with much vehemence, ' I am sick of hearing of " *dear* Lady Hamilton," and am resolved that you shall give up either her or me! ' Lord Nelson with perfect calmness said, ' Take care, Fanny, what you say. I love you sincerely; but I cannot forget my obligations to Lady Hamilton or speak of her otherwise than with affection and admiration! ' Without one soothing word or gesture, but muttering something about her mind being made up, Lady Nelson left the room, and shortly after drove from the house. They never lived together afterwards. I believe that Lord Nelson took a formal leave of her ladyship before joining the fleet under Sir Hyde Parker, but that to the day of her husband's glorious death she never made any apology for her abrupt and ungentle conduct above related, or any overture towards a reconciliation."

Messrs. Clarke and McArthur, whose life of the Admiral (1809) was patronised by Lady Nelson, state (perhaps on her authority) that before sailing to the Baltic Nelson said to her, " I call God to witness there is nothing in you or your conduct

displeasure. Mr. Nelson, however, was soon persuaded that the attachment, which Lady Nelson regarded with natural jealousy and resentment, did not in reality pass the bounds of ardent and romantic admiration; a passion which the manners and accomplishments of Lady Hamilton, fascinating as they were, would not have been able to excite, if they had not been accompanied by more uncommon intellectual endowments and a character which, both in its strength and its weakness, resembled his own.[1] It did not,

[1] This is a kinder and more correct estimate than that which has since been formed by people who have had more information than Southey and less reason to be unkind. Lord Rosebery, writing in 1905, dismissed Lady Hamilton as a " vulgar adventuress " (*United Service Magazine*, No. 923). Yet the fastidious poet Hayley, when he wrote to ask if she knew how many pictures Romney had painted of her, made use of the expression, " You were not only his *model* but his *inspirer*, and he truly and gratefully said that he owed a great part of his felicity as painter to the *angelic kindness and intelligence* with which you used to animate his diffident and tremulous spirits to the grandest efforts of art." (17th May, 1804.)
Innumerable are the books that have been written about the woman to whom Romney and Nelson admitted so profound a debt. Among these, the reader desiring further enlightenment should certainly select *Nelson's Friendships*, by Hilda Gamlin, and *Emma Lady Hamilton*, by Walter Sichel.

that I wish otherwise." We may well believe this; for the words are characteristic, and suggest a desire for mutual forgiveness. But nothing save recrimination ensued. Nelson then set out for Plymouth, and on his way penned the following epistle:

My dear Fanny, Southampton, 13th *January*, 1801.
We are arrived and heartily tired; and with kindest regards to my father and all the family, Believe me your affectionate
NELSON.

This fresh overture evoked no reply; but Nelson was not to be frustrated by silence. On 12th February he hoisted his flag in the *St. George*, and six days later received orders to proceed to Spithead *en route* for the Baltic. On 21st he reached Portsmouth, obtained leave of absence to settle his private affairs, hastened to London for " one word more," and found that Lady Nelson had shut up the house and gone away without leaving an address. This, of course, was the end.

Now it is quite in keeping with all that is known of Lady Nelson that she should prefer to dictate to her husband whom he should choose as his friends rather than draw him gently back to her side by the comforts of love and forgiveness. But that is no reason why she should forfeit the sympathy of those who read her husband's biography. Where the worldly-wise have erred, they have erred, not in the measure, but in the nature, of the sympathy they have felt and expressed. And it is Southey who has led them astray. He has said too little or else too much. He has said enough to show that Nelson lived apart from his wife; and his readers, left at liberty to conceive what they pleased, have shuddered, like the authoress of *John Halifax, Gentleman*, at imaginary wickednesses of which Nelson was incapable. Lady Nelson is to be pitied because she lost the love of one whom she never truly understood; and because she preferred to cherish her injured pride and self-esteem rather than tread the flinty road of reconciliation in search of the treasure she had lost.

Nelson has borne and will probably continue to bear the whole blame for the tragedy that ruined his home. Yet the tears were his as well as hers; and the faults not undivided. He looked for forgiveness and found none; she found misdemeanours where none had been committed. He offered her himself and she closed the door upon him; he sent her sixteen hundred a year to maintain her estate, and in a businesslike fashion she signed the receipts.

U

therefore, require much explanation to reconcile [1] him to his son—an event the more essential to Nelson's happiness because a few months afterwards the good old man died at the age of seventy-nine.[2]

Soon after the conclusion of peace, tidings arrived of our final and decisive successes in Egypt: [3] in consequence of which, the Common Council voted their thanks to the army and navy for bringing the campaign to so glorious a conclusion. When Nelson, after the action of Cape St. Vincent, had been entertained at a City feast, he had observed to the Lord Mayor that " if the City continued its generosity, the navy would ruin them in gifts." To which the Lord Mayor replied, putting his hand upon the Admiral's shoulder, " Do you find victories and we will find rewards." Nelson, as he said, had kept his word—had doubly fulfilled his part of the contract—but no thanks had been voted for the battle of Copenhagen; and feeling that he and his companions in that day's glory had a fair and honourable claim to this reward, he took the present opportunity of addressing a letter to the Lord Mayor, complaining of the omission and the injustice. " The smallest services," said he, " rendered by the army or navy to the country, have been always noticed by the great city of London, with one exception— the glorious second of April—a day when the greatest dangers of navigation were overcome, and the Danish force, which they thought impregnable, totally taken or destroyed by the consummate skill of our commanders, and by the undaunted bravery of as gallant a band as ever defended the rights of this country. For myself, if I were only personally concerned, I should bear the stigma, attempted to be now first placed upon my brow, with humility. But, my lord, I am the natural guardian of the fame of the officers of the navy, army, and marines, who fought and so profusely bled, under my command, on that day. Again, I disclaim for myself more merit than naturally falls to a successful commander; but when I am called upon to speak of the merits of the captains of His Majesty's ships,

[1] This word is unfortunate as it suggests that there had been a quarrel; whereas the mutual affection of father and son had not for a moment been disturbed.
[2] 26th April, 1802.
[3] The French armies which Napoleon took to the East and deserted after the Nile agreed to surrender and evacuate Egypt on condition that the English transported them home.

and of the officers and men, whether seamen, marines, or
soldiers, whom I that day had the happiness to command,
I then say, that never was the glory of this country upheld
with more determined bravery than on that occasion. And,
if I may be allowed to give an opinion as a Briton, then I
say that more important service was never rendered to our
King and country. It is my duty, my lord, to prove to the
brave fellows, my companions in danger, that I have not
failed, at every proper place, to represent, as well as I am
able, their bravery and meritorious conduct."

Another honour of greater import was withheld from the
conquerors. The King had given medals to those captains
who were engaged in the battles of the First of June, of
Cape St. Vincent, of Camperdown, and of the Nile. Then
came the victory at Copenhagen, which Nelson truly called
the most difficult achievement, the hardest fought battle,
the most glorious result that ever graced the annals of our
country. He, of course, expected the medal; and, in writing
to Earl St. Vincent, said, " He longed to have it, and would
not give it up to be made an English duke." The medal,
however, was not given. " For what reason," says Nelson,
" Lord St. Vincent best knows " [1]—words plainly implying a suspicion that it was withheld by some feeling of
jealousy; and that suspicion estranged him, during the
remaining part of his life, from one who had at one
time been essentially, as well as sincerely, his friend,
and of whose professional abilities he ever entertained
the highest opinion.

[1] The lack of recognition for the victory of Copenhagen seems to have been
due to a rather ludicrous desire on the part of the Ministry to prevent giving
offence to those of Sir Hyde Parker's fleet who had not actually participated in
the battle; to which motive they added a timorous feeling that they might
possibly also give umbrage to Denmark, who was now no longer a foe.

PART IX

THE CAMPAIGN OF TRAFALGAR
1803-5

CHAPTER I

THE BLOCKADE OF TOULON

[*SOUTHEY. CHAPTER VIII.—continued*]

THE happiness which Nelson enjoyed in the society of his chosen friends was of no long continuance. Sir William Hamilton, who was far advanced in years, died early in 1803; [1] [a mild, amiable, accomplished man, who has thus in a letter described his own philosophy. " My study of antiquities," he says, " has kept me in constant thought of the perpetual fluctuation of everything. The whole art is really to live all the *days* of our life; and not with anxious care disturb the sweetest hour that life affords,—which is the present. Admire the Creator, and all His works, to us incomprehensible; and do all the good you can upon earth: and take the chance of eternity without dismay."] [2] He expired in his wife's arms, holding Nelson by the hand; and almost in his last words left her to his protection; requesting him that he would see justice done her by the government, as he knew what she had done for her country. He left him her portrait in enamel, calling him his dearest friend; the most virtuous, loyal, and truly brave character he had ever known. The codicil, containing this bequest, concluded with these words, " God bless him, and shame fall on those who do not say ' Amen.' " Sir William's pension of £1,200 a year ceased with his death. Nelson applied to Mr. Addington in Lady Hamilton's behalf, stating the important service which she had rendered to the fleet at

---

[1] 6th April.
[2] The passage in brackets does not occur in the first, second, and third editions.

Syracuse: and Mr. Addington, it is said, acknowledged that she had a just claim upon the gratitude of the country. This barren acknowledgment was all that was obtained: but a sum, equal to the pension which her husband had enjoyed, was settled on her by Nelson, and paid in monthly payments during his life. A few weeks after this event, the war was renewed; and, the day after his Majesty's message to parliament, Nelson departed to take the command of the Mediterranean fleet. [1] [The war, he thought, could not be long; just enough to make him independent in pecuniary matters.] [2]

He took his station immediately off Toulon; and there, with incessant vigilance, waited for the coming out of the enemy. [The expectation of acquiring a competent fortune did not last long. " Somehow," he says, " my mind is not sharp enough for prize-money. Lord Keith would have made £20,000, and I have not made £6,000." More than once he says that the prizes taken in the Mediterranean had not paid his expenses, and once he expresses himself as if it were a consolation to think that some ball might soon close all his accounts with this world of care and vexation. At this time the widow of his brother, being then blind and advanced in years, was distressed for money, and about

---

[1] When Southey wrote this last section of his work, the menace of Napoleon's invasion scheme was still so vivid a memory in men's minds that he did not think it necessary to frame his picture in a setting of contemporaneous history. To-day, in order to understand his narrative, we need to recall the main facts of the political situation.

The Peace of Amiens in 1802 had been signed and sealed merely to be broken. Napoleon, bent on universal overlordship, was treating Holland as a subject nation; and England, who had undertaken to evacuate Malta, retained her hold upon it as the only rein whereby to curb his insolence. Napoleon attempted to browbeat her; and England amazed him by declaring war (16th May, 1803). Napoleon gathered the " Army of England" along the coast that faces the white cliffs of Dover, and certainly succeeded in instilling into the hearts of the people he hated a very real sense of fear. His legions around Boulogne numbered close upon 150,000 soldiers; and these, according to his own mendacious statement, could be embarked in boats to cross the " ditch " in a couple of hours at most.

The English seamen, who did not share the nervousness of their land-dwelling countrymen, prayed that Napoleon would be foolish enough to launch his troops in boats and put to sea. With small craft of every kind they swarmed about him, ready always to leap upon him and in that moment strike him dead. All this Napoleon thoroughly understood, and in order to rid himself of the unpleasant attentions of the English flotilla, he required the French fleets at Toulon and Brest to unite and sweep the Channel. Without being admitted into his plans, however, the Lords of the Admiralty thwarted him. They sent Admiral Cornwallis to blockade Brest, and Nelson to blockade Toulon. And so long as the French Mediterranean fleet was held a prisoner in its own port and was prevented from joining the fleet at Brest, the shores of England remained inviolable.

[2] The passage in brackets does not occur in the first, second, and third editions.

to sell her plate. He wrote to Lady Hamilton, requesting of her to find out what her debts were, and saying that, if the amount was within his power, he would certainly pay it and rather pinch himself than that she should want. Before he had finished the letter, an account arrived that a sum was payable to him for some neutral taken four years before, which enabled him to do this without being the poorer: and he seems to have felt at the moment that what was thus disposed of by a cheerful giver, shall be paid to him again. One from whom he had looked for very different conduct had compared his own wealth in no becoming manner with Nelson's limited means. " I know," said he to Lady Hamilton, " the full extent of the obligation I owe him, and he may be useful to me again; but I can never forget his unkindness to you. But, I guess many reasons influenced his conduct in bragging of his riches and my honourable poverty; but, as I have often said, and with honest pride, what I have is my own. It never cost the widow a tear, or the nation a farthing. I got what I have with my pure blood from the enemies of my country. Our house, my own Emma, is built upon a solid foundation; and will last to us, when his house and lands may belong to others than his children."

His hope was that peace might soon be made, or that he should be relieved from his command, and retire to Merton, where at that distance he was planning and directing improvements. On his birthday he writes, " This day, my dearest Emma, I consider as more fortunate than common days, as by my coming into this world it has brought me so intimately acquainted with you. I well know that you will keep it, and have my dear Horatia to drink my health. Forty-six years of toil and trouble! How few more the common lot of mankind leads us to expect! and therefore it is almost time to think of spending the last few years in peace and quietness." It is painful to think that this language was not addressed to his wife, but to one with whom he promised himself " many, many happy years, when that impediment," as he calls her, " shall be removed, if God pleased"; and they might be surrounded by their children's children.][1]

[1] The passage in brackets does not occur in the first, second, and third editions.

When he had been fourteen months off Toulon, he received a vote of thanks from the city of London for his skill and perseverance in blockading that port, so as to prevent the French from putting to sea. Nelson had not forgotten the wrong which the city had done to the Baltic fleet by their omission, and did not lose the opportunity which this vote afforded of recurring to that point. " I do assure your lordship," said he, in his answer to the Lord Mayor, " that there is not that man breathing who sets a higher value upon the thanks of his fellow-citizens of London than myself; but I should feel as much ashamed to receive them for a particular service (marked in the resolution) if I felt that I did not come within that line of service, as I should feel hurt at having a great victory passed over without notice. I beg to inform your lordship that the port of Toulon has never been blockaded by me. Quite the reverse. Every opportunity has been offered the enemy to put to sea. For it is there that we hope to realise the hopes and expectations of our country." Nelson then remarked that the junior Flag Officers of his fleet had been omitted in this vote of thanks; and his surprise at the omission was expressed with more asperity, perhaps, than an offence, so entirely and manifestly unintentional, deserved. But it arose from that generous regard for the feelings as well as interests of all who were under his command, which made him as much beloved in the fleets of Britain, as he was dreaded in those of the enemy.

Never was any commander more beloved. He governed men by their reason and their affections. They knew that he was incapable of caprice or tyranny; and they obeyed him with alacrity and joy, because he possessed their confidence as well as their love. " Our Nel," they used to say, " is as brave as a lion, and as gentle as a lamb." Severe discipline he detested, though he had been bred in a severe school. He never inflicted corporal punishment if it were possible to avoid it, and when compelled to enforce it, he, who was familiar with wounds and death, suffered like a woman. In his whole life Nelson was never known to act unkindly towards an officer. If he was asked to prosecute one for ill behaviour, he used to answer, that there was no occasion for him to ruin a poor devil, who was sufficiently his own enemy to ruin himself. But in Nelson there was more than the easiness and humanity of a happy nature. He did not merely abstain from injury; his was an active and watchful benevolence, ever desirous not only to render justice, but to do good. During the peace, he had spoken in parliament upon the abuses respecting prize-money; and had submitted plans to government for more easily manning the navy and preventing desertion from it, by bettering the condition of the seamen. He proposed that their certificates should be registered;[1] and that every man who had served, with a good character, five years in war, should receive a bounty of two guineas annually after that time, and of four guineas after eight years. "This," he said, "might, at first sight, appear an enormous sum for the state to pay; but the average life of seamen is, from hard service, finished at forty-five: he cannot, therefore, enjoy the annuity many years; and the interest of the money saved by their not deserting would go far to pay the whole expense."

To his midshipmen he ever showed the most winning kindness, encouraging the diffident, tempering the hasty, counselling and befriending both. "Recollect," he used to say, "that you must be a seaman to be an officer; and also, that you cannot be a good officer without being a gentleman." A lieutenant wrote to him to say that he was dissatisfied with his captain. Nelson's answer was in that spirit of perfect wisdom and perfect goodness which regulated his whole conduct toward those who were under his command. "I have just received your letter; and I am truly sorry that any difference should arise between your captain, who has the reputation of being one of the bright officers of the service, and yourself, a very young man, and a very young officer, who must naturally have

---

[1] The seamen were not paid what was due to them by regular wages on a fixed pay-day. They received at the end of their ship's commission a ticket or certificate on which was inscribed the amount of money to which they were entitled. This paper-coinage could only be converted into hard cash at the Ticket Office in London; and the seamen, rather than be bothered to apply themselves, would often part with their paper at a heavy discount to Jews and other speculators. This exchange led to such extensive frauds by the forging of sham certificates that the Ticket Office wearied the genuine applicant by compelling him to prove who he was. Nelson proposed the issue to all seamen of identification papers, which would not only enable them to obtain their dues, but serve by way of testimonial to character when they sought other forms of employment.

much to learn. Therefore the chance is, that you are perfectly wrong in the disagreement. However, as your present
situation must be very disagreeable, I will certainly take
an early opportunity of removing you, provided your
conduct to your present captain be such that another
may not refuse to receive you."

The gentleness and benignity of his disposition never
made him forget what was due to discipline. Being on one
occasion applied to, to save a young officer from a court
martial, which he had provoked by his misconduct, his
reply was, " That he would do everything in his power to
oblige so gallant and good an officer as Sir John Warren,"
in whose name the intercession had been made. " But
what," he added, " would he do if he were here?—Exactly
what I have done, and am still willing to do. The young
man must write such a letter of contrition as would be an
acknowledgment of his great fault; and, with a sincere
promise, if his captain will intercede to prevent the impending court martial, never to so misbehave again. On
his captain's enclosing me such a letter, with a request to
cancel the order for the trial, I might be induced to do it:
but the letters and reprimand will be given in the public
order-book of the fleet, and read to all the officers. The
young man has pushed himself forward to notice, and he
must take the consequence. It was upon the quarter-deck,
in the face of the ship's company, that he treated his captain
with contempt; and I am in duty bound to support the
authority and consequence of every officer under my command. A poor ignorant seaman is for ever punished for
contempt to *his* superiors."

A dispute occurred in the fleet, while it was off Toulon,
which called forth Nelson's zeal for the rights and interests
of the navy. Some young artillery officers, serving on
board the bomb vessels, refused to let their men perform
any other duty but what related to the mortars. They
wished to have it established that their corps was not
subject to the Captain's authority. The same pretensions
were made in the Channel fleet about the same time, and the
artillery rested their claims to separate and independent
authority on board, upon a clause in the act, which they
interpreted in their favour. Nelson took up the subject

with all the earnestness which its importance deserved. "There is no real happiness in this world," said he, writing to Earl St. Vincent as First Lord. "With all content, and smiles around me, up start these artillery boys (I understand they are not beyond that age) and set us at defiance; speaking in the most disrespectful manner of the navy, and its commanders. I know you, my dear lord, so well, that, with your quickness, the matter would have been settled, and perhaps some of them been broke. I am perhaps more patient; but I do assure you, not less resolved, if my plan of conciliation is not attended to. You and I are on the eve of quitting the theatre of our exploits; but we hold it due to our successors, never, whilst we have a tongue to speak, or a hand to write, to allow the navy to be, in the smallest degree, injured in its discipline by our conduct." To Troubridge he wrote in the same spirit, "It is the old history, trying to do away the act of parliament. But I trust they will never succeed; for, when they do, farewell to our naval superiority. We should be prettily commanded! Let them once gain the step of being independent of the navy on board a ship, and they will soon have the other, and command us. But, thank God! my dear Troubridge, the King himself cannot do away the act of parliament. Although my career is nearly run, yet it would embitter my future days, and expiring moments, to hear of our navy being sacrificed to the army." As the surest way of preventing such disputes, he suggested that the navy should have its own corps of artillery; and a corps of marine artillery was accordingly established.[1]

Instead of lessening the power of the commander, Nelson would have wished to see it increased. It was absolutely necessary, he thought, that merit should be rewarded at the moment, and that the officers of the fleet should look up to the commander-in-chief for their reward. He himself was never more happy than when he could promote those who were deserving of promotion. Many were the services which he thus rendered unsolicited: and frequently the officer, in whose behalf he had interested himself with the Admiralty, did not know to whose friendly interference he was indebted for his good fortune. He used to say, "I wish

---

[1] The Royal Marine Artillery was established in August 1804.

it to appear as a God-send." The love which he bore the navy made him promote the interests, and honour the memory, of all who had added to its glories. "The near relations of brother officers," he said, "he considered as legacies to the service." Upon mention being made to him of a son of Rodney, by the Duke of Clarence, his reply was, "I agree with your Royal Highness most entirely that the son of a Rodney ought to be the *protégé* of every person in the kingdom, and particularly of the sea officers. Had I known that there had been this claimant, some of my own lieutenants must have given way to such a name, and he should have been placed in the *Victory*. She is full, and I have twenty on my list; but, whatever numbers I have, the name of Rodney must cut many of them out." Such was the proper sense which Nelson felt of what was due to splendid services and illustrious names. His feelings toward the brave men who had served with him are shown by a note in his diary, which was probably not intended for any other eye than his own. "Nov. 7. I had the comfort of making an old *Agamemnon*, George Jones, a gunner into the *Chameleon* brig."

When Nelson took the command, it was expected that the Mediterranean would be an active scene. Nelson well understood the character of the perfidious Corsican who was now sole tyrant of France; and knowing that he was as ready to attack his friends as his enemies, knew, therefore, that nothing could be more uncertain than the direction of the fleet from Toulon, whenever it should put to sea. "It had as many destinations," he said, "as there were countries." The momentous revolutions of the last ten years had given him ample matter for reflection, as well as opportunities for observation. The film was cleared from his eyes; and now, when the French no longer went abroad with the cry of Liberty and Equality, he saw that the oppression and misrule of the powers which had been opposed to them had been the main causes of their success, and that those causes would still prepare the way before them. Even in Sicily, where, if it had been possible longer to blind himself, Nelson would willingly have seen no evil; he perceived that the people wished for a change, and acknowledged that they had reason to wish for it. In Sardinia the same burden of misgovernment was felt; and the people, like the Sicilians, were impoverished by a government so utterly incompetent to perform its first and most essential duties, that it did not protect its own coasts from the Barbary pirates. He would fain have had us purchase this island (the finest in the Mediterranean) from its sovereign, who did not receive £5,000 a year from it after its wretched establishment was paid. There was reason to think that France was preparing to possess herself of this important point, which afforded our fleet facilities for watching Toulon, not to be obtained elsewhere. An expedition was preparing at Corsica for the purpose; and all the Sardes, who had taken part with revolutionary France, were ordered to assemble there. It was certain that, if the attack were made, it would succeed. Nelson thought that the only means to prevent Sardinia from becoming French was to make it English, and that half a million would give the King a rich price, and England a cheap purchase. A better and therefore a wiser policy would have been to exert our influence in removing the abuses of the government. For foreign dominion is always, in some degree, an evil; and allegiance neither can nor ought to be made a thing of bargain and sale. Sardinia, like Sicily and Corsica, is large enough to form a separate state. Let us hope that these islands may one day be made free and independent. Freedom and independence will bring with them industry and prosperity; and wherever these are found, arts and letters will flourish, and the improvement of the human race proceed.

The proposed attack was postponed. Views of wider ambition were opening upon Bonaparte, who now almost undisguisedly aspired to make himself master of the continent of Europe; and Austria was preparing for another struggle, to be conducted as weakly and terminated as miserably as the former.[1] Spain, too, was once more to be involved in war by the policy of France: that perfidious government having in view the double object of employing the Spanish resources against England, and exhausting

[1] The allusions are to Mack's surrender at Ulm on 20th October, 1805, and to the defeat of the Austro-Russian forces at Austerlitz on 2nd December in the same year.

them, in order to render Spain herself finally its prey.[1] Nelson, who knew that England and the Peninsula ought to be in alliance, for the common interest of both, frequently expressed his hopes that Spain might resume her natural rank among the nations. " We ought," he said, " by mutual consent, to be the very best friends, and both to be ever hostile to France." But he saw that Bonaparte was meditating the destruction of Spain; and that, while the wretched court of Madrid professed to remain neutral, the appearances of neutrality were scarcely preserved. An order of the year 1771, excluding British ships of war from the Spanish ports, was revived, and put in force; while French privateers, from these very ports, annoyed the British trade, carried their prizes in, and sold them even at Barcelona. Nelson complained of this to the Captain-General of Catalonia, informing him that he claimed for every British ship or squadron the right of lying, as long as it pleased, in the ports of Spain, while that right was allowed to other powers. To the British ambassador he said, " I am willing to make large allowances for the miserable situation Spain has placed herself in; but there is a certain line, beyond which I cannot submit to be treated with disrespect. We have given up French vessels taken within gun-shot of the Spanish shore, and yet French vessels are permitted to attack our ships from the Spanish shore. Your excellency may assure the Spanish government that in whatever place the Spaniards allow the French to attack us, in that place I shall order the French to be attacked."

During this state of things, to which the weakness of Spain, and not her will, consented, the enemy's fleet did not venture to put to sea. Nelson watched it with unremitting and almost unexampled perseverance. The station off Toulon he called his home. " We are in the right fighting trim," said he. " Let them come as soon as they please. I never saw a fleet altogether so well officered and manned. Would to God the ships were half as good! The finest ones in the service would soon be destroyed by such terrible weather. I know well enough that, if I were to go into

[1] Spain joined France in October 1804, and declared war against England shortly afterwards. Months earlier she had betrayed where her sympathies lay; and by opening her ports to the shipping of France she had already torn to shreds her pretence of neutrality.

Malta, I should save the ships during this bad season: but
if I am to watch the French, I must be at sea; and, if at
sea, must have bad weather: and if the ships are not fit to
stand bad weather, they are useless." Then only he was
satisfied, and at ease, when he had the enemy in view. Mr.
Elliot, our minister at Naples, seems, at this time, to have
proposed to send a confidential Frenchman to him with
information. " I should be very happy," he replied, " to
receive authentic intelligence of the destination of the
French squadron, their route, and time of sailing. Anything
short of this is useless; and I assure your Excellency, that
I would not, upon any consideration, have a Frenchman
in the fleet, except as a prisoner. I put no confidence in
them. You think yours good; the Queen thinks the same.
I believe they are all alike. Whatever information you can
get me I shall be very thankful for; but not a Frenchman
comes here. Forgive me, but my mother hated the French."

M. Latouche Tréville, who had commanded at Boulogne,[1]
commanded now at Toulon. " He was sent for on purpose,"
said Nelson, " as he *beat me* at Boulogne, to beat me again:
but he seems very loath to try." One day,[2] while the main
body of our fleet was out of sight of land, Rear-Admiral
Campbell, reconnoitring with the *Canopus, Donegal*, and
Amazon, stood in close to the port; and M. Latouche,
taking advantage of a breeze which sprang up, pushed out
with four ships of the line and three heavy frigates, and
chased him about four leagues. The Frenchman, delighted
at having found himself in so novel a situation, published
a boastful account; affirming that he had given chase to
the whole British fleet, and that Nelson had fled before
him![3] Nelson thought it due to the Admiralty to send
home a copy of the *Victory's* log upon this occasion. "As
for himself," he said, " if his character was not established
by that time for not being apt to run away, it was not
worth his while to put the world right."—" If this fleet
gets fairly up with M. Latouche," said he to one of his

---

[1] See above, pp. 252–6.

[2] 24th May, 1804.

[3] As Nelson himself with the bulk of his ships was far out of sight, Admiral
Campbell restrained the pugnacity of the *Donegal*, who was prepared to fight the
whole French fleet by herself, and led his little force to join the main body, hoping
to deliver the French into Nelson's hands. He was commended by the Admiral
for his sagacity.

correspondents, "his letter, with all his ingenuity, must be different from his last. We had fancied that we chased him into Toulon; for, blind as I am, I could see his water line, when he clued his topsails up, shutting in Sepet. But from the time of his meeting Captain Hawker, in the *Isis*,[1] I never heard of his acting otherwise than as a poltroon and a liar. Contempt is the best mode of treating such a miscreant." In spite, however, of contempt, the impudence of this Frenchman half angered him. He said to his brother, " You will have seen Latouche's letter; how he chased me, and how I ran. I keep it: and if I take him, by God he shall eat it."

Nelson, who used to say that in sea-affairs nothing is impossible, and nothing improbable, feared the more that this Frenchman might get out and elude his vigilance; because he was so especially desirous of catching him, and administering to him his own lying letter in a sandwich. M. Latouche, however, escaped him in another way. He died,[2] according to the French papers in consequence of walking so often up to the signal-post upon Sepet, to watch the British fleet. " I always pronounced that would be his death," said Nelson. " If he had come out and fought me, it would, at least, have added ten years to my life." The patience with which he had watched Toulon, he spoke of, truly, as a perseverance at sea which had never been surpassed. From May 1803 to August 1805 he himself went out of his ship but three times; each of those times was upon the King's service and neither time of absence exceeded an hour. [In 1804 the *Swift* cutter going out with dispatches

[1] The frigate *Iris* (*sic*) met Latouche-Tréville in the frigate *Hermione* off Sandy Hook on 7th June, 1780. After a close action, lasting one hour and twenty minutes, the French frigate made off under all the sail she could carry. The *Iris* pursued for three-quarters of an hour, but was then compelled to desist on account of injuries to her rigging. Latouche-Tréville thereupon informed his countrymen that he had attacked the *Iris* and would have taken her, but that her superior speed enabled her to take refuge in New York.

Nelson, of course, was on the far side of the Atlantic during the American War (see above, pp. 16-30), and may have recalled the incident from his memory. He may even have remembered the correct name of the English frigate; but his original letter to Captain Sutton of the *Amphion*, here quoted, exists only in Clarke and McArthur's transcript (Vol. II. p. 367), which may very well have been faulty. If the original letter could be found it might possibly throw light on the obscure phrase, " shutting in Sepet," which has never been accurately explained; though it probably means no more than that Nelson had ocular proof that his opponent had snuggled safely behind the harbour defences.

[2] 18th August, 1804. He was succeeded in his command by Vice-Admiral Villeneuve.

was taken,[1] and all the dispatches and letters fell into the hands of the enemy. " A very pretty piece of work! " says Nelson, " I am not surprised at the capture, but am very much so that any dispatches should be sent in a vessel with twenty-three men, not equal to cope with any row-boat privateer. The loss of the *Hindustan* was great enough ; [2] but for importance it is lost [3] in comparison to the probable knowledge the enemy will obtain of our connections with foreign countries.[4] Foreigners for ever say (and it is true), ' We dare not trust England. One way or other we are sure to be committed.' " In a subsequent letter, he says, speaking of the same capture, " I find, my dearest Emma, that your picture is very much admired by the French Consul at Barcelona; and that he has not sent it to be admired, which I am sure it would be, by Bonaparte. They pretend that there were three pictures taken. I wish I had them. But they are all gone as irretrievably as the dispatches; unless we may read them in a book, as we printed their correspondence from Egypt.[5] But from us what can they find out? That I love you most dearly, and hate the French most damnably. Dr. Scott went to Barcelona to try to get the private letters; but I fancy they are all gone to Paris. The Swedish and American Consuls told him that the French Consul had your picture and read your letters: and, the Doctor thinks, one of them probably read the letters. By the master's account of the cutter, I would not have trusted an old pair of shoes in her. He tells me she did not sail, but was a good sea-boat. I hope Mr. Marsden will not trust any more of my private letters in

---

[1] Sent out from England to carry Admiralty dispatches to Nelson. She had only eight four-pounders, and relied entirely on her speed. She was overhauled by the French xebec *L'Esperance* and captured on 3rd April, 1804. Her commander, William Martin Leake, defended his ship with great gallantry and managed to sink his dispatches before he laid down his life (*cp.* James, *Naval History*, Vol. III. p. 263).

[2] The *Hindustan*, with stores for Nelson, was accidentally destroyed by fire in Rosas Bay on 2nd April, 1804. Her captain was honourably acquitted of all blame, and the court martial complimented him for his skill in smothering the fire twelve leagues from shore and saving the lives of all his company. (Nicolas, Vol. V. p. 503.)

[3] Insignificant.

[4] From the *Swift's* dispatches, which Nelson wrongly believed that the enemy had secured.

[5] " Unless we read them in a book as the French may have read those which were captured by us during the Egyptian campaign "—*i.e.*, *Copies of Original Letters from the Army of General Bonaparte in Egypt Intercepted by the Fleet under the Command of Admiral Lord Nelson*. London, 8vo. 1798.

such a conveyance. If they choose to trust the affairs of the public in such a thing, I cannot help it."

While he was on this station],[1] the weather had been so unusually severe, that he said the Mediterranean seemed altered. It was his rule never to contend with the gales; but either run to the southward to escape their violence, or furl all the sails, and make the ships as easy as possible. The men, though he said flesh and blood could hardly stand it, continued in excellent health, which he ascribed, in great measure, to a plentiful supply of lemons and onions. For himself, he thought he could only last till the battle was over. One battle more it was his hope that he might fight. "However," said he, "whatever happens, I have run a glorious race." ["A few months' rest," he says, "I must have very soon. If I am in my grave, what are the mines of Peru to me? But to say the truth, I have no idea of killing myself. I may, with care, live yet to do good service to the state. My cough is very bad, and my side, where I was struck on the 14th of February,[2] is very much swelled; at times a lump as large as my fist, brought on occasionally by violent coughing. But I hope and believe my lungs are yet safe."][3] He was afraid of blindness ;[4] and this was the only evil which he could not contemplate without unhappiness. More alarming symptoms he regarded with less apprehension, describing his own "shattered carcase" as in the worst plight of any in the fleet: and he says, "I have felt the blood gushing up the left side of my head: and, the moment it covers the brain, I am fast asleep." The fleet was in worse trim than the men, but when he compared it with the enemy's, it was with a right English feeling. "The French fleet yesterday," said he in one of his letters, "was to appearance in high feather, and as fine as paint could make them. But when they may sail, or where they may go, I am very sorry to say is a secret I am not acquainted with. Our weather-beaten

---

[1] The passage in brackets does not occur in the first, second, and third editions.

[2] In a letter to Sir Gilbert Elliot immediately after the battle of St. Vincent Nelson wrote, "Amongst the slightly wounded is myself, but it is only a contusion and of no consequence, unless an inflammation takes place in my bowels, which is the part injured." (Nicolas, Vol. II. p. 350.)

[3] The passage in brackets does not occur in the first, second, and third editions.

[4] The nerves of the eyes are so closely connected that the injury which Nelson received in Corsica was causing intense pain in his "one good eye" and beginning seriously to impair his powers of vision.

x

ships, I have no fear, will make their sides like a plum-pudding." [" Yesterday," he says, on another occasion, " a Rear-Admiral and seven sail of ships put their nose outside the harbour. If they go on playing this game, some day we shall lay salt upon their tails."] [1]

Hostilities at length commenced between Great Britain and Spain. That country, whose miserable government made her subservient to France, was once more destined to lavish her resources and her blood in furtherance of the designs of a perfidious ally. The immediate occasion of the war was the seizure of four treasure-ships by the English. The act was perfectly justifiable; for those treasures were intended to furnish means for France. But the circumstances which attended it were as unhappy as they were unforeseen. Four frigates had been dispatched to intercept them. They met with an equal force. Resistance, therefore, became a point of honour on the part of the Spaniards, and one of their ships soon blew up, with all on board. Had a stronger squadron been sent, this deplorable catastrophe might have been spared: a catastrophe which excited not more indignation in Spain, than it did grief in those who were its unwilling instruments, in the English government, and in the English people.[2] On the 5th of October [3] this unhappy affair occurred, and Nelson was not apprised of it till the 12th of the ensuing month. He had, indeed, sufficient mortification at the breaking out of this Spanish war; an event which, it might reasonably

---

[1] The passage in brackets does not occur in the first, second, and third editions.

[2] The point that Southey touches here is a favourite topic with students of international law. Was Great Britain justified in chastising the Spaniards before she had announced her intention of doing so? As a matter of English naval usage, a blow at the Spanish treasure previous to a formal declaration of war had been our regular procedure ever since Drake set the fashion in 1585.

In the present instance Commodore Moore, with his broad pendant in the *Indefatigable*, had three other frigates in company when he disposed of the four home-coming galleons from Monte Video. Southey argues that if the English frigates had been more numerous, the Spaniards would have surrendered to superior force and no blood would have been spilled. But such reasoning, though attractive, is logically unsound.

If Moore had the right to capture the Spanish squadron with forty ships, he had an equal right to capture it with four. A fire broke out on board the *Mercedes*, and it was through the fire that the explosion occurred. This accident was not the fault of the English Government; and it was they who gave Moore his orders. They were justified in giving them by the constant aggressiveness of a power which enjoyed all the immunities of a neutral. The destruction of the *Mercedes* was the fortune of war; and when fortune is cruel, pity is universal. That really is all that need be said.

[3] 1804.

have been supposed, would amply enrich the officers of the Mediterranean fleet, and repay them for the severe and unremitting duty on which they had been so long employed. But of this harvest they were deprived; for Sir John Orde was sent with a small squadron, and a separate command, to Cadiz.   Nelson's feelings were never wounded so deeply as now.   " I had thought," said he, writing in the first flow and freshness of indignation; " I fancied,—but nay; it must have been a dream, an idle dream;—yet, I confess it, I *did* fancy that I had done my country service; and thus they use me!—And under what circumstances, and with what pointed aggravation!—Yet, if I know my own thoughts it is not for myself, or on my own account chiefly, that I feel the sting and the disappointment.   No! it is for my brave officers: for my noble-minded friends and comrades. Such a gallant set of fellows! Such a band of brothers! My heart swells at the thought of them."[1]

[1] As a regular thing, the Mediterranean command extended backwards into the Atlantic as far as Cape St. Vincent.   Not only that, but the stretch of sea between Cape St. Vincent and the Strait of Gibraltar was considered the richest prize-making station in the whole wide world.   To rob the Mediterranean fleet of its avenue to wealth was hard; but to hand over the avenue to Sir John Orde, whom Nelson considered his *bête noir* (*cp.* above, pp. 118 and 203), was not only hard, but injudicious and unkind.

CHAPTER II

THE PURSUIT OF VILLENEUVE

18th January—19th August, 1805

[SOUTHEY. CHAPTER VIII.—continued]

WAR between Spain and England was now declared; and on the 18th of January,[1] the Toulon fleet, having the Spaniards to co-operate with them, put to sea.[2] Nelson

[1] 1805.

[2] Nelson's rigid blockade of Toulon, balanced as it was by Cornwallis's still more rigid blockade of Brest, had convinced Napoleon that he would have to modify his scheme for uniting these squadrons and sweeping the Channel. By sheer compulsion he dragged Spain into the war; and the consequent acquisition of Carthagena, Cadiz and Ferrol (with the fleets they contained) certainly improved his chances of success. Not content with these additions, he prepared a new French squadron at Rochefort; while the subjection of Holland put at his disposal the Dutch fleet in the Texel. With such a remarkable range of possibilities, he convinced himself that the sceptre of the seas was in his grasp. But he still required to concentrate the squadrons enumerated, or as many as time and fortune would allow.

Remembering Nelson's precipitate rush round the Mediterranean when his own expedition sailed for Egypt in 1798, he persuaded himself that the surreptitious departure of seven Napoleonic fleets would set the various contingents of the British Navy playing an extended game of " Blind Man's Buff ": and in the resulting confusion he believed it possible that his own squadrons might happily unite and co-operate with him at Boulogne.

His likeliest scheme would have left each Franco-Spanish unit free to " escape " when occasion offered. But against this procedure there was the obvious objection that all detachments ought to reach the rendezvous at the same moment. His programme underwent various changes while its details were being hammered out; but the consummation which Napoleon dreamed of took eventually some such shape as the following. The Toulon fleet, evading Nelson, would raise the blockade both of Carthagena and Cadiz, and, thus strengthened, sail for the secret rendezvous. The Brest fleet, if it could elude Cornwallis, would pick up the Spanish contingent at Ferrol, and sail for the same place. These two fleets, Napoleon hoped, would find there the Rochefort squadron awaiting them, and the grand armada, sweeping round the British Isles, would join the Dutch fleet in the North Sea, and convey across the Strait of Dover the army for the conquest of England.

The secret rendezvous (which Napoleon deliberately set at a distance from Britain) was the French island of Martinique. There was little enough reason to suppose that such a hiding-place would be suspected. But as in six weeks a search-party could easily cross the Atlantic, Napoleon (to make security doubly sure) told the Toulon fleet to curtail its stay in the West Indies. If in forty days there was no sign of the Brest contingent, the Mediterranean ships were to return to the coast of Spain, release the fleet at Corunna-Ferrol, and, raising the blockade of Brest, bring a sufficient force up Channel to achieve the grand purpose.

On paper the scheme looked rather attractive. But in reality it was the creation of a landsman who knew little or nothing of sea-campaigning. Even if every

was at anchor off the coast of Sardinia,[1] where the Madalena Islands form one of the finest harbours in the world,[2] when, at three in the afternoon of the 19th, the *Active* and *Seahorse* frigates brought this long-hoped-for intelligence. They had been close to the enemy at ten on the preceding night, but lost sight of them in about four hours.

The fleet immediately unmoored and weighed, and at six in the evening ran through the strait between Biche and Sardinia:[3] a passage so narrow that the ships could only pass one at a time, each following the stern lights of its leader. From the position of the enemy, when they were last seen, it was inferred that they must be bound round the southern end of Sardinia.[4] Signal was made the next morning to prepare for battle. Bad weather came on, baffling the one fleet in its object, and the other in its pursuit. Nelson beat about the Sicilian seas for ten days, without obtaining any other information of the enemy than that one of their ships had put into Ajaccio, dismasted; and having seen that Sardinia, Naples, and Sicily were safe, believing Egypt to be their destination, for Egypt he ran. The disappointment and distress which he had experienced in his former pursuits of the French through the same seas were now renewed. But Nelson, while he endured

detail had worked to perfection, and every Franco-Spanish unit got clear away to Martinique, the effect would not have been the dispersal of the British contingents, but their concentration in the mouth of the English Channel. Here they would quietly have awaited the pleasure of destroying Napoleon's armada when it returned in utter weariness from its double passage across the Atlantic. Nelson, it is true, had rushed from place to place during the campaign of 1798; but if on the present occasion he did so again, and (unlike other British Admirals) disobeyed the injunction to retire on home waters, the probabilities were strong that he would run the allied fleet to earth, and hack it to pieces with Egyptian relish as he had done aforetime at the Nile.

[1] Nelson's blockade was not quite so close as Cornwallis's, because his fleet was too small for the task confronting it. To have sent away a detachment (however small) for purposes of refitting would have rendered impotent the fraction that stayed with his flag. He preferred, before all things, to keep his ships together; and therefore, when one could no longer keep the sea, he took his whole force into harbour. This necessary withdrawal he excused to himself by the hope that it would coax the mouse from its hole; and, by keeping his frigates in front of Toulon, he believed himself able to spring on his prey almost as soon as it stirred. Compare his remarks in his letter to the Lord Mayor; above, p. 267.

[2] The principal advantage of the anchorage was its double entrance. With a fairway to the east of him and another to the west, Nelson was little likely, whichever way the wind might blow, to be imprisoned by foul weather. The islands are off the north-east corner of Sardinia. See above, map, p. 52.

[3] That is to say, the eastern exit.

[4] Nelson thought at this time (the wind being west) that the enemy were projecting fresh mischief in the Levant. He had, of course, no acquaintance with Napoleon's actual designs.

these anxious and unhappy feelings, was still consoled by the same confidence as on the former occasion—that, though his judgment might be erroneous, under all circumstances he was right in having formed it. " I have consulted no man," said he to the Admiralty. " Therefore the whole blame of ignorance in forming my judgment must rest with me. I would allow no man to take from me an atom of my glory had I fallen in with the French fleet; nor do I desire any man to partake any of the responsibility. All is mine, right or wrong." Then stating the grounds upon which he had proceeded, he added, " At this moment of sorrow, I still feel that I have acted right." In the same spirit he said to Sir Alexander Ball,[1] " When I call to remembrance all the circumstances, I approve, if nobody else does, of my own conduct."

Baffled thus, he bore up for Malta, and met intelligence from Naples that the French, having been dispersed in a gale, had put back to Toulon. From the same quarter he learned that a great number of saddles and muskets had been embarked; and this confirmed him in his opinion that Egypt was their destination. That they should have put back in consequence of storms, which he had weathered, gave him a consoling sense of British superiority. " These gentlemen," said he, " are not accustomed to a Gulf of Lions gale. We have buffeted them for one-and-twenty months, and not carried away a spar." He, however, who had so often braved these gales, was now, though not mastered by them, vexatiously thwarted and impeded; and on February 27, he was compelled to anchor in Pula Bay, in the Gulf of Cagliari. From the 21st of January the fleet had remained ready for battle, without a bulkhead up,[2] night or day. He anchored here that he might not be driven to leeward.[3] As soon as the weather moderated he put to sea again; and, after again beating about against contrary winds, another gale drove him to anchor in the Gulf of Palmas, on the 8th of March. This he made his rendezvous. He knew that the French troops still remained embarked,

---

[1] Captain Ball had been knighted in 1801.

[2] Bulkheads were wooden partitions erected to subdivide the deck space into separate rooms and cabins. When battle was imminent, the risk of splinters made them dangerous; and they were in consequence taken down and stowed in the hold.

[3] That is, to the east again; the wind being squally at N.W.

and, wishing to lead them into a belief that he was stationed upon the Spanish coast, he made his appearance off Barcelona with that intent.

About the end of the month, he began to fear that the plan of the expedition was abandoned; and, sailing once more towards his old station off Toulon, on the 4th of April, he met the *Phœbe*, with news that Villeneuve had put to sea on the last of March [1] with eleven ships of the line, seven frigates, and two brigs. When last seen, they were steering toward the coast of Africa. Nelson first covered the channel between Sardinia and Barbary, so as to satisfy himself that Villeneuve was not taking the same route for Egypt which Gantheaume had taken before him, when he attempted to carry reinforcements thither. [2] Certain of this, he bore up on the 7th for Palermo, lest the French should pass to the north of Corsica, [3] and he dispatched cruisers in all directions. On the 11th, he felt assured that they were not gone down [4] the Mediterranean; and sending off frigates to Gibraltar, to Lisbon, and to Admiral Cornwallis who commanded the squadron off Brest, he endeavoured to get to the westward, beating against westerly winds. After five days, a neutral gave intelligence that the French had been seen off Cape de Gatte [5] on the 7th. It was soon after ascertained that they had passed the Straits of Gibraltar on the day following; and Nelson, knowing that they might already be half way to Ireland, or to Jamaica, exclaimed that he was miserable. One gleam of comfort only came across him in the reflection, that his vigilance had rendered it impossible for them to undertake any expedition in the Mediterranean.

Eight days after this certain intelligence had been obtained, he described his state of mind thus forcibly, in writing to the governor of Malta, " My good fortune, my dear Ball, seems flown away. I cannot get a fair wind or even a side wind. Dead foul!—Dead foul!—But my mind

---

[1] Villeneuve put to sea, not on the last day of March, but on the last day but one.

[2] In April 1801 Gantheaume had sailed *via* Leghorn and the Strait of Messina to carry to Egypt reinforcements for the army which Napoleon had left behind him there.

[3] With a view to reaching the eastern Mediterranean by way of the Strait of Messina.

[4] Into the Levant.

[5] To the westward of Carthagena.

is fully made up what to do when I leave the Straits, supposing there is no certain account of the enemy's destination. I believe this ill-luck will go near to kill me; but as
these are times for exertion, I must not be cast down,
whatever I may feel." In spite of every exertion which
could be made by all the zeal and all the skill of British
seamen, he did not get in sight of Gibraltar till the 30th of
April; and the wind was then so adverse, that it was impossible to pass the Gut. He anchored in Mazari Bay, on
the Barbary shore; obtained supplies from Tetuan; and
when, on the 5th, a breeze from the eastward sprang up at
last, sailed once more, hoping to hear of the enemy from
Sir John Orde (who commanded off Cadiz) or from Lisbon.
" If nothing is heard of them," said he to the Admiralty,
" I shall probably think the rumours which have been
spread are true, that their object is the West Indies: and,
in that case, I think it my duty to follow them,—or to the
Antipodes, should I believe that to be their destination."
At the time when this resolution was taken, the physician
of the fleet had ordered him to return to England before
the hot months.

Nelson had formed his judgment [1] of their destination,
and made up his mind accordingly, when Donald Campbell,
at that time an admiral in the Portuguese service, the same
person who had given important tidings to Earl St. Vincent
of the movements of that fleet from which he won his title,
a second time gave timely and momentous intelligence to
the flag of his country. He went on board the *Victory*, and
communicated to Nelson his certain knowledge that the
combined Spanish and French fleets were bound for the
West Indies. [2]

[1] It should be noted that Nelson had, by his genius for sea-strategy, thus early
divined the most secret item of Napoleon's privy plan. The following must have
been his train of thought:

(*a*) The Toulon fleet, we have proved, has not gone into the eastern Mediterranean, and England has nothing at stake in the western.

(*b*) The enemy were seen at Gibraltar a month ago, and in the interim no
news has come from the English squadrons that stretch from Cadiz to the
Channel. Villeneuve has therefore not gone north.

(*c*) It is unlikely that he is bound at the present moment for the Cape of
Good Hope and the south.

(*d*) Therefore the rumour (otherwise worthless) that the Toulon fleet is
bound for the West Indies is probably correct.

[2] When Nelson reached the West Indies, he received positive information as
to Villeneuve's whereabouts from the general officer commanding-in-chief in the
Leeward Isles. The authority was unimpeachable; and yet the intelligence was

Hitherto all things had favoured the enemy. While the British commander was beating up against strong southerly and westerly gales, they had wind to their wish from the N.E.; and had done in nine days what he was a whole month in accomplishing. Villeneuve, finding the Spaniards at Carthagena were not in a state of equipment to join him, dared not wait, but hastened on to Cadiz. Sir John Orde necessarily retired at his approach.[1] Admiral Gravina, with six Spanish ships of the line and two French, came out to him, and they sailed without a moment's loss of time. They had about three thousand French troops on board, and fifteen hundred Spanish: six hundred were under orders, expecting them at Martinique, and one thousand at Guadeloupe. General Lauriston commanded the troops. The combined fleet now consisted of eighteen sail of the line, six forty-four-gun frigates, one of twenty-six guns, three corvettes, and a brig. They were joined afterwards by two new French line-of-battle ships and one forty-four.[2] Nelson pursued them with ten sail of the line and three frigates. " Take you a Frenchman apiece," said he to his captains, " and leave me the Spaniards. When I haul down my colours, I expect you to do the same,—and not till then."

The enemy had five-and-thirty days' start; but he calculated that he should gain eight or ten days upon them

entirely false. The reader should therefore guard against a natural inclination to accept the statement in the text as final and conclusive.

When Nelson was at Gibraltar, he certainly saw Admiral Donald Campbell and received from him (according to Captain Hargood of the *Belleisle*) " important information as to the destination of the French squadron." But there is nothing in the Nelson papers to confirm Hargood's statement; and there is unimpeachable evidence to show that, four days after his interview with Campbell, Nelson still retained an open mind on the matter. The truth is that when a small man holds the same opinion as a great man and the great man listens to what the small man says, the small man attaches to the interview more importance than the interview will bear. " It was myself," he grandiloquently informs his friends, " who put that notion into his head."

Campbell's statement was but as a grain of dust in the scales that Nelson was balancing.

[1] Sir John Orde fell back on Cornwallis at Brest according to prearranged plans (see above, Note 2, p. 280). With only five ships he could not compete with the odds against him. If, however, he had clung to Villeneuve's skirts, he might have discovered where the Allies were going, and so robbed Nelson of some of his glory.

[2] The first ships to evade the English and start for Martinique were the ships from Rochefort. They set sail on January 11, and reached their destination on 20th February. But after five weeks of waiting they returned home again, thereby lending the problem that confronted their foes an element of mystification. The two battleships and the frigate mentioned here were a second contingent from the same port.

by his exertions.[1] May 15th he made Madeira, and on
June 4th reached Barbados,[2] whither he had sent dispatches
before him: and where he found Admiral Cochrane,[3] with
two ships, part of our squadron in those seas being at
Jamaica. He found here also accounts that the combined
fleets had been seen from St. Lucia on the 28th,[4] standing
to the southward, and that Tobago and Trinidad were
their objects. This Nelson doubted; but he was alone in
his opinion, and yielded it with these foreboding words,
" If your intelligence proves false, you lose me the French
fleet." [5] Sir William Myers [6] offered to embark here with
two thousand troops. They were taken on board, and the
next morning he sailed for Tobago. Here accident confirmed the false intelligence which had, whether from
intention or error, misled him. A merchant at Tobago, in
the general alarm, not knowing whether this fleet was
friend or foe, sent out a schooner to reconnoitre, and
acquaint him by signal. The signal which he had chosen
happened to be the very one which had been appointed by
Colonel Shipley of the Engineers to signify that the enemy
were at Trinidad; and as this was at the close of day, there
was no opportunity of discovering the mistake. An American
brig was met with about the same time, the master of which,
with that propensity to deceive the English and assist the
French in any manner which has been but too common
among his countrymen, affirmed that he had been boarded
off Grenada a few days before by the French, who were
standing towards the Bocas [7] of Trinidad. This fresh
intelligence removed all doubts. The ships were cleared
for action before daylight, and Nelson entered the Bay of
Paria on the 7th, hoping and expecting to make the mouths
of the Orinoco as famous in the annals of the British Navy

[1] Villeneuve crossed the Atlantic in thirty-four days, and Nelson in twenty-four.
[2] See above, map, p. 19.
[3] Admiral Sir Alexander Cochrane, G.C.B., uncle of the famous seaman, the
Earl of Dundonald, had been sent to the West Indies with half-a-dozen ships to
protect British interests from the waspish attentions of the Rochefort squadron
(see above, Note 2, p. 285). When the Rochefort squadron returned to its base,
Cochrane remained as a safeguard to Jamaica and the Leeward Isles; but the
paucity of his ships rendered him powerless in the face of such a force as Villeneuve's.
[4] Of May. This was the positive intelligence of General Brereton (Commander-
in-Chief of the forces in the Leeward Isles) mentioned above in Note 2, p. 284.
[5] Villeneuve was still at Martinique when Nelson spoke these fateful words.
[6] Commander of the troops at Barbados.
[7] Islands off the north-west point of Trinidad.

as those of the Nile. Not an enemy was there; and it was
discovered that accident and artifice had combined to lead
him so far to leeward that there could have been little hope
of fetching to windward of Grenada for any other fleet.
Nelson, however, with skill and exertions never exceeded,
and almost unexampled, bore for that island.[1]

Advices met him on the way, that the combined fleets
having captured the Diamond Rock,[2] were then at Martinique, on the 4th,[3] and were expected to sail that night for
the attack of Grenada. On the 9th Nelson arrived off that
island; and there learned that they had passed to leeward
of Antigua the preceding day, and taken a homeward-
bound convoy. Had it not been for false information, upon
which Nelson had acted reluctantly, and in opposition to
his own judgment, he would have been off Port Royal [4]
just as they were leaving it, and the battle would have
been fought on the spot where Rodney defeated De Grasse.[5]
This he remembered in his vexation: but he had saved
the colonies, and above two hundred ships laden for Europe,
which would else have fallen into the enemy's hands; and
he had the satisfaction of knowing that the mere terror of
his name had effected this, and had put to flight the allied
enemies, whose force nearly doubled that before which they
fled. That they were flying back to Europe he believed,
and for Europe he steered in pursuit on the 13th, having disembarked the troops at Antigua, and taking with
him the *Spartiate*, seventy-four; the only addition to the
squadron with which he was pursuing so superior a force.
Five days afterwards the *Amazon* brought intelligence that

[1] It must be understood that Nelson at this time knew nothing of the projected
rally of Franco-Spanish fleets at Martinique. He supposed that Villeneuve had
come to the West Indies (as the French admirals had done in the American War,
1778–83) in order to plunder convoys and capture islands. In this conjecture he
was not wholly incorrect, as Villeneuve, in his days of waiting for the fleet from
Brest, had orders to do the maximum of mischief to British property. North of
Tobago came the English island of Grenada, and thither Nelson sped, still supposing that the French were south of St. Lucia (*cp.* map above, p. 19). His
anxiety for the moment was lest the Easterly Trades (*cp.* above, Part II. pp. 15
and 19) should prevent him from attacking the enemy when found.
[2] A splintered pinnacle or islet standing out of the sea near the entrance to
Fort Royal, Martinique. It had been seized by a handful of bluejackets, who had
christened it H.M. Sloop *Diamond Rock*, and with a gun or two had held it against
all French efforts to dislodge them.
[3] Of June.
[4] Fort Royal, the French naval base at Martinique.
[5] The battle of the Saints, 12th April, 1782.

she had spoke a schooner who had seen them, on the evening of the 15th, steering to the N.; and, by computation, eighty-seven leagues off. Nelson's diary at this time denotes his great anxiety, and his perpetual and all-observing vigilance. —" June 21. Midnight, nearly calm, saw three planks, which I think came from the French fleet. Very miserable, which is very foolish." On the 17th of July he came in sight of Cape St. Vincent, and steered for Gibraltar.— " July 18th," his diary says, " Cape Spartel in sight, but no French fleet, nor any information about them. How sorrowful this makes me! but I cannot help myself." The next day he anchored at Gibraltar; and on the 20th, says he, " I went on shore for the first time since 16th June, 1803; and from having my foot out of the *Victory*, two years, wanting ten days."

Here he communicated with his old friend Collingwood; who, having been detached with a squadron, when the disappearance of the combined fleets and of Nelson in their pursuit, was known in England, had taken his station off Cadiz.[1] He [2] thought that Ireland was the enemy's ultimate object; that they would now liberate the Ferrol squadron, which was blocked up by Sir Robert Calder; call for the Rochefort ships, and then appear off Ushant with three- or four-and-thirty sail; there to be joined by the Brest fleet. With this great force he supposed they would make for Ireland,—the real mark and bent of all their operations: and their flight to the West Indies, he thought, had been merely undertaken to take off Nelson's force,[3] which was the great impediment to their undertaking.

Collingwood was gifted with great political penetration. As yet, however, all was conjecture concerning the enemy; and Nelson, having victualled and watered at Tetuan,

---

[1] Replacing Sir John Orde, who (it will be remembered) had at Villeneuve's approach fallen back on the Channel.

[2] Collingwood. The letter which he wrote to Nelson (for Nelson refused to stop and talk) is printed in full in *Correspondence and Memoir of Lord Collingwood*, G. L. Newnham Collingwood, p. 109.

[3] " I have considered the invasion of Ireland as the real mark and butt of all their operations. Their flight to the West Indies was to take off the naval force, which proved the great impediment to their undertaking."

These words of Collingwood, when exactly quoted, will not bear out Southey's construction that Villeneuve crossed the Atlantic in order to draw Nelson after him. The force that covered Ireland was not Nelson's squadron, but the Grand Fleet under Cornwallis.

stood for Ceuta [1] on the 24th, still without information of their course. Next day intelligence arrived that the *Curieux* brig [2] had seen them on the 19th, standing to the northward. He proceeded off Cape St. Vincent, rather cruising for intelligence than knowing whither to betake himself: and here a case occurred that more than any other event in real history resembles those whimsical proofs of sagacity which Voltaire, in his *Zadig*, has borrowed from the Orientals. [3] One of our frigates spoke an American, who, a little to the westward of the Azores, had fallen in with an armed vessel, appearing to be a dismasted privateer, deserted by her crew, which had been run on board by another ship, and had been set fire to; but the fire had gone out. A log-book and a few seamen's jackets were found in the cabin; and these were brought to Nelson. The log-book closed with these words, " Two large vessels in the W.N.W.": and this led him to conclude that the vessel had been an English privateer, cruising off the Western Islands. But there was in this book a scrap of dirty paper, filled with figures. Nelson, immediately upon seeing it, observed, that the figures were written by a Frenchman; and, after studying this for a while, said, " I can explain the whole. The jackets are of French manufacture, and prove that the privateer was in possession of the enemy. She had been chased and taken by the two ships that were seen in the W.N.W. The prize-master, going on board in a hurry, forgot to take with him his reckoning. There is none in the log-book; and the dirty paper contains her work for the number of days since the privateer last left Corvo, with an unaccounted-for run, which I take to have been the chase, in his endeavour to find out her situation by back reckonings. By some mismanagement, I conclude, she was run on board of by one of the enemy's ships, and dismasted. Not liking delay (for I am satisfied that those two ships were the advanced ones of the French

---

[1] Ceuta and Gibraltar are what the ancients called the two " Pillars of Hercules," the rocky doorposts of the Mediterranean. Nelson sought between them for scraps of evidence that would show whether Villeneuve was returning to his starting-place.

[2] This information (if delivered in this form) was quite false. The *Curieux* had sighted the combined fleet, but on the 19th of June, not July. For the adventures of this brig see next chapter.

[3] *Zadig*, in Voltaire's romance, was gifted with great powers of divination.

squadron), and fancying we were close at their heels, they set fire to the vessel, and abandoned her in a hurry. If this explanation be correct, I infer from it, that they are gone more to the northward; and more to the northward I will look for them." [1] This course accordingly he held, but still without success. Still persevering, and still disappointed, he returned near enough to Cadiz to ascertain that they were not there; traversed the Bay of Biscay; and then, as a last hope, stood over for the north-west coast of Ireland, against adverse winds, till, on the evening of the 12th of August, he learned that they had not been heard of there. Frustrated thus in all his hopes, after a pursuit, to which, for its extent, rapidity, and perseverance, no parallel can be produced, he judged it best to reinforce the Channel fleet with his squadron, lest the enemy, as Collingwood apprehended, should bear down upon Brest with their whole collected force. On the 15th he joined Admiral Cornwallis off Ushant. No news had yet been obtained of the enemy; and on the same evening he received orders to proceed, with the *Victory* and *Superb*,[2] to Portsmouth.

[1] Southey transcribed this rather intricate story from Clarke and McArthur (Vol. II. pp. 417–18) with rather less than his usual care. The language of navigation is, to the lay mind, always obscure; and when obsolete terminology is employed and copyist's errors left uncorrected, the modern reader may well confess himself defeated.

What Nelson required to know was Villeneuve's position. Scraps of evidence were laid before him in the shape of an abandoned privateer, injured by collision, and partly destroyed by fire; a neglected log-book that closed with the words " Two large vessels in the W.N.W.!"; a piece of paper with calculations indecipherable by English and Americans; and a few seamen's jackets of unfamiliar cut. Almost immediately he converted the broken bits of imagery into a complete picture, and a picture which told him exactly what he wanted to know.

An English privateer had been cruising off the Azores, when she sighted two French vessels to windward. She made off as quickly as she could; but her two enemies overhauled her, boarded her, and carried her off with them. The prize-master, in taking charge, had no reliable data as to his position; and in consequence had made no immediate entry of his own in the privateer's log; but, since leaving the Azores, had jotted down on a piece of paper his changes of course, etc., so that he could work out a correct position and eventually enter it in the book. He was prevented, however, from doing so by an accident. One of the French ships had collided with the prize and gravely injured her. Some reason or other rendered repairs out of the question. The prize-crew in consequence had been removed; the privateer had been set on fire, and the two French ships had made off. Why? Because they realised that Nelson's fleet was on their traces, and might at any moment spring upon them.

The tell-tale figures gave the direction and course of the two French ships, who were part of the fleet returning from the Indies.

Villeneuve was to the north of him, and northward Nelson turned.

[2] The plucky way in which this ship accompanied Nelson all the way to Trinidad and back again, though her very timbers groaned aloud for want of repair, has been immortalised by Sir Henry Newbolt in his poem " The Old *Superb*."

This chapter serves to illustrate in a very striking way the impossibility of appreciating at their proper worth historical events in the hour of their unfolding. Mighty transactions, like lofty buildings, can best be seen at a distance. Southey examines Nelson's pursuit of Villeneuve, and finds in it matter which excites in turn his sympathy and pity. He calls attention to the constant disappointment and failure; the futile searchings, the vexatious gropings in the darkness of ignorance. He contrasts with Nelson's uncertainty a chance guess of Collingwood's and finds therein the evidence of great political penetration; and then, as if he had said too much, he reminds his readers that, though the subject of his biography had been unhappily led astray, he had for all that "saved the colonies and above two hundred ships" and displayed in his pursuit a "rapidity" and "perseverance" without parallel.

It never occurred to Southey that he was sitting in judgment on the maritime strategy of England and France and plumbing depths which he was powerless to fathom. It never occurred to him that his compunction was uncalled for and his sympathy out of place. It never occurred to him that Nelson's transatlantic cruise set the crown on a great career.

Napoleon desired that his several fleets should combine at a secret rendezvous; and, returning therefrom, occupy the Channel, in order to cover his invasion of England. The choice of Martinique as a trysting-place fulfilled a double purpose. It was the last spot, in his opinion, that the English would suspect, if they had the wit to guess what was afoot; and the withdrawal thither of his fleets from their customary stations could not fail, he thought, to set his enemies scattering in all directions.

The British admirals as a body no doubt were mystified by the behaviour of their opponents; but they knew exactly where their duty called them; and, when a French contingent disappeared, they quietly fell back on the Brest blockade, and with their reinforcements enabled Cornwallis to bid defiance to any Franco-Spanish fleet that dared set a course for Boulogne.

But Nelson behaved differently from everyone else, and solved the enigma which Napoleon thought insoluble. Though the flat-bottomed boats were ready at Boulogne to embark the legions that were to conquer England; though Napoleon announced that, as soon as Villeneuve arrived, he should cross the Channel and occupy London; and though the boldest Londoners trembled at the doom that overshadowed them; Nelson turned his back alike on Britons and Boulogne and made sail across the wide Atlantic. If Villeneuve had actually gone to Boulogne, then Nelson's reputation was ruined for ever. But if, for some reason then to Britons unintelligible, Villeneuve also was crossing the Atlantic, then the strategic intuition that carried Nelson after him eclipses completely the display of genius he had given in the campaign that preceded the Nile.

To-day Southey's picture still lives in the nation's memory, because people are unable to put aside what none of their ancestors possessed—the knowledge of where Villeneuve was going, and what he was attempting to do. The facts, therefore, that need emphasis are these:

On 4th April, 1805, Nelson learnt that the Toulon fleet had

escaped; and on 19th August he landed in England. In the interval of time that separates these dates he did not once catch so much as a glimpse of Villeneuve's ships. And yet, strategically blindfold, he had followed them across the world and back again, never faltering in his pursuit, never more than a day or two astern. Napoleon's rendezvous was no rendezvous; Napoleon's schemes were mere worthless imaginings; when the greatest Admiral in the world's history laid them bare as fast as they were hidden.

A combination of fleets, Napoleon said, would safeguard the Channel, and enable him to cross. Such a combination of fleets was actually effected, for when Gravina joined Villeneuve they had at their disposal twenty sail of the line. Yet Nelson, with a storm-beaten group of ten, including the rickety *Superb*, drove his adversaries in panic and confusion before him, as a lion puts cattle to flight.

For years after Southey completed his book it was an accepted tradition that the battle of Trafalgar saved England from invasion. But it was in the hour in which Nelson completed his chase and came home for a few days' rest that Napoleon abandoned his scheme of conquest and marched away from Boulogne. That confession of failure is the completest gauge of Nelson's great success.

Quite recently Thomas Hardy in *The Dynasts* has repeated Southey's strategic blunder, and asserted in a new form the time-honoured heresy that Nelson was led astray.

CHAPTER III

DRAMATIC PAUSE BEFORE THE CATASTROPHE

19th August—9th October

[*SOUTHEY. CHAPTER IX*]

At Portsmouth Nelson, at length, found news of the combined fleet. Sir Robert Calder, who had been sent out to intercept their return, had fallen in with them on the 22nd of July, sixty leagues west of Cape Finisterre.[1] Their force consisted of twenty sail of the line, three fifty-gun ships, five frigates, and two brigs: his, of fifteen line-of-battle ships, two frigates, a cutter, and a lugger. After an action of four hours, he had captured an eighty-four and a seventy-four, and then thought it necessary to bring-to the squadron, for the purpose of securing their prizes. The hostile fleets remained in sight of each other till the 26th, when the enemy bore away.[2] The capture of two ships from so superior a force would have been considered as no inconsiderable victory a few years earlier; but Nelson had introduced a new era in our naval history; and the nation felt, respecting this action, as he had felt on a somewhat similar occasion.[3] They regretted that Nelson, with his eleven

---

[1] Just before Nelson left the West Indies, he dispatched the *Curieux* brig to carry home his news. The *Curieux* overtook Villeneuve on 19th June (see above, Note 2, p. 289); and, making a memorandum of his latitude and longitude, sped to England brimful of information. Lord Barham, the octogenarian but energetic First Lord, roused out of bed in the early hours, at once discerned where the combined fleet was making for, and sent Calder at Ferrol tidings and reinforcements which enabled him to grapple with Villeneuve's fleet as it reached its journey's end.

Calder was not " sent out " from England to the coast of Spain; but " sent out " from his station further seawards so as to fight the fleet in front of him without interruption from the fleet behind.

[2] Calder's battle was fought in a fog and hardly anyone could know what was actually going on. In the end, two of the Spanish ships fell to leeward and, as the text relates, were captured. Calder seems to have been genuinely anxious to continue the battle, but to have been unable to regain contact with the enemy. In his dispatch he emphasised the difficulty of his position with the Ferrol fleet in his rear; and people, with human fallibility, jumped to the conclusion that this was the real reason why he had not renewed the engagement. In consequence he was summoned home to stand his trial by court martial.

[3] Hotham's action in the Gulf of Genoa, see above, pp. 70–74.

ships, had not been in Sir Robert Calder's place; and their disappointment was generally and loudly expressed.

Frustrated as his own hopes had been, Nelson had yet the high satisfaction of knowing that his judgment had never been more conspicuously approved, and that he had rendered essential service to his country by driving the enemy from those islands where they expected there could be no force capable of opposing them. The West India merchants in London, as men whose interests were more immediately benefited, appointed a deputation to express their thanks for his great and judicious exertions.

It was now his intention to rest awhile from his labours, and recruit himself after all his fatigues and cares in the society of those whom he loved. All his stores were brought up from the *Victory*; and he found in his house at Merton the enjoyment which he had anticipated.

Many days had not elapsed before Captain Blackwood, on his way to London with dispatches, called on him at five in the morning. Nelson, who was already dressed, exclaimed, the moment he saw him, " I am sure you bring me news of the French and Spanish fleets! I think I shall yet have to beat them!" They had refitted at Vigo, after the indecisive action with Sir Robert Calder; then proceeded to Ferrol, brought out the squadron from thence, and with it entered Cadiz in safety. " Depend on it, Blackwood," he repeatedly said, " I shall yet give M. Villeneuve a drubbing." But, when Blackwood had left him, he wanted resolution to declare his wishes to Lady Hamilton and his sisters, and endeavoured to drive away the thought. He had done enough, he said,—" Let the man trudge it who has lost his budget!" His countenance belied his lips; and as he was pacing one of the walks in the garden, which he used to call the quarter-deck, Lady Hamilton came up to him, and told him she saw he was uneasy. He smiled, and said, " No, he was as happy as possible; he was surrounded by his family; his health was better since he had been on shore, and he would not give sixpence to call the King his uncle." She replied, that she did not believe him; that she knew he was longing to get at the combined fleets; that he considered them as his own property; that he would be miserable if any man but himself did the business; and that he ought to have them as the price and reward of his two years' long watching and his hard chase. " Nelson," said she, " however we may lament your absence, offer your services. They will be accepted, and you will gain a quiet heart by it. You will have a glorious victory, and then you may return here, and be happy." He looked at her with tears in his eyes:—" Brave Emma!—Good Emma!— If there were more Emmas there would be more Nelsons."

His services were as willingly accepted as they were offered; and Lord Barham, giving him the list of the navy, desired him to choose his own officers. " Choose yourself, my lord," was his reply. " The same spirit actuates the whole profession. You cannot choose wrong." Lord Barham then desired him to say what ships, and how many, he would wish, in addition to the fleet which he was going to command, and said they should follow him as soon as each was ready. No appointment was ever more in unison with the feelings and judgment of the whole nation. They, like Lady Hamilton, thought that the destruction of the combined fleets ought properly to be Nelson's work; that he, who had been

> Half around the sea-girt ball,
> The hunter of the recreant Gaul,[1]

ought to reap the spoils of the chase which he had watched so long, and so perseveringly pursued.

Unremitting exertions were made to equip the ships which he had chosen, and especially to refit the *Victory*, which was once more to bear his flag. Before he left London he called at his upholsterer's, where the coffin which Captain Hallowell had given him was deposited; and desired that its history might be engraven upon the lid, saying that it was highly probable he might want it on his return. He seemed, indeed, to have been impressed with an expectation

[1] This quotation is from *Songs of Trafalgar*, by the Right Hon. J. W. Croker, M.P. (1805). *Cp.* " Dedication " above, p. xli.

> High then the monumental pile
> Erect for Nelson of the Nile,
> Of Trafalgar, and Vincent's heights,
> For Nelson of the hundred fights—
>
> For him alike on shore and surge
> Of proud Iberia's power the scourge,
> And half around the sea-girt ball
> The hunter of the recreant Gaul.

that he should fall in the battle. In a letter to his brother, written immediately after his return, he had said " We must not talk of Sir Robert Calder's battle. I might not have done so much with my small force. If I had fallen in with them, you might probably have been a lord before I wished; for I know they meant to make a dead set at the *Victory*." Nelson had once regarded the prospect of death with gloomy satisfaction. It was when he anticipated the upbraidings of his wife, and the displeasure of his venerable father. The state of his feelings now was expressed in his private journal in these words:—" Friday night (September 13), at half-past ten, I drove from dear, dear Merton; where I left all which I hold dear in this world, to go to serve my King and country. May the great God, whom I adore, enable me to fulfil the expectations of my country! And if it is His good pleasure that I should return, my thanks will never cease being offered up to the throne of His mercy. If it is His good providence to cut short my days upon earth, I bow with the greatest submission; relying that He will protect those so dear to me, whom I may leave behind! His will be done. Amen! Amen! Amen! "

Early on the following morning he reached Portsmouth; and having dispatched his business on shore, endeavoured to elude the populace by taking a by-way to the beach. But a crowd collected in his train, pressing forward, to obtain a sight of his face. Many were in tears, and many knelt down before him, and blessed him as he passed. England has had many heroes; but never one who so entirely possessed the love of his fellow-countrymen as Nelson. All men knew that his heart was as humane as it was fearless; that there was not in his nature the slightest alloy of selfishness or cupidity; but that, with perfect and entire devotion, he served his country with all his heart, and with all his soul, and with all his strength; and, therefore, they loved him as truly and as fervently as he loved England. They pressed upon the parapet, to gaze after him when his barge pushed off, and he was returning their cheers by waving his hat. The sentinels, who endeavoured to prevent them from trespassing upon this ground, were wedged among the crowd; and an officer, who, not very prudently upon such an occasion, ordered them to drive the people down with their bayonets, was compelled speedily to retreat; for the people would not be debarred from gazing, till the last moment, upon the hero—the darling hero of England!

He arrived off Cadiz on the 29th of September—his birthday. Fearing that, if the enemy knew his force, they might be deterred from venturing to sea, he kept out of sight of land, desired Collingwood to fire no salute, and hoist no colours; and wrote to Gibraltar, to request that the force of the fleet might not be inserted there in the *Gazette*. His reception in the Mediterranean fleet was as gratifying as the farewell of his countrymen at Portsmouth. The officers who came on board to welcome him, forgot his rank as commander, in their joy at seeing him again.

On the day of his arrival, Villeneuve received orders to put to sea the first opportunity.[1] Villeneuve, however, hesitated, when he heard that Nelson had resumed the command. He called a council of war; and their determination was, that it would not be expedient to leave Cadiz unless they had reason to believe themselves stronger by one-third than the British force. In the public measures of this country secrecy is seldom practicable, and seldomer attempted. Here, however, by the precautions of Nelson, and the wise measures of the Admiralty, the enemy were for once kept in ignorance; for as the ships appointed to reinforce the Mediterranean fleet were dispatched singly, each as soon as it was ready,—their collected number was not stated in the newspapers, and their arrival was not known to the enemy. But the enemy knew that Admiral Louis, with six sail, had been detached for stores and water to Gibraltar. Accident also contributed to make the French Admiral doubt whether Nelson himself had actually taken the command. An American, lately arrived from England, maintained that it was impossible,—for he had seen him only a few days before in London; and, at that time, there was no rumour of his going again to sea.

The station which Nelson had chosen was some fifty or sixty miles to the west of Cadiz, near Cape St. Mary's. At

[1] Napoleon, who had abandoned his invasion scheme, and was unaware of Nelson's proximity to Cadiz, desired Villeneuve's help in the Mediterranean, where fresh business was already afoot.

this distance he hoped to decoy the enemy out, while he guarded against the danger of being caught with a westerly wind near Cadiz, and driven within the Straits. The blockade of the port was rigorously enforced, in hopes that the combined fleet might be forced to sea by want. The Danish vessels, therefore, which were carrying provisions from the French ports in the bay, under the name of Danish property, to all the little ports from Ayamonte [1] to Algeçiras, from whence they were conveyed in coasting boats to Cadiz, were seized. Without this proper exertion of power, the blockade would have been rendered nugatory, by the advantage thus taken of the neutral flag. The supplies from France were thus effectually cut off. There was now every indication that the enemy would speedily venture out. Officers and men were in the highest spirits at the prospect of giving them a decisive blow; such, indeed, as would put an end to all further contest upon the seas. Theatrical amusements were performed every evening in most of the ships; and *God save the King* was the hymn with which the sports concluded. " I verily believe," said Nelson (writing on the 6th of October), " that the country will soon be put to some expense on my account; either a monument, or a new pension and honours; for I have not the smallest doubt but that a very few days, almost hours, will put us in battle. The success no man can ensure: but for the fighting them, if they can be got at, I pledge myself. The sooner the better. I don't like to have these things upon my mind."

At this time he was not without some cause of anxiety. He was in want of frigates—" the eyes of the fleet," as he always called them—to the want of which the enemy before were indebted for their escape, and Bonaparte for his arrival in Egypt. He had only twenty-three ships. Others were on the way—but they might come too late; and, though Nelson never doubted of victory, mere victory was not what he looked to. He wanted to annihilate the enemy's fleet. The Carthagena squadron might effect a junction with this fleet on the one side; and on the other it was to be expected that a similar attempt would be made by the French from Brest; in either case a formidable

---

[1] Midway between Cadiz and Cape St. Vincent.

contingency to be apprehended by the blockading force. The Rochefort squadron did push out, and had nearly caught the *Agamemnon* and *l'Aimable*, on their way to reinforce the British Admiral. Yet Nelson at this time weakened his own fleet. He had the unpleasant task to perform of sending home Sir Robert Calder, whose conduct was to be made the subject of a court martial, in consequence of the general dissatisfaction which had been felt and expressed at his imperfect victory. Sir Robert Calder and Sir John Orde [1] Nelson believed to be the only two enemies whom he had ever had in his profession—and, from that sensitive delicacy which distinguished him, this made him the more scrupulously anxious to show every possible mark of respect and kindness to Sir Robert. He wished to detain him till after the expected action; when the services which he might perform, and the triumphant joy which would be excited, would leave nothing to be apprehended from an inquiry into the previous engagement. Sir Robert, however, whose situation was very painful, did not choose to delay a trial, from the result of which he confidently expected a complete justification: and Nelson, instead of sending him home in a frigate, insisted on his returning in his own ninety-gun ship; ill as such a ship could at that time be spared. Nothing could be more honourable than the feeling by which Nelson was influenced. But at such a crisis, it ought not to have been indulged.

On the 9th Nelson sent Collingwood what he called, in his diary, " The Nelson Touch." [2] " I send you," said he, " my plan of attack, as far as a man dare venture to guess at the very uncertain position the enemy may be found in; but it is to place you perfectly at ease respecting my intentions, and to give full scope to your judgment for carrying them into effect. We can, my dear Coll, have no little

---

[1] Sir Robert Calder, who was flag-captain to Jervis at St. Vincent, had publicly criticised Nelson's disobedience during that battle in leaving his place without orders; Sir John Orde had, as already noted, protested against the selection of an officer subordinate to himself for the command of the fleet which won the victory of the Nile.

[2] The original " Memorandum," filling two sheets or eight pages of quarto size, written throughout in Nelson's hand and amended by his chaplain, Dr. A. J. Scott, is one of the treasures of the British Museum. It may be obtained in pamphlet form at the Museum bookstalls, and will be found in Sir Harris Nicolas's seventh volume, pp. 89-92.

jealousies. We have only one great object in view, that of annihilating our enemies, and getting a glorious peace for our country. No man has more confidence in another than I have in you; and no man will render your services more justice than your very old friend, Nelson and Bronte." The order of sailing was to be the order of battle: the fleet in two lines, with an advanced squadron of eight of the fastest sailing two-deckers.[1] The second in command, having the entire direction of his line, was to break through the enemy, about the twelfth ship from their rear; he [2] would lead through the centre, and the advanced squadron was to cut off three or four ahead of the centre. This plan was to be adapted to the strength of the enemy, so that they should always be one-fourth superior to those whom they cut off. Nelson said, " That his admirals and captains, knowing his precise object to be that of a close and decisive action, would supply any deficiency of signals, and act accordingly. In case signals cannot be seen or clearly understood, no captain can do wrong if he places his ship alongside that of an enemy." [3] One of the last orders of this admirable man was that the name and family of every officer, seaman, and marine, who might be killed or wounded in action, should be, as soon as possible, returned to him, in order to be transmitted to the chairman of the patriotic fund, that the case might be taken into consideration, for the benefit of the sufferer, or his family.

[1] On the day of battle Nelson had not so many ships as he had anticipated. He was therefore obliged to abandon the idea of the advanced squadron of eight.

[2] Nelson.

[3] Since the death of Nelson no question connected with his thought and work has caused so much discussion as the " Tactics of Trafalgar." Indeed, an official judgment on the issues involved was not made known until the Government issued a Blue Book on the subject in October 1913.

But of such discussion Southey knew nothing. In his allusion to Nelson's " Memorandum " he mentions that its chief tactical innovation was the employment of two separate and independent fleets, and with that he dismisses the topic. Nor is there any need to supplement here his casual reference; for strange as it must appear to modern readers, Southey makes no attempt to describe Trafalgar as he describes the Baltic and the Nile. Not only does he tell us nothing of the adventures of Collingwood's force, but he does not even describe what happened to the ships under Nelson's own command. From this point onward he has no eyes except for the *Victory* and the hero whom she carried through death to immortality.

Those who would pursue the subject at large are advised to turn to the Blue Book in question, Cd. 7120, and to the " Documents and Books " which it tabulates on page v. Those who prefer the material predigested will find an epitome in the second Appendix to the present editor's *Sea Kings of Britain*, Vol. III.

CHAPTER IV

THE BATTLE

19th–21st October

[SOUTHEY. CHAPTER IX.—continued]

ABOUT half past nine in the morning of the 19th,[1] the *Mars*, being the nearest to the fleet of the ships which formed the line of communication with the frigates inshore, repeated the signal that the enemy were coming out of port. The wind was at this time very light, with partial breezes, mostly from the S.S.W. Nelson ordered the signal to be made for a chase in the south-east quarter. About two, the repeating ships announced that the enemy were at sea.[2] All night the British fleet continued under all sail, steering to the south-east.[3] At daybreak they were in the entrance of the Straits, but the enemy were not in sight. About seven, one of the frigates made signal that the enemy were bearing north.[4] Upon this the *Victory* hove to;[5] and shortly afterwards Nelson made sail again to the northward. In the afternoon the wind blew fresh from the south-west, and the English began to fear that the foe might be forced to return to port. A little before sunset, however, Blackwood, in the *Euryalus*, telegraphed, that

---

[1] Saturday.

[2] At eight on Saturday morning the enemy began to hoist their topsails, and this news reached Nelson, who was fifty miles away, in an hour and a half. But almost as soon as the Franco-Spanish fleet put itself in motion, the wind fell to nothing and there was a dead calm. The tidings which Nelson received at 2 o'clock (sent off by the frigates shortly after midday) was to the effect that nine of the enemy were out of harbour. But these ships, the only ones that put to sea on Saturday, were obliged to anchor where they were and wait till Sunday for the rest.

[3] Nelson knew, almost as well as if he had been told, that Villeneuve was making for the Mediterranean.

[4] This does not mean that the enemy were moving in a northerly direction, but that the British frigates (who lay between Nelson and Cadiz) sighted the vanguard of the Franco-Spanish fleet to the north of them.

[5] Came to a stop. Nelson had already succeeded in his first object and cut off his foe from the Straits.

they appeared determined to go to the westward,[1] " And
that," said the Admiral, in his diary, "they shall not do,
if it is in the power of Nelson and Bronte to prevent them."
Nelson had signified to Blackwood that he depended upon
him to keep sight of the enemy.[2] They were observed so
well, that all their motions were made known to him; and
as they wore twice, he inferred that they were aiming to
keep the port of Cadiz open, and would retreat there as
soon as they saw the British fleet:[3] for this reason he was
very careful not to approach near enough to be seen by
them during the night.

At daybreak the combined fleets were distinctly seen
from the *Victory's* deck, formed in a close line-of-battle
ahead, on the starboard tack, about twelve miles to leeward,
and standing to the south.[4] Our fleet consisted of twenty-
seven sail of the line, and four frigates; theirs of thirty-
three, and seven large frigates. Their superiority was
greater in size, and weight of metal, than in numbers. They
had four thousand troops on board; and the best riflemen
who could be procured, many of them Tyrolese, were dispersed through the ships. Little did the Tyrolese, and little did
the Spaniards, at that day, imagine what horrors the wicked
tyrant whom they served was preparing for their country.

Soon after daylight Nelson came upon deck. The 21st of
October was a festival in his family, because on that day [5]
his uncle, Captain Suckling, in the *Dreadnought*, with two
other line-of-battle ships, had beaten off a French squadron
of four sail of the line, and three frigates. Nelson, with that
sort of superstition from which few persons are entirely

---

[1] This was only a momentary impression. Villeneuve's course, if he could make
it, lay due south. It must be remembered that at this time, thanks to Nelson's
care, no English craft except the signalling ships were visible.

[2] During the pitchy blackness of Sunday night. Blackwood tells us that his
difficult task was greatly facilitated by the glow of lamps from the enemy's stern
cabin windows.

[3] When the enemy's fleet wore, they went about in the opposite direction; so
that after twice wearing they would resume their original course. To the British,
whose one desire was to strike, these movements naturally suggested a wriggling
apprehensiveness. But Villeneuve, who knew that every moment was precious
after the English frigates had laid him under observation, was merely dressing
his line in the night watches so as to reach the Mediterranean in good order at the
earliest possible moment.

[4] The ships of the combined fleet were separated one from another by short
intervals, and were advancing to the southward with the wind to the right of
them, with their keels in one and the same straight line, and about twelve miles
to the eastward of Nelson's fleet, who enjoyed the advantage of the weather berth.

[5] 1757, the year before Nelson was born.

exempt, had more than once expressed his persuasion that this was to be the day of his battle also; and he was well pleased at seeing his prediction about to be verified. The wind was now from the west, light breezes, with a long heavy swell. Signal was made to bear down upon the enemy in two lines; and the fleet set all sail. Collingwood, in the *Royal Sovereign*, led the lee line [1] of thirteen ships; the *Victory* led the weather line of fourteen. [2] Having seen that all was as it should be, Nelson retired to his cabin, and wrote the following prayer:

" May the great God, whom I worship, grant to my country, and for the benefit of Europe in general, a great and glorious victory, and may no misconduct in any one tarnish it; and may humanity after victory be the predominant feature in the British fleet! For myself individually, I commit my life to Him that made me; and may His blessing alight on my endeavours for serving my country faithfully! To Him I resign myself, and the just cause which is entrusted to me to defend. Amen! Amen! Amen! "

Having thus discharged his devotional duties, he annexed, in the same diary, the following remarkable writing:

" *October* 21, 1805.—*Then in sight of the combined fleets of France and Spain, distant about ten miles.*

" Whereas the eminent services of Emma Hamilton, widow of the Right Honourable Sir William Hamilton, have been of the very greatest service to my King and country, to my knowledge, without ever receiving any reward from either our King or country.

" First, that she obtained the King of Spain's letter, in 1796, to his brother, the King of Naples, acquainting him of his intention to declare war against England; from which letter the ministry sent out orders to the then Sir John Jervis to strike a stroke, if opportunity offered, against either the arsenals of Spain or her fleets. That neither of these was done is not the fault of Lady Hamilton; the opportunity might have been offered.

---

[1] The wind was a little to the north of west; and, as the two English squadrons were sailing parallel to one another, Collingwood's (the more southerly) was to leeward of Nelson's.

[2] Collingwood had fifteen ships, and Nelson twelve.

"Secondly, the British fleet under my command could never have returned the second time to Egypt, had not Lady Hamilton's influence with the Queen of Naples caused letters to be wrote to the Governor of Syracuse that he was to encourage the fleet's being supplied with everything, should they put into any port in Sicily. We put into Syracuse and received every supply, went to Egypt and destroyed the French fleet.

"Could I have rewarded these services I would not now call upon my country; but as that has not been in my power, I leave Emma Lady Hamilton therefore a legacy to my King and country, that they will give her an ample provision to maintain her rank in life.

"I also leave to the beneficence of my country my adopted daughter, Horatia Nelson Thomson; and I desire she will use in future the name of Nelson only.

"These are the only favours I ask of my King and country at this moment when I am going to fight their battle. May God bless my King and country, and all those I hold dear! My relations it is needless to mention; they will, of course, be amply provided for.

"NELSON AND BRONTE.

"*Witness,* { HENRY BLACKWOOD.
{ T. M. HARDY." [1]

[1] It is a matter of common knowledge and a matter for deep and lasting regret that Government deliberately declined to carry out the wishes here expressed. Lady Hamilton believed that the fault lay with Nelson's eldest brother, who took no steps in the matter until he had secured, for himself and his heirs, an earldom, an annuity of £5000, and a grant of £120,000 with which to purchase an estate. A careful examination of facts and figures, however, lends little support to this view.

Captain Hardy brought home the codicil and handed it safely to Nelson's brother on 6th December. At that time Mr. Pitt was lying seriously ill; and not unnaturally the newly-made Earl for a while postponed action. In January 1806 the Prime Minister died; and on 15th February Earl Nelson (according to his own account, Pettigrew, Vol. II. p. 626) surrendered the document to Pitt's successor, Lord Grenville, who commended him for so doing. By that time an annuity of £2000 had already been made to Lady Nelson: but the more copious grants for the endowment of the earldom were not proposed until 28th March, nor ratified till May (Cobbett's *Parliamentary Debates*, Vol. VI. p. 564).

Attempts have been made, especially by Sir John Laughton, R.N. (*The Nelson Memorial*), to prove that the services enumerated in the codicil were not actually performed by Lady Hamilton. Even if this were true—and the opinion was not shared either by Mr. Canning, Mr. Rose, or even by Lord Grenville—the fact remains that Government in confining their generosity to those who bore the Admiral's name were ignoring, not Lady Hamilton's claim, but Nelson's dying wishes.

The reasons for their decision can at best be made the subject for conjecture. Some, indeed, have stated very confidently that the scheme miscarried owing to the King's disapproval, and that Pitt, who alone would have dared to run counter to the royal wishes, was not there to see justice done. But, on the other hand, it

The child of whom this writing speaks was believed to be his daughter, and so, indeed, he called her the last time that he pronounced her name. She was then about five years old, living at Merton, under Lady Hamilton's care. The last minutes which Nelson passed at Merton were employed in praying over this child, as she lay sleeping. A portrait of Lady Hamilton hung in his cabin: and no Catholic ever beheld the picture of his patron saint with devouter reverence. The undisguised and romantic passion with which he regarded it amounted almost to superstition; and when the portrait was now taken down, in clearing for action, he desired the men who removed it to "take care of his guardian angel." In this manner he frequently spoke of it, as if he believed there was a virtue in the image. He wore a miniature of her also next his heart.

Blackwood went on board the *Victory* about six. He found him in good spirits, but very calm; not in that exhilaration which he had felt upon entering into battle at Aboukir and Copenhagen. He knew that his own life would be particularly aimed at, and seems to have looked for death with almost as stoic an expectation as for victory. His whole attention was fixed upon the enemy. They tacked to the northward, and formed their line on the larboard tack; thus bringing the shoals of Trafalgar and San Pedro under the lee of the British, and keeping the port of Cadiz open for themselves.[1] This was judiciously done: and Nelson,

must be remembered that Lady Hamilton (before leaving her ungrateful native land to die obscurely at Calais) made her last appeal in the days, not of George III., but of the Prince Regent.

The reply she received runs as follows:

Madam,   Whitehall, *6th March*, 1813.

It is very painful to me to acquaint your Ladyship that after full communication with Lord Liverpool on the subject of your memorial . . . I am unable to encourage your hopes that the object of it can be accomplished. His Lordship sincerely regrets the embarrassments which you have described, but on comparing them with representations now before him of difficulty and distress in many other quarters, and upon view of the circumstance with which they are attended, he finds it impossible so to administer the scanty means of relief and assistance which, under the authority of the Prince Regent, are at his disposal as to satisfy his own sense of justice to others and at the same time give effect to your Ladyship's application. I have the honour to be, Madam,

Your Ladyship's obedient servant,

SIDMOUTH.

[1] Nelson was rushing down upon the allied fleet in two separate squadrons moving parallel to one another. Villeneuve suspected a massed attack upon the rear, and an intention to cut him off from Cadiz. By turning about, he hoped to keep the door of Cadiz open, and to receive the impact of the enemy with his leading ships, so that the remainder could in time move up to their support.

aware of all the advantages which it gave them, made signal to prepare to anchor.[1]

Villeneuve was a skilful seaman, worthy of serving a better master, and a better cause. His plan of defence was as well conceived, and as original, as the plan of attack. He formed the fleet in a double line; every alternate ship being about a cable's length to windward of her second ahead and astern.[2] Nelson, certain of a triumphant issue to the day, asked Blackwood what he should consider as a victory. That officer answered, that, considering the handsome way in which battle was offered by the enemy, their apparent determination for a fair trial of strength, and the situation of the land, he thought it would be a glorious result if fourteen were captured. He replied, " I shall not be satisfied with less than twenty." Soon afterwards he asked him, if he did not think there was a signal wanting. Captain Blackwood made answer that he thought the whole fleet seemed very clearly to understand what they were about. These words were scarcely spoken before that signal was made, which will be remembered as long as the language, or even the memory, of England shall endure—Nelson's last signal—" ENGLAND EXPECTS EVERY MAN WILL DO HIS DUTY! " [3] It was received throughout the fleet with· a shout of answering acclamation, made sublime by the spirit which it breathed, and the feeling which it expressed. " Now," said Lord Nelson, " I can do no more. We must trust to the great Disposer of all events, and the justice of our cause. I thank God for this great opportunity of doing my duty."

He wore that day, as usual, his Admiral's frock coat,

[1] Villeneuve signalled his fleet to tack at 8.0 a.m. Nelson warned his ships that he might want them to anchor, but his warning was not signalled until noon.

[2] Villeneuve showed sound sense in reversing his line; but that is all there is to be said. Southey's lavish praise is out of place; for he has not expounded the merits of Nelson's tactical scheme, and the reduplication of the enemy's line was the accidental result of a hurried change of disposition.

[3] Southey got the signal wrong in every edition. In the first he wrote, " England expects every man to do his duty." The actual words were " England expects that every man will do his duty " (Cd. 7120, p. 102). The signal was made at 11.48, eight minutes after Collingwood opened fire, and a quarter of an hour before the *Victory* fired her first broadside. There were, altogether, twelve hoists; because " DUTY," being Nelson's own selected word, was not then in the Vocabulary (numeral code). " England (253) expects (269) that (863) every (261) man (471) will (958) do (220) his (370) d (4) u (21) t (19) y (24)."

bearing on the left breast four stars [1] of the different orders with which he was invested. Ornaments which rendered him so conspicuous a mark for the enemy were beheld with ominous apprehensions by his officers. It was known that there were riflemen on board the French ships; and it could not be doubted but that his life would be particularly aimed at. They communicated their fears to each other ; and the surgeon, Mr. Beatty, [2] spoke to the chaplain, Dr. Scott, and to Mr. Scott the public secretary, desiring that some person would entreat him to change his dress, or cover the stars. But they knew that such a request would highly displease him. " In honour I gained them," he had said when such a thing had been hinted to him formerly, " and in honour I will die with them." Mr. Beatty, however, would not have been deterred by any fear of exciting his displeasure from speaking to him himself upon a subject in which the weal of England, as well as the life of Nelson, was concerned,—but he was ordered from the deck before he could find an opportunity. This was a point upon which Nelson's officers knew that it was hopeless to remonstrate or reason with him; but both Blackwood, and his own captain, Hardy, represented to him how advantageous to the fleet it would be for him to keep out of action as long as possible; and he consented at last to let the *Leviathan* and the *Téméraire*, which were sailing abreast of the *Victory*, be ordered to pass ahead. Yet even here the last infirmity of this noble mind was indulged, for these ships could not pass ahead if the *Victory* continued to carry all her sail; and so far was Nelson from shortening sail, that it was evident he took pleasure in pressing on, and rendering it impossible for them to obey his own orders. A long swell was setting into the bay of Cadiz. Our ships, crowding all sail, moved majestically before it, with light winds from the south-west.[3] The sun shone on the sails of the enemy; and their well-formed line, with their numerous three-deckers, made an appearance which any other assailants would have thought formidable. But the British sailors

---

[1] The Order of the Bath (English), the Order of San Ferdinand (Neapolitan), the Order of San Joachim (Sardinian), and the Order of the Crescent (Turkish).
[2] In this part of the work I have chiefly been indebted to this gentleman's *Narrative of Lord Nelson's Death*, a document as interesting as it is authentic. —SOUTHEY'S NOTE.
[3] N.W. or W.N.W.

only admired the beauty and the splendour of the spectacle; and, in full confidence of winning what they saw, remarked to each other, what a fine sight yonder ships would make at Spithead!

The French Admiral, from the *Bucentaure*, beheld the new manner in which his enemy was advancing—Nelson and Collingwood each leading his line; and pointing them out to his officers, he is said to have exclaimed, that such conduct could not fail to be successful. Yet Villeneuve had made his own dispositions with the utmost skill, and the fleets under his command waited for the attack with perfect coolness. Ten minutes before twelve they opened their fire. Eight or nine of the ships immediately ahead of the *Victory*, and across her bows, fired single guns at her, to ascertain whether she was yet within their range. As soon as Nelson perceived that their shot passed over him, he desired Blackwood, and Captain Prowse of the *Sirius*, to repair to their respective frigates; and, on their way, to tell all the captains of the line-of-battle ships that he depended on their exertions; and that if by the prescribed mode of attack they found it impracticable to get into action immediately, they might adopt whatever they thought best, provided it led them quickly and closely alongside an enemy. As they were standing on the front of the poop, Blackwood took him by the hand, saying he hoped soon to return and find him in possession of twenty prizes. He replied, " God bless you, Blackwood. I shall never see you ¹ again."

Nelson's column was steered about two points² more to the north than Collingwood's, in order to cut off the enemy's escape into Cadiz: ³ the lee line, therefore, was first engaged. " See," cried Nelson, pointing to the *Royal Sovereign*, as she steered right for the centre of the enemy's line, cut through it astern of the *Santa Aña*, three-decker, and

---

¹ " Speak to you."
² A point is $\frac{1}{32}$ of a complete turn or revolution. The line of Nelson's advance made with the line of Collingwood's advance an angle of $22\frac{1}{2}°$.
³ The accepted view to-day is that this northerly movement was intended to puzzle and confuse the enemy, whose attention Nelson desired to divert from Collingwood's attack.
That Southey and others deduced from the tactical " Memorandum " motives which it was never intended to convey only goes to prove (what is now very generally admitted) that Nelson's plans for his own squadron were as puzzling to his friends as to his enemies.

engaged her at the muzzle of her guns on the starboard side, " See how that noble fellow, Collingwood, carries his ship into action! " Collingwood, delighted at being first in the heat of the fire, and knowing the feelings of his commander and old friend, turned to his captain, and exclaimed, " Rotherham, what would Nelson give to be here! " Both these brave officers, perhaps, at this moment thought of Nelson with gratitude, for a circumstance which had occurred on the preceding day. Admiral Collingwood, with some of the captains, having gone on board the *Victory*, to receive instructions, Nelson inquired of him where his Captain was and was told in reply that they were not upon good terms with each other. " Terms! " said Nelson. " Good terms with each other! " Immediately he sent a boat for Captain Rotherham; led him, as soon as he arrived, to Collingwood; and saying, " Look; yonder are the enemy! " bade them shake hands like Englishmen.[1]

The enemy continued to fire a gun at a time at the *Victory*, till they saw that a shot had passed through her maintopgallant sail. Then they opened their broadsides, aiming chiefly at her rigging, in the hope of disabling her before she could close with them. Nelson, as usual, had hoisted several flags, lest one should be shot away. The enemy showed no colours till late in the action, when they began to feel the necessity of having them to strike.[2] For this reason, the *Santissima Trinidad*, Nelson's old acquaintance as he used to call her, was distinguishable only by her four decks; and to the bow of this opponent he ordered the *Victory* to be steered. Meantime an incessant raking fire was kept up upon the *Victory*. The Admiral's secretary was one of the first who fell; he was killed by a cannon-shot while conversing with Hardy. Captain Adair of the marines, with the help of a sailor, endeavoured to remove the body

---

[1] I have never been able to discover any confirmation of this story, which is inherently improbable. Collingwood was adored by his officers; he and Rotherham were fast friends, and had been dining together on board the *Victory* only a short time before (Nicolas, Vol. VII. p. 57).

[2] This is a curious mistake. Southey is confusing the word " flag " as used ashore with the word as used at sea. The combined fleet, like the British, had their colours hoisted; but the Admirals commanding (Villeneuve, Gravina, Alava, and the rest) did not fly the banners indicative of their rank until the battle began in earnest. Their object was to confuse Nelson, who (they rightly guessed) would have designs upon them. The *Santissima Trinidad*, however, could not hide her bulk, and showed Nelson where one Flag Officer might be found.

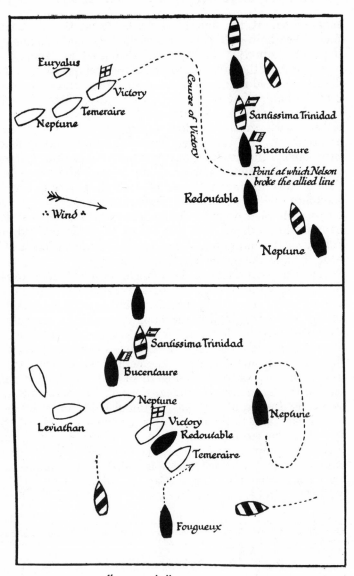

THE " VICTORY'S " PART AT TRAFALGAR

from Nelson's sight, who had a great regard for Mr. Scott. But he anxiously asked, " Is that poor Scott that's gone? " and being informed that it was indeed so, exclaimed: " Poor fellow! " Presently, a double-headed shot [1] struck a party of marines who were drawn up on the poop, and killed eight of them: upon which Nelson immediately desired Captain Adair to disperse his men round the ship, that they might not suffer so much from being together. A few minutes afterwards a shot struck the fore-brace bitts [2] on the quarter-deck, and passed between Nelson and Hardy, a splinter from the bitt tearing off Hardy's buckle and bruising his foot. Both stopped, and looked anxiously at each other; each supposed the other to be wounded. Nelson then smiled, and said, " This is too warm work, Hardy, to last long." [3]

The *Victory* had not yet returned a single gun. Fifty of her men had been by this time killed or wounded, and her maintopmast, with all her studding sails [4] and her booms, [5] shot away. Nelson declared that, in all his battles, he had seen nothing which surpassed the cool courage of his crew on this occasion. At four minutes after twelve, she opened her fire from both sides of her deck. It was not possible to break the enemy's line without running on board one of their ships. Hardy informed him of this, and asked him which he would prefer. Nelson replied, " Take your choice, Hardy, it does not signify much." [6] The master was ordered to put the helm to port, and the *Victory* ran on board the *Redoutable*, [7] just as her tiller

---

[1] This is still preserved at the Royal United Service Institution Museum, Whitehall, Exhibit 2021.

[2] The fore-braces were ropes attached to the ends of the yard which spread the foresail. When not being used to alter the position of the yard, they were made fast to their " bitts," a framework of upright timbers bolted securely to the deck.

[3] Nelson was still deliberately choosing the point at which he should break the allied line. The galling enfilade that the enemy poured into the *Victory* made it perilous to protract the agony much longer.

[4] Lateral extensions of the ordinary sails to increase their wind-surface in light airs.

[5] " Their booms," first, second and third editions.

[6] " It does not signify which."—BEATTY's *Narrative*.

[7] The narrative is at this point rather misleading. The combined fleet had braced itself to withstand the shock of the attack, and the line looked unpierceable. The *Victory*, however, shouldered her way between the *Bucentaure* (Villeneuve's flagship) and the *Redoutable*; and as she did so, she fired into both her foes with desolating unanswerable force. Once through the line her principal antagonist for a while was the *Neptune*, who had moved to leeward of her friends

ropes were shot away.[1] The French ship received her with a broadside; then instantly let down her lower deck ports, for fear of being boarded through them, and never afterwards fired a great gun during the action.[2] Her tops, like those of all the enemy's ships, were filled with riflemen. Nelson never placed musketry in his tops. He had a strong dislike to the practice; not merely because it endangers setting fire to the sails, but also because it is a murderous sort of warfare, by which individuals may suffer and a commander now and then be picked off, but which never can decide the fate of a general engagement.

Captain Harvey, in the *Téméraire*, fell on board the *Redoutable* on the other side. Another enemy was in like manner on board the *Téméraire* ;[3] so that these four ships formed as compact a tier as if they had been moored together, their heads lying all the same way. The lieutenants of the *Victory*, seeing this, depressed their guns of the middle and lower decks, and fired with a diminished charge, lest the shot should pass through, and injure the *Téméraire*. And because there was danger that the *Redoutable* might take fire from the lower-deck guns, the muzzles of which touched her side when they were run out, the fireman of each gun stood ready with a bucket of water; which, as soon as the gun was discharged, he dashed into the hole made by the shot. An incessant fire was kept up from the *Victory* from both sides; her larboard guns playing upon the *Bucentaure* and the huge *Santissima Trinidad*.[4]

in order to greet Nelson with a raking fire (see map); but, ten minutes after she had broken the allied line, the *Victory* put up her helm, and the resulting movement brought her down upon the *Redoutable*, with whom she was quickly locked in fierce embrace.

[1] From the rudder-head the tiller passed through the stern of the ship into the gun-room. Attached to its fore end were actuating ropes that led upwards to the drum of the steering-wheel under the break of the poop. These ropes, when they reached the upper deck, were exposed to the enemy's fire; and though the tiller could, after special tackle had been fitted, be worked from the gun-room, the loss of the tiller-ropes was extremely serious and marked a moment which all would remember.

[2] Here again subsequent information has proved to us that Southey's facts were wrong. Captain Lucas of the *Redoutable* was specialising in small arms, and hoped to capture the *Victory* by clearing her upper deck with musketry and hand-grenades (*cp*. Nelson's capture of *San Nicolas* and *San Josef* at St. Vincent). He closed his gunports because he did not intend to employ artillery, and was holding his gunners in reserve so as to reinforce his upper works and board the enemy.

[3] The *Fougueux* (Spitfire).

[4] Except, of course, when an English vessel intervened; see plan.

CHAPTER V

THE DEATH OF NELSON

[*SOUTHEY. CHAPTER IX.—continued*]

IT had been part of Nelson's prayer, that the British fleet might be distinguished by humanity in the victory which he expected. Setting an example himself, he twice gave orders to cease firing upon the *Redoutable*, supposing that she had struck because her great guns were silent; for, as she carried no flag, there was no means of instantly ascertaining the fact. From this ship, which he had thus twice spared, he received his death.[1] A ball fired from her mizzentop, which, in the then situation of the two vessels, was not more than fifteen yards from that part of the deck where he was standing, struck the epaulette on his left shoulder, about a quarter after one, just in the heat of action. He fell upon his face, on the spot which was covered with his poor secretary's blood. Hardy, who was a few steps from him, turning round, saw three men raising him up. " They have done for me at last, Hardy," said he. " I hope not," cried Hardy. " Yes! " he replied; " my backbone is shot through." Yet even now, not for a moment losing his presence of mind, he observed, as they were carrying him down the ladder, that the tiller ropes, which had been shot away, were not yet replaced, and ordered that new ones should be rove immediately. Then, that he might not be seen by the crew, he took out his handkerchief, and covered his face and his stars. Had he but concealed these badges of honour from the enemy, England, perhaps, would not have had cause to receive with sorrow the news of the battle of Trafalgar.

[1] The gunners of the *Victory* ceased firing from time to time because it seemed to them unsportsmanlike to pour their broadsides into a vessel that, with her ordnance at least, made no reply. But the *Redoutable*, though silent below, was pugnacious enough above (see Note 2, p. 312), and it was in accordance with her set scheme to clear the *Victory's* upper deck that her sharpshooters levelled their pieces at Nelson. The great attempt of the plucky French vessel to carry her opponent by boarding took place quite a long time after the " fatal wound."

The cockpit was crowded with wounded and dying men; over whose bodies he was with some difficulty conveyed, and laid upon a pallet in the midshipmen's berth. It was soon perceived, upon examination, that the wound was mortal. This, however, was concealed from all except Captain Hardy, the Chaplain, and the medical attendants. He himself being certain, from the sensation in his back and the gush of blood he felt momently within his breast, that no human care could avail him, insisted that the Surgeon should leave him, and attend to those to whom he might be useful; "for," said he, "you can do nothing for me." All that could be done was to fan him with paper, and frequently to give him lemonade to alleviate his intense thirst. He was in great pain, and expressed much anxiety for the event of the action, which now began to declare itself. As often as a ship struck, the crew of the *Victory* hurrahed; and at every hurrah, a visible expression of joy gleamed in the eyes, and marked the countenance of the dying hero. But he became impatient to see Captain Hardy; and as that officer, though often sent for, could not leave the deck, Nelson feared that some fatal cause prevented him, and repeatedly cried, "Will no one bring Hardy to me? He must be killed! He is surely dead!"

An hour and ten minutes elapsed from the time when Nelson received his wound, before Hardy could come to him. They shook hands in silence; Hardy in vain struggling to suppress the feelings of that most painful and yet sublimest moment. "Well, Hardy," said Nelson, "how goes the day with us?" "Very well," replied Hardy; "ten ships have struck, but five of the van have tacked, and show an intention to bear down upon the *Victory*. I have called two or three of our fresh ships round, and have no doubt of giving them a drubbing." "I hope," said Nelson, "none of our ships have struck?" Hardy answered there was no fear of that. Then, and not till then, Nelson spoke of himself. "I am a dead man, Hardy," said he: "I am going fast. It will be all over with me soon. Come nearer to me. Let my dear Lady Hamilton have my hair, and all other things belonging to me." Hardy observed that he hoped Mr. Beatty could yet hold out some prospect of life. "Oh no!" he replied: "it is impossible. My back is shot through. Beatty will tell you so." Captain Hardy then, once more, shook hands with him; and, with a heart almost bursting, hastened upon deck.

By this time all feeling below the breast was gone; and Nelson, having made the surgeon ascertain this, said to him, " You know I am gone. I know it. I feel something rising in my breast,"—putting his hand on his left side,— " which tells me so." And upon Beatty's inquiring whether his pain was very great, he replied, " So great, that he wished he was dead. Yet," said he, in a lower voice, " one would like to live a little longer too! " And after a few minutes, in the same undertone, he added, " What would become of poor Lady Hamilton, if she knew my situation! " Next to his country she occupied his thoughts. Captain Hardy, some fifty minutes after he had left the cockpit, returned; and, again taking the hand of his dying friend and commander, congratulated him on having gained a complete victory. How many of the enemy were taken he did not know, as it was impossible to perceive them distinctly; but fourteen or fifteen at least. " That's well," cried Nelson, " but I bargained for twenty." And then, in a stronger voice, he said, " Anchor, Hardy; anchor." Hardy, upon this, hinted that Admiral Collingwood would take upon himself the direction of affairs. " Not while I live, Hardy," said the dying Nelson, ineffectually endeavouring to raise himself from the bed. " Do you anchor! " His previous order for preparing to anchor had shown how clearly he foresaw the necessity of this. Presently, calling Hardy back, he said to him in a low voice, " Don't throw me overboard "; and he desired that he might be buried by his parents, unless it should please the King to order otherwise. Then reverting to private feelings, " Take care of my dear Lady Hamilton, Hardy. Take care of poor Lady Hamilton.— Kiss me, Hardy," said he. Hardy knelt down and kissed his cheek: and Nelson said, " Now I am satisfied. Thank God I have done my duty." Hardy stood over him in silence for a moment or two, then knelt again and kissed his forehead. " Who is that? " said Nelson; and being informed, he replied, " God bless you, Hardy." And Hardy then left him—for ever.

Nelson now desired to be turned upon his right side, and

said, " I wish I had not left the deck; for I shall soon be gone." Death was, indeed, rapidly approaching. He said to the chaplain, " Doctor, I have *not* been a *great* sinner ": and after a short pause, " Remember that I leave Lady Hamilton and my daughter Horatia [1] as a legacy to my country." His articulation now became difficult; but he was distinctly heard to say, " Thank God, I have done my duty." These words he repeatedly pronounced; and they were the last words which he uttered. He expired at thirty minutes after four,—three hours and a quarter after he had received his wound.

Within a quarter of an hour after Nelson was wounded, above fifty of the *Victory's* men fell by the enemy's musketry. They, however, on their part, were not idle; and it was not long before there were only two Frenchmen left alive in the mizzen-top of the *Redoutable*. One of them was the man who had given the fatal wound. He did not live to boast of what he had done. An old quarter-master had seen him fire; and easily recognised him, because he wore a glazed cocked hat and a white frock. This quarter-master and two midshipmen, Mr. Collingwood and Mr. Pollard, were the only persons left in the *Victory's* poop. The two midshipmen kept firing at the top, and he supplied them with cartridges. One of the Frenchmen, attempting to make his escape down the rigging, was shot by Mr. Pollard, and fell on the poop. But the old quarter-master, as he cried out, " That's he—that's he," and pointed at the other who was coming forward to fire again, received a shot in his mouth and fell dead. Both the midshipmen then fired at the same time, and the fellow dropped in the top. When they took possession of the prize, they went into the mizzen-top and found him dead, with one ball through his head, and another through his breast.

The *Redoutable* struck within twenty minutes after the fatal shot had been fired from her. During that time she had been twice on fire,—in her fore-chains and in her fore-castle. The French, as they had done in other battles, made use in this of fire-balls and other combustibles; implements of destruction which other nations, from a sense

[1] In the codicil to his will Nelson says, " I also leave to the beneficence of my country my *adopted* daughter Horatia Nelson Thompson; and I desire she will in future use the name of Nelson only."

of honour and humanity, have laid aside; which add to the
sufferings of the wounded without determining the issue
of the combat; which none but the cruel would employ
and which never can be successful against the brave. Once
they succeeded in setting fire, from the *Redoutable*, to some
ropes and canvas on the *Victory's* booms. The cry ran
through the ship, and reached the cockpit: but even this
dreadful cry produced no confusion. The men displayed
that perfect self-possession in danger by which English
seamen are characterised. They extinguished the flames on
board their own ship, and then hastened to extinguish them
in the enemy, by throwing buckets of water from the gangway. When the *Redoutable* had struck, it was not practicable to board her from the *Victory*; for, though the two
ships touched, the upper works of both fell in so much, that
there was a great space between their gangways; and she
could not be boarded from the lower or middle decks, because her ports were down. Some of our men went to
Lieutenant Quilliam, and offered to swim under her bows,
and get up there; but it was thought unfit to hazard brave
lives in this manner.

What our men would have done from gallantry, some of
the crew of the *Santissima Trinidad* did to save themselves.
Unable to stand the tremendous fire of the *Victory*, whose
larboard guns played against this great four-decker, and
not knowing how else to escape them, nor where else to
betake themselves for protection, many of them leaped
overboard, and swam to the *Victory*; and were actually
helped up her sides by the English during the action. The
Spaniards began the battle with less vivacity than their
unworthy allies, but they continued it with greater firmness.
The *Argonauta* and *Bahama* were defended till they had
each lost about four hundred men; the *San Juan Nepomuceno* lost three hundred and fifty. Often as the superiority
of British courage has been proved against France upon
the seas, it was never more conspicuous than in this decisive
conflict. Five of our ships were engaged muzzle to muzzle
with five of the French. In all five the Frenchmen lowered
their lower-deck ports, and deserted their guns; while our
men continued deliberately to load and fire, till they had
made the victory secure.

Once, amidst his sufferings, Nelson had expressed a wish that he were dead; but immediately the spirit subdued the pains of death, and he wished to live a little longer—doubtless that he might hear the completion of the victory which he had seen so gloriously begun. That consolation—that joy—that triumph, was afforded him. He lived to know that the victory was decisive; and the last guns which were fired at the flying enemy were heard a minute or two before he expired.

The ships which were thus flying were four of the enemy's van, all French, under Rear-Admiral Dumanoir. They had borne no part in the action; and now, when they were seeking safety in flight, they fired not only into the *Victory* and *Royal Sovereign* as they passed, but poured their broadsides into the Spanish captured ships, and they were seen to back their topsails, for the purpose of firing with more precision. The indignation of the Spaniards at this detestable cruelty from their allies, for whom they had fought so bravely, and so profusely bled, may well be conceived. It was such, that when, two days after the action, seven of the ships which had escaped into Cadiz came out, in hopes of retaking some of the disabled prizes, the prisoners, in the *Argonauta*, in a body, offered their services to the British prize-master, to man the guns against any of the French ships: saying, that if a Spanish ship came alongside, they would quietly go below; but they requested that they might be allowed to fight the French, in resentment for the murderous usage which they had suffered at their hands. Such was their earnestness, and such the implicit confidence which could be placed in Spanish honour, that the offer was accepted, and they were actually stationed at the lower-deck guns. Dumanoir and his squadron were not more fortunate than the fleet from whose destruction they fled. They fell in with Sir Richard Strachan, who was cruising for the Rochefort squadron, and were all taken. In the better days of France, if such a crime could then have been committed, it would have received an exemplary punishment from the French government. Under Bonaparte, it was sure of impunity, and, perhaps, might be thought deserving of reward. But, if the Spanish court had been independent, it would have become us to have delivered Dumanoir and his captains up to Spain, that they might have been brought to trial, and hanged in sight of the remains of the Spanish fleet.[1] The total British loss in the battle of Trafalgar amounted to one thousand five hundred and eighty-seven. Twenty of the enemy struck. But it was not possible to anchor the fleet, as Nelson had enjoined.[2] A gale came on from the south-west. Some of the prizes went down, some went on shore; one effected its escape into Cadiz; others were destroyed; four only were saved, and those by the greatest

---

[1] In this rather unfortunate paragraph Southey deserts the excellent authority of Dr. Beatty, and includes some tittle-tattle from Gibraltar, which seems to have been acceptable to him, because (as he wrote) Englishmen and Spaniards were combining against the French in the Peninsula.

The allied van, consisting of ten ships under Dumanoir, were by the ingenuity of Nelson's tactics left out of the battle altogether. They were ahead of the *Bucentaure* and *Santissima Trinidad*, and could not participate in the affray unless they turned themselves about. Repeated signals were made to them to do so, and after a while Dumanoir was able to obey. But the process of altering course consumed much time; and in the process the ten ships separated into two independent, and consequently useless, squadrons. Of the five with Dumanoir one was made prize as she passed the scene of action; but the other four eventually escaped, only to be captured ten days later, as the text relates, by Sir Richard Strachan.

This group may be regarded as the weather squadron; for its units, having tacked, kept to seaward of the battlefield. The other squadron, being to leeward, was more deeply involved. Three of its vessels succeeded in reinforcing Gravina, and of these the *Héros* eventually reached Cadiz; but the *Intrépide* and *San Augustino*, entering the lists in the hour of Britain's triumph, yielded to superior numbers and the hard necessity of war.

[2] In the former editions it was said that " unhappily the fleet did not anchor," implying an opinion that Nelson's orders ought to have been followed by his successor. From the recently-published *Correspondence and Memoir of Lord Collingwood*, it appears that this was not practicable, and that if it had been practicable, and had been done, the consequences, from the state of the weather (which Nelson could not foresee), would, in all likelihood, have been more disastrous than they were.

Having thus referred to Lord Collingwood's *Life*, I may be allowed to say that the publication of that volume is, indeed, a national good; it ought to be in every officer's cabin, and in every statesman's cabinet.—SOUTHEY'S NOTE, Fourth Edition.

In his first edition Southey wrote:

" Twenty of the enemy struck. Unhappily the fleet did not anchor, as Nelson, almost with his dying breath, had enjoined."

Newnham Collingwood's defence of his father-in-law was occasioned, not by Southey's statement, but by James's amplification of it in his *Naval History*, Vol. IV. Unhappily the world has not followed Southey's advice about reading these memoirs, and the belief that some remissness on Collingwood's part led to the loss of the prizes is a belief that still prevails. The technical evidence adduced in Collingwood's biography, by its very completeness, makes quotation difficult; but everyone who has read it admits, with Southey, that it is quite unanswerable. James completed his *History* in 1824, and its sententious, dogmatic and prejudiced pages were described by the impeccable *Edinburgh Review* as approaching " as nearly to perfection . . . as any historical work ever did." Collingwood's *Memoir*, published in 1828, advanced the first of a series of damning indictments, which have been levelled against it ever since.

exertions.[1] The wounded Spaniards were sent ashore, an assurance being given that they should not serve till regularly exchanged; and the Spaniards, with a generous feeling, which would not, perhaps, have been found in any other people, offered the use of their hospitals for our wounded, pledging the honour of Spain that they should be carefully attended there. When the storm, after the action, drove some of the prizes upon the coast, they declared that the English, who were thus thrown into their hands, should not be considered as prisoners of war; and the Spanish soldiers gave up their own beds to their shipwrecked enemies.[2] The Spanish Vice-Admiral, Alava, died of his wounds.[3] Villeneuve was sent to England, and permitted to return to France. The French government say that he destroyed himself on the way to Paris, dreading the consequences of a court martial. But there is every reason to believe that the tyrant, who never acknowledged the loss of the battle of Trafalgar, added Villeneuve to the numerous victims of his murderous policy.[4]

It is almost superfluous to add that all the honours which a grateful country could bestow were heaped upon the memory of Nelson. His brother was made an earl, with a grant of £6,000 a year; £10,000 were voted to each of his sisters: and £100,000 for the purchase of an estate.[5] A public funeral was decreed, and a public monument. Statues and monuments also were voted by most of our principal

[1] Eighteen of the enemy were accounted for on the day of battle, and four were subsequently taken by Sir Richard Strachan. Total twenty-two. Then outside Cadiz, on 23rd October, the *Rayo* added one to the list of captures, and two that had escaped and came out again were wrecked. Total twenty-five. From this figure we must deduct three, because one prize slipped through the English fingers, and two were recaptured in the mêlée on the 23rd. Of the gross figure, fourteen found a grave on the battlefield and eight (including Strachan's four) were eventually carried home.

[2] Here and elsewhere the careful reader will observe the tenderness of Southey for the inhabitants of the land which he knew and loved so well, and from which he drew the inspiration for many of his works in poetry and prose.

[3] Gravina, the Spanish Admiral, died of his wounds; Alava, the Vice-Admiral, survived for many years.

[4] The Admiral, who was staying at the Hôtel de la Patrie at Rennes, was found in bed on the morning of 22nd April, 1806, with a knife in his heart. His door was locked on the inside; and his servant averred that for some days his master's manner had been so strange that he had taken it upon himself to unload the Admiral's pistols. The same witness gave evidence that Villeneuve had applied to Napoleon for an interview and had been refused. On the whole, then, there is little enough reason to believe that the unhappy victim died by any hand but his own.

[5] "Trafalgar," Downton, near Salisbury.

cities. The leaden coffin in which he was brought home was cut in pieces, which were distributed as relics of Saint Nelson—so the gunner of the *Victory* called them—and when, at his interment, his flag was about to be lowered into the grave, the sailors who assisted at the ceremony with one accord rent it in pieces, that each might preserve a fragment while he lived.

The death of Nelson was felt in England as something more than a public calamity. Men started at the intelligence and turned pale, as if they had heard of the loss of a dear friend. An object of our admiration and affection, of our pride and of our hopes, was suddenly taken from us; and it seemed as if we had never, till then, known how deeply we loved and reverenced him. What the country had lost in its great naval hero—the greatest of our own and of all former times—was scarcely taken into the account of grief. So perfectly, indeed, had he performed his part, that the maritime war, after the battle of Trafalgar, was considered at an end. The fleets of the enemy were not merely defeated, but destroyed. New navies must be built, and a new race of seamen reared for them, before the possibility of their invading our shores could again be contemplated. It was not, therefore, from any selfish reflection upon the magnitude of our loss that we mourned for him. The general sorrow was of a higher character. The people of England grieved that funeral ceremonies, and public monuments, and post-humous rewards were all which they could now bestow upon him, whom the King, the legislature, and the nation would have alike delighted to honour; whom every tongue would have blessed; whose presence in every village through which he might have passed would have wakened the church bells, have given school-boys a holiday, have drawn children from their sports to gaze upon him, and " old men from the chimney corner " to look upon Nelson ere they died. The victory of Trafalgar was celebrated, indeed, with the usual forms of rejoicing, but they were without joy. For such already was the glory of the British navy, through Nelson's surpassing genius, that it scarcely seemed to receive any addition from the most signal victory that ever was achieved upon the seas. And the destruction of this mighty fleet, by which all the maritime schemes of France were totally frustrated, hardly appeared to add to our security or strength; for, while Nelson was living, to watch the combined squadrons of the enemy, we felt ourselves as secure as now, when they were no longer in existence. There was reason to suppose, from the appearances upon opening the body, that, in the course of nature, he might have attained, like his father, to a good old age. Yet he cannot be said to have fallen prematurely whose work was done; nor ought he to be lamented, who died so full of honours, and at the height of human fame. The most triumphant death is that of the martyr; the most awful that of the martyred patriot; the most splendid that of the hero in the hour of victory. And if the chariot and the horses of fire had been vouchsafed for Nelson's translation, he could scarcely have departed in a brighter blaze of glory. He has left us, not indeed his mantle of inspiration, but a name and an example, which are at this hour inspiring thousands of the youth of England: a name which is our pride, and an example which will continue to be our shield and our strength. Thus it is that the spirits of the great and the wise continue to live and to act after them; verifying, in this sense, the language of the old mythologist,

Τοὶ μὲν δαίμονές εἰσι, Διὸς μεγάλου διὰ βουλὰς,
'Εσθλοί, ἐπιχθόνιοι, φύλακες θνητῶν ἀνθρώπων.[1]

[1] The quotation is from Hesiod's *Works and Days*, and may be turned into English as follows:

To His elect, while still their bodies sleep,
God gives a spirit incorruptible,
That they may walk on earth and still inspire
The feeble sons of men, whose need He knows.

FINIS

APPENDIX

QUESTIONS ON PART I

1. How far is it just to say that this part is less a chapter of biography than a narrative of polar exploration?

2. At what age did Nelson become a midshipman, and at what age a lieutenant? How many years of his life are reviewed in this part, and how were they spent? Make a chronology with the aid of the notes.

3. Read carefully Note 2, p. 8; and then explain why Nelson in the middle watch needed a mist, under cover of which to stalk his bear. (N.B.—The expedition reached lat. 80° N. on 10th June and was released from the ice-pack on 10th August.)

4. This part is largely an account of Nelson's training and education. Show what were the chief causes that contributed to make him the practical seaman he was when he passed his lieutenant's examination.

5. Which do you prefer—the story of Nelson and the bear, or the stories of Nelson's infancy as told on pp. 2-3? The story of the bear is undoubtedly true. What of the story of the grandmamma, or the legend of the pears? Would you admire Nelson any the less if these could be proved untrue?

QUESTIONS ON PART II

1. Select from this part examples to illustrate (a) Nelson's human sympathy and thoughtful kindness for others; (b) his prompt resource in sudden emergencies; (c) his readiness to sacrifice on the altar of duty even his chosen career and all hopes of advancement; (d) his tenacity of purpose; (e) his tactfulness in dealing with a difficult situation; (f) his charm of manner; (g) his magnanimity.

2. What other qualities in him have you already noticed in addition to those mentioned in Question I?

3. It has been said that Southey was always too prone to forsake

the thread of a story if a congenial topic presented itself. Is there anything in Part II. to support this contention?

4.   "Admirals all they said their say;
       The echoes are ringing still."—NEWBOLT.

Select from this part sayings of Nelson which in your opinion deserve to be had in remembrance.

5. Name the two most eminent people with whom Nelson was brought into contact between 1777 and 1787. What opinions did they express concerning him?

6. You may have begun your study of Nelson by supposing that such a hero very soon attained honour and glory. Work out from the dates given in Parts I. and II. and from the date of Trafalgar which you already know:

(a) What age he was when he died.

(b) How many years of his life the narrative has so far covered.

7. Three of Nelson's lifelong friends and companions in arms were Troubridge, Collingwood, and Cornwallis. Explain the circumstances under which he first made the acquaintance of each.

8. Explain the views which Southey, in common with other men of 1812, held with regard to the making of an Isthmian Canal.

QUESTIONS ON PART III

1. In 1905 a small work appeared under the title *The True Account of Nelson's Famous Signal*. Its author by citations from contemporary documents endeavoured to show that Nelson could not have put his glass to his blind eye at Copenhagen, for the simple reason that he saw as well with one eye as with the other. How far are you prepared to accept this argument, and how far is your view of the Admiral's appearance affected by what you have read?

2. Draw from your imagination some kind of a plan to illustrate Nelson's duel with the *Ça Ira*.

3. Give Southey's opinions as expressed in this part with regard to:

(a) Napoleon.

(b) The monarchies of Europe, 1794–96.

(c) The French Revolution.

4. How far are Southey's opinions as expressed in this part entertained by thoughtful people to-day?

5. Compose a speech supposed to have been delivered by Admiral Sir John Jervis to the ship's company of the *Agamemnon* (when

that ship at last left the Mediterranean command) calling attention
to the variety and value of her exploits.

6. Write an imaginary letter from Nelson to his wife contrasting
the character of Admiral Hotham with that of Admiral Lord Hood.

QUESTIONS ON PART IV

1. Admiral of the Fleet Earl Beatty, in his Jutland dispatch,
speaks of Hood as bringing his squadron into action "in a most
inspiring manner, worthy of his great naval ancestors."
How far does this chapter lend weight to the remark that naval
valour is hereditary in the family of Hood?

2. Turn to Nelson's enumeration of his services on pp. 114-15.
Arrange them in the form of a list, and write against each (or
against as many as you can) such particulars as your memory retains.

3. Imagine yourself to be Lieutenant Josiah Nisbet, R.N., and
write to your mother an account of what occurred on the night of
24th July, 1797.

4. Which was the more important event—the battle of St. Vincent
or that attack on Teneriffe? Of which does Southey write the better
account?

5. Draw a plan of your own devising to show what happened in
the Bay of Santa Cruz.

6. Write a little leaderette, supposed to be taken from *The Times*
of 25th November, 1797, and having for its theme the unique
character of Nelson's bravery.

7. What evidence does this part supply of the estimation in which
Nelson was held by the ordinary seamen?

8. Who was the Duke of Clarence, and what were the circumstances that had made him so completely Nelson's friend?

9. What sort of picture does Southey draw of the state of the
Spanish navy? Suggest any reason that would (in our own country's
interest) have made it advisable to censor his story of the Madrid
pasquinade?

10. Describe the part that Troubridge played in the attack upon
Santa Cruz.

11. Write a brief report (supposedly from Nelson to Admiral the
Earl of St. Vincent) recommending Sykes for a lieutenancy and
giving reasons for the recommendation.

12. The story of Sir Richard Grenville's last fight tells us that the

2 A

326   LIFE OF NELSON

Spaniards made gallant antagonists. How far is this view endorsed by the story of Nelson's attack on Teneriffe?

13. Admiral Jervis, Admiral Parker, and Captains Collingwood, Frederick and Troubridge all played remarkable parts at the battle of St. Vincent. Why does popular opinion ascribe the credit almost exclusively to Nelson?

QUESTIONS ON PART V

1. Write in Nelson's name a letter to Captain Benjamin Hallowell, thanking him for his *memento mori*. Endeavour to imitate, as far as you can, the Admiral's whimsical turn of phrase.

2. Imagine yourself to be a seaman of the *Vanguard* wounded in the early part of the fight. Write, as an eye-witness would do, what happened when Nelson was brought down into the cockpit.

3. Explain (with the help of a diagram) the claim put forward by Southey on behalf of Captain Foley of the *Goliath*, and show how such a claim robs Nelson of his hardly-won renown.

4. Nelson was fond of calling those who fought with him at the Nile his "band of brothers." Turn to Shakespeare's *Henry V*. (Act IV. Sc. iii.) and rewrite the King's speech, beginning with the words "Then shall our names," substituting those of Nelson's captains without spoiling the metre.

5. Draw a plan of the Mediterranean, inserting a red line to illustrate Nelson's cruising track in the year 1798.

6. Write from memory a list of the presentations made to Nelson after the battle of the Nile.

7. Compose a speech, supposed to have been delivered by William Pitt in the House of Commons, proposing the grant of a peerage to Admiral Nelson and a pension of £2000.

8. Which do you prefer, Mrs. Hemans' *Casabianca* or Southey's description of the destruction of the *Orient*? Give reasons for your preference.

9. What were frigates used for? If Nelson had possessed as many as he required in 1798, how would the history of the world have been changed?

10. What was the substance of Captain Ball's advice to Nelson, and what were the circumstances under which it was offered?

11. Upon what grounds did Nelson base his contention that, without the help of Troubridge and Lady Hamilton, he could never have won the battle of the Nile?

12. Explain: Mizzen-peak, rake, braces, langridge, athwart-hawse, port-fire, to wear, carpenter.

13. "Where there is room for an enemy's ship to swing, there is room for one of ours to anchor."
Collect from this part half-a-dozen pithy sayings of Nelson which, like the one quoted, deserve to be treasured in the memory.

QUESTIONS ON PART VI

1. Write a letter from Sir William Hamilton to his nephew and heir, Charles Grenville, describing the escape of King Ferdinand and Queen Maria Carolina from Naples to Palermo.

2. Describe in a word or two, as playwrights do in their *Dramatis Personæ*, the following characters: Méjean, Mack, Pius VI., Championnet, Ruffo, Masaredo.

3. While Nelson was staying at Naples, he sat for his portrait to an artist called Guzzardi. The finished picture, which differs widely from the pleasing canvases of Beechey, Romney, and Abbott, shows a face pinched with care and anxiety. Can you suggest any reasons for this?

4. Do you consider the trial and execution of Caracciolo justifiable? State the grounds for your opinion.

5. Explain the meaning of the words "armistice" and "capitulation," and show clearly what stage had been reached in the negotiations between Cardinal Ruffo and the insurgent fortresses when Nelson dropped anchor in Naples Bay.

6. Criticise the sources from which Southey derived the material on which, in this chapter, he based his attack on Nelson's conduct.

7. Write a leading article, such as would appear in an outspoken magazine of to-day, on the appointment of Lord Keith to the Mediterranean command in place of the victor of the Nile.

8. Was England right or wrong to befriend, in 1799, a state whose cruelty and corruption brought it half a century later to an unregretted overthrow?

9. Contrast Southey's treatment of Nelson in this chapter with his treatment of Sir Thomas Troubridge. Point your remarks with appropriate quotations.

10. Summarise the work done by the British fleet from the time of Nelson's arrival in Naples to the hour of his return to England.

11. Write an imaginary letter from Nelson in London to his friend Captain Ball in Malta describing his journey home.

QUESTIONS ON PART VII

1. What new information about Nelson's character and habits have you gleaned from these last chapters?

2. Describe a court martial on Captain Robert D. Fancourt (of the *Agamemnon*) for his failure to bring his ship into the firing line.

3. "I feel very sorry for Sir Hyde, but no *wise* man would ever have gone with Nelson or over him, as he was sure to be in the background in every case."
Discuss the justice of this saying of Lady Malmesbury's.

4. Compose a leading article for *The Times* of 10th July, 1801, estimating the political effects of Nelson's Baltic campaign upon the Northern powers.

5. Explain the meaning of: Vail, topsail breeze, a quarter less five; and the significance of signals 16 and 39.

6. Quote from memory the order in which Nelson desired his ships to enter battle; and show how far this order was changed or upset.

7. With the aid of your imagination describe in detail the scene on board the *Elephant*:
   (a) When Nelson was writing his first letter to the Crown Prince; or
   (b) When Sir Hyde Parker broke at the *London's* masthead the signal of recall.

8. Reproduce from memory as closely as you can the letter which Nelson wrote to Sir Hyde Parker while they were still in the Cattegat.

9. Draw a plan of part of the Sound, showing Copenhagen, Amag Island, Saltholm, and the Middle Ground; and show how Nelson approached the Danish fleet, and where he dropped anchor on the night of 1st April.

10. In what manner did Nelson's eventual plan of attack resemble his earlier proposal to pass through the Great Belt?

11. Give as many reasons as you can for thinking that the chapter in which he describes the battle of Copenhagen is Southey's best effort up to this point.

12. Quote from memory any notable sayings of Nelson from the time he left England for the Baltic to the time of his return.

13. In the character of Olfert Kofod, a Danish fisherman, describe the scene at the jetty when Nelson came ashore to visit the Crown

Prince. Afterwards (if possible) compare your own pen-picture with a reproduction of Thomas Davidson's painting.

14. Read Campbell's *Battle of the Baltic* and then criticise it:
    (*a*) as a patriotic poem,
    (*b*) as a picture of the battle.

15. Why did not the Admiralty reprimand Nelson for disobeying Sir Hyde Parker as they had done in the case of Lord Keith? What other example of "inspired disobedience" can you furnish from Nelson's career?

16. Write a letter, supposedly from Nelson, enclosing a contribution to Riou's monument, and drawing the attention of the public to the splendour of the frigate-captain's services.

QUESTIONS ON PART VIII

1. Write a letter from the Admiral to his father (Rev. Edmund Nelson), inviting him to come and stay at Merton, and expatiating upon its comforts and delights.

2. What evidence does this chapter contain of Nelson's liberality and care for the afflicted?

3. Nelson, while he was at home, by no means settled down entirely in one place. In addition to London, he visited Oxford (where he received an honorary D.C.L.), Blenheim, Hereford, and Worcester.

What reason can you offer by way of explanation for Southey's lack of interest in the Admiral's home life?

4. What steps would have to be taken by the enemies of England before they could successfully invade this country?

5. Nearly every inn that fronts the sea between Orfordness and Beachy Head has a suite of rooms which it claims to have put at Nelson's disposal during the autumn of 1801.

What credit would you attach to these claims? In the character of Jonathan Oldbuck write a report to the Society of Antiquaries upon the authenticity of the claims of the "Three Cups" at Harwich which you have investigated for yourself.

QUESTIONS ON PART IX

1. Attempt to write down from memory the entry that Nelson made in his journal on leaving Merton for the last time.

2. Quote in their own words the seamen's character of "Admiral

Nel," and support the truth of their words by examples selected from any part of this book.

3. To what extent should Nelson's disappointment with his own performance be our guide in estimating the value of his pursuit of Villeneuve?

4. Describe Nelson's departure from Portsmouth for his last battle as if you had seen it with your own eyes.

5. Write a caustic leading article for *The Times* of 1st June, 1809, dealing with M. Latouche-Tréville's report (received *via* Paris) that he had been in pursuit of Nelson's fleet.

6. In what sense is it true to say that a battle with Villeneuve in June 1805 on the spot where Rodney defeated de Grasse would have been a less effective illustration of Nelson's genius than the events that actually occurred?

7. Give any reasons that you may have for preferring Chapter III. of this section to Chapter II.

8. Describe with the help of a diagram what Napoleon expected his fleets to do after they had joined at Martinique; and explain why it was that he did not dare to cross the Channel before his projected armada arrived.

9. Suppose yourself to be the fortunate possessor of a couple of pages from Nelson's diary at the time when he was blockading Toulon. With the help of your imagination write down what you can remember of them.

10. Write some verses in the manner of Mr. Croker's *Songs of Trafalgar* in commemoration of any episode in Nelson's career.

11. Compose a memorandum as from the ship's company of H.M.S. *Arrow* (dated 7th November, 1804), imploring Lord Nelson not to send you home in spite of your vessel's defects.

12. Draw a sketch-map of western Europe showing where Napoleon's numerous fleets were based at the beginning of 1805, and inserting the names of the British admirals who were maintaining the blockade.

13. Set Southey's appreciation of Nelson in Chapter III. §7 of this part beside his detraction in Part VI. (see above, pp. 186–7), and ask yourself whether the two characters thus drawn by him are reconcilable, or mutually destructive.

14. Give in the form of an extract from his *Memoirs* Napoleon's reasons for breaking camp at Boulogne in August 1805.

15. Quote from memory any notable entries made by Nelson in his diary during his pursuit of Villeneuve.

16. Draw a plan to show the position of the *Victory* and the ships immediately around her at the moment when the *Redoutable* lowered her flag.

17. Compose a dialogue between Nelson and Captain Blackwood of the *Euryalus* frigate during the last hours that these friends were together.

18. Write down from memory:
(*a*) Nelson's last prayer.
(*b*) Southey's last paragraph.

19. Draw an enlarged map of the Spanish coast between Cadiz and Gibraltar, and by dotted lines show the movements of the British and combined fleets before the battle of Trafalgar began.

20. Reproduce, if possible word for word, the letter that Nelson wrote to the lieutenant who was dissatisfied with his captain.

INDEX

ACRE, 100 n., 123, 202
Adair, Captain, 309, 311
Addington, Henry, Lord Sidmouth, 206 and n., 264, 265, 305
Addison, Joseph, xix
Adventures of Harry Richmond, 9
Ajaccio, 281
Alava, 309 n., 320 and n.
Alberoni, 55
Alexander I., Czar, 246, 247
Alexandria, 123 and n., 126, 127, 141 n., 148, 150, 168, 176
Amadis de Gaul, xviii
Amag Island, 210 n., 214, 219, 230, 231, 242, 244
American Independence, War of, 15, 129 n.
Amiens, Peace of, 111 n., 258, 265 n.
Andersen, Hans, xx
Anson, xxxi, 26 n.
Antibes, 65 and n.
Antigua, 33 and n., 41, 287
Antipas, 185
Arethusa, Fountain of, 126 and n.
Argyle, Ninth Earl of, 166
Aristotle, xxix
Armed Neutrality of 1780, 15, 25
Armed Neutrality of 1800, 206 n., 208 n., 240
"Army of the Faith" 151, 152
Augustus, Prince, 51
Austerlitz, 272 n.
Azores, 289, 290 n.

Baffin, 5 n.
Ball, Sir Alexander, xi, 119, 121 and n., 124, 125 and n., 136, 139 and n., 142, 150, 151, 160, 168, 196, 199, 200, 282 and n.
Ballad for a Boy, 12 n.
Barbados, 32, 33 n., 35, 286 and n.
Barcelona, 273, 276, 283
Barham, Lord, 41, 44, 293 n., 295
Barras, 89
Barrie, Sir J. M., xix, xx
Barrington, Admiral, 15, 129 and n.
Bastia, 49, 56, 62, 63, 64, 65, 66, 92, 93, 115
Bath, 16, 24, 25 n., 31, 46.
Battles:
Camperdown, 115 and n., 263
Chesapeake, 16
Copenhagen, xxv, xxxv, 5, 206, 208, 209 and n., 210 and n., 212, 232 n., 235 n., 251, 262, 263, 305
First of June, 145 n., 263
Grand Cul de Sac, 129 n.
Grenada, 16
Gulf of Genoa, 69
Hyères, 69, 76 n., 77 n.
Jutland, xxxiv, xxxv
Nile, xxx, 117–148, 125 n., 127 and n., 129, 131, 145 n., 158, 159, 161, 163, 167, 183 n., 201, 234, 235 n., 259, 281 n., 291 n., 300 n., 305
Saints, the, xxv, 15, 16–26 n., 28 n., 92 n., 133 n., 287 n.

Battles—continued
St. Vincent, xxx, xxxviii, 96–116, 145 n., 160
Teneriffe, 96
Trafalgar, xxx, xxxviii, 156, 229 n., 291 n., 300 n., 305, 313, 319, 321
Beatty, Doctor, xxiv, 307, 314, 315, 319 n.
Belt, Great, 210 and n., 212 and n., 214
Bequières, 128, 132, 141
Bercet, M. de, 255
Berry, Sir Edward, 101 and n., 103, 121 and n., 130 n., 132 and n., 133 n., 137, 144 n., 207 and n.
Berwick, Duke of, 94
Bexley, Lord, 208 n.
Bibliography:
Annual Register (1798), 133 n.
Authentic Narrative, Dr. Beatty, xxiv, xxvii, 307 n., 311 n.
Authentic Narrative, Rear-Admiral Sir Edward Berry, 130 n.
Cambridge Modern History, Vol. VIII., 157 n.
Cobbett's Parliamentary Debates, Vol. VI., 304 n.
Correspondence and Memoir of Lord Collingwood, G. L. N. Collingwood, xxxvii, 103 n., 319 n.
Dictionary of National Biography, 227 n.
Dispatches and Letters of Lord Nelson, Sir Harris Nicolas, xxxiii, 43 n., 85 n., 132 n., 155 and n., 163 n., 164 n., 172 n., 180 n., 182 n., 183 n., 202 n., 212 n., 256, 260, 276, 299 n., 309
Dynasts, The, Thomas Hardy, 291 n.
Emma, Lady Hamilton, Walter Sichel, 261 n.
English Review, Vol. XIV., No. 2, 159
Letters of Lord Nelson to Lady Hamilton, xxxvii, 252–3, 256, 258, 266, 276
Life of Nelson, Geoffrey Callender, 159
Life of Nelson, Clarke and McArthur, xxii, xxiii, xxv, xxvi, xxvii, xxxi, 17 n., 44 n., 65 n., 72 n., 103 n., 120 n., 125 n., 133 n., 135 n., 187 n., 188 n., 220 n., 260, 275 n., 290 n.
Life of Nelson, Harrison, xxi, xxiv, 104 n., 156, 252–3, 294–5
Life of Saumarez, Sir John Ross, 133 n.
Memoirs of Lord Nelson, T. J. Pettigrew, xxxiii, 304 n.
Memoirs of the Earl of St. Vincent, Jedediah Tucker, 103 n.
Memorie storiche sulla vita del Cardinale Ruffo, Domenico Sacchinelli, 157 n.
Morrison Manuscripts, xxxiii
Naples in 1799, Constance Giglioli, 157 n.
Naval Biography, James Ralfe, xxxvii, 212 n., 227 n.
Naval Biography of Great Britain, John Marshall, xxxvii, 133 n.
Naval Chronicle, Clarke and McArthur, xxiii, 17, 103 n.
Naval Chronology, Isaac Schomberg, 43 n.

Bibliography—*continued*
Naval History, Capt. Edward Brenton, xxxvii
Naval History, William James, xxxvii, 276 *n.*, 319 *n.*
Navy Records Society, Vols. XVIII. and XLVI., 97 *n.*, 227 *n.*
Nelson, the Embodiment of the Sea Power of Great Britain, Admiral Mahan, xxxiii
Nelsonian Reminiscences, Lieut. G. S. Parsons, R.N., 201 *n.*, 226 *n.*
Nelson Memorial, Sir John Laughton, 304 *n.*
Nelson's Friendships, Hilda Gamlin, 261 *n.*
Nelsons of Burnham Thorpe, M. Eyre Matcham, 46
Sea Kings of Britain, Geoffrey Callender, 300 *n.*
Sketches of the State of Manners and Opinions in the French Republic, Helen Maria Williams, xxxiv, 156 *n.*
Songs of Trafalgar, J. W. Croker, 295 *n.*
Trafalgar Blue Book (Cd. 7120), 300 *n.*
Treatise of the Principles and Practice of Naval Courts Martial, John McArthur, xxii, 187 *n.*
Ulm and Trafalgar, George Canning, xxxv *n.*, xlii
Voyages in the Mediterranean, Willyams, 148 *n.*
Voyage up the Mediterranean, Chaplain of the *Swiftsure*, 130 *n.*
Biscay, Bay of, xxv, 290
Blackwood, Captain Henry, 125 *n.*, 294, 301, 302 *n.*, 303, 304, 305, 306, 307, 308
Blake, xxxi, 107 and *n.*
Bochetta Pass, 79, 85 *n.*, 86, 87
Bomba, King, 159
Book of the Church, xviii
Bornholm, 244 *n.*, 245, 246
Boscawen, 4 *n.*
Boswell, 54 *n.*
Boulogne, 253, 265 *n.*, 274, 280 *n.*, 291 *n.*
Bowen, Capt., 108, 109, 110, 111 and *n.*
Bowen, Rear-Admiral James, 111 *n.*
Brazil, History of, xx, xxxi
Brereton, General, 286 *n.*
Briarly, Alexander, 222 *n.*, 224 *n.*
Bronte, Duke of, 160, 193, 198, 231 *n.*, 233 *n.*, 300, 302, 304
Browning, Robert, 226 *n.*
Brueys, Admiral, 127 and *n.*, 129 *n.*, 130 *n.*, 132 and *n.*, 135, 136 *n.*, 138
Bruix, Admiral, 151, 160, 180 *n.*
Burnham Thorpe, I, 45 *n.*, 144
Byron, Admiral John, 15
Byron, Lord, xv, xvi, xviii, xix, xx, xxvi, 20 *n.*

Cagliari, 282
Calabria, 151, 174, 176
Calder, Sir Robert, 288, 293 and *n.*, 294, 296, 299 and *n.*
Calvi, 49, 66, 67, 115
Calvirrano, Duke of, 184
Campbell, Rear-Admiral D., 274 and *n.*, 284, 285 *n.*
Campo Formio, Peace of, 167 *n.*, 171 *n.*
Candia, 123 and *n.*, 126, 127
Canning, xxxv, xlii, 304 *n.*
Capua, 155, 160, 174, 188, 190, 191
Caracciolo, Francesco, 70, 153, 154, 155, 157, 158, 159, 160, 183 and *n.*, 184 and *n.*, 185 and *n.*, 186 and *n.*, 187 *n.*, 188
Carlscrona, 244, 245
Carnot, 89 *n.*

Carroll, Lewis, xix, xx
"Cartel's ship," 65, 140
Casabianca, 139
Castellana, 171
Cataract of Lodore, xix
Cato, Addison's, xix
Ceuta, 289 and *n.*
Championnet, 174, 175
Charles III. of Spain, 194
Charles VI., Emperor, 54
Chatham, Lord, 48, 74
Chatterton, xix
Chelingk, 143 and *n.*, 144
"Christian Army," 176, 181
Christian VII. of Denmark, 213, 215 *n.*, 233 and *n.*, 245
Cid, The, xviii
Clarence, Duke of, xxiii, xxx, 28 and *n.*, 40, 43, 44 *n.*, 48, 109, 114, 189, 190, 197, 271
Clarke, Rev. Dr. James S., xxii, xxiii, xxiv, 141
Clerk of Eldin, xxx
Cochrane, Admiral Alexander, 286 and *n.*
Cockburn, Admiral Sir George, 90, 94
Coke of Norfolk, 46 *n.*
Coleridge, viii–ix, xi, xii, xiii, xviii, xxviii, 200
Collingwood, Lord, 17, 18, 24, 35, 37, 100 and *n.*, 103 and *n.*, 224, 288 and *n.*, 290, 291 *n.*, 297, 299, 300 *n.*, 303 and *n.*, 306 *n.*, 308 and *n.*, 309 and *n.*, 315, 319 *n.*
Colloquies, xviii, xxxvi
Cordova, Don Joseph de, 97
Cornwallis, Admiral Hon. Wm., 15, 24, 265, 280 *n.*, 283, 285 *n.*, 288 *n.*, 290, 291 *n.*
Corsica, xxvii, 53, 54, 55, 56, 57, 58, 59, 60, 61, 64, 69, 70, 74, 88, 91, 92, 93, 160, 272, 277 *n.*, 283
Corunna-Ferrol, 280 *n.*
Council of the Indies, 18 *n.*
Cowper, Life of, xix, xxxi
Cowper's Letters, xx, xxxi
Croker, Rt. Hon. J. W., xli, 295 *n.*
Cronstadt, Vice-Admiral, 245, 246, 247
Crown Batteries, 218, 220, 225
Cruikshank, George, xxxvi
Cuba, 28 *n.*
Curse of Kehama, xvii, xix, xxi

d'Aubant, General, 62, 64
Darby, Captain H. D. E., 122, 135
Davis, John, xxxi, 32 *n.*
Davison, Alexander, 27, 30, 147, 181, 251
Davy, Sir Humphrey, xxv, 259 *n.*
Decline and Fall, xii, xiii
De Grasse, 129 *n.*, 287
De Koster, xxxvi
Denmark, Crown Prince of, 243 *n.*, 249
Denmark, King of, *see* Christian VII.
De Quincey, xiii–xiv
Despard, 22
d'Estaing, Count, 15, 18, 129 and *n.*
Deux Ponts, Count de, 29, 31
de Vins, General, 69, 76, 81, 82, 83 and *n.*, 85, 86, 87, 90
Diamond Rock, 287
Digby, Admiral Robert, 28
Directory, The, 162, 179
Dog Watches, 8 *n.*
Domett, Captain, 212 and *n.*, 225, 226 *n.*
Drake, Sir Francis, xxxi, 278 *n.*
Duc d'Enghien, 124 *n.*
Duckworth, Admiral, 159, 176, 179 *n.*, 188
"Duke of Thunder," 194
Dumanoir, Rear-Admiral, 318, 319 and *n.*

Duncan, 115, 145 n.
Dundas, General, 62, 63, 65 n.
Dundonald, Earl of, 54, 286 n.
" Duty," 306 n.

Edinburgh Review, xvi, xvii, xxiv, xxxvi, 319 n.
Edith Southey, see Fricker
Egalité, Philippe, 166
Elba, 50 n., 88, 91, 94, 106 n., 107
Elliot, Sir Gilbert, 61 and n., 92, 274, 277 n.
Elsinore, 16, 25, 210, 213, 214, 215
" England expects every man will do his duty,"
    306 and n.
English Harbour, 33 n., 42, 43 n.
Epictetus, xiii, xv
Epistles, Casaubon's, xix
Erskine, Sir James St. Clair, 175, 197
Espriella, Don Manuel, xix
Esterhazy, Prince of, 204

Falkland Islands, 4 and n.
Fanny, see Nelson, Frances Viscountess
Farmer, Captain, 12, 13 n.
Ferdinand IV., King of Naples, 50 n., 51 n.,
    150, 151, 153, 154, 155, 160, 164, 165, 168,
    169, 171–3, 176–7, 179, 182 n., 183 n., 184,
    186, 188, 192, 193, 194, 196, 200, 303
Ferrol, 280 n., 293 n., 294
Finland, Gulf of, 243 n., 247
Foley, Captain Thomas, xxx, 122, 132, 133 n.,
    213, 219, 227 and n., 232
Foote, Captain, xxxiv, 150, 152, 153, 156, 180,
    181, 182 and n., 183 and n., 189
Four Georges, xx, xxi
Fox, Charles James, xviii
Francis II., Emperor, 171, 179 and n.
Frederick, Captain T. L., 100 n.
Frederick II., 214
Fremantle, Captain, 106, 109, 110, 111, 220,
    232, 238
Fremantle, Mrs., 109, 111
French Revolution, xxviii, 45 n., 60, 149, 155
Fricker, Edith (Southey's wife), ix, xvᵉ
Frock-coat, Nelson's, 306

Gaffori, 56, 57
Gallinazos, 24
Gantheaume, 283 and n.
George III., 43, 203, 240, 245, 304 n., 305 n.,
    321
George IV., xx, xxii, 305 and n.
Germaine, Lord George, 20
Gibbon, Edward, xviii
Gillespie, Dr. Leonard, xxvi
Girondins, xxviii
Glover, Captain, 24
" God Save the King," 298
Golfe Juan, see Gourjean
Goodall, Vice-Admiral, 73
Gould, Capt. Davidge, 122, 134
Gourjean Roads, 49, 65, 129 n., 131
Graham, Colonel, 197, 198
Graves, Admiral, 15, 216, 227 and n., 246
Gravina, Admiral, 285, 292 n., 309 n., 319 n.,
    320 n.
Grenada, 15, 20 n., 286, 287 and n.
Grenville, Lord, xxxi, 304 n.
Grimm's Fairy Tales, xx
Gulf of Finland, 245
Gustavus IV., 245

Hallowell, Captain Benjamin, 122, 136, 141
    and n., 142, 148 n., 180, 195, 196, 203, 295
Hamilton, Emma Lady, xxi, xxviii, xxxiv,
    50, 51, 125 and n., 126, 150, 158, 160, 161,

162, 163, 164, 173, 174, 178, 180, 182 and n.,
    183 n., 184, 185 n., 186 and n., 187 n., 194,
    198, 204, 205, 232 n., 251, 252, 256, 258–9,
    260 n., 261 and n., 264, 266, 276, 294, 295,
    303, 304 and n., 305 and n., 314, 315, 316
Hamilton, Sir William, 50, 73 n., 126, 150, 160,
    161, 162, 163, 165, 172, 173, 178, 182 and n.,
    184, 198, 200, 201, 204, 251, 258–9, 264
Hamlet, 215
Hardy, Captain, 125 n., 137, 184, 219, 220, 238,
    304 and n., 306, 309, 311, 313, 314, 315
Hardy, Thomas, 291 n.
Hargood, Captain, 285 n.
Harvey, Captain Eliab, 312
Hawke, xxxiv, 17 n.
Hayley, 261 n.
Hébert, 166
Helvoetsluys, 254
Herod Philip, 185 n.
Hill, Margaret, vii
Hill, Rev. Herbert, viii–x
History of the Great Rebellion, 107 n.
Hood, Admiral Viscount, xxii, xxx, 15, 16,
    28, 48, 50 and n., 61, 62, 63, 64, 65, 66 and n.,
    67, 69 and n., 74, 83, 89, 129 n., 131
Hood, Capt. Samuel, 112 and n., 113, 122, 127,
    132 n., 133 and n., 140, 142, 148
Horatia, see Thompson, Horatia Nelson
Hotham, Admiral, 69 and n., 70, 72 n., 73 and
    n., 74, 75 and n., 76, 77 n., 79, 81 and n., 83,
    85, 89, 153, 293 n.
Howard of Effingham, xxxi
Howe, xxxi, xxxiv, 32, 43, 44, 145
Hughes, Admiral Sir Richard, 32, 33 and n.,
    35, 36, 37
Hughes, Lady, 32

Inman, Captain, 228
Ionica, 12 n.
Irish Saints, Colgar's, xiv
Irving, Dr., 6 and n.
Isle St. Honoré, 65
Isle Ste. Marguerite, 65

Jacobins, 66, 79, 91, 149, 150–1, 153–5, 159,
    166, 192, 249
Jamaica, 14, 15, 17 n., 20, 21, 24, 25 n., 41, 45,
    283, 286 and n.
James II., xxii
Joan of Arc, xvii
John Halifax, Gentleman, 261
Johnson, Dr., xix, xxxi, 54 n.
Jortin, 144 n.
Joseph Bonaparte, 179 and n.
Josiah, see Nisbet

Keith, Lord, 158, 160, 179, 190, 191, 200–1
    and n., 206 n., 265
Keppel, Admiral, 26 and n.
King's Deep, 200 n., 235 n., 236 n.
Kioge Bay, 246, 247
Kirke White, xix
Knights of St. John of Jerusalem, 122 n.
Kronborg Castle, 208, 210, 212, 214, 215 and n.,
    218
Kronstadt, 207, 246

Lamb, Charles, xv
Landor, W. S., xv, xviii
Landscrona, 214
Latouche-Tréville, 274, 275 n.
La Valette, 200, 201
Lazzaroni, 164, 173, 174
Leake, William Martin, 276 n.

Leghorn, 87, 88, 91, 93, 150, 159, 160, 169, 172, 176, 201 *n.*, 204, 283 *n.*
Leonidas, 24
Lesser Antilles station, 15, 32 *n.*, 33 *n.*
Letters from England, xix
Lincoln's Inn, 30
Lindholm, Danish Adjutant-General, 232, 233, 234, 242, 243 and *n.*
Linzee, Commodore, 51 and *n.*, 53, 61
Liverpool, Lord, 305 *n.*
Lives of the Admirals, Campbell's, xxxviii
Lives of the British Admirals, Southey's, xix
Locke, 166
Locker, Captain William, 14, 17 and *n.*
Louis, Captain T., 122, 135, 137, 191, 196, 297
Louis XVI., 50 *n.*, 149
Lucas, Captain, 312 *n.*
Lutwidge, Captain, 6, 9

McArthur, John, xxii–xxiii
Macaulay, xvii, xviii, xxiv, xxv, xxvi, xxix, xxxiv, xxxvi
Mack, General, 149, 150, 169, 170, 171, 172, 174, 272 *n.*
M'Cormick, Father, 171
Madalena Islands, 281
Madeira, 286
Madoc, xvii, xviii
Mahan, xxix, xxxiii, xxxiv, xxxviii, 12 *n.*, 97 *n.*
Man, Admiral Robert, 75
Manœuverer, The, 30
Marat, 166
Maria Carolina, Queen of Naples, 51 *n.*, 125, 150, 151, 159, 160, 162, 165, 169, 173, 178, 183 *n.*, 193, 194, 204, 304
Marie Antoinette, 50 *n.*, 149, 162
Mariner's Mirror, 47
Marryat, Captain, 14 *n.*
Marsden, William, 276
Martinique, 15, 33, 34, 35, 280 *n.*, 281, 285 and *n.*, 287 and *n.*, 291 *n.*
Masaniello, 188
Masaredo, 151, 179, 179 *n.*
Masefield, John, xxxii
Massacre of St. Bartholomew, 4 *n.*
Matcham, M. Eyre, 46
Matilda, Queen, 215
Mazari Bay, 284
Mecklenburg Strelitz, Duke of, 248
Méjean, Citoyen, 189
Melville, Lord, 66 *n.*
Memorandum, Nelson's, 299 *n.*, 308 *n.*
Meredith, George, 9
Merton, 258, 266, 294, 296, 305
Messina, Straits of, 151, 168, 176, 197, 198, 283 *n.*, 284
Middleton, Sir Charles, *see* Barham, Lord
Miller, Capt. R. W., 97, 100 *n.*, 101, 105, 112, 122, 134
Milton, xxix
Minorca, 26 *n.*, 75, 158, 159, 176 *n.*, 181, 188, 189, 190, 191, 192, 195, 197
Minto, Earl of, *see* Elliot, Sir Gilbert
Monastic Orders, xiii, xviii
Monk, xxxi
Monmouth, 166
Monody, Canning's, xxxv
Montego Bay, Jamaica, 18
Moore, Commodore, 278 *n.*
Moore, Sir John, 61
Morte d'Arthur, xix
Moutray, Resident Commissioner, 33 and *n.*
Murray, John, xxv, xxvii, xxxvi, xxxviii

Mutiny, Great, 105 *n.*
Myers, Sir William, 286

Napier, Sir William, xviii
Napoleon, xv, xxviii–xxix, 50 *n.*, 88–91, 117, 120, 123–4, 127 and *n.*, 128, 148 *n.*, 149, 150, 158, 167, 171 *n.*, 195, 201, 202 *n.*, 203 and *n.*, 206 *n.*, 252, 262 *n.*, 265 *n.*, 276 and *n.*, 280 *n.*, 281 *n.*, 283–4, 291 *n.*, 292 *n.*, 297–8, 318
Naufragia, Dr. Clarke's, xxii
Navigation Act, 34 and *n.*, 35, 37, 39 *n.*, 46
Navy Board, 6 *n.*, 14 *n.*
Navy Office, 14 *n.*
Nelson, Frances Viscountess, xxviii, 39–40, 45, 46, 47, 114, 115, 117, 123 *n.*, 137, 143, 205, 259–60, 261 and *n.*, 304 *n.*
Nelson, Horatio Viscount: born at Burnham Thorpe, 1; captain's servant to his uncle Maurice Suckling, 3; from whom he receives a nautical education, 4–5; accompanies an expedition to the Arctic, 5–12; receives a commission, 14; and is appointed to the *Lowestoft*, 14; boards a prize in a storm, 16–17; appointed to his first ship, *Badger*, 18; rescues the crew of a burning ship, 18; made post into the *Hinchinbrook*, 18; escorts an expedition to Nicaragua, 20–4; meets Lord Hood and becomes his disciple, 28; and puts down illegal trading in the West Indies, 32–42; on half-pay, 1787–93, 42–8; receives command of his first battleship, *Agamemnon*, 48; sails with Lord Hood to the Mediterranean, 50; fights La Melpomène and four other ships, 51–3; distinguishes himself in the conquest of Corsica, 53–68; loses the sight of his right eye, 66–7; conducts an audacious duel with the *Ça Ira*, 70–4; takes part in the battle of Hyères, 76–7; sees prolonged service off the coast of Genoa, 80–91; superintends evacuation of Corsica, 92–3; captures *La Sabina*, 94; greatly distinguishes himself at the battle of St. Vincent, 96–104; receives his flag and the Order of the Bath, 105; fights a hand-to-hand encounter with a Spanish launch, 106; conducts an expedition to Santa Cruz, 108–13; and loses his right arm, 110–16; given an independent command in the Mediterranean, 117–18; unravels the secret of Napoleon's Eastern campaign, 119–27; and annihilates his fleet at the battle of the Nile, 127–42; created a peer, 144–5; co-operates with Naples against France, 161–73; carries the king and queen into safety in Sicily, 173–4; returns to Naples and cancels the flag of truce, 181–2; receives surrender of insurgent fortresses, 183; convenes a court martial on Caracciolo, 183–5; and as consenting authority executes sentence, 186–8; restores Ferdinand IV. to the throne, 188, 191; summoned by Lord Keith to defend Corsica and declines to obey, 188–9; created Duke of Bronte, 193–4; captures *Le Généreux*, 200; and *Guillaume Tell*, 201; returns home by land with the Hamiltons, 203–4; lands at Yarmouth and is rapturously received, 205; in the Baltic campaign of 1801, 206; acts as second to Sir Hyde Parker, 206–8; but secures the real command for himself, 209–17; utterly defeats the Danes at Copenhagen, 217–35; and by skilful diplomacy obtains from them all that England requires, 237–49; attacks the Boulogne flotilla, 252–6; purchases Merton and enjoys a spell ashore, 258–65; at the

outbreak of the Napoleonic war receives command of the Mediterranean, 265; and for two years enforces the blockade of Toulon, 267–79; chases Villeneuve to the West Indies, 280–7; and back, 287–90; pays his last visit to Merton and London, 294–6; venerated by the Portsmouth mob, 296; annihilates the Franco-Spanish fleet at Trafalgar, 297–312; but is mortally wounded, 313–15; and dies in the cockpit of the *Victory*, 316

Nelson, Maurice, 47
Nelson, Rev. Edmund,'xxxii, 1, 2, 117
Nelson, Rev. William, 1–3, 251, 304 *n.*
" Nelson Touch," the, 299
Newbolt, Sir Henry, 290 *n.*
Nicknames, ships', 50 *n.*
Niebuhr, 235 *n.*
Nisbet, Josiah, 39, 49, 51, 109 and *n.*, 110, 114 and *n.*, 259–60
Nootka Sound, 47
Nore, 6, 42, 254
North, Lord, 26 *n.*
Nova Scotia, 35
Nuovo, Fort, 152, 156, 160, 181, 183 *n.*

Oldfield, Captain, 108
Orde, Admiral Sir John, 118 and *n.*, 203 and *n.*, 279 *n.*, 284, 285 and *n.*, 299 and *n.*
Otway, Admiral Sir R. W., Bart., 212 *n.*, 227 *n.*

Palermo, 150–1, 153, 156, 158–9, 174, 178, 180–1, 182 *n.*, 183 *n.*, 184 *n.*, 192–3, 199, 283
Palmerin of England, xviii
Paoli, Pasquale de, 53 and *n.*, 54 and *n.*, 57–9, 60 and *n.*, 61, 69 *n.*
Parker, Admiral Sir Hyde, xxxv, 79, 85, 97, 206, 207 *n.*, 208, 209, 210, 212 and *n.*, 225, 226 *n.*, 227 and *n.*, 231 *n.*, 232, 235, 237, 240, 244–6, 248, 263
Parker, Captain, 255–6
Parker, Sir Peter, 17
Parker, Sir William, 118 and *n.*
Parsons, Lieutenant G. S., 201 *n.*
" Parthenopeian Republic," 150, 184
Paul, Czar, 143, 179 *n.*, 198, 206, 245–7
Peary, 6 *n.*
Peninsular War, Southey's, xviii, xx
Peyton, Captain John, 122, 135
Phipps, Captain, 6, 7, 10
Pignatelli, Prince, 174
Pitt, William, 9, 44, 118 *n.*, 144 and *n.*, 145, 149, 206 *n.*, 304 *n.*
Pius VI., Pope, 149, 195, 196
Pocock, Nicholas, xxiii
Pole, Admiral Sir Charles Maurice, 13, 249
Port Royal, 20–21, 24, 287
Porto Ferrajo, 91, 94–5, 105 and *n.*
Portugal, History of, Southey's, xvii, xviii, xxv
Pre-Raphaelites, xxxvi
Progress of Maritime Discovery, Dr. Clarke's, xxii
Puerto Cabello, 29
Pula Bay, 282

Quadrant, 32 and *n.*
Quarterly Review, xvi, xxiv, xxv
Quebec, 26, 27
Quilliam, Lieutenant, 317

Raleigh, Sir Walter, xxxii, 6 *n.*
Rathbone, John, 4, 5
Register Act, 39
Religious Ceremonies, Picart's, xii
Richardson, Samuel, xxiv

" Right of Search," 15, 206 *n.*
Riou, Captain, 208, 218–20, 225 and *n.*, 227–8, 232
Ripperda, 55
Riviera di Genoa, 79–80, 96
Robinson Crusoe, xxxviii
Rochefort, 280 *n.*, 285 *n.*, 286 *n.*, 299, 318
Roderick the Last of the Goths, xvii
Rodney, xxv, xxxi, 15, 28 and *n.*, 133 *n.*, 271, 287
Roland, Madame, 155
Romney, 261 *n.*
Rosebery, Lord, 261 *n*
Rosetta, 140
Rotherham, Captain, 309 and *n.*
Rousseau, ix, xii, 58
Rowley, Captain, 77
Royal Society, 6 *n.*
Ruffo, Cardinal, 151–3, 156–8, 160, 176, 181–2, 182 *n.*, 183 *n.*, 184, 195
Ruskin, xxxvi
Russell, Lord William, 166

St. Angelo, Castle of, 171, 195
St. Antonio, 192
St. Elmo, Castle, 152, 155, 160, 181, 188, 189, 190
St. Eustatius, Roads of, 34
St. Januarius, 175 and *n.*, 192
St. Kitts, 36 and *n.*, 129 *n.*
St. Lucia, 41, 129 and *n.*, 286, 287 *n.*
" St. Nelson," 321
St. Omer, 31
St. Vincent, Earl, xxxi, 88, 89, 91 *n.*, 92, 94 *n.*, 95, 96, 98 and *n.*, 99, 100 *n.*, 103 and *n.*, 104 and *n.*, 106 *n.*, 107, 113, 117, 118 and *n.*, 122, 125, 144 *n.*, 145 *n.*, 148, 158, 160, 161, 164, 180 and *n.*, 190, 201, 202, 203 and *n.*, 207 and *n.*, 240, 242, 246, 257, 263, 270, 277 *n.*, 284, 299 *n.*, 303, 312 *n.*
Saltholm, 210 *n.*, 214, 218, 244
San Bartolomeo, 22, 23
San Domingo, 20 and *n.*, 28 *n.*
San Fiorenzo, 56, 61, 62, 63, 64. 76 and *n.*, 88
San Juan, Castle of, 22, 23, 24
San Remo, 79, 82
Sandwich, Lord, 6 and *n.*, 26 and *n.*
Sangro, Duke di, 169
Santa Cruz, 107 *n.*, 108, 109, 118 *n.*, 132 *n.*
Saratoga, 15
Saumarez, Admiral Lord de, 121 and *n.*, 133 and *n.*, 148
Savona, 84, 86, 87
Savonarola, 159
Schérer, 89
Schomberg, Isaac, 43 *n.*, 44 *n.*
Schroedersee, 229
Scott, Doctor, xxvi, 276, 299 *n.*, 307, 314
Scott, Mr., 307, 311
Scott, Sir Walter, xv, xviii, xxi, xxxi
Sextant, 32 *n.*
Shakespeare, xxxviii, 9
Shelburne, Lord, 59
Shelley, xv
Ships:
  Agamemnon, xxii, 48, 49, 50 and *n.*, 52, 53 and *n.*, 62, 65, 71, 72 and *n.*, 73, 76 *n.*, 77, 81, 84 *n.*, 85, 86, 87, 88, 89, 160, 180, 205, 222 and *n.*, 225 *n.*, 271, 299
  Aimable, 299
  Albemarle, 16, 25, 26 and *n.*, 27, 28, 29, 31
  Alcmene, 148, 220
  Alexander, 119, 136, 139, 146, 163
  Amazon, 208, 218, 220 *n.*, 228, 274, 287
  Amphion, 275 *n.*

Ships—*continued*
Aquilon, 135
Ardent, 222 *n.*, 223 *n.*, 230
Argonauta, 317
Arrow, 220
Audacious, 122, 133 *n.*, 134
Badger, 16, 17 *n.*, 18
Belleisle, 285 *n.*
Bellerophon, 122, 135, 136, 148 *n.*
Bellona, 222 and *n.*, 223 and *n.*, 224 and *n.*, 225 *n.*, 228, 234
Blanche, 94, 208 *n.*, 220
Blenheim, 100 and *n.*
Boreas, 31, 32, 33, 34, 37, 42
Bristol, 16, 17, 18
Bucentaure, 308, 311 *n.*, 312, 319 *n.*
Ça Ira, 70, 72 and *n.*, 73 and *n.*, 74
Canopus, 274
Captain, 88, 97, 100, 101 *n.*, 103, 104 *n.*, 106 *n.*
Carcass, 6, 8, 13 *n.*
Censeur, 73 and *n.*, 74
Conquérant, 133, 134
Courageux, 73, 85
Culloden, 85, 97, 100 and *n.*, 122, 136, 137, 140, 146, 163
Curieux, 289 and *n.*, 293 *n.*
Dannebrog, 230 and *n.*, 232 *n.*, 234, 236 *n.*
Defence, 122, 135, 232
Defiance, 222 *n.*, 223 *n.*, 233
Désirée, 228, 234
Diamond Rock, 287 *n.*
Diane, 140 *n.*
Dolphin, 13 and *n.*, 14, 114 *n.*
Dreadnought, 1 *n.*, 4 and *n.*, 302
Edgar, 222 and *n.*, 224 *n.*
Elephant, 213, 220 *n.*, 222 *n.*, 223 and *n.*, 227 and *n.*, 230, 231 and *n.*, 232, 233 and *n.*, 234, 237, 245
Emerald, 112, 119, 148
Euryalus, 301
Excellent, 100 and *n.*
Foudroyant, 154, 155, 160, 182 *n.*, 183 *n.*, 184 and *n.*, 185 *n.*, 186 *n.*, 187 *n.*, 188, 201
Fougueux (Spitfire), 312 *n.*
Fox, 108, 109, 111
Franklin, 134, 135, 136, 137
Ganges, 222 *n.*, 223 *n.*, 232, 233
Généreux, 139 and *n.*, 160, 200, 201 and *n.*
Glatton, 222 *n.*, 223 *n.*, 230, 233
Goliath, 122, 132, 133, 148
Guerrier, 133, 134, 135
Guillaume Tell, 139 and *n.*, 160, 201
Hermione, 275
Héros, 319
Hinchinbrook, 16, 17 *n.*, 18, 21, 24
Illustrious, 73
Inconstant, 71
Intrépide, 319 *n.*
Invincible, 213
Iris, 232 *n.*, 275 *n.*
Isis, 222 and *n.*, 228, 275
Jean Barras, 71, 72 *n.*
Justice, 140 *n.*
Latona, 33 and *n.*
Leander, 122, 136
Leviathan, 307
Lion, 16, 24, 201
London, 227 *n.*, 212 *n.*, 233
Lowestoft, 14, 15, 16, 17 and *n.*, 18
Majestic, 122, 135
Mars, 232 *n.*, 301
Mediator, 35, 37
Medusa, 253
Meleager, 90

Ships—*continued*
Melpomène, 49, 52, 53 *n.*
Minerve, 88, 94, 153, 155, 185 and *n.*, 186 *n.*
Minotaur, 122, 135, 137, 191
Monarch, 215, 222 *n.*, 223 *n.*, 229, 233
Mutine, 136
Neptune, 311 *n.*
Orient, 135, 136, 137, 138, 139, 141, 143 *n.*, 148 *n.*
Orion, 119, 121 *n.*, 133
Pegasus, 43 *n.*
Penelope, 201
Peuple Souverain, 134
Polyphemus, 222 and *n.*, 228
Quebec, 12 *n.*
Racehorse, 6, 8, 11
Raisonnable, 1 and *n.*, 3, 4, 48
Ramillies, 232
Rattler, 37
Redoutable, 229 *n.*, 311 and *n.*, 312 and *n.*, 313 and *n.*, 316, 317
Royal Sovereign, 303, 308, 318
Russell, 222 *n.*, 223 and *n.*, 224 and *n.*, 225 *n.*
Sabina, 52, 88, 94
St. George, 89, 213, 237, 244, 261 *n.*
Salvador del Mundo, 100
San Augustino, 319 *n.*
San Isidro, 100
San Josef, 96, 100, 101 and *n.*, 103 *n.*, 312 *n.*
San Juan Nepomuceno, 317
San Nicolas, 96, 100, 101 and *n.*, 103 *n.*, 312 *n.*
Sans-Culottes, 71, 72 *n.*
Santa Aña, 308
Santissima Trinidad, 97, 100, 309 and *n.*, 312, 317, 319 *n.*
Seahorse, 12, 109, 111, 151, 156, 180, 181, 182, 281
Sirius, 308
Spartiate, 135, 148 *n.*, 287
Superb, 290, 291 *n.*
Swift, 275, 276 *n.*
Swiftsure, 122, 130 *n.*, 136, 139, 141, 146, 148
Téméraire, 1 *n.*, 312
Theseus, 100 *n.*, 106 and *n.*, 109, 111, 122, 134, 140
Tonnant, 135
Triumph, 4, 5 and *n.*, 13 *n.*
Vanguard, 117, 119, 120 and *n.*, 121 and *n.*, 126, 129, 135 and *n.*, 137, 160, 163, 164, 174, 178
Victory, 233, 271, 284, 288, 290, 294, 296, 300 *n.*, 301, 302, 303, 305, 306 *n.*, 307, 308, 309 and *n.*, 311 and *n.*, 312 and *n.*, 313 *n.*, 314, 316, 317, 318, 321
Zealand, 229, 237, 240
Zealous, 89, 122, 127, 132 and *n.*, 133 and *n.*, 140, 148
Shirley, Major-Gen. Sir Thomas, 35, 36 and *n.*
Sidmouth, Viscount, *see* Addington
Sidney, Algernon, 166
Simple, Peter, 14 *n.*
Smeerenberg Harbour, 11
Smith, Sir Sidney, 100 *n.*, 176, 202 and *n.*
Smollett, xxiv
Sound, 209, 210 and *n.*, 212, 213, 215, 218, 220
Southey, Criticism of, xvii–xxi, xxv–xxxi, xxxiii–xxxix, 1, 12 *n.*, 50 *n.*, 51 *n.*, 54, 65 *n.*, 72, 76, 78, 79, 84 *n.*, 85, 87 *n.*, 96, 97 *n.*, 98 *n.*, 99 *n.*, 103 *n.*, 104–5 *n.*, 106 *n.*, 108 *n.*, 118 *n.*, 127 *n.*, 130 *n.*, 131 *n.*, 132 *n.*, 133 *n.*, 135 *n.*, 149, 153, 156, 164 *n.*, 179 *n.*, 180 *n.*, 182 *n.*, 183 *n.*, 185 *n.*, 186 *n.*, 187 *n.*, 201, 206 *n.*, 220 *n.*, 223 *n.*, 233 *n.*, 261 *n.*, 306 *n.*, 308 *n.*, 309 *n.*, 319 *n.*
Southey, Essay on (Macaulay), xxxvi

Southey's connection with Spain, ix, x, xiii, 318, 320
Southey, Thomas, xxv, xxx, 226 *n.*
Specimens of Later English Poets, xix
Spence, Mr., Maritime Surveyor, 254
Spencer, Countess, 260
Spencer, Earl, 97 *n.*, 114, 118 and *n.*, 126, 146, 155, 157, 173, 201
States General, 155
Stewart, Hon. Colonel, 220, 223 *n.*, 227 *n.*
Strachan, Sir Richard, 319 and *n.*, 320 and *n.*
Stuart, Don Jacopo, 94
Stuart, General Sir Charles, 66, 176
Suckling, Capt. Maurice, 1, 2, 3, 4 and *n.*, 14 and *n.*, 28, 110, 308
Suffren, Bailli de, 12 *n.*
Suvaroff, 167, 188, 195
Swin Channel, 5 and *n.*, 254
Sykes, John, 106
Syracuse, 125, 126 and *n.*, 163, 168

Tactics of Trafalgar, 300 *n.*
Teneriffe, 96–116, 107 *n.*, 164 *n*, 180, 259
Texel, 280 *n.*
Thackeray, xx, xxi
Thalaba the Destroyer, xvii, xviii, xxi
Thesiger, Captain Sir Frederic, 232 and *n.*, 233
Thompson, Horatia Nelson, 266, 304, 316 *n.*
Thompson, Sir Thomas Boulden, 110, 111, 122, 136, 222–3
Thura, Captain, 229
Thura, Count, 154, 185, 187 *n.*
Ticket Office, 268 *n.*
Tobago, 286, 287 *n.*
Toulon, 50 *n.*, 51, 52, 61–2, 65, 73 *n.*, 77 *n.*, 88, 117, 120, 150, 182, 265, 266, 267, 271–3, 275, 280 *n.*, 282 *n.*, 284 *n.*, 291 *n.*
Traffics and Discoveries, xxxviii
Trees of Liberty, 149
Tregoyen, Don Miguel, 106
Trekroner, 209 and *n.*, 210 *n.*, 222 *n.*, 225 *n.*, 228, 231, 232 *n.*, 233, 235 *n.*, 237, 242
Trinidad, 286 and *n.*, 290 *n.*
Trollope, Anthony, xix
Troubridge, Admiral Sir Thomas, 13, 100 and *n.*, 108, 112, 113, 122, 126, 132 *n.*, 136, 142, 146, 151, 155, 160, 176–8, 180, 189–92, 195–9, 201–2, 224 *n.*, 257, 270
Tunis, Dey of, 51 *n.*

Turin, 90, 120
Tuscany, 69, 91, 176
Tuscany, Grand Duke of, 169, 172
Tycho Brahe, 214
Tyler, Elizabeth, vii–ix, xii

Ulm, 149, 272 *n.*
Ulm and Trafalgar, xxxv
Uovo, 152, 156, 160, 181, 183 *n.*
Uranienburg, 214 *n.*
Ushant, 288, 290

Vado Bay, 67, 79 and *n.*, 82, 84, 87, 90
Valetta, 200 *n.*
Vansittart, Mr., 208 and *n.*, 209
Vendémiaire, 89 *n.*
" Vesuvian Republic," 150–1
Victory's log, 274
Vigo, 294
Villemoes, 229, 239
Villeneuve, xxix, 139 *n.*, 275 *n.*, 283 and *n.*, 284 *n.*, 285 and *n.*, 286 *n.*, 287 *n.*, 288 *n.*, 290 *n.*, 291 *n.*, 292 *n.*, 293 *n.*, 294, 297, 301 *n.*, 302 *n.*, 305 *n.*, 306 and *n.*, 308, 309 *n.*, 311 *n.* , 320 and *n.*
Vision of Judgment, xvii–xviii
Voltaire, 289

Walden's Island, 9
Wallis, General, 86 *n.*
Walpole, Lord, 1 and *n.*
Walpole, Sir Robert, 1
Wandle, 258, 259
Waterloo, 5 *n.*
Wellington, 145 *n.*
Wesley, Life of, Southey's, xix, xx, xxxi
Westall, Richard, R.A., xxiii
Westcott, Captain G. B., 122, 135, 140
William IV., *see* Clarence, Duke of
Williams, Miss Helen Maria, xxxiv, 155, 156
Windham, Mr., 145 *n.*, 170, 171
Wordsworth, xiii–xiv, xxv
Works and Days, 322

Yarmouth, 160, 205, 207, 208, 213, 249

Zadig, 289 and *n.*
Zante, 194
Zealand, 210 *n.*, 214